# SECURITY
# AND
# CRIME PREVENTION

# SECURITY
# AND
# CRIME PREVENTION

## ROBERT L. O'BLOCK, Ph.D.

Department of Political Science/Criminal Justice,
Appalachian State University,
Boone, North Carolina

*Illustrated*

## The C. V. Mosby Company

ST. LOUIS · TORONTO · LONDON    1981

MOSBY

1906 **75** 1981
YEARS

A TRADITION OF PUBLISHING EXCELLENCE

Printed in the United States of America

The C. V. Mosby Company
11830 Westline Industrial Drive, St. Louis, Missouri 63141


**Library of Congress Cataloging in Publication Data**

O'Block, Robert L., 1951-
    Security and crime prevention.

    Bibliography: p.
    Includes index.
    1.  Crime prevention.   2.   Industry—Security
measures.   I.   Title.
HV7431.O24      364.4      81-1353
ISBN  0-8016-3738-4      AACR2


VT/D/D  9  8  7  6  5  4  3  2  1      01/A/024

# Foreword

Professor O'Block's *Security and Crime Prevention* is a text that has been needed for some time. Rising crime rates of all types have brought an awareness to both the public and criminal justice professionals that crime prevention is the only logical approach to this problem. There are two main reasons that crime prevention is the preferred antidote to crime. First, crime prevention is economical. With restricted local, state, and federal government budgets, it is neither practical nor possible to control crime by placing hundreds of police officers in every neighborhood. It is practical and possible however to utilize the skills and talents of citizens in an organized manner, for example, neighborhood watch programs, to help prevent crime. Crime prevention is also more economical from another standpoint involving crimes against businesses. Most consumers would agree that it is better to take steps to reduce losses resulting from shoplifting, bad checks, credit card fraud, and employee theft rather than pass those losses on to consumers in the form of higher prices.

Second, crime prevention techniques reduce opportunities for individuals to exhibit criminal behavior. This is perhaps the most important aspect of crime prevention, since an overwhelming majority of crime is thought to involve semiskilled or unskilled amateurs, and center around opportunities created by the victims themselves. Individuals unconsciously or unknowingly invite crime through careless behaviors such as leaving doors unlocked, flashing cash and credit cards in public, leaving car keys in the ignition, and venturing onto dark and unfamiliar streets alone. These behaviors create or increase vulnerabilities to crime, thus making people more prone to criminal attack. On the other hand, crime prevention strategies can decrease the risk of being victimized, without confinement within a self-created police state.

As intelligent and reasonable citizens, we know that crime prevention is both the most logical and economical approach to take in crime control. The preventive approach to crime uses common sense in many respects and is seemingly so simple and practical that, in the past, it was often overlooked as an element essential to crime control. However, those who are familiar with crime prevention will not assert that it is easy to implement, that it can be achieved overnight, or that any preventive technique or device is foolproof. But we know that some tenets are essential to the success of any crime prevention program. These are:

1. The police must be the pivotal point for all crime prevention programs.
2. Citizens must carry out most crime prevention activities. A crime prevention program that does not require citizen involvement and participation will most probably fail.
3. While crime prevention can be one of the most effective tools for police-community relations, this should not become an end in itself.
4. All police officers must become experts in crime prevention techniques; all citizens must become involved in crime prevention activities.
5. Public awareness and education are essential to citizen involvement. Public education programs and materials must be developed professionally and must always reflect proven and practical experience.
6. A level and cool-headed attitude must permeate the crime prevention approach. Creating a state of public panic about crime would be ineffective and counterproductive.

*Security and Crime Prevention* has recognized the principles involved in crime prevention and has thoroughly discussed many, many types of community programs that have been successful in reducing crime. Also expertly addressed are crime prevention theories and specific steps citizens and businesses can take to reduce opportunities for victimization. Also presented is a much needed discussion of the role of criminal justice agencies in preventing crime. Perhaps most importantly, information gleaned from the use of this well-rounded text provides criminal justice educators, students, and professionals, as well as individual citizens, with the means to curb the increase of crime in their communities. Action taken by these groups to prevent crime can be more important than the combined efforts of all government workers and elected officials in the country. Crime prevention strategies as described in this book provide people with the power to stop crime and to stop the economic loss and human suffering that result from crimes against property and violent crimes against people. We have the wisdom to prevent many of these crimes. The human agony, loss of years of hard work and savings, and loss of pride and confidence in ourselves and our communities provide the incentive to put this wisdom to work for us. Preventing crime in this country is not a goal set too high, nor is it a goal that is unachievable. But it will take the time and effort of millions of Americans and the persistence and competent leadership of criminal justice personnel to accomplish this goal. The payoff, however, will be great, perhaps much greater than one might first expect. This should be kept in mind as this book is used and as crime prevention programs are implemented throughout the nation.

**L. D. Hyde**

*Director, Crime Prevention Division,*
*Department of Crime Control and Public Safety,*
*State of North Carolina*

# Preface

This book is concerned with the security and safety of the community, our businesses, and individual persons. It is possible for security to be achieved through crime prevention activities. This book does not consider our criminal justice system as the sole answer to crime prevention. In fact, it probably has a less significant impact on crime than do the roles of the family, the school, and the individual citizen.

This book is divided into four major sections. The first section, An Interdisciplinary Perspective, covers the general nature of crime prevention, current theories of crime prevention, and the effect that the family, school, and peer groups play on both crime causation and crime prevention.

Section II, Personal Crime Prevention, examines measures that individuals can take to prevent crime and protect themselves, their families, and their homes from victimization. This section covers not only violent street crimes but also such nonviolent crimes as deceptive advertising, medical quackery, and various other frauds. This section also devotes an entire chapter to crime prevention for the elderly who may not be victimized as often as the under-65 age group, but, when victimized, suffer much more devastating effects.

Section III, Business Crime Prevention, looks at crime prevention for business with an in-depth examination of both internal and external security problems. Effects of corruption in both business and government are covered, as well as the use of security surveys and target hardening procedures.

Section IV, Community-Based Crime Prevention, examines environmental design, various community programs, the role and relationship of criminal justice agencies, and new directions in crime prevention in which a discussion of promising new ideas, approaches, and strategies on the forefront is included.

A variety of research techniques was utilized for this book, including a review of the literature, observation, and interviews with crime prevention officers, private security administrators, and convicted criminals. Some information, such as that included in the chapter on corruption, was necessarily obtained under the Freedom of Information Act. Included in this book are chapters that some of my behavioral science colleagues may feel are too practical, such as the chapters on personal and home security. To this criticism, my only hope is that these critics never have to suffer any of the traumas of victimization.

In 1936, Sheldon and Eleanor Glueck of Harvard University wrote that the title of their book, *Preventing Crime,* was "frankly optimistic, and that some may regard it as unduly so." As with this book 45 years later, crime prevention is still a goal for optimists, the same kind of optimists who have discovered the secrets of flight, the cure of diseases, and knowledge of the mysteries of the body and who are unraveling the secrets of the universe. To those of you who are the achievers in life, set your goals, go forward, and be optimistic in this endeavor.

**Robert L. O'Block**

# Contents

Crime is a social problem that is interwoven
with almost every aspect of American life.
Controlling it involves improving the quality of family life,
the way schools are run, the way cities are planned,
the way workers are hired. Controlling crime
is the business of every American institution.
Controlling crime is the business of every American.

      *—The Challenge of Crime in a Free Society*

# Section I

# AN INTERDISCIPLINARY PERSPECTIVE

# Chapter 1

# The nature of crime prevention

Before the trouble comes, advice obtain;
After it has come, advice in vain.

Those words by Joseph Zabara, a thirteenth century Spanish Hebrew physician and poet, are as true today as when they were written. This phrase truly reflects an attitude of prevention and alludes to the consequences if preventive measures are ignored. There has been an interest in preventing crime for at least 4,000 years as evidenced by an ancient Egyptian hieroglyphic, which advises young men how to stay out of trouble.[1] Mankind has long been concerned with the problem of crime and its prevention. Crime as a major social problem has been attacked through the years by a number of approaches; most of the emphasis has been on seeking causation, punishment, and correction.

Jails and penitentiaries have been overcrowded for decades and, as the 1921 writings of Kate O'Hare point out, the "crime wave" is nothing new:

> Newspapers and magazines have been busy for the past few months discussing a disturbing social phenomena which they call the "crime wave." Judging from the reports of the press, crime has increased in the United States in an alarming manner during the last year. The jails are full, the criminal court dockets are overburdened and penitentiaries are crowded to capacity. Rare indeed is the newspaper that has not demanded more effective policing, more stringent laws, and more drastic penalties for the detection and punishment of crime.[2]

For many years the field of medicine has been trying to prevent disease. One might ask why a similar effort has not been applied to crime prevention. Unfortunately, there is still a great deal of emotionalism associated with crime, and this interferes with our ability to make unbiased decisions and to

---

[1]Burma, John H., *How To Understand Criminology and Penology.* Girard, Kansas: Haldeman-Julius Publications, 1943, p. 1. Little Blue Book No. 1819.
[2]O'Hare, Kate Richards, *Crime and Criminals.* Girard, Kansas: Frank P. O'Hare, Haldeman-Julius Collection, 1921, p. 1.

conduct unbiased research. Crime is not merely a physical problem with one direct cause as are many illnesses. Crime involves complex emotional, psychologic, social, and environmental variables and, therefore, prevention is not simply a matter of developing a "vaccine" or "antidote" to crime.

The crime prevention movement in America is only now beginning to achieve a new permanence as increasing crime rates make more and more streets unsafe, and more and more courts and penitentiaries become overcrowded. Since crime is a *social* problem, the police are unable to contain the crime problem within a socially tolerable level by themselves. Therefore, alternatives to arrest, conviction, punishment, and rehabilitation of criminals are being sought as methods of prevention. There are now many forces involved in crime prevention, as Fig. 1-1 demonstrates.

The general public still does not totally recognize that the causes of crime lay within such variables as societal structures, socioeconomic conditions, lack of self-discipline, methods of child-rearing, and the very home environment that parents provide for their children. Before it was realized that diseases are caused by bacteria and viruses, people employed witch doctors and medicine men to effect a cure by driving out evil spirits. Similarly, until the

**Fig. 1-1.** Approaches to crime prevention.

knowledge of crime causation filters down into the elementary school books and becomes a common basis of knowledge, we will continue to see a reactive approach to crime rather than the proactive approach of prevention. Any approach to dealing with crime other than prevention is self-defeating.

## DEFINITIONS OF CRIME PREVENTION

There have been several definitions offered for crime prevention. It has been described as "any organized activity aimed at keeping unlawful behavior from occurring originally or keeping such behavior to a minimum and thus avoiding police intervention; or any organized activity aimed at deterring unlawful behavior."[3] Akers and Sagarin define crime prevention as "actions taken to forestall crime beyond or instead of the threatening or the application of legal penalties."[4] Empey has defined crime prevention as an attempt to: (1) identify those institutional characteristics and processes most inclined to produce legitimate identities and nonpredatory behaviors in people; (2) restructure existing institutions or build new ones so that these desirable features are enhanced, and (3) discard those features that tend to foster criminal behaviors and identities.[5] The National Crime Prevention Institute defines crime prevention as "the anticipation, recognition and appraisal of a crime risk and the initiation of some action to remove or reduce it."[6] Vestermark and Blauvelt state, "prevention means, practically speaking, reducing the probability of criminal activity."[7] Although there are slight variations of the definition of crime prevention, most of them are explained in goal-oriented language, that goal being the prevention of crime.

## INTERDISCIPLINARY NATURE OF CRIME PREVENTION

The field of crime prevention by its very nature transcends the bounds of any one discipline. It does not fall totally within the bounds of pure criminal justice since many concerns of security and crime prevention also include psychosocial, economic, and architectural aspects. Security and crime prevention are true eclectic subjects; criminology itself draws from all areas of

---

[3]Pursuit, Dan G., et al., editors, *Police Programs for Preventing Crime and Delinquency.* Springfield, Illinois: Charles C Thomas, 1972, p. xi.

[4]Akers, Ronald L., and Sagarin, Edward, editors, *Crime Prevention and Social Control.* New York: Praeger Publishers, 1972, p. viii.

[5]Empey, Lamar T., "Crime Prevention: The Fugitive Utopia," in *Crime: Emerging Issues,* James A. Inciardi and Harvey A. Siegal, editors. New York: Praeger Publishers, 1977, p. 104.

[6]"Understanding Crime Prevention." *The Practice of Crime Prevention.* Louisville, Ky.: National Crime Prevention Institute Press, Vol. 1, 1978, no. 1-2.

[7]Vestermark, Seymour D., Jr., and Blauvelt, Peter D., *Controlling Crime in the School: A Complete Security Handbook for Administrators.* West Nyack, N.Y.: Parker Publishing Co., Inc., p. 115.

society—science, education, law, religion, sociology, social work, political science, economics, and public administration.[8]

## Crime prevention disciplines

Crime prevention must be approached in an interdisciplinary manner if it is to be effective. The contributions of the major fields involved in the crime prevention effort are listed in the following section.

**Education.** Early recognition of young students experiencing problems in school can help prevent juvenile delinquency. School-related difficulties are highly indicative of problems at home that interfere with learning and ability to complete school work. Learning disabilities or defects in the socialization process can also contribute to future delinquency.

In addition, criminal justice education must be increased and advanced at the college level. Improved training courses as well as advancements made regarding the academic understanding of various social problems can contribute to crime prevention.

**Architecture.** Architecture can play a role in crime prevention through the design of safer buildings using more crime-resistant materials. The importance of crime prevention measures in the incorporation of building and home designs must be realized by all architects.

**Psychology.** Psychology is making continuing contributions in the area of crime prevention by increasing our understanding of human behavior.

**Criminal justice.** As a new academic discipline, criminal justice is in the forefront of promoting crime prevention. Criminal justice is also critically examining the various components of our criminal justice system and promoting the upgrading of its personality.

**Systems analysis.** By directing a proper amount of attention toward a systems approach, research in the crime prevention area will be increased, thereby assuring that efforts and measures have been evaluated as to their effectiveness before being implemented. Therefore, programs and projects would have a demonstrated impact on crime and delinquency problems and would be undertaken with more confidence. Ineffective programs would be avoided without a waste of resources.

**Law.** Formulating laws that are in the public interest, expediting court processes, and establishing laws for the betterment of the citizenry are ways in which the discipline of law can improve crime prevention efforts.

**Biology and medicine.** By increasing our knowledge of the anatomy and physiology of the human body and its reactions to various stimuli, and by

---

[8]Inciardi, James A., and Siegal, Harvey A., editors, *Crime: Emerging Issues.* New York: Praeger Publishers, 1977, p. 1.

coming forward as expert witnesses in cases of medical quackery, for example, biologists and medical personnel can do much to help prevent crime.

**Electronics.** The field of electronics has played a significant role in crime prevention through the development of security and protection devices that both enhance personal safety and protect physical structures.

**Political science.** Political scientists seek to identify political strategy and solutions to the crime problem usually by the allocation of resources.

**Sociology.** By broadening our understanding of society, its interactions, and processes, and using this knowledge to reduce the need and motivation of individuals to deviate, sociology has contributed much to crime prevention.

Crime prevention as a field of study and inquiry should not be limited to the most obvious crimes, such as burglary, robbery, and rape, but should also include the study of other ways through which individuals are criminally victimized. These include such nonviolent crimes as deceptive advertising, medical quackery, confidence games, corruption in government, restraint of trade, and efforts by professional associations to stifle competition and thereby criminally set artificial prices. The principles of prevention of crime in this book are meant to include those circumstances in which the individual is victimized by another individual, group, organization, business, or government, both violently and nonviolently.

## ROLE OF PRIVATE INDUSTRY IN PREVENTION
### Private security

The goal of private security has always been to prevent or deter crime, while the statutory goal of the police has been—and still is—to enforce the law. The job of private security personnel is not to apprehend anyone after a crime has been committed; they seek to prevent the crime from ever occurring. While it is true that police spend a major portion of their time in "preventive patrol," the effectiveness of this procedure has recently been questioned, and prevention is still regarded as a secondary goal of law enforcement. Although many police chiefs have expressed interest in prevention, their efforts until now have been hampered by the lack of a suitable knowledge base. The private security industry will continue to play a critical role in crime prevention. Facilities such as nuclear power plants, as well as many other businesses and industries, must continue to be protected by the private security industry.

### Insurance industry

The insurance industry can also be a major force in crime prevention. Both private security and the insurance industries have a vested interest in controlling crime. Further, each also has more potential financial resources available for implementation of programs than do many municipalities. Since the private sector is more interested in cost-effectiveness than in bureaucratic red tape, some very efficient crime prevention programs have been developed by insurance companies for their clients.

### Cost of crime prevention versus cost of crime

Can we afford *not* to prevent crime? The answer to this question is obviously no. No one can put a monetary value on human life or personal safety that is at risk during the commission of violent crimes. Even those crimes in which the victim and offender do not come into direct contact are costing this country billions of dollars every year in economic losses.

Crime prevention does not always have to be expensive. Many crimes are committed against residential structures by unauthorized entry through unlocked doors and windows. Therefore, the simple locking of doors and windows, which will cost the individual nothing, can be an effective crime prevention measure. Many other crime prevention measures, such as changing a key-in-knob lockset to a deadbolt lock will require only minimal investment but will tremendously increase the physical safety of the structure and therefore the safety of those who occupy the building. A home or building that complies with recommended security precautions may also be eligible for decreased insurance premiums, which will help offset the cost of the increased security. Crimes of opportunity are crimes that can be prevented. If police resources and time could be spent preventing these crimes rather than reacting to them—responding, investigating, and making arrests, in addition to the time spent in the courts during criminal trials—the savings could be passed on to all citizens in the form of lower taxes. Also, if many of the crimes that cause businesses to go bankrupt could be prevented, there would be increased revenues, less unemployment, and more legitimate channels for everyone to achieve a satisfying livelihood. The cost of implementing various crime prevention programs, purchasing security hardware, and providing increased assistance to social agencies that help prevent crime is far less than the cost of crime in many respects. In this book various approaches to crime prevention will be described. Some measures of prevention require no expenditures while others require substantial investment. However, all will ultimately help reduce the cost of victimization, both in terms of economic losses and human losses—physical injury and death.

### STEPS IN CRIME PREVENTION

One frustrated police chief is quoted as saying, "But what can I do about crime prevention? Who is the expert? Where do I find the information?"[9] If it

---

[9]McGowan, J. F., "The Empty Shelf." *Police*, May-June, 1966, pp. 82-84.

is any consolation, he can rest assured that crime prevention is not just the responsibility of the police, the courts, and the prisons. Crime cannot be controlled without the active support of individual private citizens, schools, businesses, and labor unions. Crime has an effect on everyone, not just the criminal and the victim.[10] The National Crime Commissions Report, *A National Strategy to Reduce Crime* (1973), recommended four priorities for reducing crime: (1) preventing juvenile delinquency, (2) improving delivery of social services, (3) reducing delays in the criminal justice process, and (4) securing more citizen participation in the criminal justice system.

Massive community efforts will be required, and law enforcement's role in these efforts should be to lead, encourage, and assist, but not to take sole responsibility. Crime is a community problem and it will take various community resources to meet the problem head-on. In fact, one can imagine the ineffectiveness of any police program that fails to secure community participation beforehand. Further, all segments of society must be represented so that all groups will have an opportunity to develop crime prevention measures specifically tailored to meet their needs. The elderly, for example, have particular needs that can neutralize their vulnerability to crime; in order to serve this population satisfactorily, crime prevention programs must seek their participation and cooperation.

*The Challenge of Crime in a Free Society*, a result of a Presidential Commission on Law Enforcement, offers seven major steps toward crime prevention:

1. Society must seek to prevent crime before it happens by assuring all Americans a stake in the benefits and responsibilities of American life, by strengthening law enforcement, and by reducing criminal opportunities.
2. Society's aim of reducing crime would be better served if the system of criminal justice developed a far broader range of techniques with which to deal with individual offenders.
3. The system of criminal justice must eliminate existing injustices if it is to achieve its ideals and gain the respect and cooperation of all citizens.
4. The system of criminal justice must obtain more people and better people— police, prosecutors, judges, defense attorneys, probation and parole officers, and corrections officials—with more knowledge, experience, initiative, and integrity.
5. Research into the problems of crime and criminal administration, by those both within and without the system of criminal justice, must be intensified.
6. The police, courts, and correctional agencies must be given substantially greater amounts of money if they are to improve their ability to control crime.
7. Individual citizens, civic and business organizations, religious institutions,

---

[10]Lewin, Stephen, editor, *Crime and Its Prevention*. New York: The H. W. Wilson Company, 1968, p. 3.

and all levels of government must take responsibility for planning and implementing the changes that must be made in the criminal justice system if crime is to be reduced.[11]

These are general steps which, if taken, can contribute to crime reduction. In addition, I suggest:

1. Providing preventive services by schools for children who appear to be heading toward delinquency. This should be positive intervention and must begin by the fifth grade at the latest and continue through the high school years.
2. Reducing the recidivism rate among adults. As with providing positive intervention to the troubled juvenile, we are dealing with persons known to us (rather than an unknown figure in the shadow and alleyways). There must be improved correctional services to reduce the number of repeat offenders.

Examples of measures that can be taken to accomplish the above two goals include various social work services, counseling, psychologic assessments, visiting teacher services, special education programs, Big Brother/Big Sister programs, student-centered education, guidance programs, providing positive role models, and a whole array of various other school, community, and police programs that are described in the following chapters.

## RECIDIVISM AND CRIME PREVENTION

The individual who commits a felony in most cases has already committed a previous felony. In fact, the FBI estimates the recidivism rate to be 75%. Although a major source of crime is repeat offenders, the solution to recidivism is not long prison sentences. This has only helped to stigmatize, label, and teach additional criminal behavior to the imprisoned. First offenders in particular must be kept away from the hardened criminals who are housed in our jails and prisons. Therefore, "more effective" sentencing, not necessarily traditional and lengthy sentencing, is a partial answer to the recidivism problem. First offenders could realize the magnitude and seriousness of their crime but would not be exposed to additional criminal behavior.

C. R. Jeffery maintains that self-actualization of human potential should be the goal of crime prevention. If such a goal were met, we would not walk the streets in fear of the rapist or mugger, children would not be beaten to death by their parents, or old persons would not be assaulted, and we would not have to put criminals in cages for years. By using the self-actualization of human potential, according to Jeffery:

> We need not resort to police or prison brutality to control the human potential nor waste billions of dollars a year trying to keep the old system afloat with

---

[11]*Challenge of Crime in a Free Society.* Washington, D.C.: Superintendent of Documents, Summary, 1967, pp. v-vi.

this model. The only question remaining then is: If the present model is so stupid, why do we resist all attempts to change it? This question I cannot answer.[12]

## CRIME PREVENTION IN THE CLASSROOM

Crime prevention as an academic subject not only should be included in every criminal justice, sociology, or political science curriculum, but also it should be a required course for all students regardless of major. Crime prevention is important because it directly affects the life and safety of individuals, neighborhoods, cities, states, and the nation. The more the general population and our future leaders know about crime prevention, the better off they and everyone else will be. Crime prevention must be incorporated into all criminal justice programs. It addresses such variables as environmental design, lighting, alarms, and locks, but it also looks at the nature of human behavior, why persons commit crimes, and what can be done through social programs to prevent and deter criminal behavior. Therefore, it is vital that college students who will be our future lawyers, physicians, legislators, social workers, law enforcement practitioners, architects, and business leaders, have knowledge as to the current state of the art.

## CONCLUSION

While there will never be 100% success in combatting crime, crime has been reduced very significantly on many fronts. The improved security at airports has reduced actual skyjackings to an infrequent incident. Other successful crime prevention measures include the direct deposit of checks, two-key safes for money in public conveyances, and the practice by service station attendants of not carrying change at night. Crime prevention encompasses a broad range of activities and must involve a wide range of services. Since crime affects everyone either directly or indirectly, efforts to prevent it must involve everyone. Although crime cannot be eliminated entirely, most authorities believe it can be significantly reduced in many areas. The purpose of this book is to provide the principles of crime prevention that will enable us to achieve this goal.

---

[12]Jeffery, C. Ray, *Crime Prevention Through Environmental Design.* Beverly Hills: Sage Publications, Inc., 1977, p. 10.

Chapter 2

# Crime prevention theory

Formulation of theory in the behavioral sciences—including crime prevention—is still in its infancy. Theorists in crime prevention are at about the same state as when Newton lay half-asleep under the apple tree wondering why the apples did not fall up. Current theories would probably be more correctly labeled propositions or at best theorems. Although there are many theories of crime causation that have been grouped into various schools, there is a deficiency of theories of crime prevention with testable hypotheses.

## IMPORTANCE OF THEORY

Kerlinger has defined a theory as a set of interrelated constructs (concepts), definitions, and propositions that present a systematic view of phenomena by specifying relations among variables, with the purpose of explaining and predicting the phenomena.[1] Without a body of crime prevention theories and testable hypotheses, we will always be wondering the equivalent of why apples do not fall up. Therefore, the scientific approach in the long run will prove to be the only rational approach. It has been said of criminal justice that, unlike other fields, large amounts of money are spent without knowing what works. Less than 1% of all criminal justice expenditures goes for research. Despite the lack of funding, individual researchers in the field of crime prevention are beginning to develop a body of scientific knowledge with workable theories. This scientific approach is a systematic method for the attainment of knowledge. The scientific method has built into it the advantage of self-correction with continual verification and replication by other scientists. Even when a hypothesis seems to be confirmed, the scientist will compare it to alternative hypotheses that have also been tested. The scientist will not accept a statement as true, even if it sounds completely logical, until he or she has experimentally tested it. More than anything else,

---

[1]Kerlinger, Fred N., *Foundations of Behavioral Research.* New York: Holt, Rinehart, and Winston, Inc., 1973, p. 9.

12

a lack of basic research is the reason why crime on a massive scale will be with us for many years to come. The purpose of this chapter is to present a brief exploration of several of the current theories being expounded today.

During the mid-1960s, the era of the President's Crime Commission, the United States government asked social scientists for help in dealing with and understanding crime. As noted by Wilson, "there was not in being a body of tested or even well-accepted theories as to how crime might be prevented or criminals reformed, nor was there much agreement on the 'causes' of crime except that they were social, not psychological, biological, or individualistic."[2] The situation today has not changed dramatically. As Wilson commented, "Only later did I realize that criminologists, and perhaps all sociologists, are part of an intellectual tradition that does not contain built-in checks against the premature conversion of opinion into policy."[3] According to Wolfgang and associates, nearly half of the theoretical works in criminology are polemical, without much structure and with little usefulness in developing hypotheses. Another one-fourth may be designated as formal theory, and one out of four of the works contains some empirical referents. Wolfgang et al. perceive most of the theoretical research to be of limited scope, either with regard to a specific phenomenon or to a type of individual.[4] In addition, these authors point out that very few of the theoretical propositions within the framework of the theoretical writings have been demonstrated, and only one fourth include suggestions for verification; in 60% of the cases, testability is not even referred to as a problem. The construction of novel and innovative theory, conceptualization, or methodologies appears infrequently in these theoretical works.[5]

Presently there are three broad categorizations into which criminologic theories can be placed.[6] The first group includes theories that focus upon the blockage of individuals' striving for goals and the consequent alienation individuals experience when goals cannot be met. Some of these approaches apply most centrally to violent crime such as homicide but most are directly related to property crimes. The second categorization pertains to subcultural conditions, roles, and behavioral patterns conducive to crime. From this perspective, crime is a consequence of both a lack of socially accepted role models and behavior patterns and a prevalence of role models and behaviors that encourage the learning of criminal behaviors. The third group of theories

---

[2]Wilson, James Q., *Thinking about Crime*. New York: Basic Books, Inc., 1975, p. 58.
[3]Ibid, p. 62.
[4]Wolfgang, Marvin E., Figlio, Robert M., and Thornberry, Terence P., *Evaluating Criminology*. New York: Elsevier, 1978, p. 143.
[5]Ibid.
[6]Palmer, Stuart, *The Prevention of Crime*. New York: Behavioral Publications, 1973, p. 64.

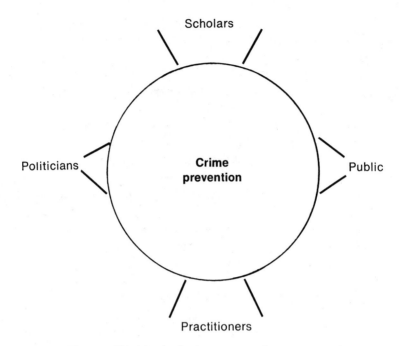

**Fig. 2-1.** Divisions of crime prevention awareness.

emphasizes two related matters: (1) the functions that crime serves, particularly as a contributor to social organization, and (2) the social controls that society establishes in order to both perpetuate and prevent crime. Labeling individuals as criminal before the fact, crime in prisons and reformatories, and inappropriate punishment are all examples of controls that contribute to crime.

Lunden argues that at present there is no theory of crime prevention, only a number of theories of crime *causation*.[7] He believes that a theory of criminality is a *why* question whereas the issues in prevention are *how* questions. The problem also appears to be one of perspective. There are four major groups concerned with the problems of crime prevention: (1) politicians, (2) law enforcement practitioners, (3) the public, and (4) scholars. Each group has a limited view on crime prevention, as is illustrated in Fig. 2-1: The politician's view is generally limited to financial and political aspects; practitioners (i.e., police officers, probation officers, security executives, etc.) deal with the problem on a case-by-case method; the public's perceptions are blurred by fear, biases, and prejudices; scholars with true theoretical ability are too far removed from the other groups to be effective.

---

[7]Lunden, Walter A., "The Theory of Crime Prevention." *British Journal of Criminology*, Vol. 2, Jan. 1962, pp. 213-228.

We have not traditionally been a preventive society. In general, action is taken only after a problem has attained large-scale proportions. For example, the medical community, although changing its emphasis in recent years, has been oriented primarily toward treating ill individuals rather than pursuing broad preventive measures; mental health practitioners emphasize psychiatric intervention into the lives of emotionally disturbed individuals, but there is very little emphasis on preventing mental illness before this intervention becomes necessary. Unfortunately, the same has also been true with the crime problem.

Only the permanence of the crime prevention movement will assure that we are making a deliberate, planned, and organized attempt to prevent crime rather than continuing the most inefficient practices of apprehending, arresting, convicting, and punishing criminals. Even when outdated methods and solutions fail and problems deteriorate into crisis situations, antiquated solutions are still tried, such as no-knock entry, preventive detention, and wiretapping. All of these methods have been used in the recent past in vain attempts to reduce crime.[8] It should be apparent that now more than ever, with the skyrocketing crime statistics, new theories are needed. However, scientific research methods must be used at the same time so that assumptions and untested hypotheses will be avoided.

Many scholars and practitioners have written articles and books expressing their own version of the cause of crime and how it can best be prevented. For example, many state "If only we didn't label individuals," or "We need to get tough with criminals," or "If everyone had access to legitimate opportunity," there would be much less crime. However, many of these and similar statements are not theories but beliefs, and in some cases, very primitive beliefs. In order to be more scientific, we must start evaluating these statements to determine their validity.

## Test of a good theory

The following test can be used to determine whether or not a statement is an actual theory or is the writer's personal belief, an assumption, an insight, a way of looking at something, an ideology, or an approach:

1. Does the "theory" have testable hypotheses?
2. Have the hypotheses been tested?
3. Has the research been replicated by others in different locations?
4. Have the results been consistent?
5. Does the "theory" make prediction possible at a rate of probability that is better than chance?

---

[8]Flournoy, Roy, *New Crime Controls: Savings for Taxpayers and Victims.* Denver: Church of the Cross, 1977, p. 91.

Crime prevention is in a continual state of evolution.[9] Therefore, a number of different approaches are currently being used, including reducing opportunities for crime, various police/citizen actions to discourage crime, intervention programs for populations identified as being high risk for criminal activities, target hardening, and removal of environmental or personal causes of crime.

### THEORETICAL APPROACHES

In the prevention of crime, several theoretical approaches have been suggested. Some of the more current approaches are discussed below.

### Labeling theory

There has been much discussion about the role of labeling as a self-fulfilling prophecy and its role in crime. This may prove to be particularly important in the treatment of young offenders who are labeled as delinquents or criminals. It would seem that this practice would do little to discourage criminal behavior since any latent criminal tendencies would tend to be stimulated. Labeling, therefore, should be used only in specifying individuals as nonoffenders rather than as criminals and delinquents. At present, the relative importance of labeling in crime prevention is undetermined and remains an untested theory. Perhaps if nonlabeling is accompanied by other variables, such as the provision of socially approved role models and a reduction of criminal subcultures, a major impact in crime prevention will be realized.

### Learning theory

Jeffery,[10] who has examined the implications of learning theory and crime prevention, believes that a logical approach to crime prevention involves removing or reducing any reinforcements thought or known to perpetuate criminal activity. This approach would not rely upon conventional (and ineffective) or rehabilitative approaches, such as prisons, executions, or therapy programs, to prevent further crimes. This premise is very similar to the concept of secondary gain, which has long been recognized by the medical profession as a major contributing factor in the development of many psychosomatic illnesses. Removing the secondary gains such as sympathy, attention, flowers, cards, and gifts sometimes greatly inhibits the expression or development of physical complaints of psychosomatic origin.

---

[9]Adams, Gary, "Crime Prevention: An Evolutionary Analysis." *The Police Chief,* Dec. 1971, p. 52.
[10]Jeffery, C. Ray, *Crime Prevention Through Environmental Design.* Beverly Hills: Sage Publications, Inc., 1977.

Jeffery introduced a profit-loss or pleasure-pain model and put this dichotomy in terms of a probability model, since future consequences of behavior are always in terms of probability statements. Therefore, according to Jeffery, criminal behavior (CB) is the probability of reinforcement (Rp) minus the probability of pain or punishment (Pp), or:

$$CB = Rp - Pp$$

The Jeffery theorem is the type of paradigm that needs to be experimentally tested and either verified or rejected. If over the last 2000 years the field of medicine had continually insisted on using the same procedures on patients that made them worse instead of better, our health care system would obviously be very primitive and leave much to be desired. But that is exactly what the criminal justice system has done with the use of prisons to "correct" offenders. This comparison merely reminds us of the need for further basic research and scientifically tested hypotheses rather than assuming a new proposal to be fact before it has been properly tested.

## Displacement theory

Displacement theory could be called a negative theory of crime prevention. This theory postulates that while crime may be prevented in one neighborhood by the use of neighborhood watch and target hardening programs, the criminals simply move to another neighborhood where the crime rate then increases. Crime prevention through these tactics only displaces crime from one neighborhood to another. This theory is somewhat plausible since crime is largely a matter of opportunity. Therefore, crime prevention measures cannot be taken in only one area but will be necessary throughout a community, and programs and strategies aimed at reducing motivations for criminal conduct will also have to be utilized. Displacement theory at this time is still generally regarded as a theory and not proved scientific fact.

## Marxist theory

There are still a number of persons who subscribe to the Marxist view of crime prevention, in which crime is considered to be the result of economic exploitation by the group in power. Cramer, pointing to the work of Chambliss, believes that on a theoretical level, there exists a perspective that does not hold control and prevention of crime as a goal.[11] In fact, according to the Marxian viewpoint, crime may serve several purposes for the ruling class. For example, many individuals, such as law enforcement officers, judges, criminal justice educators, private security personnel, and many other individuals in-

---

[11]Cramer, James A., editor, *Preventing Crime.* Beverly Hills: Sage Publications, 1978, p. 9.

cluding the criminals, are employed because of crime and, therefore, their livelihood is dependent upon the fact that crime exists. This view suggests that crime exists and/or is created by members of society who would have to make large sacrifices if it did not exist. The Marxist theory also maintains that crime diverts deviant energies of members of the lower socioeconomic class away from the exploitation by the higher economic classes and keeps these energies directed toward other members of the same class.

However, it is quite apparent that this argument is erroneous since a great deal of crime also exists in Marxist and Communist countries. Further, many crimes are not caused by economics, but by passion, jealousy, distrust, and revenge.

### Environmental design theory

The major theorists linking crime with the physical environment have been Newman,[12] Jeffery,[13] and Gardiner.[14] According to Gardiner, the concept of territoriality is the most widely recognized theory linking the physical environment with criminal activity. The concept of territoriality must involve at least three conditions: (1) all residents must take a genuine interest and feel a certain amount of responsibility for an area that goes beyond that of their own front door; (2) residents must be willing to take action when they believe this territory to be threatened by intruders; and (3) the above two factors must be strong enough so that potential offenders are able to perceive the fact that any intrusion is likely to be noticed. Therefore, they are less likely to commit a criminal act. In all of its various forms, territoriality is a desired condition or goal in achieving environmental security.[15] Fig. 2-2 is a schematic representation of the interrelationships of environments and crime.

Based on the environmental design theory, design criteria for redesigning the physical environment should be established to allow and encourage the development of individual and group territoriality. In order for this to be accomplished, we must examine a number of peripheral factors including the residence of the victim, the residence or source of the offender, and the location of the offense. This information will determine both the geographic area of the environment in which the crime took place and the reason why the victim and offender came into contact. Many elements within the environment may be responsible for bringing victim and offender together; these are

---

[12]Newman, Oscar, *Defensible Space*. New York: The Macmillan Co., 1972.
[13]Jeffery, op. cit.
[14]Gardiner, Richard A., *Design for Safe Neighborhoods*. Washington, D.C.: National Institute of Law Enforcement and Criminal Justice, Law Enforcement Assistance Administration, U.S. Department of Justice, 1978.
[15]Ibid.

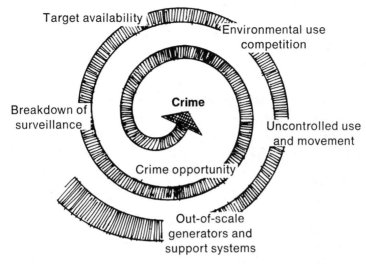

**Fig. 2-2.** Interrelationship of environment to crime. (From Gardiner, Richard A., *Design for Safe Neighborhoods*. Washington, D.C.: National Institute of Law Enforcement and Criminal Justice, LEAA, U.S. Department of Justice, 1978.)

referred to as crime generators. There are basically three categories of opportunity crime generators within an environment that must be considered as affecting the level of environmental security:

1. Known crime generators—"hot spots" or areas in which crime is known to occur frequently, such as bars, drug dealing points, parks
2. Service generators—public or private facilities and elements that attract potential victims as well as potential offenders, such as open spaces, parks, public facilities, hospitals, high schools, and commercial locations
3. Movement generators—public conveyances that attract potential victims/offenders, such as subways, bus stops, walkways, parking lots

As interaction among people takes place within an environment, some will become victims and some will become offenders. Therefore, identification of crime generators plays a major role in analyzing the cause and effect phenomena and in developing solutions to the problem. By relating the location of the crime generators with the structure of the environment and how and by whom the environment is used, it is possible to speculate on a probable cause-and-effect relationship between certain patterns of crime.

Decisions to locate or relocate high schools, hospitals, commercial developments, parks, playgrounds, etc., should be made on the basis of these factors and the resultant interrelationships of persons who will be using the environment. For example, a factory that will employ a large number of persons should not be located in a high crime area so that interrelationships between potential victims and offenders can be minimized. Unfortunately, this aspect of site selection is often not considered, and the potential for harm and crime impact remains unrecognized or ignored by city planners.

The California Crime Technological Research Foundation[16] has taken a technological approach to various types of threats to environmental security and developed an equation for determining the margin of safety:

$$E = \left[\frac{R}{M} - 1\right] \times 100$$

where

    E  = Entry security safety margin (%)
    R  = Resistance to entry
    M  = Man's threat

As Grenough notes, environmental design offers new avenues of thought and development for those who are attempting to thread their way effectively and sensitively between two undesirable extremes—high crime rates and a police state.[17] Specific crime prevention techniques of environmental design are discussed in Chapter 12.

## TAP theory

Response time, or the amount of time it takes the police to respond to a crime, is dependent upon three distinct timing activities: (1) detection time, or the time from the beginning of the commission of the crime until it is detected and an alarm sounded; (2) reporting time, or the time interval between activation of the alarm or detection by other means (passersby, guards, etc.) and the receipt of the information by police; and (3) police response time, or the time interval from the receipt of the information by the police dispatcher until the police patrol arrives at the scene of the crime. The culmination of these three responses, or the total interval between the detection of the criminal act and the arrival of police officers at the scene, is known as time of arrival of police (TAP). As stated by Mandelbaum, "TAP includes the time of arrival of other counterforce elements, such as guards and watchmen, as

---

[16]*A Technological Approach to Building Security.* California Crime Technological Research Foundation, Office of Criminal Justice Planning, Law Enforcement Assistance Administration, U.S. Department of Justice, 1974, p. 5.

[17]Grenough, John L., "Crime Prevention: A New Approach—Environmental Psychology and Criminal Behavior." *Journal of Police Science and Administration*, Vol. 2, No. 3, 1974, p. 343.

well as the police; however, because the great majority of responses to criminal alarms are by the police, TAP is used as the basic criterion."[18]

In a report for the Small Business Administration,[19] an equation is offered for TAP theory which is expressed:

$$Cd = f(TAP, ti)$$

This equation reads that crime deterrence is a function of time of arrival of police and the time of intrusion.

As discussed in Chapter 12, a key concept in cutting crime is to increase the time of intrusion and escape of the intruder. The complexity and length of time necessary to gain unauthorized entry are crucial in determining whether a criminal will accept the risk. Prior to 1972, these factors were not given particular attention by most architects and still are not enforced today by mandatory building codes. If the criminal decides to accept the risk and does enter successfully, the next most important factor affecting TAP becomes detection and capture. This principle involves a systems approach, utilizing detection and transmission devices at the site, communication lines to commercial central stations and/or the police, opportunities for passersby to observe criminal activity, and the arrival of police at the scene of the crime.

Results of recent studies are indicating that the most critical factor is the reporting time of the crime. If this is done automatically, response from the police can begin instantaneously. But victims and witnesses have been known to wait twenty minutes or more before calling the police. The further development of accurate and automatic reporting devices will prove to be a great asset and partial solution to this problem.

## Random area search theory

Probably no other aspect of crime prevention is so frequently used as random area search, or "patrol." However, there is no scientific proof that such searches do, in fact, prevent crime. The basic theory of random area search is the probability of detecting an event (crime) that takes place within a given area by an observer (the patrol), moving continuously in the area in a random manner. This theory is expressed in the following equation:[20]

$$P = 1 - EXP\ (-qtnv/c)$$

---

[18]Mandelbaum, Albert J., *Fundamentals of Protective Systems*. Springfield, Illinois: Charles C Thomas, Publisher, 1973, p. 49.

[19]Mandelbaum, Albert J., et. al., *Protective Devices Systems*. Senate Documents, Volume 1, 91st Congress, 1st Session, Washington, D.C.: U.S. Government Printing Office, 1969, p. VII.

[20]Elliott, J. F., and Sardino, Thomas J., *Crime Control Team*. Springfield, Illinois: Charles C Thomas, Publisher, 1971, p. 13.

where

P = Probability that patrol will intercept the crime

EXP = Exponent

q = Probability of detecting the crime if the patrol visits the location during the commission of the crime

t = Time required to carry out the crime, plus the time that the perpetrator remains in the area and is identifiable by the patrol as the perpetrator of the crime

n = Number of patrol units in the area

v = Velocity of the patrol unit

c = Length of the area that is vulnerable to attack and is being protected by the patrol (the sum of the lengths of all of the streets and alleys in the area)

The use of patrol as a means of crime prevention dates back to the earliest days of security. It also serves other functions, which include the detection of criminal activity, and a rapid means of reaction to criminal attack. However, the recent Kansas City patrol experiment has questioned the value of traditional police patrol, but further validation and replication of this experiment will be necessary before firm conclusions can be reached.[21]

## Information theory

Willmer suggests that many different forms of information about criminal activity are emitted, some even by criminals themselves.[22] The strength of the signals emitted will depend on the decision, skill, and experience of the criminal. The expected level of payoff also influences the strength of the signals emitted. According to this theorist, several forms of deterrence can be achieved by reducing the level of payoffs for committing the criminal act and by increasing the strength of the signal the criminal has to emit in order to perpetrate the crime. This could be accomplished by target hardening, for example. Another type of deterrence can be obtained if the police can make a criminal change his or her method of operation or the type of crime generally committed.

In management terms, the level of payoff can be thought of as the point of cost effectiveness of committing the crime. In other words, is the risk of getting caught worth the risk involved in committing the crime? The strength of the signal the criminal emits can also depend on the way he prepares for a crime, his skill in executing it, the methods used to dispose of stolen property, etc. An example of decreasing payoffs is provided by the all-night conve-

[21]Kelling, George, et al., *The Kansas City Preventive Patrol Experiment: A Summary Report.* Washington, D.C.: The Police Foundation, 1974.

[22]Willmer, M. A. P., *Crime and Information Theory.* Edinburgh: Edinburgh University Press, 1970, p. 67.

nience store that advertises the fact that no more than $50 is kept in cash or that it takes two persons and two keys to unlock the safe. An example of reading a criminal's signals is the "skyjacker profiles" used by security personnel at major airports. Information theory appears logical, but conclusive judgments cannot be reached until research indicates levels of performance for the optimal types of crimes toward which this theory is oriented.

## Stress theory and Transcendental Meditation (TM)

Lanphear formulates an interesting hypothesis regarding stress theory and TM in the causation and prevention of crime.[23] Lanphear believes that all of the competing theories of crime causation are correct but that they do not go far enough. For example, all of the various theories emphasizing unemployment, anxiety, low intelligence, and unequal opportunity are correct, but they do not consider the ultimate cause—stress. Lanphear provides the analogy that any machine will break down if it is taxed beyond its limits. The breakdown caused by stress in human terms could certainly be displayed in the form of criminal activity. One factor that produces stress is the emphasis in our society upon the acquisition of wealth, big homes, fancy cars, stylish clothes, gourmet foods, and expensive entertainment; however, to many people these are unattainable within legal means. This fact along with other pressures in society produces stress. Thus, according to Lanphear, stress is the ultimate cause of criminal behavior, and the relieving of stress through transcendental meditation is the means to prevention. TM can be accomplished without the use of drugs, confinement, force, coercion, or expense. As an individual activity, it can be practiced anywhere. TM is now being taught to inmates in a few prisons but conclusive data have not yet been formulated on its effectiveness as a crime prevention technique. It will be interesting to compare the recidivism rates of prisoners who practice TM and those who have never been exposed to it.

## Deterrence theory

Deterrence theory can be defined simply as the threat of punishment to inhibit wrongful behavior.[24] The theory of deterrence has been the subject of much debate since the time mankind first carved penal codes onto stone tablets. Penal codes may have changed drastically over the years but the arguments concerning the effectiveness of this most volatile subject continue to exist. There is rarely any agreement between the opposing sides of the vast

[23]Lanphear, Roger G., *Freedom From Crime Through the T.M.-Sidhi Program.* New York: Nellen Publishing Co., 1979.
[24]Levine, James P., Musheno, Michael C., and Palumbo, Dennis J., *Criminal Justice, A Public Policy Approach.* New York: Harcourt Brace Jovanovich, Inc., 1980, p. 353.

issues that relate to deterrence theory, and scientific research concerning this subject has not been done with the same energy and dedication as with other areas in the law enforcement field. It has been studied and researched to a limited extent, however, and criminologists of today have made a distinction between special and general deterrence. *Special deterrence* refers to the threat of further punishment of one who has already been convicted and punished for crime; *general deterrence* is the threat of punishment that is applicable to all citizens, including convicted criminals.[25] Special deterrence would include threats to dissuade the criminal from recidivism, such as threat of the same or more severe punishment should the criminal behavior be repeated. General deterrence, which applies to all members of society, includes such punishments as traffic tickets for not obeying traffic laws or threats of punishment for evading income taxes.

According to Wilson, criminologists have only recently given serious empirical attention to the deterrent and accessibility aspects of crime.[26] This is both unfortunate and inexcusable. However, Gibbs and Erickson provide the following three propositions:[27]

1. Pp $\longleftrightarrow$ De
2. De $>\!\!-\!\!<$ Cr
3. Pp $>\!\!-\!\!<$ Cr

where

Pp is some property of legal punishment
De is deterrence
Cr is some kind of crime rate
$\longleftrightarrow$ signifies a direct relation
$>\!\!-\!\!<$ signifies an inverse relation

Given the first two propositions, the third is derived, as Gibbs and Erickson state, because the specific assertion is not testable. It does not distinguish between actual and prescribed punishments let alone specify any particular property of punishment, such as celerity, certainty, and severity.[28] As these authors suggest, because deterrence is an inherently unobservable phenomenon, we will never see or hear any individual being deterred and therefore we will never be able to directly measure this phenomenon. We can study it only inferentially.

---

[25]Morris, Norval, and Hawkins, Gordon, *The Honest Politician's Guide to Crime Control.* Chicago: The University of Chicago Press, 1970, p. 255.
[26]Wilson, James Q., *Thinking About Crime.* New York: Basic Books, Inc., 1975, p. 55.
[27]Gibbs, Jack, and Erickson, Maynard L., "Capital Punishment and the Deterrence Doctrine," in *Capital Punishment in the United States,* Hugo Bedau and Chester Pierce, editors, New York: AMS Press, Inc., 1975, p. 303.
[28]Ibid.

The notion that deterrence does not actually work against the criminally inclined has long been questioned. In 1913, Thomas Mosby stated that when individuals commit crimes they either: (1) expect to avoid detection and escape all punishment or (2) are usually acting on the spur of the moment and are governed by one or more social and individual factors that render the prospect or possibility of punishment wholly inoperative at the time of the commission of the crime.[29]

Several recent studies have found that the likelihood of punishment has little deterrent effect.[30] Blumstein concluded, based on a review of available studies, that there is no useful evidence on the deterrent effect of capital punishment.[31] According to Erickson and Gibbs there is virtually no relationship between perceived certainty of punishment and crime rate when social disapproval of the offense is controlled.[32] However, Minor indicates that a consistent finding in deterrence research is that higher levels of certainty of punishment are associated with lower levels of crime, although the effectiveness of severity in punishment is not clearly understood.[33] Other investigations reveal that fear of arrest and imprisonment may deter many from crime but fear of long imprisonment does not.[34] Webb has stated that the acts classified as impulsive or compulsive in motivation will not be responsive to legal deterrence but rather the individual's perception of the act or behavior and the situation in which it occurs are the crucial variables in determining or understanding human actions, whether they be criminal or noncriminal.[35] Deterrence will have little effect in reducing many types of crimes because the situational motivation of the offender is not considered. Thus the existence of social disapproval may well serve a function equally as important as the deterrent effect of punishment. It should also be mentioned that there is a big difference between likelihood of punishment and certainty of punishment, which could account for the differing positions taken by researchers on the general effectiveness of deterrence.

**Negative aspects of deterrence.** Our society is more concerned with pun-

---

[29]Mosby, Thomas S., *Causes and Cures of Crime.* St. Louis: The C.V. Mosby Co., 1913, p. 252.

[30]Lotz, E., Regoli, R. M., and Raymond, P., "Delinquency and Special Deterrence," *Criminology,* Vol. 15, No. 4, Feb. 1978, pp. 539-548.

[31]Blumstein, A., "Deterrent and Incapacitative Effects," *Journal of Criminal Justice,* Vol. 6, No. 1, Spring, 1978, pp. 3-10.

[32]Erickson, M. L., and Gibbs, J. P., "Objective and Perceptual Properties of Legal Punishment and the Deterrence Doctrine." *Social Problems,* Vol. 25, No. 3, Feb. 1978, pp. 253-264.

[33]Minor, William W., "Deterrence Research: Problems of Theory and Method," in *Preventing Crime,* James A. Cramer, editor. Beverly Hills: Sage Publications, 1978, p. 25.

[34]McCormick, Mona, *Robbery Prevention: What the Literature Reveals.* La Jolla, Calif.: Western Behavioral Sciences Institute, 1974, p. 20.

[35]Webb, Stephen D., "Deterrence Theory: A Reconceptualization." *Canadian Journal of Criminology,* Vol. 22, No. 1, Jan. 1980, p. 33.

ishing the offender than with understanding why he or she broke the law.[36] According to Shaw, some major objections to deterrence are (1) it necessarily leaves the interests of the victim wholly out of account; (2) it injures and degrades the offender; (3) it destroys the offender's reputation, without which he or she cannot seek employment; (4) it atrophies an offender's powers of fending for himself when imprisonment is applied.[37]

Supposedly the greatest deterrent of all, the death penalty, does not seem to be very effective, possibly because it is used so infrequently. Abe Fortas[38] has put forth another reason of why capital punishment may not serve as much of a deterrent: A potential murderer who rationally weighs the possibility of punishment by death (if there is such a person) would figure that he or she has better than a 98% chance of avoiding execution in the average capital punishment state. From 1960 to 1967, a murderer's chances of escaping execution were better than 99.5%. The professional or calculating murderer is not apt to be deterred by such odds.[39]

According to Jacoby[40] deterrence from criminal activity may result more from the normative values of the community, church, schools, peers, or economic institutions than from punishment likely to be invoked by the criminal justice system. As Jeffery has pointed out, on the basis of present research, the most that can be expected from deterrence is that some individuals are deterred in some situations from some crimes by some punishments. There are variations in individuals, crime situations, crimes, and punishments, all of which must be included in the equation for deterrence.[41]

Even so, armed robbers, rapists, and murderers cannot be let go scot-free, but we need to realize that the threat of receiving prison sentences is not going to prevent crime; therefore, it cannot be used as a crime prevention tool. In addition, rarely is there a prison that indirectly contributes to crime prevention through appropriate rehabilitative programs. Therefore, we need to look for other alternatives.

During this discussion several reasons pointing to the failure of deterrence have been given. However, the main reason that deterrence is highly ineffective is because it is directed at adults. If an adult commits an armed

---

[36]Abrahamsen, David, *Who Are The Guilty: A Study of Education and Crime.* New York: Rinehart and Co., 1952, p. 3.

[37]Shaw, Bernard, *Doctor's Delusions, Crude Criminology, and Sham Education.* London: Constable and Co., 1931 (reprinted in 1950), pp. 181-182.

[38]Fortas, Abe, "The Case Against Capital Punishment," in *The Death Penalty,* Irwin Isenberg, editor. New York: The H. W. Wilson Co., 1967, p. 111.

[39]Ibid.

[40]Jacoby, Joan E., "The Deterrent Power of Prosecution," in *Preventing Crime,* James A. Cramer, editor. Beverly Hills: Sage Publications, 1978, p. 139.

[41]Jeffery, op. cit.

robbery and is convicted, the individual may go to jail for five to ten years, and according to the deterrence theory, the penalty should prevent a person from commiting an armed robbery. However, that penalty only applies to adults— those persons who are over eighteen years of age; juveniles are responsible for the commission of half of all crime and more than half of all serious crime. Since juveniles are handled by the juvenile court, they are generally immune to long prison sentences. No matter how severe the penalties are for adults, it simply does not affect the youngsters who commit a healthy portion of crime. Further, a basic characteristic of many adolescents is that they do *not* consider the consequences of their actions. Therefore, taking the negative approach (punishment) is self-defeating; rather, we should be working with youngsters at the very early ages of four or five, teaching them self-discipline, self-control, and respect for other people.

## CONCLUSION

At present, there are numerous theories of crime causation but there still exists a need for additional theories that genuinely propose valid and reliable methods of preventing crime. This can only be accomplished through scientific research into the field and a willingness by scholars, practitioners, and the public to give up those traditional theories or hypotheses found to be ineffective. There will perhaps need to be an integration of existing theories since crime, being a complex problem, will require a complex theory of prevention. In addition, there are interrelationships between crime causation and crime prevention that need further exploration. Perhaps from this exploration, additional information on crime prevention theories can be extrapolated and researched.

We must not be too eager to accept certain proposals as fact until they have been validated. Research and evaluation of present theories must be intensified as must the search for new theories. The theories that have been presented in this chapter all have their strengths and weaknesses, advocates and opponents. At present, none of these theories can answer all of our questions, but serve only as our best attempts to work with the prevention aspects of crime.

# Chapter 3

# Cutting crime at the roots

The major premise of cutting crime at the roots lies in the prevention of juvenile delinquency. The period of childhood is a period in which either socially accepted or criminal behavior is established, depending upon the child's experiences, parental attitudes, and various other factors. There are myriad variables that can affect the eventual molding and shaping of a child's attitudes toward crime, attitudes that will influence behavior for the rest of his or her life. Theodore Roosevelt once stated, "If you want to do anything permanent for the average man, you must begin before he is a man. The chance of success lies in working with the boy, not the man."[1]

Serious attention must be given to the problem of juvenile delinquency and methods to prevent it. Statistics indicate that more than one half of violent crime is committed by youths. There is also strong evidence that the majority of ordinary crime against individuals and property is committed by youths and adults who have had previous contact with the criminal or juvenile justice system.[2] Fortunately, most juvenile delinquents do not become adult criminals, although most adult criminals were juvenile delinquents. As shown in Fig. 3-1, crime is a young person's activity, and its prevention should be of paramount importance rather than waiting to correct and rehabilitate adult offenders. Six years of hearings and investigations in Washington and throughout the country by former Senator Birch Bayh's Subcommittee To Investigate Juvenile Delinquency have led him to two important conclusions:

> The first is that our present system of juvenile justice is geared primarily to react to youthful offenders rather than to prevent the youthful offense.
>
> Second, the evidence is overwhelming that the system fails at the crucial point when a youngster first gets into trouble. The juvenile who takes a car for a joy ride, or vandalizes school property, or views shoplifting as a lark, is confronted

---

[1]Cited in Glueck, Sheldon, and Eleanor Glueck, *Preventing Crime*. New York: McGraw-Hill Book Co., 1936, p. 234.
[2]*A National Strategy to Reduce Crime*. National Advisory Commission on Criminal Justice Standards and Goals, Washington, D.C.: U.S. Government Printing Office, 1973.

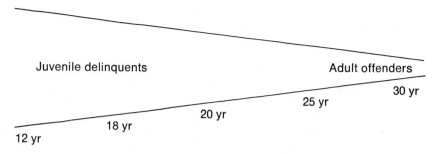

**Fig. 3-1.** Proportion of juvenile delinquents to adult offenders.

by a system of justice often incompletely incapable of responding in a constructive manner.

We are all too aware of the limited alternatives available to juvenile court judges when confronted with the decision of what to do with a case involving an initial, relatively minor offense. In many instances the judge has but two choices—send the juvenile back to the environment which helped create the problems in the first place with nothing more than a stern lecture, or incarcerate the juvenile in a system structured for serious, multiple offenders where the youth will invariably emerge only to escalate the level of violations into more serious criminal behavior.[3]

Before discussing prevention, we should elaborate on the Subcommittee's second conclusion. The juvenile justice system presents serious inadequacies but by no means are these inadequacies a new phenomenon. The Gluecks, in 1936, recognized the need to revise the juvenile justice system when they called for the following recommendations, many of which are still not being heeded today by a majority of communities and institutions:

1. Crime prevention programs should take into account the evidence that most criminals show definite antisocial tendencies of attitude and behavior early in childhood.
2. In most instances, children should be kept away from the typical contacts with police stations, courts, and correctional institutions until more scientific and sympathetic efforts have failed.
3. An experimental attitude should govern the establishment and conduct of crime prevention programs.
4. It cannot be definitely concluded as yet that any one type of crime prevention activity is necessarily superior to, or should be exclusive of, any other.
5. While much good can be accomplished by whatever qualified agency in a community assumes the leadership in crime prevention, the public schools can play an especially significant role.
6. Although not indispensable, a crime prevention bureau in a police department has certain unique values.

[3]Bayh, Birch, *The Congressional Record.* Vol. 123, No. 47, March 17, 1977, S4235.

7. Crime prevention efforts should be discriminating in technique (implying that mass treatment is undesirable).
8. A crime prevention program should recognize that children must have ample outlets for their energies.
9. Other psychologic and behavior traits of children should be taken into account in planning and carrying out crime prevention programs.
10. In intensive work with problem children and delinquents, the attitudes and prejudices of parents should not be ignored.
11. Trained personnel should be liberally employed in crime prevention activity.[4]

The Gluecks brought up the importance of many factors, such as preventing contact between juveniles and hardened criminals, parental attitudes, and the importance of the school as a major influence upon children. It is imperative that contact by young offenders with the criminal justice system, particularly the corrections aspect, be minimized. The vicious cycle of recidivism must be interrupted as soon as possible. Incarceration has not proved to be an effective method of correction. Jails crowded with juveniles, first offenders, and hardened criminals can only serve as "schools of crime," since people tend to imitate the behavior of those closest to them. Further, as a juvenile sinks deeper and deeper into the criminal justice process, it becomes harder and harder to steer him or her away from a criminal career.

People, juveniles in particular, tend to become what they are told they are, and the stigma that involvement with the criminal justice system creates only helps to confirm their beliefs about themselves. There are any number of ways in which society displays its distaste for those so involved, such as rejection by peers, expressions of hostility or distrust by school officials, increased police surveillance, and discriminatory employment practices. These actions by society only increase the chances that legitimate channels to attain a fulfilling and satisfying life will be blocked for the juvenile, which in turn only serves to increase the chances that illegitimate channels to achieve these goals will be sought.

As the Subcommittee to Investigate Juvenile Delinquency states—and the Gluecks long ago pointed out—alternatives must be made available, but certain changes in societal attitudes and practices within the criminal justice system must take place first. These changes do not include abandoning the use of confinement for certain individuals, for until more effective means of treatment are available, chronic and dangerous delinquents will necessarily be locked up to protect society. However, society must begin to use means of controlling and supervising young offenders that will best serve to keep them out of the recidivist cycle while still adequately protecting the community. This means that the juvenile justice system must look for optimal programs

---

[4]Glueck and Glueck, op. cit., p. 6.

outside of institutionalization for those who do not need confinement. This is certainly a step in the right direction but such goals are oriented to treatment rather than prevention. The ideal goal should be to prevent juvenile delinquency altogether, since then the problems of recidivism and social isolation of delinquents would not exist. The establishment of a large number of prevention efforts and programs must reflect this goal if delinquency is to be prevented.

A very broad definition of delinquency prevention is offered by Martin, who states: "Anything that contributes to the adjustment of children and to their healthy personality development prevents delinquency."[5]

The roles of the family, school, and peers in preventing juvenile delinquency have had considerable attention during the last several years and have been recognized by most researchers and scholars as vital influences in delinquency prevention. Offenders become offenders for some reason. Perhaps the reason is not always identifiable, but it is only natural to look to the most prominent influences in a child's life for the answer, and these influences are the family, school, and peers. As Abrahamsen has stated, however, "This is not to say that there is no weakness in the person who commits the crime. But as we examined case after case we invariably asked ourselves: 'Where were the parents, the school, the community, when this crime was committed?'"[6] Thus it has been evident for many years, although not widely acted upon, that the primary thrust of delinquency prevention, or cutting crime off at the roots, must be aimed toward family life, the school, and peer relations. These three major influences will be discussed in further detail in the following pages.

## INFLUENCES OF FAMILY AND HOME LIFE

The home should be considered the paramount institution. There has been a great deal of research into the role of the family in delinquency prevention. Just after the turn of the century, the role of the family in delinquency causation was being explored. Asbury wrote in 1906 that the typical delinquent was misunderstood and thus mistreated by parent, playmate, neighbor, and teacher, and that the black sheep of the family was usually made black by the family, a result of trying to bring up an uncommon boy by common methods.[7] Asbury's contemporary, Cesare Lombroso, one of the founding fathers of criminology, said ". . . the family relies upon the school

---

[5]Martin, John M., "Three Approaches to Delinquency Prevention: A Critique." *Crime and Delinquency,* Jan. 1961, p. 16.

[6]Abrahamsen, David, *Who Are The Guilty: A Study of Education and Crime.* New York: Rinehart and Co., 1952, p. 3.

[7]Asbury, George B., *The Cure and Prevention of Crime.* Jeffersonville, Indiana: Indiana Reformatory Trade School Press, 1906, p. 2.

for the care of education, while the schoolmaster, for his part, who in any case could do little because of the great number of pupils demanding his attention, counts upon what the family is supposed to accomplish."[8] Many years later in 1928 Benjamin Glassberg predicted that, "As long as parents will not regard their home interests as paramount and continue to avoid their responsibility and to thrust it upon the schools, social agencies and the courts, we shall continue to have a large group of cases for the courts to deal with."[9] By 1928 it had already been concluded that:

> The right kind of home . . . is one where the relationship between the parents is normal and healthy, which has not been marred by divorce or desertion, where there is no overindulgence or repression; where there is no extreme poverty, extreme parental neglect, excessive quarreling, alcoholism, obscenity, immorality, criminalism or mental disease. It has been the experience of child care workers that the children from broken homes whether because of death, divorce or desertion are more likely to come to the attention of juvenile courts. This impression is here amply corroborated. In such homes the necessary discipline is absent. Forty percent of the delinquents came from families where the proper sort of discipline was entirely absent.[10]

Harry Elmer Barnes, writing in 1929, recognized the importance of adequate living conditions and the need for legitimate channels to be available for everyone to earn a "decent" living: "Highly unfortunate living conditions which generate these bad habits that lead to crime, should be rapidly and thoroughly eliminated. This would require not only better housing conditions, better facilities for recreation, and better educational methods, but also such a fundamental reorganization of economic life and motives as would lead to the possibility for every able-bodied individual to earn a decent livelihood."[11]

It is estimated that 95% of learning is through imitation, and since most children are around their parents and other family members the majority of the time, particularly during the preschool years, they naturally imitate and thus learn more from their parents than from anyone else. Very young children are emotionally and physiologically dependent upon others and thus very receptive to imitating the actions and attitudes of others. Most people who have children consider themselves good parents and, fortunately, most probably are or there would no doubt be even more juvenile delinquency.

---

[8]Lombroso, Cesare, *Crime, Its Causes and Remedies.* Montclair, N.J.: Patterson Smith Inc., reprinted 1968, p. 303.

[9]Glassberg, Benjamin, et al., *Prisons or Crime Prevention?* Girard, Kansas: Haldeman-Julius Publications, 1928. Little Blue Book No. 1271.

[10]Ibid, p. 13.

[11]Barnes, Harry Elmer, *How To Deal With Crime.* Girard, Kansas: Haldeman-Julius Publications, 1929, p. 26. Little Blue Book No. 1468.

But some parents, as Abrahamsen has stated, create "illness, future unhappiness, and the beginnings of crime in their children."[12] Parenthood, one of the most difficult but potentially rewarding jobs in the world, requires absolutely no training or experience for which to qualify.

### Delinquent parents

Much interest has developed concerning the notion that juvenile delinquency is a vicious cycle passed along from generation to generation. Parents of delinquents have themselves often been subjected to adverse parental influences, such as emotional abnormalities, alcoholism, and criminal behaviors, as had their parents before them. We know this to be a factor in child abuse and alcoholism, and it certainly would act as a strong influence in the development of other antisocial and criminal behaviors. Thus interrupting this cycle of damaging familial influences becomes a major challenge for many social agencies. Psychiatric, social, religious, educational, and other social agencies will need to become involved in a holistic approach in treating both the delinquent and the family, since it would be futile to treat one deviant member apart from others who may have contributed to the problem.

The need for these services may be greater than ever before since the majority of families today are nuclear, comprised of parents and children only, as opposed to extended families in which as many as four generations lived in the same household. In extended families new parents received the benefit of guidance, support, and assistance of their more experienced elders in raising children, and thus stresses of parenthood were reduced or at least shared among all the family members.

Another change in families today is their size. Families today have an average of two children compared to the pre-Depression era when there were as many as fourteen children in many families. In this situation, the older children were generally expected to assist in rearing the younger ones. They received the obvious benefit of having some experience and knowledge in childrearing when the time came for them to raise their own families. This change, although necessary for economics and population control, has resulted in a situation in which young parents of today do not know as much about childrearing, nor have they had as much contact with young children as adults as did their parents and grandparents.

A third stress upon families of today, which certainly affects parenting, is that there are more and more one-parent families, either through death, divorce, separation, desertion, or institutionalization of one parent. Coupled with the complexities of modern city living, particularly in underprivileged

---

[12]Abrahamsen, op. cit., p. 292.

areas, it is no wonder that some parents are failing at the important job of raising children, and are themselves delinquent in many respects.

### Early mother-child relationships

Much interest has been shown in determining the effect of the very earliest mother-child relationships in contributing to the development of juvenile delinquency. For example, maternal bonding, or the development of close, protective bonds between mother and baby immediately after delivery, has been shown to be of paramount importance. It is thought that lack of maternal bonding may be instrumental in the development and expression of hostility, resentment, and child abuse by the mother during periods of stress.

The field of psychiatry also alludes to the importance of early and satisfying mother-child relationships. Most psychiatrists, psychologists, and social scientists have recognized that negative maternal attitudes toward a child's early instinctual reactions may be considered instrumental in the formation of antisocial behaviors by the child. The effects of such a dissatisfying relationship may lead to the development of what psychiatry has termed the "reality principle," in that such children develop an inability to distinguish between reality and fantasy.

### Other predisposing factors

Poverty is one of the factors that undermine the ability of the family to prevent delinquency since it produces many of the conditions conducive to crime. Emotional disturbance or mental illness can make parents psychologically unfit for childrearing. Inappropriate discipline, either too much or too little, can also be a factor in producing delinquency. With too much leniency a child will grow up undisciplined, but a child disciplined too severely may become rebellious during the teenage years.

### Family-oriented prevention

There are many complex factors that interfere with the family remaining a stable unit capable of preventing delinquency. We also have long realized that family efforts are the heart of a delinquency prevention program, and that preventive efforts that bypass the family will be of little or no value. Psychotherapy and behavior modification are not the answer to prevention. (If this were true, this would be a very short chapter.) Different approaches that include each family member and not merely the child offer the most promise at present.

One such program is Parental Effectiveness Training (P.E.T.), which instructs individuals in more effective parenting techniques. Many parents need information about the normal growth and development of children and how to administer fair and firm discipline not accompanied by anger. Many parents need help in realizing the importance of early parent-child relationships and how they play a role in forming the child's basic personality traits that are eventually carried into adulthood.

Parents who are experiencing difficulty may also benefit from a somewhat different approach—Alderian counseling. Alfred Alder, originator of the program, suggests that all behavior, even "problem" behavior, has a purpose. Alderian family counseling is based on the theory that we all have mistaken ideas of how to belong that come from childhood interpretations. The objective of Alderian family counseling is to point out these mistakes. Another assumption is that everyone is entitled to equality and the right to dignity and respect, although this does not mean that everyone has to be the same. Recommendations centered on the family are given during the counseling sessions and usually begin with helping family members accept one another just as they are. As the counseling sessions progress, recommendations focus on problem behavior, using the system of logical consequences. The third phase of recommendations centers on encouraging events that have happened within the family, as well as concerns still present.

Coffey suggests that "family-related prevention efforts have two major focuses: (1) prevention of crimes precipitated by family crisis, and (2) exercise of social control within the family to discourage criminal and delinquent behavior on the part of its members and to reduce the possibility of family crisis that could lead to crime."[13] Providing unemployment insurance during periods of unemployment of the breadwinner is an example of the first type of preventive effort. Also, the police and various other agencies have a primary role in preventing crimes within the family that may result from family violence precipitated by the crisis. The second focus involves internal control by the family, which generally is accomplished through parental control. Coffey suggests that adequate parental control includes such specifics as: enforcement of a family curfew, continual awareness of each child's location, familiarity with each child's activities and associates, assurance of adequate supervision, and parental models of responsible authority, consistent moral system, and consequence-oriented behavior.[14]

The importance of strengthening the family unit by both external and (more desirably) internal controls must receive much more emphasis if crime is to be cut at the roots. Although the family has been recognized as very important to this aim for several decades, many more resources have been devoted to apprehension, confinement, and correction of offenders than to

---

[13]Coffey, Alan R., *The Prevention of Crime and Delinquency.* Englewood Cliffs, N.J.: Prentice-Hall, Inc., 1975, p. 56.
[14]Ibid, p. 62.

stabilizing, strengthening, and preserving the family. If delinquency is to be prevented, we must strive to develop new and enhance existing family-oriented counseling and treatment programs and to bring these programs to locales where they are not yet realities.

## INFLUENCE OF LEARNING INSTITUTIONS
### Historical perspective

Seven years before Auguste Comte coined the word "sociology" in his *Positive Philosophy*,[15] educators were already studying the problems of crime and delinquency and proposing preventive measures. In 1835, Francis Lieber, a member of the Philadelphia Society for Alleviating the Miseries of Public Prisons, wrote:

> The more we can prevent the future growth of a feeling of separation from society or, with which in fact, this feeling often ends in its natural progress of opposition to the rest of society, the more we shall also prevent the various acts of selfishness, of absorbing egotism, of crime. It is for this reason, among others, that instruction in our political duties ought to form a branch of instruction in all schools. Let us teach and convince everyone that he forms an integral part of the community upon the faithful performance of whose duties its welfare partially depends, and we shall increase his self-esteem, and thereby afford him one of the best preservatives against crime.[16]

Lieber also stated, "The best preservatives against crime will always be a well trained mind, early application and industrious habits, together with good example . . . It is easy to judge how much a sound school education contributes to a regular training of the youthful mind." Then he asked, "Is there no test then by which we may ascertain whether universal education tends to prevent crime or whether ignorance promotes it?"[17] The test Lieber suggested can be conducted by simply going into any jail and determining the educational level of the inmates. Most persons in jail are there for committing the more violent street crimes, and the vast majority of these offenders do not have a high school education. Their average reading level is equivalent to that of a fifth grader. On the other hand, embezzlers and other white collar criminals who are educated tend to be released on bail or are given probationary sentences. Therefore, for the large body of crimes that the public fears most, Lieber's "test," which he proposed in 1835, is still valid today.

---

[15]Comte, Auguste, *Positive Philosophy.* Cited in Marvin, Francis S., *Comte, the Founder of Sociology.* New York: Russell & Russell, Publishers, 1965.

[16]"The Relation Between Education and Crime." Letter to the Right Rev. William White, D.D. by Francis Lieber, L.L.D., published by the Philadelphia Society for Alleviating the Miseries of Public Prisons, Philadelphia, 1835. Library of American Civilization, Microfiche No. LAC 40028.

[17]Ibid, p. 9.

Beccaria, an eighteenth century criminologist, stated "It is better to prevent crimes than to punish them." He believed that in order to do this, virtue should be rewarded and every effort should be made to increase and extend knowledge since enlightenment should accompany human liberty. "The most effective method for the prevention of crime is a perfect system of education."[18] Clarence Darrow, another early pioneer, once wrote that, "If there is to be any permanent improvement in man and any better social order, it must come mainly from the education and humanizing of man."[19]

Many early scholars recognized and argued for the importance of education in crime prevention, and that argument is still being advanced. Shaw may have been one of the first to bring attention to the fact that education, to offer any potential in this goal, must be appropriate, interesting, and stimulating. In 1931, Bernard Shaw suggested that children should be granted a constitution conferring rights and liberties.[20] Speaking on the unnatural surroundings of most classrooms, he commented:

> That children should be herded together for hours every day, and beaten or otherwise punished if they fidget, talk, or are inattentive to an uninteresting teacher whom no adult audience would tolerate for five minutes, is taken as a matter of course, and called instruction. It is, of course, nothing of the sort. It is grotesque, unnatural cruelty, both to the teacher and the children, who hate each other as no human beings possibly could hate each other in natural and humane relations.[21]

In 1954, Albert Einstein noted the consequences of repressive conditions and policies:

> To me the worst thing seems to be for a school principally to work with methods of fear, force, and artificial authority. Such treatment destroys the sound sentiments, the sincerity, and the self-confidence of the pupil. It produces the submissive subject.[22]

The problem of obtaining a quality education is still with us, as Clifford notes:

> The simple multiplication of teaching institutions and formal qualifications may not be education at all. Quality is no less important. Education may well prove to be the key to the prevention of increased crime—if it is education for

---

[18] Cited in Mannheim, Hermann, editor, *Pioneers in Criminology*. Chicago: Quadrangle Books, Inc., 1960, p. 47.

[19] Darrow, Clarence, *Crime, Its Cause and Treatment*. Montclair, N.J.: Patterson Smith, Inc., reprinted 1972, p. 281.

[20] Shaw, Bernard, *Doctor's Delusions, Crude Criminology and Sham Education*. London: Constable and Co., reprinted in 1950, p. 339.

[21] Ibid, p. 340.

[22] Einstein, Albert, *Ideas and Opinions*. New York: Bonanza Books, 1954, p. 61.

life and not for social recognition by diploma gathering. The two are related but not inextricable.[23]

We now know that schools must offer an atmosphere of structure coupled with flexibility, and an atmosphere where the creativeness of the not-so-common student will not be stifled. Forcing certain types of children into the conventional patterns and routines results in tension, frustration, and aggression, characteristics that contribute to delinquency. Therefore, schools have an obligation to society to make their curricula more flexible so that a variety of satisfying experiences for each student is provided. Unfortunately, this is not always the case, and as Reckless and Dinitz have stated, disadvantaged youths may perceive legitimate prospects as grim and therefore reject them.[24]

It is recognized that a lot of services other than education are expected from our schools. Today's school systems are expected to provide transportation, feed children breakfast and lunch, and provide after-school programs to keep the children of working parents occupied until the parents arrive home. These services certainly have proved necessary and worthwhile, for if they did not exist, many children could not get to school and would have nothing to eat. Although the school can never become all things to all people—and it still remains second to the family in effecting socialization—it must begin to share a larger responsibility in the prevention of juvenile delinquency, particularly if the family fails at its task to maintain control over the children. In the following pages we will discuss how and why the school acts as such an important influence in preventing juvenile delinquency, as well as deficiencies and successes in meeting this latest expectation.

### Why the school should play a role in delinquency prevention

The school is the only social institution that by law demands compulsory attendance of children. Thus children must spend a fairly large portion of their time attending school, in addition to time spent in voluntary school-related activities. Because of this, the school is in a unique position both to identify children with behavioral and socialization problems and to set examples for law-abiding behavior.

No other organizations or institutions, including churches, are in a position to take advantage of the opportunities the schools have to promote socialization and law-abiding behavior. The school is accepted by most parents as an intervening agency. It has vast community support and confidence, and it is regarded as an integral component of the community. Persons having

---

[23]Clifford, William, *Planning Crime Prevention*. Lexington, Mass.: Lexington Books, 1976, p. 32.
[24]Reckless, Walter C., and Dinitz, Simon, *The Prevention of Juvenile Delinquency, An Experiment*. Columbus, Ohio: Ohio State University Press, 1972, p. 6.

the most contact with students during school are well educated, are in positions to get to know the students well, and therefore can recognize and try to understand the "whys" of maladjusted behavior. Most teachers like children and can develop strong personal relationships with each student, even to the extent of functioning as a parent surrogate, yet can retain a certain measure of objectivity and distance.

Teachers are in a position to maintain close contact with the student's home without this contact being interpreted by family members as a threatening outside intervention. Therefore, teachers are in an ideal position to intervene, using special services of counselors, psychologists, school nurses, and social case workers, and to act as positive role models with which children can identify. The school also provides an opportunity for parent-teacher interrelationships and a source for parental instruction. Teachers can no longer be concerned only with "readin', writin', and 'rithmetic," but must strive to develop maximal potentialities, maintain emotional stability, and encourage proper social adjustment among students.

Khleif found that teachers have a fairly high degree of accuracy in determining which children need to be referred for psychological services.[25] When teachers make derogations of a student, they can usually be placed in one of eight content categories: (1) misconduct, (2) objectionable personality traits, (3) withdrawn personality traits, (4) poor work habits, (5) poor attitude toward schooling, (6) poor attendance, (7) poor ability to do grade level work, and (8) poor academic achievement.[26] Teachers represent one of the best sources of diagnostic ability and the school is able to offer many intervening services to children identified as having such problems.

Despite these many assets, however, there still exist some deficiencies in many school systems, even to the extent that they may be contributing to delinquency rather than preventing it. Therefore, such factors are brought to the reader's attention since schools cannot be regarded as a panacea for delinquency prevention.

## Deficiencies in the school system

Schools that fail to rewrite their educational objectives to include the aforementioned responsibilities will contribute to juvenile delinquency. However, the fault does not lie solely with these schools since some communities do not support liberal programs by the schools that are not directly related to the more traditional objectives. There is sometimes a reluctance by

---

[25]Khleif, B. B., "Teachers as Predictors of Juvenile Delinquency and Psychiatric Disturbance," in *Prevention of Delinquency, Problems and Programs*, John R. Stratton and Robert M. Terry, editors. New York: The Macmillan Co., 1968, p. 84.

[26]Ibid, p. 87.

the public to provide sufficient funds for adequate teaching staffs, competitive salaries, and appropriate equipment. This results in larger classes, a larger teaching load per teacher, and an impersonal relationship between teacher and students. Generally, it also stifles attempts to relate education to the real world. Education that does not incorporate or address employment opportunities contributes to the dropout rate, which in turn contributes to the development of delinquency among out-of-school and out-of-work youths. In addition, many schools fail at the important task of teaching students to make decisions. This contributes to their dependence upon others, which inhibits maturity. Immaturity in turn is a characteristic of delinquent behavior.

Some school personnel fail to identify or recognize symptoms of delinquent behavior. Teachers need to conscientiously study behaviors of children and be able to recognize those that appear symptomatic of delinquency. Stubbornness, disobedience, lying, destructive behavior, use of "bad" language, poor reading ability, poor work habits, and general maladjustment are considered as predictive factors of juvenile delinquency by many researchers. There has also been much interest in the past few years in recognizing certain attitudes toward school as indicative of delinquent tendencies. Negative attitudes toward school, for example, are very characteristic; delinquents almost invariably attest to the fact that they "hate" school. Desires and ambitions of delinquents for formal education or vocational training are not nearly as strong as those of nondelinquents. In studies using a semantic differential scale I have found that delinquents have significantly more negative attitudes toward school than do nondelinquents. An inability by school officials to recognize these attitudes or failure to bring attention to the problem deprives the child of preventive intervention and further contributes to the incidence of juvenile delinquency.

Negative attitudes toward school are often demonstrated by disruptive behavior problems and truancy. In tracing school misbehavior of delinquents, the Gluecks found that nine in ten of the delinquents persistently (and often seriously) misconducted themselves in school.[27] Truancy may likewise become a problem when students find the curriculum perplexing or irrelevant to their needs, or they are not able to keep up academically. Frustration ensues as humiliating experiences within the school increase. Unfortunately, school administrators do not react to truancy logically. Expulsion from school is the usual punishment, making the punishment identical to the crime. Truancy may eventually lead to the child dropping out of school, which in turn means a decreased ability to obtain desirable employment. It also con-

---

[27]Glueck, Sheldon, and Glueck, Eleanor, *Delinquents in the Making.* New York: Harper and Brothers Publishers, 1952, pp. 76-77.

tributes to the opportunity for juveniles to commit crimes they would not have committed had they been in school. For this reason, truancy is considered one of the first signs of delinquency.

The policy of expelling truants from school is far from the solution to the problem. Efforts must be made to understand the underlying causes of why the child "played hookey" and each case must be treated individually. Every effort must be made to keep these children in school rather than to expel them. Truants are in particular need of meaningful school experiences, counseling services, and follow-up assistance. Merely throwing a youngster out of school for truancy turns him or her into a community problem. The child becomes more vulnerable to the influence of street gangs, has more unsupervised free time, and becomes negatively labeled by peers and school officials. Many school officials are now beginning to realize that much, if not most, vandalism is caused by truants and dropouts aimlessly "hanging around" school grounds with nothing to do. Even though the school may be perceived as a problem, it may represent the only sense of belonging within a community for the truant or dropout. As Empey has stated, "Even dropouts, despite their feelings of alienation, congregate at the school during lunch, recess, or other free periods. It remains a place of considerable salience to them."[28] Therefore, the practices of suspension and expulsion should be severely restricted because they are not in the best interest of either the community or the individual.

Additional negative attitudes toward school may be expressed through hostile, inappropriate, uncooperative, or antisocial behaviors within the classroom. Such behaviors undoubtedly arise from the need for attention, and negative attention or punishment that results as a consequence of disruptive behavior is better than no attention at all. Students on the verge of dropping out of school tend to withdraw first from school activities. They may not identify with their middle class teachers and feel inadequate or resentful toward the demands of school. There is usually no identification with the school, and potential dropouts appear emotionally troubled, living in a state of anomie. Their actions are characterized by a lack of confidence and they often express anger at the world. To try to escape frustrations, they drop out only to find that they are not equipped to cope with the outside world. This in turn increases their feelings of hopelessness and frustration. Individuals react differently to this situation. Very few return to school, some withdraw into the drug culture, others strike out in anger by committing street robberies and other violent acts, and others demonstrate self-destructive behavior such as alcoholism.

---

[28]Empey, Lamar T., "Crime Prevention: The Fugitive Utopia." In *Crime: Emerging Issues*, James A. Inciardi and Harvey A. Siegal, editors. New York: Praeger Publishers, 1977, p. 115.

Many strong and elaborate forces have been offered as motivators of deviant behavior (e.g., too early or too rigid toilet training, unsatisfactory resolution of the Oedipal conflict) but much of human behavior can be explained simply as a desire to get attention. Owning a van with murals painted on the side, wearing flashy clothes, or walking a tightrope between two tall buildings are all attempts of various degrees to gain attention. Throwing a brick through a window is also a bid for attention. It is certainly an indication that the child needs help, although he or she may be asking for it unconsciously and indirectly. Adults have the same need for attention, only most have legitimate opportunities and less harmful means of getting it, and it is usually referred to as recognition rather than attention. The idea that the need for attention may be a motivator for deviant behavior has not received the degree of scholarly concern that it should, while more than enough emphasis has been placed upon the possibility of more deeply rooted psychologic motivating forces.

After recognizing that deviant behavior does exist and perhaps even determining the reason for its existence, schools create yet another deficiency in their treatment of such students. Programs that are oriented toward high-risk youngsters and exclude other students contribute to the labeling process, which many scholars believe actually causes delinquent behavior. Programs that are specifically designed to prevent delinquency and that are primarily oriented toward certain groups do not necessarily have to be referred to as such; they probably will receive more participation from target students if they are not overtly designated as having a preventive function. Aspects other than prevention, such as opportunities for recreation, socialization, or new learning experiences, should be emphasized.

Last but not least, there are also failures of the school system to properly educate some students. In many cases youths are passed from one grade to the next without knowing how to read or write. These students may eventually find themselves graduating in this same illiterate condition. This is particularly true of school athletes who in some cases are given passing grades so that they may remain on the team, regardless of their real academic standings. In the end, students who make it through high school in this manner have not been given any favors, since most suffer severely when exposed to the real world where they must depend solely on their own abilities.

In general, there are many areas in which schools need improvement, regarding both policy and curricula. New and different kinds of educational experiences for youth are needed, as well as enlightened treatment of children recognized as having behavior problems leading to delinquency. There must be a willingness of teaching personnel to develop interdisciplinary approaches to broad areas of knowledge. Approaches to the learning process that utilize real life experiences as the tool for teaching should be tried. Labeling or otherwise stigmatizing students must be halted, and methods to deal with disruptive students and truants must be revised. Various programs, policies, and services that show success or promise in preventing delinquency are discussed in the next section.

## DELINQUENCY PREVENTION PROGRAMS
## IN THE SCHOOLS

As we have seen, the school has a responsibility in bringing up responsible and law-abiding citizens, and it must be many things to many people. Schools must not only educate, but also link the world of employers, community programs, and colleges to the student to enhance the relevance of education. In addition, the school must assure all children access to health, legal, social, and employment services so that they will remain in school and function to the best of their ability. In order to meet these responsibilities additional services and programs within the school system are needed, many of which are discussed in the following pages.

### Community education

Extension of educational services into the community can help both students and community members. Talents and services of community leaders, members of the business community, and representatives of other professions can be utilized to bring the working world closer to the school world. Also, citizens who may feel alienated or out of touch with the school system are given a means of becoming a part of the educational process. Effective utilization of resources and facilities within the community promotes development of diversified programs, with a great potential of learning opportunities for youngsters. The community education concept should be expanded and implemented into every school district encompassing both affluent and disadvantaged neighborhoods.

### Social work services

Not every school system presently has the benefit of social work services, but the need for them is great. Many poverty areas where social services are desperately needed still do not have them. School social workers can help to close the gap between family and school by identifying problems within the home environment that may be causing a child's behavior problems in school. They can help the family obtain assistance from various community services that can help stabilize the family unit. School social workers can also help to assure that no child misses school because of financial need and that disadvantaged children receive proper medical attention.

## Job placement

Obtaining employment is a main concern for many secondary school students. Assistance in finding compatible employment for students has proved to be particularly important in school systems that have a high dropout rate and where career education is limited to jobs that are available within the student's immediate environment. The staff of the job assistance program should be well versed on job opportunities available not only within the community but also throughout the state as well as the qualifications required to fill those jobs. The job placement staff can also serve as effective public relations tools on behalf of the school, since they should keep in close contact with businesses, trade unions, community organizations, and government agencies. Other responsibilities of the job placement program include assisting in career curricula development and working with school counselors to better meet the career needs of all students but giving particular attention to potential dropouts.

## School health services

Providing health services to students is a very important school function since many students come from families that cannot afford medical care. Some families may not be aware of the significance of certain symptoms, or the child may have been physically or sexually abused and parents are reluctant to seek medical attention for fear of disclosure. School nurses and psychologists can do much to improve the health care of students, particularly emotionally disturbed children. Children not given proper health care often suffer from undetected defects that can interfere with their ability to learn. Children with vision or hearing problems that have not been detected may be mistakenly labeled as underachievers or slow learners. Therefore, providing screening programs with adequate follow up of children referred for further evaluation or treatment is very important.

School psychologists also play a very important role in preventing delinquency, since they work with a number of emotionally disturbed children and children with learning disabilities who may present serious problems. It is often up to the school psychologist to try to prevent the development of hostility, resentment, withdrawal, or violence among these children. Psychologists must also work with the families of children who are having problems, since they may be part of the problem and must understand the necessity of services provided or recommendations made. In addition, school psychologists must work with teachers in helping them to recognize serious behavior problems so that they may refer the children for help.

There is much interest in the relationship of learning disabilities (LD) to delinquency. According to Allan Berman, a researcher-psychologist, subtle

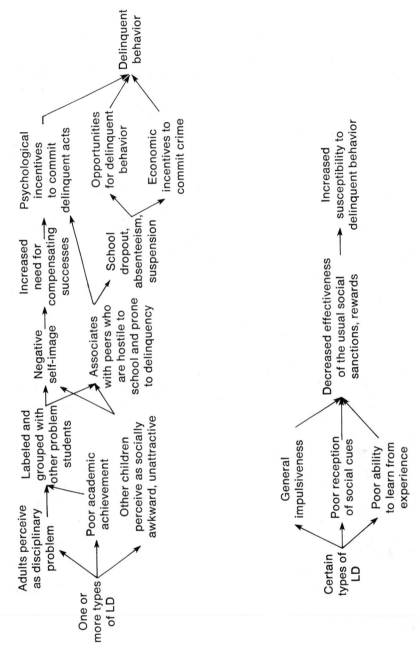

**Fig. 3-2.** Proposed chains between LD and JD. (Adapted from Murray, Charles A., et al., *The Link between LD and JD, Current Theory and Knowledge, Executive Summary.* Washington, D.C.: American Institute for Research, 1976, pp. 6-7.)

brain deficiencies responsible for learning disabilities often go unnoticed in elementary school children but in many cases they are responsible for triggering delinquent behavior years later.[29] The "typical" delinquent, according to Berman's research results, is a youth who has had difficulty in making sense of the world around him. Delinquent youths generally lack verbal skills that are necessary to function effectively with people. As a consequence, the youth has difficulties in making complex interpersonal solutions important in life. Berman believes that children at high risk to develop delinquent behavior can be identified by the third grade, based on four critical factors: (1) Some children doing poorly in school (mainly because of LD problems) begin to associate with other children who are also doing poorly; (2) delinquency-prone children show significant deficiencies on the Halstead-Reitan battery in the trail marking test (connecting dots between letter and number sequences), tactile performance, and speech sounds perception test; (3) delinquency-prone youths do more poorly on the perceptual and hand-eye coordination aspects of the Wechsler intelligence scale; and (4) nondelinquents tend to have "attentive, supportive" families.[30]

The notion that there is a link between education and juvenile delinquency certainly deserves more exploration. Research in this area is still fragmentary and although it cannot be concluded that there is a causal relationship between LD and delinquency, a causal chain has been implied. Learning disabilities produce effects that in turn produce second-order effects, which eventually produce delinquent behavior.[31] Two routes of this implied chain have been hypothesized by proponents of the learning disabilities–juvenile delinquency (LD-JD) link and are illustrated in Fig. 3-2.

Critics of the LD-JD link object mainly to the notion that any one cause accounts for a significant portion of delinquent behavior, since delinquency is a very complex problem, entailing other variables such as poverty, broken homes, social disadvantages, etc. This objection should be well taken but clearly indicates that this is an area that demands further research, since there does exist a definite relationship between school failure and delinquency as well as myriad other variables.

### Visiting teacher programs

The visiting teacher program has developed in some schools as a result of the need to further link home with school. Visiting teachers work with parents

---

[29]"Delinquency as a Learning Disability." *Science News,* **114**(11):180, Sept. 9, 1978.
[30]Ibid, p. 181.
[31]Murray, Charles A., et al., *The Link Between LD and JD, Current Theory and Knowledge, Executive Summary.* Washington, D.C.: American Institute for Research, U.S. Department of Justice, Law Enforcement Assistance Administration, 1976, p. 2.

and teachers to help the child with any emotional difficulties and to make their experiences in school happy and satisfying. Hopefully, the visiting teacher can help the child and family with problems at their inception, before maladjustment and delinquency become symptomatic. Therefore, visiting teacher programs are emphasized a great deal in elementary schools but there is also a need for careful study and follow-up of students in junior and senior high levels.

The work of the visiting teacher enables school personnel to further understand the child's social background and to understand the child's behavior. The visiting teacher must combine the services of teacher with social case worker. As a member of the school staff, the visiting teacher must also emphasize his or her function as being available to the student's family to discuss their problems. Generally, students who give evidence of lack of success (whether academic or otherwise), those who present serious behavioral problems, and those who show obvious personality deviations (excessive shyness, suspicion, resentment, aggressiveness, withdrawal) are targets of the visiting teacher. Usually such students are referred to the visiting teacher by teachers, principals, school nurses, counselors, and psychologists.

### School-police programs

Many larger police departments have developed classes for youths held in conjunction with the school. The Los Angeles County Sheriff's Department, for example, conducts four such classes for students at various educational levels. The department's Student and the Law program presents high school students with an opportunity to become acquainted with the criminal justice system. It is a one-semester, voluntary course with the following objectives: to promote a better understanding of the law and the role of law enforcement as it applies to youths, to provide youth with an opportunity to express their views and ask questions regarding law enforcement, to teach youth about the laws that affect them, and to bring an awareness to youth of the crime and drug problems and how they are affected.

Some school systems are also offering crime prevention as a course of study. In Kentucky, crime prevention is being taught in over 5,000 elementary schools. Teachers are assisted with ten crime prevention lessons and flip charts prepared by the Office of Crime Prevention, Kentucky Department of Justice.[32] The school system of Oakland, California also teaches crime prevention to elementary students through its Officer Friendly program, in which first graders learn how to avoid becoming a victim of crime and that police officers are their friends.

---

[32]Dentinger, Donald, "Crime Prevention—How to Make it Work." *The Police Chief*, March 1979, p. 33.

### Police-school liaison officer

Police-school liaison officer programs are the result of the need for close police-school relationships. The idea of a liaison officer is fairly recent, originating from the Flint, Michigan police department in the late 1950s and early 1960s. Since that time, several other departments have begun police-school liaison or counselor programs modeled after Flint's program. Generally, police-school liaison officers are not in uniform and are not responsible for enforcing school regulations. Rather, they are concerned with behavior problems that occur on or around school grounds, and they have a role in counseling students and improving the image of the police among the school population. Therefore, the police-school liaison officer serves several important functions in preventing delinquency.

### Compensatory education programs

Compensatory education programs involve the identification of and assistance to pupils from culturally disadvantaged or low socioeconomic environments, who have potential for completing programs of secondary or higher education. These programs offer individualized psychologic evaluation, individualized instruction and remedial assistance, career information, and guidance and counseling of students and family members. Family members are also taught how to encourage and motivate the student. These programs also maintain liaison with community agencies and support organizations that can render assistance. Basically, the programs attempt to neutralize disadvantages among children that contribute to academic failure, dropout rates, and the development of delinquency.

### Work-study programs

These programs aim to reduce the number of dropouts by providing actual work experience outside the school while combining practical classroom instruction, oriented toward students who show signs of dropping out. Generally, the students spend half of the classroom day working and the other half in class. Work-oriented instruction is emphasized rather than achievement of academic goals.

### Remedial reading specialists

Learning to read is of utmost importance in the early years of school for all children. Many children are unable to keep pace with the teacher when reading is taught and thus fall behind in many other subjects as well. Inability to read and keep up with classmates causes frustrating and/or humiliating school experiences for the child, and his or her attitude may rapidly change from liking school to disliking it. Many times there are emotional disturbances stemming from disagreeable home conditions that interfere with a child's ability to learn to read. Some youngsters cannot concentrate or pay attention because of hyperactivity, and still others may have undetected vision or hearing problems or even brain damage that will interfere with their ability to learn. The importance of providing every opportunity for every child to learn to read can be easily recognized when one considers the fact that the typical dropout is of about average intelligence but is usually two years behind in reading and arithmetic.[33] Remedial reading specialists have become an integral part of every school system. These specialists work with children directly, giving them help their parents cannot or do not give, and also work with teachers so that reading skills are taught more effectively. A remedial reading specialist should be available at all educational levels.

There are many other programs and efforts in which community members and school officials work with parents and students to assist children. Many students performing below grade level can benefit from tutors, for example. Generally, tutors work with students to develop and enhance their talents and interests after class hours and on Saturdays. Most schools now have some type of tutorial program. Camp-school activities and various recreational programs are now utilized to improve the academic skills of the students who are failing in school. Many camp programs are also oriented to youths who are in trouble with police or are in conflict with their parents.

## THE SCHOOL AS A VICTIM OF DELINQUENCY

While education is one of the primary forces that can be used to combat crime, the school itself often becomes the victim or battleground of many types of aberrant behavior including vandalism, drug usage, bomb threats, assaults, and mass disruptions. Vestermark and Blauvelt[34] have developed an extensive handbook for school administrators on how to deal with these in-school problems.

Many different efforts have been directed at protecting the school and personnel against such deviant behavior. Some school systems have retained individuals who live on or near school grounds to keep watch over the physical structures around the clock. Some schools are protected after hours by private security forces and attack dogs who roam school grounds. Architects have also tried to "vandal-proof" new and remodeled schools or otherwise

---

[33]Mussen, Paul, Conger, John J., and Kagan, Jerome, *Child Development and Personality.* New York: Harper & Row, Inc., 1969, p. 731.

[34]Vestermark, Seymour D., Jr., and Blauvelt, Peter D., *Controlling Crime in the School: A Complete Security Handbook for Administrators.* West Nyack, N.Y.: Parker Publishing Co., Inc., 1978. See also Perry, Phillip M., *Security for Schools and Centers.* Sacramento: Creative Book Co., 1976.

make them more secure through environmental design. Corporal punishment is being used again as a form of discipline in public schools in a few states while private schools across the country have always used it as a means of increasing control over students. But whatever the punishment, school officials are recognizing that it must be clear, swift, and firm. Guards are also being employed inside the schools during class hours in an effort to curb assaults on teachers.

In an effort to decrease vandalism, lights in all San Antonio, Texas schools are turned off during closed hours, under an apparently correct assumption that lights attract youths to the school. Vandalism costs have since decreased significantly. Los Angeles schools have instituted a policy in which parents of children found guilty of vandalism must pay repair costs. Portland, Oregon crime prevention authorities sponsor an annual crime prevention week that includes a contest for elementary school children entitled Rhymes Against Crime. The following poem was chosen as one winner:

> Peter, Peter, auto stealer
> Stole a car and couldn't wheel 'er
> Crashed the car into a tree
> And now he's doing one to three[35]

Some schools have small classes in which teachers have contact with just a few students at the same time. This is done in an effort to personalize the educational climate and reduce the number of assaults on teachers.

Many other such programs are springing up across the country as the rising incidence of school-related crime has made it necessary for schools to take protective action. It is truly shameful that guards must patrol the hallways and stairwells of our nation's schools to keep teachers from being assaulted. However, until many of the preventive programs thus far described are implemented and cut crime at the roots, our schools will continue to be a breeding ground for criminal activity.

In my opinion education will turn out to be the key to crime prevention—not just to educate people about crime prevention techniques, but also to use education, especially the "community school concept," to enlighten individuals, to teach respect for one's fellow human being, to eliminate ignorance, to teach proper parenting techniques, and to give each person the necessary tools to pursue a vocation or profession which in turn will give a sense of purpose to life. School must be satisfying, not humiliating; without reinforcement many children will not stay in school and our delinquency problem will not be solved.

---

[35]Yarmon, Morton, "Ideas That Can Cut School Crime," *Parade*, Dec. 9, 1979, p. 15.

## INFLUENCE OF PEER GROUPS

By the time children enter into peer groups they have already been largely shaped by their families and school experiences. Although children begin playing together at a very early age, the importance of the peer group does not really take effect until after the child has been attending school. As the child is away from his or her parents more and more, the peer group begins to take on increased importance. Finally, in the high school years, the importance of pleasing the peer group is more important than pleasing parents.

### Role of peer groups in preventing and causing crime

Peer groups can play a strategic role in preventing or encouraging criminal activity. They can help prevent crime by negative social sanctions to those individuals who engage in infractions. The peer group will draw minor deviates back into conformity but will reject, isolate, and stigmatize serious infractions of group conduct.

The peer group can also encourage criminal activity by accepting the disregard of certain proscribed activities. They can also encourage criminal activity by rejecting a person from the group. This rejection could cause the person to react in several ways, one of which would be aberrant conduct. Why a person is rejected from a peer group is a matter that needs further study. However, the most common reason appears to be that the individual lowers the status of the group. A peer group will tolerate much from a high-status child, including changing the way they talk, act, or dress, just as long as they conform with the leader. The lower-status child does not have this advantage. If the lower-status child cannot afford to buy the latest craze in fashion, he or she will be one step closer to rejection by the group. According to Mussen et al., children of lower-status are more easily influenced than high-status children, who are more secure in their group and can better resist attempts at influencing them.[36] Likewise, a group of "rejects" can come together to form their own peer group. If this group becomes large enough, it will probably be labeled as a subculture. The norm of the participants may be to engage in a number of activities including truancy, vandalism, thefts, and drug usage. Parents can also play a large part in the shaping of the behavior of a peer group by telling their children which children they should play with and the ones they should avoid.

The child's peers become agents of socialization, although unwittingly, as reinforcers of certain behaviors, as models for imitation, and identification as a group, pressuring the child to make some modifications in behavior. Peer

---

[36]Mussen et al., op. cit., p. 582.

influence on personality development and behavior is probably second in importance only to that of parents.[37] The child will generally test social behaviors, responses, and characteristics he or she has learned and acquired in the home, all the while observing reactions of peers and teachers. It is at this point that the child may begin to deviate from what he or she has learned at home if such behaviors do not appear to please peers. From this point onward, peers will play an increasingly important role in the socialization of the child. Behaviors reinforced by peers will likely become dominant over those learned at home and reinforced by parents. Children learn very early, for example, not to wear a certain article of clothing or carry a certain type of lunchbox if they have been ridiculed by peers. Children will succumb to peer pressure if they wish to identify with the group rather than be rejected. As stated by Smart and Smart, "Children expose one another to a variety of sets of values which stem from membership of the family, class, and ethnic origin. The values of a peer group are especially compelling since a youngster has to accept them in order to be accepted as a member."[38] According to Mussen and co-workers, factors that contribute to an adolescent being rejected by a group include being ill-at-ease, lacking in self-confidence, timidity, nervousness, withdrawal, compensatory overaggressiveness, conceit, demanding attention, self-centeredness, being sarcastic or tactless, and being inconsiderate. The factors that contribute to acceptance by peers include intelligence, ability, social status, and ethnic group membership.[39]

Peer pressure should be brought into the child's life by age 4 or 5. This peer grouping must be positive since the pressure of negative peers can lead the child away from rather than toward acceptance of the approved adult patterns of behavior.[40] Einstein acknowledged that peer pressure may have negative results when he stated that excessively egotistic psychologic adjustment may become injurious for the individual and for the community.[41]

Peer pressure indeed does have injurious effects for the individual and the community. Vandalism is thought by most scholars, researchers, and practitioners to be a result of peer pressure. One such study found it definitely to be a group problem, with nine out of ten acts of vandalism carried out by persons in groups.[42] In addition to vandalism, peer pressure can also result in

---

[37] Ibid, p. 392.
[38] Smart, Mollie, and Smart, Russel, *Children: Development and Relationships.* New York: The Macmillan Co., 1972, p. 465.
[39] Mussen et al., op. cit., p. 663.
[40] Bigge, Morris L., and Hunt, Maurice P., *Psychological Foundations of Education.* New York: Harper & Row, Inc., 1968.
[41] Einstein, Albert, op. cit., p. 62.
[42] Phillips, G. Howard, and Bartlett, Kaye, *Vandals and Vandalism in Rural Ohio.* Wooster, Ohio: Ohio Agricultural Research and Development Center, Research Circular 222, Oct. 1976, p. 15.

commission of serious crimes by street gang members, shoplifting by youngsters in search of a thrill, and drug usage by youngsters searching for recognition by the group.

**Drug usage**

Drug usage among adolescents and even younger children is an extremely serious problem. Peer pressure is but one reason why youths may turn to drugs. Although attempts to get attention, retaliation against parents, escape from an unhappy home life, insecurity, and self-destructive tendencies are also applicable, users are the primary influences in many cases. Many children could not obtain drugs and would not use them were it not for associating with other youths who use drugs. Many times older children can persuade the younger ones to try drugs. Much of this occurs on school grounds during school hours when parents are not available to watch their children—and teachers are too few, too busy, and too naive to recognize the problem. Unfortunately, taking drugs is still the "in" thing to do as far as many peer groups are concerned, and children in all social classes are at risk. Efforts to stifle such usage among these group members may be of little value except in cases where peer pressure is not the overriding factor and other underlying disturbances that led to the drug problem in the first place can be identified and resolved.

There are a number of physical and behavioral clues that may alert parents and teachers to drug usage by children. Some of these include abnormal appetite, insomnia, irritability, dilated pupils, diarrhea, sudden personality changes such as short temper, withdrawal, apathy, and quickly alternating high and low moods. However, a final diagnosis of drug abuse is the responsibility of a medical doctor and the above symptoms are not always indications of aberrant behavior. If, however, they occur regularly, there is just cause to suspect a drug problem.

Since it is presently very difficult if not impossible to stop the flow and sale of drugs in this country, prevention of drug abuse lies in educating youngsters about the problems, helping them to see what drugs do to their bodies, and to see that usage of drugs is not a real means of escape from their problems. Prevention also must be shared by the family. Parents should attempt to keep lines of communication open between themselves and their children, so that problems in home life can be solved before the child turns to drugs. Troubled children must also be provided with counseling and psychologic and medical assistance, generally a responsibility of the school. Most communities have agencies from which parents of drug-abusing children can seek help. Parents who react in anger and punish their children, particularly by not letting them see their friends, are generally taking the wrong approach.

A long-term approach, which implies a genuine concern for the youngster's well-being and help in solving his or her problems, is probably the best approach that can be taken at this time.

## Television and violence

Another factor that is indirectly related to peer pressure and delinquency is television violence. Television provides us with many stars, idols, heroes, and models for behavior, but in doing so it subjects very impressionable youngsters and teenagers to an unbelievable amount of violence. Many children watch so much television that by the time they are seniors in high school, they have spent more time in front of the television than they have in the classroom. Many psychiatrists maintain that exposure to so much violence can desensitize youngsters to the effects of violence and can even encourage them to commit delinquent and aggressive acts. These concerns have been voiced to the Federal Communications Commission and television networks, and attempts have been made to persuade the networks to reduce the amount of violence in shows aired during times when children are likely to be watching. However, many violent shows still air during prime time.

## Youth service bureaus

Services available to youths in trouble are scattered, fragmented, and in most cases ineffective. In the vast majority of jurisdictions, there are youth workers in one department who may not even know who their counterparts are in other agencies. Social workers, probation officers, school counselors, and police, in many cases, work in opposition to each other. Further, when a child is in trouble, adults do not know where to turn for help. The establishment of a youth service bureau would centralize the activities of delinquency prevention and allow for more of a systems approach.[43] The purpose of a youth service bureau should not be to take over as an Orwellian big brother but rather to offer the family whatever assistance is needed to get the child back on the right track. Examples of services that should be provided are:
- □ Parental effectiveness training
- □ Individual counseling
- □ Group counseling
- □ Family counseling
- □ Liaison with the school
- □ Diagnosis of learning disabilities
- □ Diagnosis of psychologic maladjustments

---

[43]*The Challenge of Crime in a Free Society.* Washington, D.C.: U.S. Government Printing Office, 1967.

- Diagnosis of medical, dental, vision, and hearing problems
- Recommending and implementing behavioral treatment plans
- Providing financial assistance
- Providing thorough follow-up services

## CONCLUSION

Any variable that prevents a child from stable and healthy emotional growth may increase his or her proneness toward delinquency. Improving home life and strengthening families should remain the primary focus of delinquency prevention, since children spend their formative years in the home, learning from and imitating their parents. During these years, children must become accepted and loved members of the family, since paternal and maternal rejection is considered to be a strong causal factor for maladjusted behavior. Presently, there are still a number of parents who cannot adequately cope with the responsibilities of parenthood and cannot or do not provide a happy home life for their children. Broken homes, delinquent parents, child abuse, incest, poverty, lack of supervision, and nonsupport by family members are all examples of the various home life conditions that may precipitate delinquency.

The schools are the second major influence upon a child's behavior and adjustment. As an extension of the home, schools can either help prevent or contribute to delinquency. As we have seen, school programs to assist with problems at home can help reduce proneness to delinquency, but unsuccessful school experiences can lead to frustration and thereby contribute to the problem. The third major influence is the peer group, which increases in importance during the high school years. It can be either a source of prevention or a contributor to delinquent behavior.

The experiences that a child has as a result of these three influences are directly responsible for the child's behaviors, attitudes, and actions, whether they be delinquent or nondelinquent. It is these three influences that must be examined more closely to determine the underlying causes of delinquency and thus cut crime at the roots. This will not be an easy task since there are many social agencies that must become involved early in the child's life if permanent damage to the socialization process is to be avoided. Based on our current knowledge, we know that positive, early intervention offers the most promise in delinquency prevention. If the government and society decide to make a determined effort to cut crime at the roots, it must be remembered that it will take from ten to fifteen years for a noticeable effect to show up in the crime statistics. This is one reason why several chapters in this book deal with measures that can be taken here and now to reduce individual victimization.

# Section II

# PERSONAL CRIME PREVENTION

# Chapter 4

# Personal security

The underlying assumption of personal safety must partially be based upon the concept of awareness, awareness not only of the more obvious criminal opportunities, but also an awareness of one's own vulnerabilities and the precautions that can be taken to avoid potentially dangerous situations. Crimes against the person include those specific criminal activities that take place with the unwilling participation of the victim and threaten, endanger, or cause physical or emotional damage to the individual, with or without accompanying personal property loss. Crimes against the person are largely a matter of opportunity, and by reducing opportunities, many crimes can be completely avoided. This chapter discusses crime prevention measures in relation to various crimes against the individual.

The importance of avoiding potential "crime-producing" situations cannot be overemphasized. Since many crimes are opportunistic, avoiding the opportunities will drastically increase one's security. Common sense tells us to avoid such things as dark alleys and to lock our cars, and these things we can do without great sacrifice. Unfortunately, avoiding too many opportunities could make us prisoners in our own homes, and not many of us can or desire to avoid the outside world to that extent. Therefore, avoidance, although a major part of personal security, is not the total answer.

The fact that we cannot or do not wish to avoid contact from those around us makes us susceptible to victimization at one time or another. A partial "immunity" to this susceptibility can be attained by developing an attitude of awareness and alertness, although in some circumstances even this is not sufficient. This does not mean displaying a constant attitude of fright or paranoia, nor do we want a society of Lone Rangers; but it does mean developing a systematic approach for assessing more than just the obvious criminal opportunities. New situations, such as unfamiliar neighborhoods, hotel rooms, subways, recreational facilities, department stores, etc., should be evaluated in regard to other people present in the immediate vicinity, char-

**59**

acteristics of physical surroundings or evaluation of environmental design, and any other aspect of the area that makes an individual uneasy. If the area is feared too much, the individual will most likely not be willing to take the risk for whatever the expected benefit, unless there is no other alternative. Then precautions to increase personal security should be taken.

In the following pages, specific crime prevention measures are discussed. Since many crimes of a personal nature are directed against women, specific security precautions for women are discussed first.

## CRIME PREVENTION FOR WOMEN

Because women are physically weaker than men in terms of gross muscular strength and because their upbringing generally discourages physical force to counter aggression, women have historically been more vulnerable than men to crime. However, in actuality they are less often victims of crimes of violence, such as aggravated assault, robbery, and murder, than are men. The exceptions to this, of course, are sexual assaults and spouse abuse, as reflected by the Uniform Crime Reports from year to year. The fear of crime, however, which is psychologically damaging, tends to be greater among women than among men.

Every female, regardless of race, age, or social status, is a potential victim of sexual assault. Those who appear alone or easy to overpower and those who take unnecessary risks are most vulnerable. Sex crimes against women are not only damaging emotionally but usually also present a great risk for physical harm sufficient to cause death. According to Clifford a woman who submits to rape without fuss is not immune to violence because violence accompanies rape so frequently that a victim can logically expect to be killed. Those who experience rape without physical abuse are the exception rather than the rule. With or without violence there are also the very distressing possibilities of disease or unwanted pregnancy as a result of the sexual assault.[1]

### Passive sex crimes

Perhaps the only sex crime that does not involve physical contact is voyeurism. It is, however, a crude invasion of privacy by a "peeping tom" and can cause traumatic emotional shock to the victim even though no outward physical damage has been done. Another sexual assault that would probably cause no physical harm but would be very distressing emotionally is frottage. This term implies minor sexual advances, such as the intimate touching of a woman by a stranger. This behavior represents an invasion of one's personal

---

[1]Clifford, Martin, *Security*. New York: Drake Publishers, Inc., 1974, p. 205.

privacy while in public since frottage usually occurs in crowded areas such as elevators and public conveyances. If the woman is absolutely certain of the intrusion and the person responsible, her best defense is to immediately ask him in a loud voice to please keep his hands to himself. She must make it absolutely clear to him and everyone else that his actions are offensive and unacceptable. This generally embarrasses the offender so that he dare not move another muscle.

The best prevention for both the passive and violent sex crimes is to spoil the opportunities. It is fairly easy to prevent peeping toms—simply pull the shades when undressing and at night. Shades accompanied by lined draperies provide added privacy against silhouettes. All windows in the house should be similarly protected: No unshaded windows equals no window peeping opportunities.

## Rape

Rape is a sex crime far more serious and difficult to avoid once the situation has been established. Protecting oneself against rape involves more complex maneuvers than pulling shades, and in some cases all the preventive measures in the book may be to no avail. Obviously, the most desirable preventive measures are those that prevent the development of situations in which rape is likely to occur rather than relying on escaping from the rapist after he has attacked. Greater safety lies not in getting out of trouble but in avoiding trouble in the first place. In order to do this, many general precautions should be heeded by women because of their particular vulnerability. Listed below are prudent precautions, which to law enforcement officials seem to be commonsense precautions, but to the general public may not seem to be important.

### For protection on the streets
- Avoid walking on dark or deserted streets.
- Walk with someone if possible.
- Carry only a minimum of cash and avoid wearing expensive jewelry.
- Change directions if being followed, or even move into the middle of the street. Head for a well-lighted area where there are people.
- Run and scream if a suspicious person comes too close. Don't worry about appearing foolish.
- Avoid shortcuts through parks and alleys.
- Be alert while walking; do not daydream and do notice those who pass. Rapists often first pass and then turn to follow their victim.
- When being dropped off by taxi or other car get safely inside the house or apartment before the driver leaves.
- Be wary of people nearby when getting out of cars or buses.
- Stay close to the operator when riding a bus, subway, train, or other public

conveyance. Rapes on these public transportation systems, as unlikely as it may seem, can and do occur frequently.

□ Do not walk too close to buildings or parked cars.

□ Park in well-lighted areas as near the destination as possible.

□ Do not become laden down with packages. Keep your hands free—most men on the streets have their hands free.

□ Be aware of wearing apparel and dress to fit the occasion. High heels are not for walking, especially when alone. They may, however, be good for kicking. Tight skirts make running difficult, and scarves and long necklaces may make it easier for the rapist to get a strangle-hold.

□ Do not walk near or through a group of men. Cross the street if necessary to maintain distance.

□ Be alert for footsteps. If danger is near or imminent yell "Fire!" This brings more help faster since a fire could affect many people. Yelling "Help" or "Rape" confuses many people about what to do.

□ Carry a shrill whistle around your wrist and blow it if necessary.

□ Do not walk alone if upset, inebriated, or high on drugs.

□ Be aware of cars that pass by repeatedly.

**While in the car**

□ Keep the car in tip-top shape. Have plenty of gas—at least one-fourth tank at all times. A lone woman running out of gas is asking for trouble.

□ Inspect tires frequently; learn how to change flats quickly. Steel-belted radial tires are the least likely to have flats and blowouts.

□ Lock all doors and roll up windows before driving anywhere. Travel busy, well-lighted streets and plan routes carefully. Avoid rough neighborhoods even if it means taking a detour. A car in mint condition is still subject to a breakdown at any time.

□ Carry flares in the glove compartment.

□ If a breakdown does occur, get out, open the hood, get back inside, lock all doors. Keep windows rolled up. Wait patiently for law enforcement officials to arrive. Under no circumstances get out or unlock the doors for anyone else. If it is impossible not to vacate the vehicle for some reason, write on a piece of paper the time it was left, intended destination, description of anyone offering assistance, and leave in full view on car seat or dash.

□ Always lock the car when leaving and keep packages in the trunk. Packages left in the car, even if covered with newspaper or blankets, invite thieves since it is obvious there is something worth stealing. However, the trunk is also fairly easily opened so do not make a display of putting packages in it.

□ Beware of hitchhikers. Never pick them up no matter what their appearance or predicament.

□ Do not stop to offer assistance to stalled cars. Some criminals go out of their way to find victims and one can never be certain if the breakdown is legitimate. Call the police or highway patrol and report the location of the stalled vehicle.

□ Do not leave a purse on the seat. This can attract a criminal to the car. If possible, keep the purse in the glove compartment or on the floor.

□ Keep the car in gear while stopped at traffic lights or stop signs. If your safety is threatened, hold down the horn and drive away as soon as possible.

☐ Frequently check the rear view mirror. Do not turn into a driveway or stop in a deserted area if being followed. Pull over to the curb in a busy area and let the car pass. Attempt to get the license number and report it to police.

☐ If a car does follow you to the driveway, sound the horn until the car leaves or the driver is identified and his intentions are known.

☐ Do not leave keys in the ignition even if parked for only a short time.

☐ Have keys ready when getting in the car and always check the back seat so that no one could remain hidden.

**While going out**

☐ Do not be too quick to enter an elevator. Many rapes and robberies have taken place in elevators of large buildings and apartment complexes when the offender is able to attack his victim in seclusion. If there is a suspicious looking person already on the elevator, no one is obliged to enter it. It is better to wait till it comes again. If a person enters the elevator and makes a woman uneasy, she should get off immediately or at the next floor.

☐ Another precautionary measure when riding self-service elevators is to stand next to the control panel. If attacked, at least the victim has a chance of hitting the alarm button or as many buttons as she can reach.

☐ Any woman should realize it is very risky to accept an invitation to go home with someone she has just met, even if the invitation is only for a drink or snack.

☐ A woman planning to associate with a relatively new acquaintance should make sure a trusted friend knows her intended plans and the name and address of the associate.

☐ Any acquaintance who cannot provide information concerning his employment and will not introduce friends and relatives should not be trusted until more is known about his background.

☐ Women should not thumb rides or accept rides from strangers. Women who do are only putting themselves in jeopardy since there is no way of knowing who they are riding with or what they may be subjected to.

**If hitchhiking is an absolute necessity**

☐ Find out the destination of the driver before he knows your destination.

☐ Do not mention having any money or answer any personal questions.

☐ If there are signs that the driver has been drinking, such as empty beer cans in the car, pass up the ride.

☐ If possible, try not to hitchhike alone.

☐ Check door handles before entering the car. Make sure they work. If the handle is missing turn down the ride.

☐ Do not hitchhike at night.

☐ Do not accept a ride with more than one man.

☐ Make sure no one is hiding in the back seat before entering.

☐ Do not accept a ride from a man who is not fully dressed, has his pants unzipped, or cannot keep his hands on the steering wheel.

☐ Do not accept a ride from anyone who had to slam on his brakes or change directions in order to pick you up.

☐ Avoid hitchhiking to deserted or scarcely populated areas.

- Do not hitchhike in halters, see-through blouses, shorts, etc. Attire such as this may give someone the idea you are promiscuous.
- Keep the car window partly rolled down so that if screaming becomes necessary it will be more effective.

**While at home**

- If living alone, use your last name and first initial only on mailbox and phone listings.
- Never open the door to strangers. Identity can be checked through a 180-degree optical viewer. Never rely on a chain lock—they offer no security at all.
- Even the best lock cannot function if it is not locked. Doors should be kept locked during the day, while in the house, and when away—even if you will be gone only for a few minutes.
- Always check the identification of repairmen and deliverymen. Never open the door automatically. Do not be too embarrassed to make a phone call to their employer or business before allowing them inside if their identity is questionable. Children should be taught to do the same.
- Install a strong lock on the bedroom door. A telephone next to the bed will also provide psychologic comfort as well as a means of summoning assistance in case an intruder is heard.
- Lights should be left on at night even when you are away. The location of the lights left on should be varied.
- Do not allow strangers in to use the phone. Only offer to make the call for them.
- Hang up immediately on obscene phone callers.
- Do not give out personal information over the phone or let a caller know that no one else is at home. Do not give out your phone number. If a caller wants to know the number, ask "What number were you calling?" If the caller gives the wrong number, tell him so. If he gives the correct number, ask what his business is but be blunt and frank with him until his business is established as legitimate.
- Keep lights on at all entrances at night.
- Become aware of places around the home or apartment where rapists might hide.
- Make sure windows are securely locked.
- Know a few neighbors who can be trusted in an emergency.
- When alone at night and an unexpected knock comes to the door, it is sometimes helpful for a woman to exclaim, "Harry, can you answer the door?" If the person does not have legitimate intentions, this may be enough to scare him away.
- Consult Chapter 5 for additional home security precautions.

**When the rapist attacks.** First of all, every assault is different and there are as many reactions as there are situations. Only the woman being raped is aware of what action may work best in her particular case. Her response will have to be one that she is physically and emotionally capable of carrying out at the time. It should also be mentioned that the rapist is usually equipped with several advantages including, oddly enough, the law. He may be able to claim he was enticed, seduced, that the woman willingly opened her door and invited him in, or that he paid her for services rendered. In addition, the rapist is aware of the fact that many women are ashamed to report a rape and are unwilling to undergo the humiliation that publicity of the rape would bring. In too many circumstances, it is the woman's word against the accused—if he is identified at all.

These advantages, accompanied by the attacker's overpowering physical strength, make a rape almost inevitable if sufficient motivation and opportunity exist. Therefore, women should be prepared with what will turn out to be advantages for them. As stated previously, there are many possible reactions to a rape threat, and the actions taken by the woman will depend upon her physical and emotional makeup, the environmental circumstances, and the emotional and physical makeup of the attacker. The human element of emotions is of utmost importance since the purpose of any action taken by the woman should be to reduce violence from the attacker. One can see the significance of this if the would-be rapist has been rejected by women and hates them; an obviously hostile response by the woman would only add fuel to the fire and jeopardize her life further. Thus there are many variables involved, and unfortunately there is no set miracle formula of getting out of a rape threat safely. I wish to emphasize again that any actions taken by the woman should be geared toward decreasing the risk of violence against herself.

A woman's physical strength is generally no match for a man's, and unless she is certain of some form of self-defense such as karate, she might wish to employ one of several psychologic deterrents as suggested by Bennett and Clagett.[2] These tactics have been known to delay, confuse, bewilder, and (most desirably) scare off the potential attacker. Many rapists have deflated egos and, therefore, are very susceptible to compliments from women. Compliments suggesting that the rapist is desirable and probably has a lot of girlfriends may be very effective in at least stalling if not preventing the rape entirely. If the woman can get the attacker to communicate with her she may be able to learn of some of his underlying needs. Besides being a rapist he is also a person and needs to be talked with and listened to. The woman must appear to be very sincere in her compliments and communication attempts; otherwise, they may only serve to make the rapist more angry.

Another maneuver closely related to ego-building is convincing the attacker that she would enjoy having sex with him but she would like to go someplace a little more private or perhaps stop off for a drink first. This willingness to give the rapist what he wants catches him by surprise since

---

[2]Bennett, Vivo, and Clagett, Crickett, *1001 Ways to Avoid Getting Mugged, Murdered, Robbed, Raped, or Ripped Off.* New York: Van Nostrand Reinhold Co., 1977, p. 105.

most expect resistance. If the woman can convince him to hold off a little while, it allows her more opportunities for escape. This pretense to submit to the rape must also seem sincere and the woman must act in a calm manner in order to be convincing. If no opportunities occur to escape and the rapist is armed or violent, then complete submission may be the most reasonable choice.

Additional psychologic ploys include attempts to turn the rapist off. Actions such as fainting, urinating or defecating, acting insane, acting like a lesbian, or convincing the attacker he may catch venereal disease can be so unattractive to him that he no longer has the desire to commit the rape.

If the woman is equipped with a knife, gun, or any other weapon (nail file, hat pin, keys, etc), she should *not* use the weapon unless she is positive of her ability and is willing to injure and disable her attacker. It is all too easy for the rapist to overpower the woman, take the weapon, and use it against her. Even if a weapon is carried by a woman—which is illegal in any case—and she is sure of her ability to use it, it is usually kept at the bottom of her purse, which is often the first thing to be dropped during an attack. Therefore, a woman should not feel immune to crime just because she carries a weapon. One experiment that might help individuals determine if they are capable of the responsibility of carrying a weapon such as a gun is to have another person act as a rapist, then see if it would be possible to take a water pistol from a purse and get the other person wet before he can take it away. Remember, however, that this would even be easier than using a real weapon under threat.

If psychologic attempts to dissuade the rapist have failed and the rape is inevitable, there are still a few remaining options. Again, these suggestions depend upon several variables, including whether or not the rapist is armed. One of these options is running, but this should be done only if there is a place of safety to run to and the chances are good for getting away. High heels, tight skirts, and other extenuating circumstances often make this option impossible. Screaming is another option, which may frighten the attacker because of the attention it might bring. For this to be effective, help needs to be within hearing distance and it needs to be immediate and sufficient. Screaming into the attacker's ears may also result in an opportunity to escape. It is best not to scream "Rape" or "Help," since many people do not know how to respond. Screaming "Fire" will bring more people more quickly. Using one's teeth may also prove to be an effective weapon. Biting will usually cause enough pain so that the assailant must loosen his hold. A hard enough bite will draw blood, which will usually cause the assailant to run. Fingers and fingernails are also excellent weapons. Scratches by fingernails are capable of drawing blood, which will discourage the attacker and also can be used for identification purposes later. Fingers and thumbs are very effective when poked into the eyes of the assailant. Pulling his hair or ears is also another possibility for temporarily disabling the attacker. Kicking is also another good defensive maneuver. The most effective kick would cause excruciating pain to the groin area, but this is not always possible since this is also the area of his body the attacker will try to protect. A sharp kick to the assailant's shin will suffice for a groin kick since this would also cause severe pain and may enable the woman to escape. Grabbing the groin, squeezing, and turning 180 degrees should produce instantaneous pain and may be easier to accomplish than kicking. If the woman is being raped in her own home this may be the last resort in preventing the rape since many of the other tactics that stall for time would be useless.

If the rapist succeeds in knocking the woman to the ground there are still some actions that can make it more difficult for the assailant to accomplish the rape. Crossing the legs, locking the ankles, and fighting back with the hands makes it necessary for the rapist to hold down the woman's arms with his hands. As long as he must use his hands for that purpose, he cannot accomplish anything else. When the rapist attempts to remove his clothes, he will have to let go and raise up. The woman's hands will be free and the attacker will be in a vulnerable position for the groin grab. The same holds true when he attempts to disrobe the woman; her hands and arms will be free to attack any body part possible.

If the rapist is armed, a woman should not instigate violence by any action. She should strive to stay calm and assure the rapist she will not fight back. He then may become overly confident and even put his weapon aside. If this occurs and the woman is willing to fight, she may try any of the above suggestions. *Never* attack a rapist if he has a weapon, and if any defensive maneuvers are successful, do not stay around to fight. Get away and report the assault as soon as possible.

Any of the above self-defense maneuvers are legal since rape constitutes imminent jeopardy to the woman's life. Actions such as the above are those that any reasonable and prudent individual would take under the same circumstances, and therefore an individual employing any one of them would be protected by law against a counterassault suit.

**If the rapist is successful.** Actions taken by rape victims are very important in the prevention of additional rapes. The rapist rarely stops with one victim unless he is stopped with immediate and successful prosecution. Victims should not hesitate to call the police and report the crime at the earliest possible time. Much progress has been made in the prosecution of this type of charge and there is no longer any need for rape victims to feel shame, guilt, dread, or fear that they will be tried as the offender. In most areas the rape victim is interviewed by a policewoman and in some larger cities the case is prosecuted by a female assistant district attorney. The International Tribunal of Crimes Against Women has gone one step further. They have suggested that only women judges preside over rape cases.[3]

In addition to prompt reporting of the crime, victims should be cautioned against bathing or douching, even though this is generally the immediate inclination. They should demand immediate hospital care, if needed, and a physical examination. This is important to ensure the health of the victim and also for preservation of evidence to be used in prosecution. Also, the scene of the rape should be left untouched until law enforcement officers have arrived.

### A final note

It is highly unlikely that any woman could follow every single precaution all of the time, or that all women will be able to remain calm and use their heads in a threatening situation. Even if she follows some of the suggestions a woman may still be raped. However, the measures discussed above substantially reduce the risk of attack without causing undue sacrifice to personal freedom. To make the most out of crime prevention efforts, each woman should assess her weaknesses in personal security and institute measures that will fill the gaps.

### SAFETY FOR CHILDREN
### Molestation

Personal safety of children is the first and foremost responsibility of parents. Children must be protected and taught to protect themselves against the many perils of society. Molestation is second only to accidents as a threat to a child's safety. Parents have the responsibility to become aware of characteristics and habits of child molesters, which is sometimes difficult since there is no typical profile of a molester. Child molesters may look normal but they are afraid of normal sexual relations. They do not always wait in the dark and grab a child; in fact, the majority of molesters are acquainted with the victim.[4] Victims are usually young elementary school children who have not been properly instructed by their parents on what to watch for and how to avoid the child molester. Most of the sexual attacks involve children in kindergarten through the fifth grade, although toddlers and teenagers are also

---

[3]Russell, Diana E. H., and Van deVen, Nicole, editors, *Crimes Against Women*. Proceedings of the International Tribunal. Les Femmes Millbrare, Calif., 1976, p. 189.
[4]Schapper, Beatrice, "What We Know About Child Molesters." *Today's Health*, Jan. 1966, pp. 18-19.

susceptible.[5] Protecting school children during their travels to and from school has been identified as a special need in many communities.

Helping Hand and Block Parent programs have been established in many neighborhoods as a result of the need to protect young children and provide assistance in many kinds of emergencies. These emergencies include incidences of molestation, abduction, dog attacks, traffic accidents, illness, bullying by other children, and becoming lost on the way to or from school. Participating homes are easily identified by a sign familiar to all children displayed in a front window. Block Parents should be carefully screened and registered with the local law enforcement agency. The local law enforcement agency has the responsibility to make frequent checks to make sure only authorized homes display Block Parent signs.

Fortunately, molestation accompanied by violence is rare. In fact, most sexual criminals prefer to establish a relationship with a child without resorting to violence. However, if the offender fears the child may expose him, he may try to silence the child in any way possible, including murder. In actuality, however, only a very small percentage of molested children expose the offender. Why is this so? Part of the answer lies in the parents' attitudes concerning sexual matters. Many children are raised in the atmosphere of sexual secrecy and are taught to believe that sex is dirty, shameful, and forbidden. Children learn not to bring up the subject, even when they have been sexually abused. Because of the child's silence, the molester may be able to establish a long-term relationship with the child.

### Precautions for children

Children are naturally friendly, but where strangers are concerned, this friendliness should be stifled. Every child should be instructed in the following precautions for her or his own personal safety.

- A child should never accept a ride with any stranger, even if he states he was sent by the child's parents to pick the child up. Some molesters use desperate excuses to lure the child into the car, such as telling the child his parents have been in an accident and he will take the child to the hospital.
- If possible children should play outside and go to and from school with other children.
- Children should never accept money, candy, or other gifts from a stranger, even on special occasions such as Halloween.
- Parents should always know where their child will be.
- Children should never let a stranger touch them. If one tries, attempt to get away and report it to police.
- Children who are old enough for school should know the telephone number where their parents can be reached during the day, and should also know how to dial the operator.

---

[5]*National Neighborhood Watch*, Program Manual, The National Sheriff's Association, p. 21.

- Never go with men to their living quarters. This is very dangerous even if they appear friendly. They may offer candy or want to show the child something, but children should always keep away.
- Children should be accompanied by an adult when using public restrooms.
- Children should not go to movies alone. If anyone tries to touch a child in a theater, he should be instructed to tell the manager right away.
- Parents should explain to their children that they would never send a stranger to pick them up from school or any other event, even in emergencies.
- Children should not play alone in empty buildings or in deserted alleys.
- Children should be instructed never to allow new acquaintances into the house when they are there alone.
- Children should never allow anyone including friends and relatives to touch or caress private parts of their body. If someone tries, they should always inform their parents.
- A child should always take a friend when selling candy, cookies, subscriptions, etc.
- If a stranger asks a child for directions, he should be careful to maintain a good distance from the car.
- Children should attempt to get the license number of any car in which a stranger tries to get him to accept a ride.
- Children should not take shortcuts through alleys, dark streets, or empty lots where there is lots of shrubbery growing.
- Parents should make sure their child receives a gradual amount of reliable and worthwhile information concerning human sexuality, so that if something should happen, the child will be able to discuss sex and the sexual problem with his parents. If the parents are not capable of imparting this information in a mature fashion, then perhaps clergy, a counselor, the school, or carefully selected book can teach the child the necessary knowledge. No child should reach adolescence completely ignorant of sexual matters and they should certainly have an understanding of the dangers of sexual perversions.
- If a child does expose a molester, the child should not be punished. Parents need to remain calm in order to retain the trust and confidence of the child, and in order to minimize future psychological damage to the child. As much information as possible regarding the offense and the offender should be obtained.
- Unless there is specific evidence against the offender, it will be very difficult to prosecute him, and parents run the risk of libel or slander if they bring charges.
- It is the responsibility of the parents to make sure the child has no further contact with the offender or suspect.
- If evidence exists against the offender, it is the parent's duty to go to court so that future molestations can possibly be avoided.

## Other forms of sexual abuse

In addition to molestation, children may encounter other forms of sexual abuse. Sexual abuse of children covers a wide variety of behaviors including fondling, exhibitionism, incest, forcible rape, and commercial exploitation for prostitution or the production of pornographic materials. An amendment to the federal Child Abuse Prevention and Treatment Act of 1974 defines the term "sexual abuse" to include "the obscene or pornographic photographing, filming, or depiction of children for commercial purposes, or the rape, molestation, incest, prostitution or other such forms of sexual exploitation of children under circumstances which indicate that the child's health or welfare is harmed or threatened thereby."[6]

The extent of sexual abuse of children is unknown. It is thought that cases reported to appropriate authorities represent only a fraction of the cases that actually take place. Sexual exploitation of children for commercial purposes has only recently begun to receive the attention this problem deserves. At present the number of victims involved in the production of child pornography is undetermined, but it is known that the sale of these materials represents millions of dollars.

Because this type of crime is often not reported, gathering data about its scope is difficult. It is thought that many parents are reluctant to report such incidences for fear of embarrassment and an unwillingness to subject the child to further embarrassing interviews. In addition, many children do not report such incidences to their parents for fear of punishment or because of shame or guilt feelings. In fact, in many cases one of the parents is the offender. The image of the dirty old man who hides behind a bush and waits for little children is the image many would prefer to blame for the majority of sexual abuses against children, but such is simply not the case. Several studies of sexual abuse against children have demonstrated that in the majority of instances, parents, other relatives, neighbors, and acquaintances are responsible for the sexual encounter.[7]

Incest is obviously the most difficult form of sexual abuse to detect, because it tends to be kept a family secret. The most commonly reported type of incest is father-daughter or father-figure incest, although it can occur between mother-son, mother-daughter, father-son, brother-sister, cousin-cousin, etc. Complicated psychologic problems generally exist in the incestuous family. There may be such factors as social isolation, sexual incompatibility of parents, a sexually promiscuous father, a daughter who has taken over the role of the mother, a mother who consciously or unconsciously approves the incest, or a father with an abnormal desire for young children (pedophilia). Incest may even be a desperate attempt by the family to save the marriage. The child will usually cooperate with the perpetrator because he or she trusts and is dependent upon the adult. There may also be bribes of material goods or threats of physical violence if the child does not comply. The child may

---

[6]"Child Sexual Abuse, Incest, Assault, and Sexual Exploitation." A Special Report from the National Center on Child Abuse and Neglect, Department of Health, Education, and Welfare, Publication No. (OHDS)79-30166, Aug. 1978, p. 1.
[7]Ibid, p. 4.

also have needs for love and attention that are not being met through normal channels.

Most children who are victims of sexual exploitation for commercial purposes are thought to be products of incestuous families or runaways from a developing incestuous situation. This would explain their susceptibility to further exploitation; possibly this is the only way they have learned to relate to others. The long-term psychologic effects of sexual abuse upon children are inconclusive since this problem is only now beginning to be properly explored and researched. It would seem that the effects would be variable, depending upon the child, type of sexual abuse, if significant others were directly involved, and the reactions of significant others after the fact. Possible long-term effects include the repetition of self-destructive behavior patterns such as drug or alcohol abuse, self-mutilation, and the development of sexual inadequacies.

### Prevention of sexual abuse

Prevention of sexual abuse is difficult because of the problems of detecting it. The ability of professionals to recognize signs of sexual abuse is yet immature, and signs of sexual abuse are rarely clearly differentiated from signs of other problems the child may be experiencing. Many of the messages children may give to those qualified to intervene may be so camouflaged that there is no suggestion of sexual abuse. The investigator is left with only a willingness to accept the possibility that sexual misconduct might exist, even if this is contrary to what the child relates.

At present, the successful prevention of sexual abuse against children is dependent upon: further training of professionals to identify sexually abused victims, education of parents and children, and the institution of additional treatment programs to help both offender and victim. Several programs have been established that utilize extensive family and group therapy. Some of these have shown promising results in helping incestuous families. Some programs work in conjunction with police and courts, and others work closely with social and rehabilitative services. Obviously, it takes individuals who are specially trained and who are empathetic and sensitive to children's needs to deal with this type of problem. The child victim should have to undergo a minimum of questioning, and should be treated with kindness and understanding.

Telephone helplines, modeled after crises intervention hotlines, have also proved to be of major benefit in the prevention of sexual abuse. The caller has at least recognized the need for help and can use the helpline twenty-four hours a day as one method of getting it. Counselors are generally available to talk with the caller and, hopefully, help prevent a sexual attack. Those who have been victims also are encouraged to use the helpline for assistance after the assault. Education of children about their bodies, parts of their bodies that should be kept private, how to say "no" to abnormal sexual encounters, and how to ask for help when they need it will help children to protect themselves against sexual abuse. Tougher laws and greater penalties need to be passed and enforced against those who exploit children for commercial purposes. This problem will require more attention from police departments around the country if the incidence of this crime is to be halted. There is no one simple solution because the factors involved in sexual abuse are not simple. It takes an interdisciplinary approach with much dedication and effort on the part of all involved if this particular social ill is to be stopped.

## Child abuse

Child abuse may be considered any nonaccidental physical attack or physical injury, not compatible with reasonable discipline, inflicted upon children by persons caring for them. Neglect is considered to be a chronic failure on the part of an individual entrusted to a child's welfare to protect the child from obvious physical danger or to provide the basic physical, emotional, and environmental needs of the child. In order to assist in the prevention of this deplorable social problem, those in law enforcement must first know and be able to recognize characteristics of both the abused and the abuser, and factors that may relate to child abuse. A battered child probably will not tell anyone he or she is being abused and may not realize it himself. In order to help abused children the following symptoms should be noted; however, only a physician can make a final diagnosis:

### Symptoms of abuse
- Obvious malnutrition
- Minor abrasions and bruises at various stages of healing
- Presence of bite marks
- Presence of old healed lesions
- Swelling of soft tissue
- Presence of multiple fractures
- Injury to frontal dental ridge
- Presence of cigarette burn scars
- Repeated ingestion of poisons

### Behavioral characteristics
- Apprehension when contacted physically
- Cries very little even if obviously uncomfortable
- Shows lack of expectation of assurance from parents
- Does not show normal fear of strangers or distress when left alone
- Is unresponsive or stiff when held or comforted
- Shows no normal curiosity of physical environment

**Characteristics of child abusers**
- May have been subjected to similar abuse as a child
- Does not volunteer information about the child
- Contradicts self when describing how injury took place
- Becomes easily irritated when questioned about the child
- Displays anger with the child for becoming injured
- Often disappears after child has been admitted to hospital
- Tends not to visit child in hospital and shows no concern over child's condition
- Shows no indication of having any perception of how the child might feel
- May demonstrate role reversal in which parent turns to the child for nurturing, satisfaction of needs, and protection, instead of supplying this to child

In addition to recognizing signs of abuse, it is also important to have some understanding of the factors related to child abuse. Listed below are some of these factors.[8]

- Abuse may stem from disciplinary action as a result of real or perceived misconduct of the child. The disciplinary action taken may be a result of uncontrolled anger, and thus the discipline became uncontrolled as well.
- Abuse may be a result of hostility, resentment, or rejection on the part of the abuser directed toward the child.
- Atypical behavior by the child, such as hyperactivity, may provoke an attack.
- Abuse may result from a quarrel between the caretakers.
- The abuser may be under a great deal of stress, such as financial, marital, or health problems.
- Alcohol or drug intoxication may be a factor in the attack.
- Premature infants and infants who did not receive early mothering have greater susceptibility to abuse.
- Abuse may occur by babysitter, boyfriend, or other caretakers while parents are out of the home.

**Prevention of child abuse**

Abused children need the assistance of people from many disciplines and organizations—physicians, nurses, psychologists, law enforcement officers, social service workers, prosecuting attorneys, and humane societies such as the Bureau of Child Welfare. In order to prevent a repeat attack children may be temporarily placed in a foster home or an institution. Prompt reporting and rapid and thorough investigations of each family are necessary. Self-help groups such as Parents Anonymous provide an atmosphere in which abusive parents can confess their destructive tendencies and receive support in their attempts to change. There are also daycare centers where battering parents and their children can interact safely. Child abuse and neglect helplines run by hospitals, protective agencies, and voluntary agencies are also available in many areas with around-the-clock counseling services. Parents whose re-

---

[8]*Lippincott Manual of Nursing Practice.* Philadelphia: J. B. Lippincott Co., 1978, p. 1390.

lationship with their children has not yet developed into a crisis situation but who nevertheless feel it might can often benefit from such services. Follow-up of calls is also done if the parent is willing to leave his or her telephone number. Those who work with or come into contact with abusive parents need to maintain a noncritical, nonpunitive approach in order to help prevent further abuse.

## A final note

The child abuse statute protects the person who reports a possible child abuse case. Even if, upon investigation by a law enforcement agency, the report of abuse is unfounded, the person reporting the suspected child abuse is protected by law from any civil liabilities, providing the report was made in good faith. The law enforcement agency also protects the anonymity of persons reporting to protect them from acts of reprisal. Many persons are in a position to observe the battered and neglected child; if they feel that a child is being mistreated, they should not hesitate to contact a social or law enforcement agency. The earlier a problem is referred to appropriate persons for help, the greater the opportunity for helping the child and family.

## OTHER CRIMES AGAINST THE PERSON
### Robbery

Robbery has become a more commonly committed offense in recent years and the use of deadly weapons in robberies has increased. The victim's life is always in immediate jeopardy since a robber must have deliberate, planned, personal contact with the victim in order to commit the crime. The fact that robbers often have volatile personalities and are easily provoked makes this crime a serious threat to personal security. The prevention of robbery, as with most other crimes, lies in one's being aware of and avoiding situations in which robberies are likely to occur. This requires the development of certain habits and practices, which are listed below:

- If possible, carry money in an inside pocket rather than in a purse or wallet.
- Walk in an aware manner, against the flow of traffic.
- Keep records of credit cards at home in a safe place.
- Do not go to laundromats or a laundry room in an apartment house alone at night. Such places are frequented by robbers also.
- Do not stop for a conversation with a stranger.
- Do not display large sums of cash or other valuables.
- Avoid cars parked along the street with the motor running.
- Avoid crowds of adolescents.
- Do not become distracted when buying something or opening a purse or wallet.
- Do not get into elevators with strange persons.
- Do not wait for the bus or taxi alone on a deserted street at night.

□ When going out, it is a good idea to carry a loud, shrill whistle or other body alarm.

A fairly inexpensive body alarm is one that is combined with a flashlight and sounds a loud high-pitched buzz; another type is a horn on top of a bottle of compressed gas which makes a siren noise. A more expensive body alarm is the "panic button," which looks and works similar to a hand control for a garage door opener. It works in conjunction with an alarm system in the individual's home or car and has a range of 200 feet. It is particularly effective if an alarm is needed when one is working in the yard or walking to the car. Eventually this type of alarm system may be incorporated into the present pocket pager. The panic button could alert others that an emergency is taking place, and as technology increases, the pocket pager could become a necessity, allowing for two-way communication to summon help and to pinpoint the user's exact locale.

The reader is referred to Chapter 6, Crime Prevention for the Elderly, and Chapter 8, Business Security, for further crime prevention measures for robbery.

## Automobile theft

Automobile or bicycle theft usually does not involve direct contact of the victim with the offender but nevertheless will be considered as a crime against the person, since vehicles are personal property, and their loss very often results in considerable insult and inconvenience to the victim. The automobile is a major investment to most persons and represents the main source of private transportation. Cars parked on the street (most are out of necessity) are particularly vulnerable to theft or vandalism. Glass can be easily broken, key switches bypassed, and wheels, tires, hubcaps, etc., can be easily removed. Even a locked car can be quickly opened using something as simple as a coat hanger. Any unattended vehicle is subject to theft and each motorist must help law enforcement curb the rising incidence of this problem.

Most automobiles are stolen by professional car theft rings and are never recovered. Others are taken by juveniles for the purpose of joyriding and are often badly damaged in crashes or vandalized before being abandoned. In addition, joyriding often results in serious injury to the youngsters and many youngsters who joyride often commit more serious crimes in later life.

There are nearly one million motor vehicles stolen each year; nearly one in five is left unlocked with the keys still in the ignition.[9] Most of the thefts

---

[9]"Your Car Could Be Stolen This Year." National Automobile Theft Bureau, 390 North Broadway, Jericho, N.Y., 1977.

take place at night in residential areas. Many precautions to reduce the risk of auto theft have been recommended by the National Automobile Theft Bureau (NATB). These recommendations include:

- Park in well-lighted areas.
- Always remember exactly where the car is parked.
- Park with wheels turned sharply to the right or left so that it is difficult for the car to be towed away.
- Lock all doors and keep windows rolled up. Many areas have local laws prohibiting keys to be left in unattended cars, and tickets are issued for such offenses.
- Activate any auto alarms or antitheft devices.
- Keep packages, tape decks, and citizen band radios out of sight. Expensive items in full view invite theft even if the car is locked.
- Avoid transferring valuable items to the trunk at the location where the car is to be parked.
- Use a garage if possible and lock both car and garage.
- Know the license number, model, year, and make of the car.
- Do not keep licenses and registrations in the car itself. If stolen these documents could be used to impersonate the owner.
- Do not leave money, checkbooks, wallets, or credit cards in the car at any time.
- Leave only the ignition key with the attendant of a commercial parking lot.
- Consider installing numerous antitheft devices (such as those designed to interrupt the fuel or electrical system, sound alarms, or lock the brakes, doors, or steering) and door locks that are difficult to open with wire.
- Put some form of personal identification on or in the car in an inconspicuous place. Manufacturer's identification numbers are being increasingly removed by professional car thieves, and determining ownership then becomes difficult if no other form of identification exists. Identification marks can easily be engraved into several hard-to-spot places; the owner's name and address can be placed behind the instrument panel, a floor mat, or door interior.

### When purchasing a used car, beware of the following

- New paint jobs on late model cars
- No fixed address or job of the seller
- Manufacturer's identification number that appears to have been tampered with. (This number can be found on a metal plate over the driver's dash section, visible from the outside at the bottom of the windshield.)
- Replacement sets of keys for late model cars. The buyer should get at least one set of original manufacturer's keys.
- Inspection stickers that are out of date or issued by another state.
- Evidence of forgery or alteration of the title.
- Old plates on a new car.
- Signs of break-in such as replaced glass, sprung doors, tool marks, chipped glass, or poorly closing windows.

Locking the car and pocketing the key is the most important behavior motorists can develop in order to prevent car thefts. This action alone can substantially decrease the number of cars stolen each year, while representing no sacrifice to personal freedom at all. Again, car thievery is mainly one of opportunity, and if all motorists are committed to protecting themselves and their cars against criminals, the automobile thief can be put out of business.

## Bicycle security

Rising fuel costs coupled with increased leisure time have brought a resurgence of bicycle popularity. The increased demand for bicycles, their light weight, easy mobility, and attractive resale value has made them prime targets for theft. Bicycles have become a fairly expensive item to purchase and there are a few people who would rather steal one. Bikes can be stolen from just about anywhere that anyone would park a bike, and most bikes that do get stolen are not locked. Again, bicycle theft is also related to the opportunities available to steal one.

To protect bicycles against those who would be tempted to steal one, the following precautions are advised:

- Keep bicycles locked any time they are unattended with a good case-hardened padlock and cable. Hook the cable through the frame, front and rear wheels, and around a solid fixed object (preferably not a wooden post).
- Check the lock by pulling on it to make sure it is secure.
- With an engraving pencil mark an identifying number on unpainted major bike components.
- During the day at home, keep the bike out of sight, or at least at the rear of the house.
- At night and when not at home, keep the bike inside a locked structure.
- Retain all evidence of purchase.
- Be able to identify the bike not only by its color but also its features.
- Have one or more close-up color photographs of the bike and its owner on hand.
- Register the bike in community registration programs if available.
- Never loan a bicycle to strangers.
- Try to avoid parking a bicycle in high crime, deserted, or poorly lit areas.

## Crime prevention during travel

Traveling, whether for business or pleasure, has become part of the American way of life. Jets, trains, buses, cruisers, the automobile, motorcycles, and even bicycles have made it possible for one to go just about anywhere in the world. Unfortunately, there is no area in the world where one is safe from criminal activities. Criminal opportunities accompany travelers and are there to greet them when they arrive at their destination. Therefore, crime prevention measures for the traveler are just as important or perhaps more important as crime prevention precautions one should take when on home territory. A trip cannot be accompanied by a false sense of security just because one is "away from it all" on vacation, and travelers must remember that other countries are also experiencing problems with rising crime rates. This is not to say that a majority of tourists are victimized. In fact, the percentage is still quite low, but for those who are, victimization means inconvenience, some degree of financial loss, and threats to physical safety. Unfamiliar areas, people, and situations make a tourist particularly vulnerable to criminal opportunity. There is perhaps no other time when a person could have so much to lose, since travelers probably carry more cash with them on a trip than they would to the local grocery store. Some travelers are victims of rings of thieves, who, for example, have been known to follow rented cars from airports into the city, puncture a rear tire, and wait to rob the occupants when they have the trunk open and the wheel upon the jack.

Travel tip campaigns have assisted in making some tourists better prepared and more vigilant than in previous years. Happy trips and vacations take planning, thought, and awareness, and in some instances one may still find oneself unprepared for strange situations. In the following pages, travel safety precautions are discussed, which should lend assistance to anyone on any trip.

### Before the trip

- Plan the trip and let trusted family members or friends know the itinerary.
- Make sure to carry an up-to-date medical insurance card.
- Place identification tags inside and on the outside of luggage. Use first initials and last name only. Tie a bright ribbon around luggage that is a common style and color.
- Persons under 21 years of age should carry a written permission slip signed by parents or guardians authorizing emergency medical treatment.
- Persons having medical problems should wear a medi-alert necklace or bracelet explaining the nature of their illness.
- Make a record of credit card numbers. Consider temporary insurance to cover loss of credit cards while traveling.
- Learn as much as possible about the location of the trip or vacation beforehand.
- If going overseas, learn a few words of the language in case of an emergency and help is needed.
- Avoid bulging suitcases that may easily pop open if dropped.
- Do not carry any more confidential business papers in a briefcase than absolutely necessary.

### After arriving

- Make sure all luggage is loaded on the same bus or limosine service. If for some reason the luggage must wait until the next available taxi, wait with it. Do not leave it unattended at any time.

- Leave money, passports, rail passes, airline tickets, and valuables in the hotel safe.
- Women should avoid carrying handbags that make easy targets; if they are carried, stay away from curbs.
- Do not keep a list of serial numbers of travelers' checks in the same handbag, wallet, or briefcase as the checks themselves.
- Never carry large amounts of cash. Keep large bills separated from smaller ones and avoid flashing bills in public places.
- Women traveling alone should register in hotels giving first initial and last name only.
- If renting a car, do not stop to ask pedestrians directions.
- Do not rent the largest automobile available unless it is really needed.
- Do not invite strangers to your hotel room.
- Do not engage in lengthy conversations with strangers.
- Do not participate in tours not conducted by public agencies or resorts.
- Take tours scheduled with a group when possible since there is safety in numbers.
- Be wary of strangers or new acquaintances who appear too eager to listen or who ask a lot of casual questions about your plans for specific events. This person may be trying to assess if your hotel room is worth breaking into and, if so, when would be the best time.
- Use operator-type elevators, if possible. Do not use stairways unless going with a group.
- Do not become overly friendly with persons who live overseas but are United States citizens. The comfort of talking with someone without an accent could result in the person finding out more than he or she should know about your personal business.
- Do not leave jewelry and expensive gear in view at any time in the hotel room.
- Do not open the door to any repairman without first checking with the desk clerk.
- Do not participate in groups or parades in the street, no matter how much fun they are having.
- Do not stray too far from the main tourist attractions at night or when alone.

**When traveling by automobile**
- Have the automobile checked by a reputable mechanic to make sure it is in tip-top working condition and that the tires are safe.
- Avoid late night driving.
- Do not pick up hitchhikers.
- Look for a gas station before the gasoline gauge indicates the tank is one-fourth full. Plan travel mileage to reach a sizable town with a gas station.
- Avoid shortcuts; use well traveled roads.
- Keep car doors locked at all times.
- If traveling long distances alone, arrange a couple of pillows with a coat and hat over them to make it look like someone is sleeping.
- Women who drive alone at night should wear a man's hat to disguise their sex.
- Keep valuables out of sight when the car is parked.
- Do not drive a convertible with the top down at night.

□ If lost, stop at a well-lighted, reputable, major-brand service station for directions.

□ Do not take maps into public places to look over the route.

□ Use extreme care if it becomes necessary to pull off the road to sleep.

□ Stay only in approved campsites when camping.

### When traveling via public transportation

□ Stand in well-lighted areas when waiting for a bus or taxi.

□ Stand close to the entrance when waiting for a subway or ferryboat.

□ When traveling in a train, choose a car with several other occupants.

□ Taxis can usually be considered safe to ride in alone, day or night.

□ Disembark from the ferry immediately when it reaches the dock.

### While at the hotel

□ Keep jewelry in the hotel's vault, obtain pieces for the evening just before going out, and put the jewelry on in the hotel lobby.

□ Consider using portable alarm devices and portable travel locks. Several varieties are available that are fairly inexpensive. If neither travel lock or alarm is available, nightstands, chairs, etc., can be moved in front of the door and anchored between the floor and the doorknob.

□ Do not leave cameras, jewelry, and other expensive items lying around the hotel room even when occupied. Such things may tempt hotel employees or even passing guests.

□ Use a key to lock the hotel door if possible. When leaving, hang the Do Not Disturb sign on the outer doorknob if the maid has already made up the room.

□ Do not assume because the door is locked the hotel room is safe. Burglars know that many hotels do not bother to change the lock if a key is not returned.

□ Keys to the hotel room should be kept rather than being left with the hotel desk clerk when going out.

□ Leave a portable radio and a light on in the room when no one will be there.

□ Do not reveal room numbers to strangers or casual acquaintances.

□ Do not reveal plans for the day to other guests.

□ Men traveling alone should beware of the nice lonely girl in the cocktail lounge; she may turn out to be not so nice or so lonely.

□ Use extra precautions to protect money, checks, and wallets. Take time to tape them to the underside of a dresser drawer before going to sleep at night; use a money belt when going out.

□ In addition to these precautions, many hotels and motels have posted warning signs alerting guests of common thefts. These should be read carefully and their advice followed to the full extent.

Traveling security precautions will not guarantee an absolutely safe trip every time even if each and every precaution is followed all the time. But it will significantly turn the odds in favor of the traveler instead of the criminal. However, personal security may still be threatened more when on a trip than when at home, because the dangers when traveling are easily ignored or forgotten.

### Kidnapping

Kidnapping is a very complex, unsettled, and serious crime, which often leads to death for the victim even if all ransom demands are met. Release of a victim seriously jeopardizes the future safety of the abductor. Preventing identification of the kidnapper by the victim is a primary motive for the victim's death. The situations and circumstances are extremely variable, and the extremely volatile behavior of many kidnappers makes this a very challenging crime for law enforcement officials, whose goal is always to free the victim unharmed.

Many kidnappers have a strong need for recognition; others are devoted to impractical causes. The majority of those demanding ransom are laborers or unemployed. Some have haphazardly decided to kidnap or to fake a kidnapping; others have taken extreme care in planning their crime. Many kidnappings are phony, just as are many bomb threats, but because there is no sure way of knowing the difference, all kidnap threats need to be taken seriously.

Anyone is subject to be kidnapped, but persons providing the most motivation for a kidnapping to take place, and who therefore are most vulnerable, include corporate executives, bank officials, celebrities, persons of considerable political influence, and children of wealthy parents or those kidnapped by an ex-spouse. Additional victims include robbery hostages, members of poor families held for small ransoms, passengers on hijacked public transportation facilities, and victims held hostage for the release of prison inmates or exiled political leaders. A memorable example of the latter was provided in late 1979 when Iranian students overpowered United States Marines, took over the American Embassy in Iran, held sixty Americans hostage, and demanded the return of the Shah of Iran, who at the time was undergoing cancer treatment at New York's Cornell University. The students threatened to kill their hostages at the slightest indication of forcible maneuvers against them.

The apprehending and convicting of kidnappers is by itself a deterrent, but much greater precautions are necessary. The prevention of kidnapping and abduction is the responsibility of many. By far, parents have the major responsibility for their children's safety, but schools and children, by obeying their parents, also share some of this responsibility. In the following pages, prevention of kidnapping and responsibilities for parents and schools are discussed. Security precautions for executives follow this discussion.

**Kidnap prevention for children.** Each family must assess their own vulnerabilities and make a determination of how likely each member is to become a victim of kidnapping. Many of the precautions to be discussed should become routine for all families, while other precautions may only be needed in special circumstances or when a family feels particularly afraid or vulnerable to kidnapping. Schools should follow rules that apply to them and can often get assistance in doing so from an experienced police officer or security consultant. Ideally, school security programs should be set up through the Parent Teacher Association. Rules for parents and educators alike have been published by the Federal Bureau of Investigation and are distributed by several publishing organizations. Basic rules for preventing a kidnapping are discussed below.

### Rules for parents

- Have children travel in groups or pairs, especially to and from school.
- Instruct children to walk along heavily traveled streets and to avoid isolated areas.
- Instruct children to refuse automobile rides from strangers and to refuse to accompany a stranger anywhere on foot.
- Have children play in city-approved playgrounds where recreational activities are supervised by responsible adults and police assistance is readily available.
- If there is any reason to fear a kidnapping, escort service for the child should be provided. Teachers and principals should be told exactly who will pick the child up. Public transportation should be avoided.
- Immediately report anyone who molests or annoys your children.
- Instruct children to never leave home without telling parents where they will be and who will accompany them.
- Instruct children to cry loudly for help if a stranger attempts to detain them unwillingly.
- Know names, addresses, and telephone numbers of the child's usual playmates.
- Do not allow children to travel on the streets at night unless accompanied by a reliable adult.
- Divorced parents may wish to provide school principals with a picture of their ex-spouse in case he or she should come for the child during school hours.

### While at home

- Make certain that outside doors, windows, and screens are securely locked before retiring at night.
- Keep the door to the child's room open so that any unusual noises can be detected more readily.
- The child's room should not be readily accessible from the outside.
- Young children should never be left alone and parents need to make certain that caretakers are trustworthy and reliable.
- Parents should tell children to always keep the doors and windows locked and never to open them to strangers.
- Children should be taught how to call police in case strangers attempt to gain entrance.
- The house should be kept well-lighted when older children are left home alone.
- Hired hands should be instructed not to allow strangers inside the house.
- Family finances, practices, and habits should not be discussed openly, or with bartenders, hairdressers, etc.

- If parents are particularly worried about their child's safety, or if a child must travel long distances to and from school alone, he or she should be instructed to telephone the parents at specified intervals during the day. The child should be provided with enough dimes, plus an extra one taped inside a shoe for emergencies.

### Responsibilities of the school

- Before releasing a child to anyone except the parents during the regular school day, a teacher or other school official should first obtain approval from one of the child's parents or guardians.
- When a parent telephones to request that the child be dismissed early from school, the identity of the caller should be verified before the child is released. If the parent is calling from home, the school can confirm the request by a return telephone call. In the event the telephone call is not coming from the child's home, the school official should ask the caller questions such as the child's birthday, courses of study, names of teachers and classmates, and similar facts that should be known to the parents.
- School personnel should be alert to observe suspicious persons who loiter in school buildings and on the grounds. Anyone who cannot provide an excuse for his or her presence should be immediately reported to police. The identity and a description of suspicious persons should be obtained.
- Adult supervision should be provided for all after-school programs and playground areas.

### In case of kidnapping

- Telephone the Federal Bureau of Investigation. The telephone number of the nearest FBI office is listed in front of each telephone directory. Use a neighbor's phone in case the victim's has been tapped.
- Maintain absolute secrecy. Do not permit any of the details of the kidnapping or demands for ransom to become known to anyone outside the immediate family and the investigating officers.
- Do not touch or disturb anything at the kidnapping site.
- Try to avoid panic. Go about daily routines in the usual fashion as much as possible. Rely on leadership provided by law enforcement officials.
- If telephone contact with the kidnapper is made, ask to speak to the victim to make sure of his or her identity and that the person is safe. Give the abductor a code word to use when making further telephone contacts. In this way those who had nothing to do with the abduction but nevertheless would like to capitalize on the situation by demanding a ransom cannot do so.
- Assist law enforcement officials in every way possible. Their main objective is the safe return of the victim.

### Precautions for executives

- Evaluate corporation and branches as to risks (i.e., history of kidnappings, bombings, or other terrorist activities; labor disputes; political or social difficulties).
- Evaluate access routes to premises.
- Evaluate protection available from local, state, and federal law enforcement agencies.

- Rehearse for panic situations. Have leaders within the company well trained for emergency situations.
- Have well-defined procedures for calling police, taping calls, communicating with the kidnapper, and paying the ransom.
- Complex security problems within the corporation itself should be left to professional security consultants or a corporate security executive.
- Install proper alarms, locks, and other safeguards for maximum home and office security.
- Keep personal publicity to a minimum.
- Warn employees not to give out information about executives, other employees, or their families. Questions about employees by someone who does not have a need to know should not be answered.
- Do not grant personal interviews with freelance reporters.
- Vary routes to work, times of arrival, lunch hours, places to eat lunch, etc.
- Be wary of occupants in nearby parked cars, signs of forced entry into a car, anything underneath a car, and look for persons hiding in the rear of the car.
- Avoid working alone in an empty office or plant, or walking through less traveled corridors.
- Take the left lane on multilane highways, install a radio-telephone in the car, and follow car safety precautions listed previously in this chapter.
- Arrange a duress signal with chauffeurs or other drivers.
- Telephone the office when leaving home and vice versa. Inform the secretary or someone at home of the estimated time of arrival.
- Screen employees very carefully, particularly guards, menial and part-time employees, and domestic servants. Examine job history, references, personal appearance, writing abilities, etc.
- Do not publicize vacations, even to neighbors, acquaintances, or office workers.
- Do not tell strangers your name, company, or official position.
- Call the office every day when away.
- Use travel locks and follow additional suggestions of travel security given previously in this chapter.

## While traveling abroad

- Learn as much as possible about conditions in areas to be visited.
- Consult executives of foreign firms doing business in the same area about security hazards.
- Release a minimum of information about visiting experts and guests.
- Do not discuss business plans, finances, or personal plans in the presence of servants since they may also understand the English language.
- Stay away from local activities that involve getting into crowds.
- If appearing at social functions is unavoidable, leave and return with a group.

## Corporate security policies

- Method for secretary or switchboard operator to give a warning to the person being called if she or he thinks a call is suspicious in nature.
- Policies regarding who is to notify authorities, who is to tell the victim's family if a call comes at work, provisions for payment of ransom, collecting the needed cash, etc.

&#9633; Communication codes so that if a victim is allowed to speak with other corporate officials, he or she can use code words to give information without tipping the abductor.

&#9633; Instruction for executives on the behavior they should display should they become a victim.

By no means is the above list of precautions complete. Many of the suggestions provide only a foundation on which to build more detailed security programs. An entire textbook could be devoted to this one topic and indeed many have been written. For additional information concerning kidnapping, the reader is directed to these books. Following the above recommendations, however, should sharply decrease one's vulnerability to this most serious crime. These precautions against kidnapping not only reduce the opportunities by making potential victims more difficult to abduct, but also serve to speed up investigative work in case the abductor is successful. All but the most deranged kidnappers would probably pass up an opportunity if there was not more than a reasonable chance of succeeding and fulfilling their motives, whether they be money, revenge, or political leverage.

**Preventing terrorism**

Kidnapping is generally considered a form of terrorism when it reaches international attention. Jenkins defines terrorism as:

> Acts which in themselves may be classic forms of crime—murder, arson, the use of explosives—but which differ from classic criminal acts in that they are executed with deliberate intention of causing panic, disorder and terror within an organized society, in order to destroy social discipline, paralyze the forces of reaction of a society, and increase the misery and suffering of the community.[10]

Laws that deal with terrorism are weak, and numerous treaties and agreements attempting to manage the problem cover only a few terrorist acts, such as hijacking and the kidnapping of diplomats. What is terrorism to one country may be heroism in another, so there is lack of uniformity in the laws and enforcement of punishment.

Terrorism is increasing and tactics are changing from kidnappings for ransom to assassinations and murder. American businessmen and diplomats are prime targets for terrorism abroad, apparently because of their wealth and political influence. Terrorists are well financed, organized, highly mobile, and well trained. Sometimes no amount of security can deter an attack, as evidenced by the demise of former Premier Aldo Moro in Italy in 1978. There must be increased international cooperation, intelligence, and communication with tougher laws and penalties. The United States should develop

---

[10]Jenkins, Brian M., *International Terrorism*. Los Angeles: Crescent Publications, Inc., 1975, p. 1.

additional response groups who are specially trained to work against terrorism. Listed below are suggestions that might prove helpful in preventing terrorist attacks or in minimizing damage to property if an attack occurs.

- □ Corporations, schools, and other institutions should have detailed evacuation plans in case of bomb threats.
- □ Thorough bomb-search plans should be available.
- □ Screening parcels, deliveries, and just about anything else brought into a building is possible with the use of metal sensors and X-ray equipment.
- □ Taggants, tiny pieces of color-coded plastic, should be inserted into all dynamite sold. This will allow the Bureau of Alcohol, Tobacco, and Firearms to trace dynamite used in bombings back to the buyer.
- □ All institutions should consider using dogs especially trained in sniffing out bombs.
- □ Begin evacuation of buildings immediately if bomb threats are received, even if it is thought to be a hoax. Then notify authorities.

Again, the above list is not all inclusive and provides only a basic foundation for dealing with many terrorist attacks. Further, no two institutions or buildings are alike, and each one presents its own security problems and challenges for providing a safe environment whether it be a home, government institution, corporate plant, or small private business. In addition to a well-organized, thorough security program, one can only hope he or she is not at the wrong place at the wrong time if an attack occurs.

## CONCLUSION

There are many aspects to personal security, and everyone is susceptible at one time or another to some form of victimization that jeopardizes their personal safety. This does not mean that everyone is likely to be victimized, but it does mean that no one can tell who the next victim will be—not even the criminal knows unless he or she has a specific person in mind. Most offenders will choose the most vulnerable person. Therefore, no one should ever take safety for granted or believe that "it won't happen to me." In this chapter we have attempted to provide crime prevention measures to decrease the vulnerabilities of specific groups of people and to bring an awareness of the crimes that most often are directed toward these groups. Many of these suggestions may appear to be common sense but they need to be stressed so that their importance is realized. Most crime prevention measures discussed throughout the chapter do not jeopardize personal freedom, but lead to increased personal safety.

## Chapter 5

# Home security

To most of us our home and the possessions kept within it represent a lifetime investment. However, most residences provide fairly easy targets for a potential criminal. The average citizen may believe that a lock on the door is enough for a safe and secure home. However, any door or window in a home becomes a potential entryway for intruders, and rarely are doors and windows properly protected.

Suburban homes as well as inner city residences are targets; no particular location or neighborhood is ever completely safe from crime. Most crimes that take place within a residence or on the grounds involve burglary or theft, and for this reason, a large portion of this chapter will be directed toward the prevention of burglary. The reader will also note that burglary prevention efforts, if successful, serve to prevent many other types of crimes against the home, such as vandalism and theft of outdoor property.

Burglary is the fastest growing felony. Official police reports indicate that one household in every twenty-five was victimized in 1978, and it is estimated that at least as many burglaries were never reported to police.[1] This means that actually one household in every twelve was burglarized. Statistically, then, one's chances of being the victim of a burglary are about one in twelve in any one year. The incidence of burglary has in fact increased to the point that it is no longer a question of *whether* an individual will be burglarized, but *when* the burglary will take place.

Increasing crime rates have caused interest in residential security to soar and new methods of protection, from door hardware and environmental design to citizen patrol and sophisticated electronic equipment, are being explored. These approaches, along with a theoretical discussion of residential crime and a psychologic profile of the "typical" residential criminal, will be presented in this chapter.

---

[1]Michael, Edgar, *Home Security: Book One: Basic Techniques of Home Guardianship.* National Institute of Law Enforcement and Criminal Justice, Law Enforcement Assistance Administration, U.S. Department of Justice, p. 1.

## THEORETICAL DISCUSSION OF RESIDENTIAL CRIME

Residential crimes are the result of desire and opportunity. Persons having the desire to participate in criminal activity could not do so if the opportunities did not exist. Likewise, even if the opportunity did exist but the individual had no desire, the likelihood of a crime taking place is significantly decreased. A second factor regarding residential crimes is that most persons who commit these crimes follow distinctive patterns. This is not to say that there is only one modus operandi for all criminals, but rather that each criminal generally has just one criminal pattern, which he or she attempts to develop to perfection. While most burglaries are committed on the spur of the moment and the intruders look for an easy target, an individual criminal, for example, would prefer a particular type of neighborhood, a particular type of dwelling, and a particular method for gaining entrance.

A third factor involves the differences between rates and types of crime in various neighborhoods. Significant differences in crime rates exist from one neighborhood to another, and this fact can result from many variables influencing a particular neighborhood. Important variables include:

1. Environment—characteristics such as racial composition, socioeconomic class, neighborhood organization, traffic patterns, and utilization of natural resources, particularly land.
2. Police protection—amount and effectiveness of police personnel available for a given area; use of private guards.
3. Characteristics of the residence—housing characteristics, such as age, location of dwellings (whether located next to vacant lots or alleys), and overall construction design of housing units.
4. Behavior of residents—assessment of the extent to which the occupant unwittingly aids the criminal by the use of poor security precautions or the degree to which the occupant "target-hardens" the residence by establishing practical and realistic security measures.
5. Environmental design—the effectiveness of security devices such as locks, alarms, reinforced doors and windows; the perceived ease with which an intruder thinks the residence might be entered.
6. Behavior of the intruder—assessment of levels of skills, age, personality, and creed.

There have been endless debates concerning the cause of the unprecedented rise in crime. It has been attributed to increasing moral laxity, the decline of religion, the breakup of the family, and just about every other social problem. These factors may all exert an undetermined amount of influence, but three additional basic trends have been identified that point to more basic reasons for the rise in burglary rates.[2] First, there has been the

---

[2]Ibid, p. 2.

rapid increase in the number of citizens under twenty-five years of age. Since the majority of burglaries are committed by persons under age twenty-five, it should logically follow that there would be a corresponding increase in the number of available burglars. Second, there has been an increase in the number of items in the average home that are worth stealing. Prior to the postwar boom of the 1940s, few families had much worth taking. There may have been an upright radio in the living room and a fortunate few even may have had an electric mixer. But unless the family was truly well-to-do and had furs, jewelry, and money in the home, it was usually not worth the trouble of breaking in. Today, however, few households are without a color television set, a stereo, golf clubs, ten-speed bicycles, and other valuable, portable items.

Third, homes are easier to break into than they used to be. Major changes in hardware and construction methods have resulted in doors and door locks that are highly vulnerable to penetration by even the most unskilled burglar. The lock-in-knob lockset, for example, is used on ninety percent of all new homes, and has by itself made these homes vulnerable to any criminal with just a screwdriver and wrench.

The combination of these three trends results in more burglars, more goods to steal, and more opportunities to break in, which in turn results in the phenomenal rise of burglary rates. Citizens are extremely limited in their ability to do anything about the number of burglars, but there are various protective measures that can either make valuables unattractive to the burglar, or reduce opportunities for a burglar to gain entrance in the first place. Indeed, resident behavior may be one of the most important factors in preventing not only burglary but other types of crimes as well.

Clues that show that no one is at home or that the house can be entered quickly and easily makes a house an attractive target. Many homeowners fail to take even the most rudimentary steps to protect their property. They "announce" their absence from their homes by leaving a trail of telltale clues that would tempt a saint: Homes are left unlocked (in California 29% of the burglars walk right in) or, if locked at all, they are equipped with ineffectual locks.[3] Shrubbery around homes, ladders stacked against second story windows, and unlocked garage doors are other examples of opportunities for intruders to gain easy access to residences. Crimes are not only increasing in number, but criminals are increasing in gall. For example, a large portion of residential burglaries are committed in broad daylight, and forced entry often takes place through a door or window clearly visible from the street, with neighbors on both sides of the residence.

---

[3]*Your Retirement Anti-Crime Guide.* American Association of Retired Persons and National Retired Teachers Association, 1973, p. 16.

By definition, burglary is a crime against property and not against a person. The primary measure of loss is the value of property stolen or damaged, but the public's view of burglary is also influenced by the fear of confronting a burglar and the anger at knowing that a burglar has entered one's home and will probably go scot-free.

## KNOW THE ENEMY

One of the best defenses a homeowner and police personnel alike can take to reduce burglary is to get to know the facts about the average perpetrator.

Residential burglary is crime's lowest common denominator. It is an offense committed largely by the dregs of the criminal world—the unskilled, the inept, the addicted, the amateur, the stupid, the sick, and sometimes the outright insane.[4]

Criminals who cannot make it in crime's more lucrative enterprises resort to residential burglary where the pickings are relatively slim for the amount of work and risk required. Professional burglars usually specialize in commercial burglary where the rewards may be worth millions. The residential burglar, while he may steal expensive items, may only get a small percentage of the items' market value from the local fence. Thus the average residential burglar has to commit a lot of burglaries to make even a poverty income.

Today's residential burglar is most often a young, amateurish male mainly interested in an easy opportunity. These characteristics are to the homeowner's advantage since many burglars can be easily thwarted by removing opportunities. Nationwide, 83% of all burglary arrests involve persons under twenty-five years of age, and one study has indicated that 64% of burglars were under eighteen.[5] The young age of the burglar, however, does not mean that he lacks talent or normal intelligence. Most do have talent and enough ingenuity to break in, although some enter through unlocked doors and, once in, determine the most likely hiding places for valuables. The average burglar does not usually "look like" a burglar, and depending upon his degree of "professionalism" may be disguised as anyone who would fit the occasion or blend with the environment. He may be clean shaven, outfitted in expensive clothing, or dressed as a repairman.

The typical burglar wants to get richer, quicker, and without interruption. He usually does not want to hurt anyone, but it is very risky for residents to assume that burglars are inherently nonviolent. Some burglars have severe emotional problems; they may be rapists or drug addicts capable of doing great bodily harm if confronted.

---

[4]Ibid.
[5]Ibid, p. 17.

## METHODS OF ENTRY

Most burglars enter a residence through a door, many of which are unlocked; the second choice of entry is through a convenient window. Other favorites include cellar or garage doors. In many cases all doors and windows are locked but the door of the garage, where the homeowner has conveniently left all tools necessary for the burglar to break into the rest of the house. Side or rear entrances partially covered by shrubbery also provide popular sites for unauthorized entry.

Many times burglars are assisted in gaining entrance by finding "hidden" keys. Most burglars are aware of traditional hiding places and will spend a few minutes looking, particularly if he has reason to believe a key has been hidden.

Stevens[6] has described four types of attack that characterize the perpetrator's method of entry. These types are presented below:

**brute force** Pure physical force is used to gain entry, including shoulder pressure, kicking, pushing, the use of sledge hammers, axes, saws, etc.

**unskilled attack** An attack in which a novice or equivalent tries a specific attack on, for example, the lock. No special tools are used other than perhaps a screwdriver, small hammer, short pry bar, tire iron, etc.—tools normally available and usable by anyone.

**semiskilled attack** Attacker has limited special knowledge of how to defeat the particular items being evaluated. He has certain crude tools, but they are specific to the types of attack this attacker will make.

**professional** Attacker has special tools and skills. Cylinder poppers, pick sets, pick guns, master keys, punches, tapes, wire, and torches are but a few of the specially made tools to attack the item being evaluated. The professional, if determined and given enough time, will defeat just about any security device.[7]

Several different methods of gaining entry are illustrated in Fig. 5-1. From these drawings it can be seen that adequate residential security necessitates many physical security measures, in addition to the various community-based crime prevention programs discussed in Chapter 13. Doors, windows, locks, lighting, alarms, dogs, and landscaping are among the various physical considerations to be made when evaluating residential security measures.

The principles of residential security may be described by four action verbs: deter, delay, deny, and detect. The primary and most desirable goal is to deter. Many different techniques that concentrate on the exterior of the house can be employed to deter the burglar and convince him to go else-

---

[6]Stevens, Richard C., "Burglary Prevention Study." Presented at the Urban Design, Security and Crime Proceeding of NILECT Seminar, April 12, 1972.
[7]Ibid.

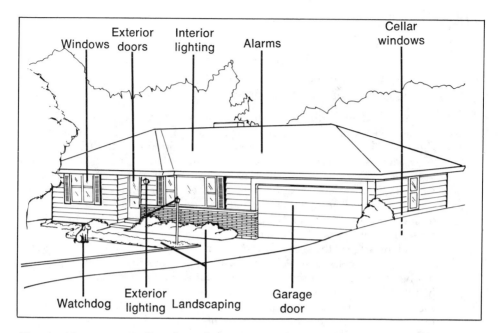

Windows Exterior doors Interior lighting Alarms Cellar windows

Watchdog Exterior lighting Landscaping Garage door

**Fig. 5-1.** Many aspects of residential security must be considered in order to maintain a crime-resistance home.

where. If the burglar is not completely deterred after an initial cursory inspection of the premises, however, he will attempt to gain entry. Delay then becomes the next important factor in determining whether or not the homeowner is successful in preventing entry. Above all, a burglar wants to avoid being caught, so the longer it takes to force a door or window, the greater the risk. A delay of approximately four minutes is generally sufficient to prevent entry into a house or apartment.[8]

If a burglar is neither deterred nor delayed, the next best thing is to deny him everything of value. Several techniques involving interior security measures can be employed. The practice of marking household property or establishing strong rooms are but two examples. Finally, detecting the burglar cannot be overlooked as an important means of crime prevention. Detection involves the use of such things as electronic and biologic alarms and various neighborhood watch programs. The extra eyes and ears of neighbors in addition to police officials have proved invaluable in detecting suspicious activity and thereby preventing crimes before they have the chance to occur.

Specific aspects regarding home security are discussed in greater detail in the following pages.

---

[8]*How to Protect Your Home.* The National Sheriffs' Association, Law Enforcement Assistance Administration, and U.S. Department of Justice, p. 2.

## DOORS

Doors are extremely important in residential security because, as mentioned previously, they are the potential intruder's first choice of entry. All exterior doors should be solid and substantial.

Three types of doors are in common use:

1. Flush wood doors: either of hollow core or solid core construction. Solid core doors provide good strength across the width of the door and add insulation and fire resistance as well as security. Hollow core doors, on the other hand, are easily penetrated, and unfortunately are used frequently in residences because they are less expensive. It is easy to hammer or kick a hole in a hollow wood door. If it is not possible to replace these doors, they should at least be reinforced. This can be accomplished by mounting a piece of sheet metal at least 0.016 inches thick and slightly smaller than the size of the door to the inside face of the door with screws spaced no more than 6 inches apart all around the edge of the sheet. This can be painted to match the woodwork, and will hardly be noticeable. A burglar who tries to kick in a hollow door which has been reinforced in this manner is in for a painful surprise when his foot hits the sheet of metal.
2. Wood panel or rail and stile doors: These doors differ in their security effectiveness depending on thickness, type of wood, and quality of fit to frame. They are generally, however, included in the types of doors to watch out for as far as security risks. It is again fairly easy for the burglar to kick out a panel, especially on doors that have large panels. Small panels are more difficult to remove by force and provide better protection, even though they are not as good as solid-core wood doors for security purposes.
3. Metal doors: These doors are superior in security terms to any wood door, but offer less insulation and are often considered aesthetically unattractive for residential use. A homeowner, however, should consider himself lucky to have such doors because of the good protection they offer.[9]

### Optical viewers

Solid doors should be equipped with a oneway peephole or viewer so that individuals coming to the door can immediately be identified. Visitors should always be identified before the door is unlocked, and under no circumstances should the door be opened if the resident is suspicious.

### Garage doors

The garage door should always be closed and locked, and the entrance door from the garage into the house should be treated as an exterior door. Not only are valuable, stealable goods kept in a garage, but also the tools neces-

[9]Sagalyn, Arnold, *Residential Security*. Washington, D.C.: U.S. Government Printing Office, U.S. Department of Justice, LEAA, National Institute of Law Enforcement and Criminal Justice, 1973, pp. 21-22.

sary to break into the rest of the house may be available and the burglar could work undetected for hours.

It is recommended that double garage doors have a rim-mounted, jimmy-resistant lock, plus flush bolts at top and bottom of the inactive door. Instead of a deadbolt, a good padlock and a case-hardened hasp can be used. If a hasp is used, it *must* be of good quality and be installed properly. The hasp should be made of hardened steel. It should be installed with long stove bolts through the door, with larger washers on the inside. Bolt heads should not be visible on any part of the hasp when it is in the locked position.

Manually operated rolling overhead doors should have slide bolts on the bottom bar, use a double cylinder deadbolt lock, or have a hole drilled to make a place to put a padlock in the door trace. An electronically opened garage door offers good security if valuable tools or equipment are kept in the garage. A mechanically operated device locks the door and can be opened only by the radio-controlled opener, which is kept in the individual's car. However, with some models the garage door can be opened at any time of the day or night by anyone who has an opener that operates on the same frequency. The dual-modulated radio equipment that operates on more than one frequency and has an opener with two buttons to be pushed in sequence is superior in terms of security. However, this equipment costs several hundred dollars.

## The frame

Unfortunately, most wooden door frames can be best described as flimsy. They are made of ¾ inch softwood and tend to split and break when force, such as a kick, is applied to the door. The door frame is installed in a rough opening in the wall, which has been deliberately measured oversize so that it is easier to install without a lot of cutting and trimming. Once the frame is erected, it is shimmed into place with small pieces of wood, leaving a gap between the frame and supporting wall. Door molding is then nailed into place with small finishing nails to cover this gap. This is not at all sturdy and causes a severe security problem.

A common burglary technique that exploits this problem is to spread the frame far enough to release the lock bolt with a prying tool. The remedy is to remove the casing surrounding the door and insert wood or metal filler pieces between the door frame and studs on both sides of the door. The fillers should extend at least 24 inches above and below the lock. In addition, the short wood screws that mount the frame should be replaced with screws about 2⅔ inches long so that the screws will penetrate the frame, the filler, and at least the first stud of the supporting wall, so that all of these components are held together as one unit. This technique substantially reduces the vulnerability of one's home to burglary.

### Hinges

Hinges as well as doors are an important but frequently overlooked security consideration. Hinges can be installed interiorly or exteriorly and most residential doors are inward-opening so that the hinges are on the inside. Doors opening outward have hinges on the outside so that all a burglar has to do is remove the hinge pins and take the door completely out of its frame. Several easy remedies to this problem have been identified and are discussed below.[10]

☐ Hinges can be replaced by "fixed-pin" or "fast-pin" hinges, which have been designed by the manufacturer so that there are no hinge pins at all, or the pin cannot be removed.
☐ Hinges may be welded to the pins. This is a permanent and effective method to secure hinges.
☐ A small hole can be drilled through the hinge and inside pin. A second pin or small nail can then be inserted flush with the hinge surface.

The homeowner who uses any of these techniques can greatly reduce the chances of doors being broken and the home entered.

### Locks

Another important aspect concerning physical security for residences is the type of locks used. Since many criminals enter through unlocked doors, the first precaution a homeowner should take is to begin locking all doors.

Locks are thoroughly discussed in Chapter 11 but will be briefly mentioned here with emphasis on residential applications. The most commonly used residential lock is the cylindrical lock, which is opened by simply inserting a key into the door knob. These locks are the least expensive and also the least effective. They offer minimal protection and should not be used when security is of the essence.

The best lock to use is the single cylinder deadbolt lock, which is used less often because of added expense. Unlike the latchbolt in a lock-in-knob lockset, the deadbolt is square-faced and cannot be easily pried or shimmied. The deadbolt lock should have a free-wheeling outer ring and the inside bolt should have a case-hardened insert that makes it impossible to saw through. The bolt connecting the two halves of the lock together should be very heavy and sturdy. The long throw deadbolt (the bolt should extend at least one full inch from the edge of the door) is excellent protection against frame spread-

---

[10]Ibid, p. 23.

ing. Better protection still is provided by an interlocking deadbolt, which, as its name implies, interlocks the door and frame so that the frame cannot be spread away from the door by a prybar. The most commonly used interlocking deadbolt lock is the vertical-throw deadlock. This type of lock also provides a decorative appearance, which homeowners are particularly concerned about.

Most supplemental deadlocks can be easily installed by most homeowners with ordinary tools. Some locks are designed to be fastened to the door with wood or sheet metal screws. Others are mounted by bolting the portion of the lock body on the inside of the door to the portion on the outside with machine screws or bolts. This through-the-door, metal-to-metal mounting is much more secure than locks that mount to the door with sheet metal or wood screws.

## WINDOWS AND SLIDING GLASS DOORS
### Locks

Locks for windows and sliding glass doors also present special problems. The most frequently used windows in homes today are the double-hung windows, which slide up and down. These windows are generally equipped with latch-type locks at the bottom of the stationary section and at the top of the movable section of the window. Unfortunately, this type of lock is extremely inadequate but can be improved with the use of a bolt-type lock. A hole can be drilled all the way through the movable section and half way through the stationary section. A bolt can then be placed in the hole, which makes it impossible to get into the window without breaking the glass. The noise resulting from the breaking window will usually cause the intruder to flee. This method of locking windows can also be used when the window is raised for ventilation. The holes can be drilled about 6 inches up and the window can then be locked when open.

Aluminum and glass sliding patio doors are a notorious security nightmare. The locks on most of them are simple spring-loaded latches, which can be lifted with a thin metal shim or quickly forced with a prybar. Some patio doors can even be lifted out of their frames from the outside. A few simple steps can greatly improve this situation, however. Sheet metal screws installed in the upper channel of the frame can prevent the door from being lifted out in the closed position. There is also a variety of special locking devices made especially for sliding glass doors which prevent them from being jimmied, lifted, or shimmied. In addition, a piece of wood can be inserted at the bottom of the door in the runners. This effectively prevents the sliding action when the door is in a closed position. The stationary section should also be reinforced with extra anchoring screws, a security measure that is usually forgotten by most homeowners. Once a burglar finds that he can neither pry the lock nor lift the door out of the frame, he will probably move on, rather than break the glass to get in. Most burglars are wary of breaking glass since the noise it makes indicates a distress signal of some type and will attract the attention of anyone within hearing distance, who may come to the scene to investigate or call the police. However, if the door is located out of view and far enough away from the neighbors, and the burglar is particularly determined to gain entry, even the thought of breaking glass may not deter him.

Windows present more complex security problems than other aspects of residential security because they come in a variety of sizes and styles and are designed for purposes other than security. The choice of the type of window selected and its placement is based primarily on lighting, ventilation, and aesthetics. In fact most windows have little security value, particularly when placed in areas that cannot be readily observed.

### Types of glass

Some windows are more vulnerable than others, depending upon their size, distance from the ground, whether they are fixed or openable, and type of glass used in their manufacture. It is desirable to use break-resistant or burglar-resistant glass, not only for windows but also for glass panels in doors. Lexan, developed by General Electric, is a fine example of a tough, break-resistant glass. It is 300 times stronger than glass and lighter than aluminum, and can be screwed into place behind the existing glass. Lexan is highly resistant to attack. The cost of burglar-resistant glass and replacement frames, however, is generally prohibitive for residential installation. But there is a little consolation in the fact that available data on the average burglar indicate that he will avoid breaking glass, not only because he is apprehensive about the noise, but also because he is concerned about injuring himself in the process of gaining entry through a broken window.[11]

Using tempered glass will also increase the security of windows. It is more resistant to shattering and safer when it is broken. Some states now require its use in the manufacture of sliding glass doors and large windows because of these safety advantages. The security value of tempered glass, however, is questionable. Although it will resist a brick or rock, it is susceptible to sharp instruments such as ice picks or screwdrivers. When attacked in this manner tempered glass tends to crumple easily and quietly, leaving no sharp edges.

Glass is not the only consideration in the security of windows. Locks are not totally ineffective in that they can serve as both a preventive and a delay-

---

[11]Ibid, p. 26.

ing tactic. A locked window will usually deter a burglar even though he could have gained entry by breaking it. But if a burglar does attempt to break a locked window, most will gamble on breaking a small area in order to reach a lock. This takes time, particularly when the burglar applies tape to muffle noise. Unused windows should always be nailed or screwed shut. Since security aspects of windows differ depending upon type and style, each will be described separately in the following pages.

### Types of windows

**Double-hung windows.** Double-hung sash windows, which operate upward and downward, have a simple sash lock that can easily be jimmied. Simple techniques such as inserting a coat hanger through a gap between the sashes is sometimes sufficient to release the latching device. Storm windows and screens offer additional protection but it is generally recommended that windows not in use be screwed shut. For windows that are in use, an inexpensive and effective method to secure them is to "pin" them on both sides. This is done by drilling a downward sloping hole into the top of the bottom window through and into the bottom of the top window and inserting a pin or nail on both sides of the window. The pin remains firmly in place and cannot be shaken free but can easily be removed from the inside when ventilation is desired.[12]

Additional security can be provided by key window locks, which also run into additional expense. This type of lock is not generally recommended by police departments because the added security protection these locks might offer is not considered enough to warrant the risk of not being able to escape during a fire.

**Casement windows.** Casement windows swing outward from the frame, and represent less of a security problem than double-hung windows because the lever-type locking mechanism cannot be opened from the outside unless the pane is cut or smashed. Even when open, most casement windows are too small for an individual to crawl through. Casement windows at ground or porch level, or those facing a fire escape should be secured with commercial locking devices especially designed for these windows.

**Sliding windows.** Sliding windows must be prevented from being forced open or being lifted up and out of the track in order to be secure. Security measures similar to those taken for sliding glass doors can also be applied to sliding windows. In addition, these windows may be pinned in the same way

---

[12]*Crime Prevention Handbook for Senior Citizens*. Washington, D.C.: U.S. Government Printing Office, National Institute of Law Enforcement and Criminal Justice, LEAA, U.S. Department of Justice, 1977, p. 22.

that double-hung windows are pinned; commercial locks are also available to reinforce sliding windows.

**Louvered windows.** Louvered windows consist of several glass slats, and have the appearance and function similar to a venetian blind. These windows are bad security risks because the glass slats can be removed quickly and quietly. These windows should be replaced with solid glass or some other type of ventilating window, or protected with a metal grate, grille, screen, or bars. These should be placed on the inside with removable screws so that they cannot be removed by intruders but can be removed by the resident in case of an emergency.

**Basement windows.** All basement windows should be closed and locked. If they are not required for ventilation, they should be permanently secured with long screws that extend through the window frame into the structure. In addition, in case entry is accomplished through basement windows, the door from the basement into the main part of the house should be treated as an exterior door.

### Grilles, bars and plastic glazing

The installation of steel bars, metal grilles, or break-resistant acrylic or polycarbonate plastic is likely to be expensive and impractical in many situations. The installation of such equipment is not a job for the average home-owner. Grilles and bars must usually be custom-made for each house, and plastic glazing often requires alterations of existing window frames so that it cannot be easily removed. Another consideration is that acrylic plastics are flammable and may be prohibited for home glazing in some areas. Since grilles and steel bars can also present a fire hazard, the hinged grilles that can be unlocked and swing open from the inside are recommended to permit rapid evacuation. Local fire codes, however, must be checked before installation of such devices. A key should be hung near the window, but out of reach and out of sight of any burglar. All members of the household should be taught to use it. In the event of a fire, one certainly does not want to be trapped by one's own security measures.

It can be seen that many fairly inexpensive, simple, and effective techniques can greatly increase the security of windows. Once a burglar has given up on the windows he will usually be frustrated enough to go elsewhere— hopefully, to another residence that is equally secure.

### LIGHTING

Burglars thrive in dark and hidden places where the likelihood of detection is slight. Therefore, another very important aspect of residential security is lighting. Outdoor lighting has been shown to be one of the most effective
Jackie

deterrents of criminal activity because it increases the chances of the perpetrator being observed, thus decreasing the probability of attack. This in turn helps to reduce fear.

All exterior doorways and shadowed areas should be well lit. Although there are no set standards for the use of lighting in residential security, a 40-watt bulb for each light should be sufficient. Front and back doors should be illuminated with two lamps in case one burns out, and these ideally should be equipped with a photoelectric control that senses the end of daylight. Tamper-proof lighting fixtures that prevent the burglar from easily breaking or disconnecting the lights are highly desirable; a variety are on the market.

The use of outdoor lighting is relatively inexpensive even with the increasing price of electricity, and provides increased protection against crime. Anyone who doubts the importance of lighting in crime prevention should recall the effects of the blackouts in the Northeast—crime rates, particularly theft and vandalism, soared as authorities frantically attempted to restore electrical power to stricken communities.

Interior lighting is also vital to good physical security for residences. Human beings are creatures of habit, and from a security standpoint, this is detrimental. Intruders can become aware of their victims' routines and know when they will not be home. Lighting can give the appearance that someone is home, thus confusing a potential burglar. This is particularly true when automatic timers, which turn on and off lights in any room in the house are used. Light alone, however, does not entirely deter criminals. If so, there would be no daytime crimes. The simulated occupancy and the increased possibility of observing intruders seem to be the two biggest benefits.

Adding lights around a home, unlike many other physical security precautions, enhances rather than detracts from the appearance of the home, which increases the crime prevention benefits—and the probability that the method will be used by the homeowner.

## ALARMS

Another aspect of physical security for residences is the use of an alarm system. Many types retailing at various prices are now on the market. Alarm systems are not for everyone, and whether a homeowner should or should not invest in one depends entirely upon individual circumstances. Alarms are described in further detail in Chapter 11.

## MAN'S BEST FRIEND

Another antiburglar investment is a dog. An alert breed that makes noise when someone comes to the door serves as one of the better and least expensive alarm systems available. Most homeowners do not need an expensive, trained, attack dog (who may hate the neighborhood children more than the burglar) because dogs are naturally protective. It is unfortunate that many individuals rush out to buy improperly trained, ferocious animals who end up giving the homeowner heartaches and lawsuits instead of protection. Another factor to consider before purchasing a dog is that buying a dog solely for the purpose of home protection is a mistake. The individual, and preferably all members of the family, should be true dog lovers. There must also be necessary facilities available and, for those living in apartments, an approving landlord. Dogs lend an advantage in home protection in that they are at home when their owners are not. Lee has described some further advantages of having a dog:

> The dog is probably the oldest burglar-alarm device known to man—and dollar for dollar is still the least expensive and most effective alarm available. Most thieves will not attempt to enter a home where there is a dog, any dog. The beasts simply make too much noise and attract too much attention to the surreptitious entry. Also, there is always the fear of being attacked, and even the unreasoned anxiety about needing painful rabies shots to counteract a potentially deadly bite (the anxiety is "unreasoned" because family pet dogs almost never have rabies).[13]

In addition to the atmosphere of fear that dogs create for strangers, their extraordinary sensory powers assist them in providing security for the residence. Their sense of smell, for example, is about 100,000 times greater than that of humans, and permits them to detect an intruder up to a quarter of a mile away. Their sense of hearing allows them to detect sounds imperceptible to the human ear. Four basic types of watch dogs are discussed below.[14]

**The alarm dog.** All that most families need is an alarm dog. Any dog that will detect, bark at, and scare an intruder or stranger will serve as an alarm dog. Even a tiny fox terrier with sharp teeth and a loud bark can be a deterrent to crime. This type of watch dog merely puts up a good front. Although he usually will not bite anyone, he barks loudly when a stranger enters his "territory." An alarm dog is also useful for a store proprietor to announce the presence of a customer if he or she is unable to watch the premises at all times.

If one's pet dog already exhibits the characteristics of a good alarm dog, nothing more needs to be done. However, if the animal is too docile, it may need training or even be unsuitable for training. A veterinarian can determine whether or not your dog has the requisite health and temperament to be a

---

[13]Lee, Albert, *Crime-Free*. Baltimore: Penguin Books Inc., 1974, p. 66.
[14]Doren, Steve, and O'Block, Robert L., "Crime Prevention: An Eclectic Approach" in *Introduction to Criminal Justice: Theory and Practice*, Dae H. Chang, editor. Dubuque, Iowa: Kendall/Hunt Publishing Co., 1979.

suitable alarm dog. He or she can also recommend a competent dog trainer. Before buying a dog to be an alarm dog it would be advisable to consult a veterinarian or a reliable kennel operator. The rise in crime has spurred the establishment of many kennels. The potential buyer should be cautious since many are simply not qualified either to offer reliable, healthy animals or to properly train them.

**The protection dog.** Dogs that are protection trained should have first met the basic requirements of the American Kennel Club Obedience Class. This will ensure their ability to sit, stay, wait, lie down, stand, and come on command. Protection dogs are trained to be good companions that will be good with children and friends. However, if the master is physically attacked, they go into action to render an attacker helpless as quickly as possible. Doberman pinschers are excellent protection dogs because of their extremely good hearing, sense of smell, and intelligence. They have also acquired a reputation that they are not to be tampered with.

Whether one selects a Doberman pinscher or a German shepherd as a protection dog, the size, health, temperament, and bloodlines of the parents of the animal should be carefully examined. A wise rule to follow is: never purchase a protection dog without first looking at the parents.

**The attack dog.** Attack dogs are used primarily by the police and military. The dog requires a handler who gives the dog orders and supervises the dog's functioning. This type of dog has been trained to be extremely vicious. It is also trained to release an intruder on command, which is necessary to save the person's life. An attack dog may also be used by a security guard who has the requisite training as a handler to patrol a building, such as a large store. The dog can easily sniff out anyone who has hidden in the building with the intention of burglarizing it after hours. The only problem with an attack dog is that if the handler's attention is diverted, the dog may exhibit poor judgment and indiscriminately bite anyone.

**The sentry dog.** The ultimate in an animal as a deterrent is a sentry dog. This type of dog is trained to patrol premises devoid of human life. The dog is usually leased rather than sold to ensure its proper use. The animal will attempt to indiscriminately kill anything or anybody who ventures onto the premises. No trainer-handler is present when the dog goes on its appointed rounds. The sentry dog is still utilized by the military to protect secret government installations and overseas bases. It is also used by some security firms on a limited basis, but is never used by police departments.

For the average family an alarm dog should be sufficient. The ultimate in a watch dog for a family would be a *protection dog* that has been purchased from and properly trained by a nationally recognized kennel. Reputable kennels, such as The House of Hoyt, of Lockport, Illinois, which specializes exclusively in Doberman pinschers, guarantee the health and performance capabilities of their dogs to the owner's complete satisfaction. The present cost of a registered, strong, healthy, one-year-old, protection-trained Doberman pinscher is about $1,500.

Based on the American Kennel Club's registration statistics, the Doberman is now one of the most popular breeds in American households, possibly because of the rising crime rates throughout the country. Despite this popularity, Dobermans remain the victim of a major fallacy: they have a reputation of turning on their masters. It is difficult to pinpoint the origin of such a misconception, although the almost exclusive use of German shepherds by the Armed Forces may contribute to it. However, many Dobermans were killed saving the lives of U.S. servicemen during World War II and have been honored in a special war dog cemetery.[15] Dogs stay in the service until they become feeble, but dog handlers sometimes change every two years. The shepherd will soon adjust to a new master, but the Doberman will not. Dobermans are a one-family dog and once they become loyal to a person or family, they remain loyal. Sometimes an adult Doberman can be given another home with success, but if the prior owner was good to the dog, he or she will *always* have first loyalty.

Dobermans do not indiscriminately turn on their masters.[16-19] They are big, strong, dominant, and extremely intelligent dogs. People who buy a Doberman because they want a mean dog have made a mistake. Dobermans are not mean but are extremely loyal and protective. However, some owners have been known to put their dog in a small cage and poke at it with a stick to make it vicious. Any dominant animal, when physically abused and painfully mistreated, will act to protect itself. If a family has a natural love for animals and buys a registered Doberman from a reputable kennel, it will have a friend for life. Indeed, it has been said that the Doberman is only a 100-pound lap dog—until someone tries to hurt its master, then *watch out!*

Dogs, as "biologic alarms," have proved to be a very effective intrusion detection system. Many individuals who do not have facilities for even a little dog have found some usefulness in tape recorded messages from our canine friends. If they hear or see suspicious activity in or around their apartment, for example, they simply turn on the recorder. It seems that almost nothing

[15]Sherer, Matt, "War Honored Dogs." *Dog World,* May 1978, p. 1.

[16]Noted Breed Authorities, *The Complete Doberman Pinscher.* New York: Howell Book House Inc., 1976.

[17]Harmer, Hilary, *The Doberman.* New York: ARCO Publishing Co., Inc., 1976.

[18]Brearley, Joan, *The Book of The Doberman Pinscher.* Neptune City, N.J.: T.F.H. Publication Inc., 1976.

[19]Walker, Joanna, et al., *The New Doberman Pinscher.* New York: Howell Book House Inc., 1978.

bothers a burglar like the sound of a yapping dog. The burglar's dislike for dogs seems not to stem from a fear of the dog itself, but a fear of the attention that the barking dog would attract. (This, by the way, is the main function of expensive electronic systems: the burglar is not afraid of the bell itself, but of the attention the sound of the bell brings.)

## STRONG ROOMS

Many homeowners have equipped their homes with a specially reinforced room or closet that provides extra security for valuables. Most valuables kept in this are too bulky for a home safe or a safe-deposit box. Criteria for a good strong room preferably include the following:

- Doors should be solid wood or metal with hinges preferably on the inside. If they are on the outside, the hinge pin should be flattened out with a ball-peen hammer so that it cannot be driven out, or inexpensive security hinge pins should be installed.
- The strong closet should be one that is in the middle of a wall with no sidewalls exposed to attack. Bold burglars might attack a convenient side wall with sledgehammers.
- The door should be equipped with a hardened steel deadbolt lock that can be opened from the inside without a key as well as locked from the inside.
- The closet can be lined with cedar to protect valuable furs or clothing.
- A fireproof filing cabinet should be placed inside for important papers, and the entire closet could be lined with gypsum board for added fire resistance.
- The closet should contain plenty of shelves, and, if one is so inclined, it could include a wine rack for storage of fine wines.
- For maximum security, a built-in wall safe may be installed for extremely valuable items used too often to be kept in a safe-deposit box. If an electronic alarm system has been installed in the rest of the house, the door to the strong room should be connected to this system.

Items that should be kept in the strong room include jewelry, furs, guns, expensive glassware, silverware, cameras, coin collections, valuable documents, or any other valuables that for some reason cannot be kept at a bank. Many persons prefer to have this strong closet inside the master bedroom. When this type of arrangement is possible it is also desirable to have a one-inch deadbolt that fits on the inside of the bedroom door. This lock would serve as extra security in emergency situations. Many persons object to the idea of being "locked-in," but this door could be left unlocked at all times except, for example, when the homeowner heard an intruder in another part of the house. In the event this happened, the individual could lock himself into the bedroom and call the police. Maximum security is obtained when the phone in the bedroom is on a separate line, since lifting one phone off its cradle will render an extension phone useless.

## LANDSCAPING

Landscaping is an important exterior deterrent since the visual appearance of the house alone is sometimes enough to discourage unauthorized entry. Most amateur burglars would rather not approach a house where they are in sight of neighbors and have no place to hide. Landscaping should be planned with both security and privacy in mind. Doorways, windows, and porches should be kept clear, and thick hedges that offer concealment between the house and street should be avoided. Ground level windows that are covered with shrubbery will be particularly attractive to the burglar, but at the same time one must not overlook the possibility of an intruder entering a second story window from a good, solid, high tree branch. Shrubbery with thorns on it may be a safeguard, however, if placed adjacent to windows or doors, since the thorns would undoubtedly cause inconvenience to a possible intruder.

## APARTMENT SECURITY

Apartment living is a community of strangers under one roof. Opportunities to steal or burglarize tend to increase in apartments when certain conditions are present. Most of the same security principles that apply to homeowners are also applicable to apartment dwellers. If the apartment door does not have a good deadbolt lock, and if the landlord will not put one on, time should not be wasted arguing about the situation. The apartment dweller should buy one and use it; after all, it is his or her personal property and welfare that are at stake. Most apartments have the policy that the residents can place extra locks on the doors, but they must stay in place, along with the keys, if the renter moves. This is a small price to pay for the additional safety these locks provide. The front door should also be equipped with a hardened steel chain lock and a wide-angle optical viewer.

● ● ●

In the preceding pages many general considerations of residential security have been described. These have primarily dealt with exterior security measures designed to make the home as unattractive to the burglar as possible. There are, however, a number of precautions that can be taken for specific items within the house, and there is also the matter of resident behavior, which can either deter or encourage the intruder to break in. These two additional aspects of residential security are the subjects of the following pages.

## WHAT TO DO BEFORE THE BURGLAR COMES

In addition to maintaining a physically secure home, a lived-in look should be maintained. Resident behaviors influence whether the home is perceived to be occupied and, therefore, directly influence whether a burglar will risk entry. Several "ideal" residential behaviors are described below:

- Leave drapes or shades in a normal open position during the day, but easily portable valuables should be left out of sight.
- Interior lights should be left on at night—bathrooms and hallways are logical places. Automatic timing devices should be used in the resident's absence.
- A radio should be left on during some of the nighttime hours, so that the home sounds occupied if the owner is away.
- Garage doors should never be left open, particularly with no car in sight. This is like a neon welcome sign to the burglar.
- Residents should participate in a neighborhood watch program.
- Good locks should be installed and, most importantly, they should be used even for short absences.
- New locks should be installed after moving to a new residence, or when house keys have been lost or stolen.
- House keys should not be carried with car keys or connected with any other form of identification.
- Notes that inform a burglar that the house is unoccupied should never be left.
- Door keys should not be left under flower pots or doormats, inside an unlocked mailbox, over the doorway, or in other obvious places.
- Persons working in the backyard should always keep the front door locked, and vice versa, when no one else is in the house.
- All doors should be locked if no one is in the main part of the house, as when residents are working in the attic or basement. Suspicious "wrong number" calls or "nobody-at-the-other-end" calls should be reported to police officials. These calls often represent burglars trying to find out if anyone is home. Other family members, especially children, should be warned not to give out any information, especially about who is home, who is out, and how long they are expected to be out.
- Names should not be displayed on the mailbox or plaques in the front yard. This only makes it easier for the burglar to look up the resident's phone number in the directory.
- Doors should not be opened to anyone who does not have business on the inside. This may be a matter of preventing robbery by force and also preventing burglars who are scouting out valuables and plan to return later when no one is home. Repairmen and others who claim to have business on the inside should show positive identification. Any doubts regarding identification should prompt a call to the individual's company or superiors to be verified.
- Persons asking to use the phone should not be allowed in under any circumstances. Even a strange child requesting to use the bathroom could be an accomplice to a burglar.
- Expected salespersons or workmen who have been admitted should not be left alone at any time.
- Obvious signs of absence, such as a stuffed mailbox or several newspapers piled up, should be avoided. These signs give burglars confidence so they can work undisturbed.
- Broken street lights should be promptly reported. Well-lit areas discourage burglars by taking away their hiding places.

- □ Ladders should not be left loose outside. If they cannot be stored inside, they should be securely locked.
- □ Outdoor articles such as lawn equipment and bicycles should not be left on sidewalks, the lawn, porch, or other areas easily accessible to the general public.
- □ Routines of the homeowner or apartment dweller should be varied. Burglars have been known to watch people's movements for weeks at a time so that they know when a house is likely to be empty.

## SECURITY PRECAUTIONS BEFORE VACATIONS

Among the burglar's favorite targets are homes of people away on vacation. He knows that he has plenty of time and does not have to pass up anything of value to him. Residents planning vacations or a prolonged absence should adhere to these additional precautions:

- □ Ideally, a trusted neighbor or friend should collect all deliveries. If this cannot be arranged, deliveries should be cancelled. However, notification to hold deliveries could possibly tip off a would-be burglar somewhere along the line.
- □ It is sometimes useful for the resident to leave a second car parked in the driveway (locked, of course) instead of putting it in the garage. This creates uncertainty about whether or not the house is occupied.
- □ Mail should be picked up or the post office should be notified to hold all mail. A stuffed mailbox and a collection of handbills is a dead giveaway that no one is home.
- □ Arrangements should be made to keep lawns raked and cut or snow shoveled.
- □ Vacation plans should not be publicized. Write-ups in the local paper about vacations should not appear until after the resident has returned.
- □ Telephones should not be temporarily disconnected. It is better for a burglar to think that the resident is out for a short time rather than know the resident is away for a prolonged period.
- □ The volume of the phone's bell should be turned as low as possible so that a burglar outside the home cannot hear an unanswered phone ring.
- □ A key should be left with a trusted neighbor so that he or she can check the house periodically.
- □ Drapes should not be left tightly closed. A few should be left partly opened, and a neighbor can readjust them from day to day.
- □ At least one light should be left burning either in the bathroom or hallway. The neighbor can also vary this. Automatic timers should be used to turn additional lights on at dusk and off at the resident's normal bedtime.
- □ Valuable items should be removed from places where they can easily be seen through windows.
- □ Before leaving, residents should notify the local police department. Although police cannot observe the residence at all times, they can make more frequent checks.
- □ Upon returning home, the residents should check for suspicious sounds, lights, and force marks before entering. If something seems wrong, they should *not* enter, but call police from a neighbor's phone at once.

## IN CASE THE BURGLAR GETS IN

If the burglar decides that security measures around the home are inadequate and he risks entry, hopefully he will not be rewarded. In other words, if it was not possible to deter the burglar through any one or a combination of exterior and interior security precautions, the next best thing is to deny him. If there is no money or convertible securities in the house, he has been denied. If not in a strong closet or home safe, for example, valuable jewelry should be kept at the bank, and furs in storage at least during the warm season.

Jewelry kept at home should not be left on dresser tops or other accessible places. All jewelry of significant value, whether kept in the bank or at home, should be photographed and marked with an identifying mark so that it could be identified if stolen and later recovered. Furs should also be marked for positive identification, but not on the label or lining. Often the entire lining of a stolen fur is replaced. The identifying mark should be made with an indelible marking pen in several places on the back of the skins.

Many other valuables such as cameras, tools, sports equipment, television sets, and kitchen appliances from the refrigerator to the toaster should be marked. Cash should not be "hidden" in traditional hiding places, because thieves have a sense of tradition too and are likely to look in such places as a sugar bowl, bureau drawer, coin banks, or behind a picture. Probably the first place a burglar would look for cash is the top drawer of a dresser or chest. It is remarkable how consistently people conceal money in socks and hankies in that top drawer. Another common place for purses is the entryway, and for wallets, still inside the pocket of the pants left hanging over the chair. This makes stealing goods as predictable as if the burglar were stealing his own mother's purse.

## RURAL CRIME PREVENTION

Crime is not limited to urban or suburban areas. Rural residents who are generally more trusting than their city friends are increasingly being victimized by burglars and thieves. In many rural areas throughout the country, crime is increasing faster than in nearby metropolitan areas. Crimes such as thefts involving equipment, tools, hay, grain, and livestock present unique crime prevention problems for farmers and sheriff's departments alike.

### Livestock mutilations

One of the most serious and unusual crimes against the farmer today is the mutilation of farm animals. This is not merely a sporadic occurrence; it is widespread and some counties report as many as 365 incidents a year, or one mutilation for every day. Various organs or other body parts are removed from the animal, and in most instances no clues or traces of evidence can be found to lead to a suspect. One hypothesis attempting to explain this aberrant behavior is that animal parts or blood are needed by certain groups known as "devil worshippers" for their rituals. Knowledge of ritualistic behavior at this point is sketchy, but it is believed that these animal parts serve as some sort of symbol. In addition, some participants have been reported to drink the animal's blood. Some authorities, both secular and religious, feel that these rituals may also be responsible for the disappearance of many children who were first thought to be lost or kidnapped for ransom.

Criminal opportunities can be reduced on the farm in much the same way that opportunities can be reduced in the city. Suggestions designed specifically for rural crime prevention are listed below:

- Engrave all personal property with an identification number.
- Expensive machinery and equipment should be kept near the farm home in a well-lighted area.
- If machinery must be left in the field, it should not be parked near the road.
- Livestock should be kept as close to the farmer's house as possible and as far away from the road as possible. In other words, the best protection for livestock is to keep them to the rear of the farmhouse where potential "cattle rustlers" and "devil worshippers" would have to physically walk past the farm house.
- The farmer should have large dogs both as alarms and for protection. While Dobermans and German shepherds are the best of the breeds to keep outside except in harsh weather, a couple of loyal large dogs from the local humane society will also serve as a very effective crime deterrent.
- Fuel supplies should be stored under padlock in a well-lighted area.
- Livestock should be branded with the same identification number used for personal property.
- Expensive tools, chemicals, and seed should be kept in a locked building.
- Rural residents should be aware of a neighbor's absence and be alert for suspicious vehicles in the area.
- Livestock should be checked frequently, particularly those located in distant fields. Any losses should be reported immediately.
- Fences and gates should be kept in good repair.
- Gates to fields where livestock are kept should be locked at all times, and good quality chains and padlocks should be placed across roads that lead to these areas.

## CONCLUSION

It is not the goal of residential security to make fortresses out of each home in the country. No home can be protected like Fort Knox, nor should it have to be. In addition, it must be kept in mind that all the locks, lights, alarms, and bars one could buy cannot totally guarantee protection. A home cannot be made crime proof, only crime resistant, which is what residential security is all about.

Burglary is a crime that occurs when the burglar has both the desire and opportunity to commit the crime. The four principles of deter, delay, deny, and detect can help reduce the opportunity and make the risk greater for the burglar. It is important to realize that most burglars devote little if any time to advance planning of any specific break-in. They pick what appears to be an easy target, and if closer examination reveals a greater risk than anticipated, they move on to a safer target. The more that is done to keep the home from looking like an easy target, the safer it and its occupants will be.

## Chapter 6

# Crime prevention for the elderly

The problems associated with aging, particularly the problem of victimization, deserve special attention. To enable senior citizens to enjoy a crime-free or at least a crime-resistant climate is one of the most challenging aspects of law enforcement today. Edward M. Davis, former Chief of Police, Los Angeles, best summed up the problem when he stated:

> If the problems associated with growing old are not properly addressed by society as a whole, we could face a future that would make today's generation of so-called "crib jobs" (crimes against the elderly that are like taking candy from a baby) look like a Sunday School picnic.[1]

A White House Conference on Aging offered several recommendations for dealing more effectively with the problem of crimes against the elderly in its report, "Towards A New Attitude on Aging":

> . . . making physical protection and crime prevention an element of the planning of facilities for the elderly; expanding police protection of minority neighborhoods; establishing formal liaison between social service agencies and police departments so that elderly victims of crime can obtain all necessary assistance; providing better street lighting; making training grants available to police officers and others to acquaint them with the special situation of the elderly and their special susceptibility to particular types of crime; and granting Federal funds to State and local prosecuting officers to expand or establish fraud units which are well acquainted with schemes used to deceive the elderly.[2]

Prior to this time, however, relatively little research was done on crime and its effects on the elderly and, consequently, specialized training for law enforcement officers was practically nonexistent. Most law enforcement officers had a compassionate interest in the elderly and were well-informed

---

[1]Davis, Edward M., "Crime and the Elderly," *Police Chief*, Vol. 44, No. 2, Feb. 1979, p. 3.
[2]"Crimes Against the Elderly." Congressional Research Service, Library of Congress, HV 6251-A, 75-230 ED, p. 3.

regarding the technical aspects of their profession, but they had difficulty communicating with older persons or working effectively with them.[3] However, through the efforts of the National Retired Teachers Association and the American Association of Retired Persons, (NRTA–AARP), much research has been done, and training seminars were instituted in 1973. The seminars were designed to impart specialized knowledge about all aspects of aging and to show how law enforcement officers can help the elderly as well as how the elderly can serve as resources of law enforcement. These seminars led to an awareness of the impact of crime on senior citizens.

It is now a well-established fact that senior citizens have varying degrees of concern about crime. For most, crime is their second greatest concern, second only to food and shelter. But for some, crime is their greatest concern, and the anxiety is so great as to make them virtual prisoners in their own homes. This withdrawal from community life in order to remain "secure" behind locked doors results in decreased personal freedom not to mention the adverse effect on the quality of life for the elderly.

In addition to numerous seminars and workshops for law enforcement officials, the realization of the impact of crime on the elderly has brought the development of numerous programs specifically designed to educate this group on crime prevention. Most cities and townships now have various programs such as Senior Citizens Anti-Crime Network, Women's Crusade Against Crime, and Neighborhood Watch programs. The NRTA–AARP have played major roles in getting these programs organized and established.[4]

## SCOPE OF THE PROBLEM

Confusion and doubt exists regarding the extent of elderly victimization, largely attributed to three factors.[5] The first factor deals with the degree to which the elderly report crimes. The reporting of crimes is inconsistent, in that many are not reported at all. Many of the elderly do not believe police can recover stolen items, especially if they were not properly identified. They believe reporting crime is a waste of the victim's and the law enforcement official's time, and they do not want to admit they have been victimized, thinking the admission may be viewed as a failure on their part.

The second factor deals with law enforcement officials' ability to meet the needs of the elderly. Because many law enforcement officials are not aware of the special needs of the elderly, changes in their attitudes and

---

[3]Sunderland, George, "National Organizations Launch Crime Prevention Programs." *Aging*, Nos. 281-282, March-April 1978, p. 32.
[4]Ibid.
[5]Malinchak, Alan, and Wright, Douglas, "The Scope of Elderly Victimization." *Aging*, Nos. 281-282, March-April 1978, pp. 12-13.

responses to elderly victims have been slow. Most departments are not concerned about the age of their victims since the victim's age is not included in
the majority of police reports. This signifies a lack of knowledge about the
special needs of older persons. An awareness among officers that the elderly
victim requires extra concern and compassion must be developed to improve
both the reporting of crime and the quality of the report itself, which should
include the victim's age.

The third factor deals with conflicting data obtained by research studies
by social scientists. Much of the data can be interpreted in a number of ways,
depending on the researcher and the situation. Victimization of the elderly
must be approached in an orderly, interdisciplinary manner, instead of a
haphazard, "bandwagon" fashion that results in unreliable data. Glen D.
King, former executive director of the International Association of Chiefs of
Police, believes most police agencies respond very positively to the problems
of the aged.[6] He further feels that law enforcement agencies, rather than
feeling the aged are a burden, feel that they have the first claim.

Although crime data that include the age of the victim are sparse, it is
generally assumed that crime rates involving older citizens are substantially
lower than crime rates involving the general population.[7] For this reason, one
might wonder for a moment why increased attention and special programs for
this problem are necessary. Why not, for example, place more resources and
manpower on crime prevention for a more frequently victimized age group
such as the young adult? The answer is readily recognized by persons familiar
with the *impact* of crime upon the senior citizen. For example, a theft of $200,
although upsetting, would not be an economic disaster for most Americans.
But for an elderly widow with limited financial resources living on a fixed
income, $200 probably means food and shelter for a month. In addition, many
crimes against the elderly are more apt to result in injuries such as broken
bones occurring from falls during the criminal attack.

A 1977 study by the Midwest Research Institute provided evidence of the
severe consequences of elderly victimization and the need for crime prevention programs.[8] Results of the study indicate that financial losses resulting
from crime forced victims to cut back or forego basic necessities in many
cases. In addition, the loss of personal property such as radios and television
sets deprived victims of the few luxuries they had, which, for most, were too

[6]"Glen D. King Shares His Views on Ways That Police Departments and the Elderly Can Work to
Combat Crime." *Aging*, Nos. 281-282, March-April 1978, p. 18.
[7]Goldsmith, Jack, and Goldsmith, Sharon, *Crime and the Elderly*. Lexington, Mass.: Lexington
Books, 1976, p. 1.
[8]*Criminal Justice and the Elderly*, National Council of Senior Citizens Legal Research and
Services for the Elderly, Summer 1978, p. 6.

**Table 6-1.** Personal and household crimes: victimization rates, by type of crime and age of victims, 1973-1976*

| Type of crime and age | 1973 | 1974 | 1975 | 1976 |
|---|---|---|---|---|
| **Personal sector**[1] | | | | |
| Crimes of violence[2] | | | | |
| 12-24 | 60.5 | 60.6 | 59.4 | 59.0 |
| 25-34 | 34.6 | 38.7 | 39.3 | 40.6 |
| 35-49 | 21.6 | 20.9 | 20.5 | 20.0 |
| 50-64 | 13.1 | 11.8 | 13.5 | 12.2 |
| 65 and over | 8.5 | 9.0 | 7.8 | 7.6 |
| Crimes of theft[3] | | | | |
| 12-24 | 154.7 | 157.4 | 155.4 | 147.3 |
| 25-34 | 99.0 | 106.6 | 109.9 | 113.2 |
| 35-49 | 72.0 | 79.3 | 80.2 | 82.6 |
| 50-64 | 46.6 | 49.4 | 51.3 | 58.6 |
| 65 and over | 22.2 | 21.9 | 24.5 | 26.0 |
| **Household sector**[4] | | | | |
| Burglary | | | | |
| 12-19 | 220.5 | 218.5 | 214.5 | 207.3 |
| 20-34 | 122.8 | 128.0 | 122.22 | 123.6 |
| 35-49 | 99.1 | 99.3 | 101.5 | 92.8 |
| 50-64 | 69.7 | 69.3 | 68.1 | 67.5 |
| 65 and over | 55.1 | 54.3 | 53.8 | 50.2 |
| Household larceny | | | | |
| 12-19 | 202.8 | 205.9 | 221.0 | 178.1 |
| 20-34 | 145.9 | 175.0 | 171.5 | 171.9 |
| 35-49 | 126.0 | 145.8 | 148.7 | 144.7 |
| 50-64 | 84.0 | 88.8 | 94.1 | 94.6 |
| 65 and over | 47.4 | 57.9 | 58.7 | 59.5 |
| Motor vehicle theft | | | | |
| 12-19 | 34.8 | 55.0 | 32.4 | 27.4 |
| 20-34 | 28.7 | 27.9 | 29.7 | 24.3 |
| 35-49 | 21.1 | 20.9 | 21.7 | 18.9 |
| 50-64 | 15.8 | 14.3 | 15.0 | 12.3 |
| 65 and over | 5.4 | 5.7 | 6.2 | 6.1 |

*From National Crime Survey.
The lower victimization rate for the elderly may relate to precautionary measures taken, and/or to self-imposed isolation designed to minimize exposure to threatening situations.
[1]Rate per 1,000 population in each age group.
[2]Includes rape, robbery, and assault.
[3]Includes personal larceny with contact and personal larceny without contact.
[4]Rate per 1,000 households headed by persons in each age group.

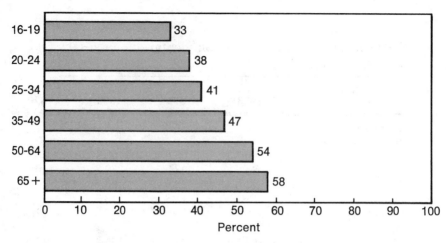

**Fig. 6-1.** Residents of twenty-six central cities: a belief that personal activities have been limited or changed because of the fear of crime, by age of respondents, 1974-1975. (From National Crime Survey.)

expensive to replace. Items of sentimental value such as jewelry given by a deceased spouse are also items often stolen, and these are certainly irreplaceable even if the victim could afford to do so. A study during 1974-1975 known as the National Crime Survey revealed that over half of the senior citizens surveyed indicated they had modified their activities because of fear of crime[9] (see Table 6-1 and Fig. 6-1). Thus it can be seen that even though the elderly generally experience lower victimization rates than other age groups, the financial, physical, and psychologic effects can be far more devastating to the older citizen than to younger members of society.

A second factor supporting crime prevention programs for the elderly deals with their particular vulnerability to criminal activity. The elderly are more open to attack in many different ways. Many are more willing to take a chance on a get-rich scheme because they are living on a fixed income; still others eagerly invest in a "miracle cure" in hopes of improving their failing health. In addition, many elderly people live alone and do not have the opportunity to consult relatives or friends before taking action on something about which they have been misinformed.

Increased vulnerability to criminal activity may also result from the fact that older persons are more trusting than younger people, having grown up in a time when people knew their neighbors and a person's word was as good as gold. Thus when a fast-talking stranger comes to the door assuring them that

[9]*Myth and Realities About Crime.* Washington, D.C.: U.S. Department of Justice, Law Enforcement Assistance Administration, U.S. Government Printing Office, p. 20.

they cannot go wrong on a deal, the elderly may easily be swayed into giving their money away.

Failing senses also place the elderly in a more vulnerable position. Since many cannot hear, see, or remember well, this would, for example, put the swindler in an ideal position when contracts are signed. According to Lawton, 40% of those over 65 years of age have some limitation of activity caused by chronic disease, more than 66% have some vision defect even with corrective lenses, less than 25% of elderly males are employed compared with 86% of men under 65 years of age, and 28% of all older people live alone, compared to 9% of those under 65 years of age.[10] These statistics are indicative of factors that limit the environmental control the elderly have upon their own lives. Physical limitations can result in crime threats going unrecognized or limit the actions the elderly can take to escape an assailant. Living alone creates social isolation, which in turn increases vulnerability. Economic insolvency also increases vulnerability since the elderly cannot afford security precautions, such as driving a car or taking a taxi instead of walking and leaving yard lights on at night.

A psychologic explanation for elderly victimization has been presented by Neugarten and associates,[11] who believe that a shift to a less active role mastery in later years influences victimization. The change from active to passive behavior or from aggression to cooperation that takes place in many elderly persons influences their attitude in such a way that they fail to take corrective action when a crime occurs.

There seems to be no limit to the exploitation of these various vulnerabilities by violent youth, con artists, and other criminals. It is no wonder that of all the generational segments of society, it is the elderly who live most in fear of crime.[12] The vulnerabilities are readily recognized by the criminals as well as law enforcement authorities, and therefore senior citizens are more prone to certain types of crime, such as purse snatch, swindling, robbery, and burglary.[13] Although the elderly have an inordinate fear of murder and rape, statistics indicate they have a very low chance of becoming victims of these crimes.[14] Types of crimes to which the elderly are most vulnerable deserve thorough analysis and will be discussed below, along with preventive techniques.

---

[10]Patterson, Arthur, "Territorial Behavior and Fear of Crime in the Elderly." *Police Chief*, Vol. 44, No. 2, Feb. 1977, p. 42.

[11]Ibid.

[12]*Criminal Justice and the Elderly*, op. cit., p. 7.

[13]Dussich, John, and Eichman, Charles: "The Elderly Victim, Vulnerability to the Criminal Act," in *Crime and the Elderly*, Jack and Sharon Goldsmith, editors. Lexington, Mass.: Lexington Books, p. 92.

[14]*Crime Prevention for the Elderly*, op. cit., p. 91.

## PREVENTIVE MEASURES FOR COMMON VIOLENT CRIMES
## AGAINST THE ELDERLY
### Burglary

Burglary has been shown to be one of the more frequent types of crimes and also the crime that poses the greatest threat to elderly citizens.[15] Not only does the intruder gain access to the person's personal belongings and worldly assets, but also there is the danger of an unexpected encounter during the commission of the burglary, which could result in injury or death of the victim.

Burglary is no longer just a crime of the inner cities. Increasingly, suburbs are becoming targets for "commuting criminals" who live in the city but drive to suburbs to commit their crimes. This affords them a better selection and enables them to make a quick getaway. Therefore, regardless of where one lives, prudent precautions should be taken.

It is believed by most law enforcement officials that burglaries could be significantly reduced if residents could learn to think in terms of the burglar's viewpoint and understood how most burglars operate. Amateur burglars and most professionals look for "easy pickings," and as a rule will not risk a well-protected home unless the possible gains are substantial. Several things as suggested by Action for Independent Maturity (AIM) can be done to a residence that will help foil a burglar.[16] There are many simple precautions costing little or no money and therefore would not cause undue strain on the elderly's fixed income. These measures have been thoroughly discussed in Chapter 5, Home Security, but will be briefly mentioned here.

**Locks.** First and foremost, secure locks should be placed on all doors and windows. These locks should consist of deadbolt and pinfall locks that cannot be forced. Snap locks with spring latches can be easily opened with a knife blade or credit card and should be avoided. Basement windows should be protected with iron bars, unless the basement is used as living quarters, in which case the windows should not be barred in case of fire. In addition to secure locks, the door should be attached to a strong frame, with sturdy hinges, a chain latch, and a peephole. Door inspection and reinforcement are of vital importance to effective minimal residential security.

Unfortunately, the cost of effective residential security devices is very high in relation to the average income of retired persons, for example, $42.50 for installation of a single deadbolt lock.[17] Purchasing cheaper locks from a

---

[15]Midwest Research Institute, *Crimes Against Aging Americans: The Kansas City Study.* Kansas City: Midwest Research Institute, 1975, pp. 3-4.

[16]*Home and Personal Safety,* Action for Independent Maturity, 1977, p. 3.

[17]"Crimes Against the Aging: Patterns and Prevention." Kansas City: Midwest Research Institute, National Clearinghouse on Aging, Administration on Aging, U.S. Department of Health, Education and Welfare, 1977, p. VIII-3.

hardware store is a questionable practice since only a false sense of security is obtained from cheap, ineffective locks. Double cylinder deadbolt locks are not recommended for older citizens since they require a key to open the door from within. The necessity of keeping track of the key and the possibility of not being able to find it during a fire make this type of lock undesirable for senior citizens.

**Locking habits.** The house or apartment doors and windows should be locked at all times, even when the resident leaves for only a short time. This is an obvious first defense against an intruder, but law enforcement authorities should not take for granted that all persons lock their homes all the time. Not too many years ago tranquil neighborhoods did exist in which many doors were left unlocked, and many people still believe it is safe to leave the door unlocked if they are away for only a short time. Most burglars enter a residence through a door, preferably an unlocked one. Police plainclothesmen who run security checks of burglary-prone neighborhoods and apartment buildings habitually find 25% to 30% of front doors unlocked.[18]

Window locks are not recommended for each and every window since at least one window should be left free as an exit in case of fire. In addition, an inexpensive and effective measure instead of locks is the use of easily removable pins as described in Chapter 5.

**Keys.** House keys should be kept with the individual at all times. Extra sets of keys should not be left under a doormat or in other "secret" hiding places around the dwelling. Burglars learn to look in these "secret" places and thus their job is made much easier for them. It is much safer for the resident to leave the key with a trusted neighbor.

If house keys are lost or stolen, locks should be changed immediately. House keys should never be left with car keys when the car is left to be tuned or repaired or even when the car is left in a commercial parking lot. Copies of such keys can be made and later used to gain entry to the individual's residence.

**Lighting.** Brightly lit neighborhoods and residences tend to deter would-be burglars since it increases their chances of being observed. Porch and yard lights provide an easy and fairly economical method of protection at night.

**Alarm systems.** There are many varieties of alarms available ranging in cost from $100 to thousands of dollars. These have been described in detail in Chapter 11. The best advice to follow when considering an alarm system is to deal with a reputable firm and to make sure the equipment has the seal of Underwriters Laboratories. In addition, if an alarm system is purchased, it

---

[18]*Your Retirement Anti-Crime Guide.* Washington, D.C.: AARP–NRTA, 1973, p. 18.

should be loud-sounding for the purpose of scaring off intruders, not for the potentially dangerous practice of bringing help to catch the intruder. Silent alarms are not recommended, especially for older people since their purpose is to lead to the apprehension of the criminal in action.

**Valuables.** Large sums of cash, valuable jewels, and other keepsakes should be kept in a safe-deposit box in a bank. If such things are kept within a household and their presence becomes known, this produces a temptation to would-be thieves regardless of preventive measures taken.

**Automatic timers.** Automatic devices that turn lights on and off while the residents are away are readily available and fairly inexpensive. Some will also turn on a radio and are somewhat more effective since lights and music are more apt to give the impression that someone is in the house or will be back shortly. Additional information on home security measures can be found in Chapter 5.

**Neighborhood programs.** Neighborhood cooperation cannot be underestimated as an effective means of crime prevention. Alert and concerned neighbors reduce the risk of vandalism or burglary substantially. These neighborhood crime prevention programs are springing up all over the country. Operation Neighborhood Watch, for example, is a federally funded program administered by the National Sheriff's Association through local county sheriff's offices. Members of the Neighborhood Watch Program organize patrols, keep an eye open for suspicious-looking strangers and cars, and listen for unusual sounds at night.

Any area that does not have a Neighborhood Watch Program can get materials and information about organizing one by contacting the county sheriff's department.

**Tips to remember for vacant homes.** It is not often possible to have someone at home at all times, and many homes are vacant for extended periods of time. Unoccupied property can be of particular interest to the criminal mind but there are a few precautionary measures that will make the residence less attractive. For example, although it is a good idea not to let mail, newspapers, and other deliveries pile up on the doorstep, the cancellation of these items could possibly tip off a potential burglar. It is best to have all deliveries collected regularly by a trusted neighbor.

Curtains should not be drawn, as this is a sure sign that the house is unoccupied. Telephone lines should be left intact since a disconnected phone would also be a sure tip-off to thieves calling to see if anyone is home.

In the event that burglars do penetrate security measures and gain access to a residence, and in the event that the owner returns home during the criminal act, a burglary could be complicated by assault and perhaps even murder. Usually, intruders do not want to hurt anyone, but they commit their crimes in a state of high tension and they are capable of physical violence if trapped, scared, threatened, or confronted. For this reason, an effective crime prevention program should educate the citizen on what to do in this situation. If either the resident or the intruder panics, the chance of confrontation increases, which is especially dangerous for the senior citizen. The consensus of law enforcement officials is that householders avoid confrontation with intruders if at all possible.[19] Therefore, citizens should be armed with knowledge of the following do's and don'ts as suggested by the New York Police Department and the New York City Department for the Aging.[20]

**Do**
- Remain calm
- Call the police from a neighbor's phone
- Discreetly attempt to see which way the burglar goes and get a description of the get-away car, if possible

**Do not**
- Go inside if the door is ajar or damaged in any way
- Antagonize or shout at the intruder
- Get a neighbor to go inside; this would only add another victim to the crime

If a resident is already home and finds that someone is attempting a break-in, the householder should make a lot of noise, such as screaming, and call the police immediately.

## Robbery

The older citizen particularly fears this crime because of direct encounter with the attacker and the possibility of sustaining serious injuries. More than 50% of crimes against the elderly are in the form of robberies.[21] Robberies can occur almost anywhere and frequently occur in one's own home.

It is not unheard of, for example, for a thief to await the return of a resident to his or her home, and as soon as the resident has unlocked the door, the attacker pushes the victim inside. Another method of gaining entrance to an occupied dwelling is to entice the resident to open the door for a delivery. The intruder then pushes his way inside.

Robberies also can occur in the short distance from door to car or from store to store. Senior citizens cannot be too careful or take preventive mea-

---

[19]*Home and Personal Safety.* Action for Independent Maturity, 1977, p. 3.
[20]"Crime Prevention for Senior Citizens." New York Police Department and the New York City Department for the Aging, Senior Citizen Anti-Crime Network, and Senior Citizen's Crime Prevention Program, p. 6.
[21]*Save Your Dollars With Senior Security.* St. Louis: Mercantile Trust Company, N.A. and the Women's Crusade Against Crime, and The Mayor's Office on Aging, p. 5.

sures too seriously. Preventive measures include the use of common sense, intuition, and awareness. Precautions to help prevent robberies are listed below:

- Always use the optical viewer or peephole. Speak through the door; never rely on the chain lock.
- Do not open the door to unexpected package deliveries. Verify the delivery first by asking for the name of the company and then call to check. Whatever the circumstance, never open the door until you are certain that the person's business is legitimate.
- Do not open the door to stated emergencies. Never allow strangers inside to use the phone, even if they state there has been an accident. The resident should instead offer to make any calls for the stranger. It is also effective to state that the police have also been called. If the stranger's business is not on the up and up, he will usually disappear very quickly.
- Plan ahead before leaving home. A trusted neighbor should know where you are going and when you are expected to return.
- When going to a car, have your keys ready and available, so that doors can be unlocked with a minimum of delay. Cars should never be left unlocked. The car should always be checked before entering for intruders hiding in the back. In addition, cars should be parked on busy, well-lighted streets if possible.
- When returning home, the grounds and front entrances should be inspected before going to the door. If anything seems amiss, do not hesitate to call the police from a neighbor's phone. Suspicious-looking characters often hang around buildings, and for this reason, apartment dwellers should be instructed to go to a neighbor's door and act like a visitor if they are already in the building. Under any circumstances, they should stay away from their own door until the stranger has gone or until his intentions are well known.

## Purse snatch

Although legally defined as a robbery, purse snatch deserves special consideration since it is a frequent crime perpetrated against elderly women.

Purse snatch is a hit-and-run operation in which speed is of the utmost importance. Usually the attacker comes from behind, grabs the purse, and disappears before anyone gets a good description of him. As with robbery, purse snatch is a street crime that can present a real danger to the elderly. This crime is largely one of opportunity, and the do's and don'ts to decrease the opportunities for purse snatch are outlined below:

### Do

- Walk against the flow of traffic.
- Plan routes; stay alert to surroundings.
- Inform someone of the route and destination so that the police can be informed if anything goes wrong.
- Choose the busiest and best-lit streets when walking at night.

- Stay away from buildings and walk next to the street.
- Divide valuables among several different pockets.
- Take only the amount of money or credit cards needed for the day or take checks when they can be substituted for money.
- Keep keys in a pocket, not in a purse. Keys to a residence combined with identification cards contained in the purse can lead to burglary.
- Carry a purse with a short loop, and hold it close to the body.
- Keep your purse on your lap while in restaurants, movies, public restrooms, etc.
- If being followed by a suspicious-looking person, carry purse upside down, holding the clasp closed with one hand. If someone does snatch the bag, its contents will fall to the ground and the thief will be thwarted. Cross the street if possible.
- Pay attention to the handbag, particularly while in crowds, elevators, trains, buses, and all other public places. It is harder for the thief to snatch the bag if the individual has her mind on it.

**Do not**
- "Keep all your eggs in one basket." In other words, money should be divided up and kept in several places on the person, the idea being that if the purse snatch cannot be prevented, at least losses can be minimized.
- Carry a purse if business can be done without one.
- Dangle a purse away from the body.
- Carry the handbag with the loop wrapped around the wrist. If a purse snatch did occur, this could result in a serious injury for the victim.
- Place handbags on the floor, another chair, or on the back of a chair in public places.
- Leave purses unattended in grocery carts in the supermarket or on counters in department stores.
- Fight back with a purse snatcher. All he usually wants is the purse, and fighting back can only result in injury. It is better not to keep too many valuables in the purse and to let it go if it is snatched.
- Run errands alone, especially those involving large sums of money.
- Carry large, bulky purses that are easiest to spot and grab.
- Carry clasp-type purses in such a way that they would open away from the body.
- Carry openweave, basket purses that allow the contents to be viewed.
- Carry a purse so that it can easily be grabbed when carrying books or packages. Take advantage of the situation by putting the purse between your body and the books or packages.
- Be naive and unaware when strangers strike up meaningless conversations. Be aware that even kindly individuals who assist with packages may have ulterior motives.
- Display large sums of cash or other valuables.
- Get caught in an area near a school at a time when school is being dismissed, since many purse snatchers are young offenders.
- Become distracted when buying something or when opening the pocketbook.

## Muggings

Muggings are usually street robberies, although they may take place in other locations such as subways, buses, or buildings. The mugger will either show a weapon or indicate that he or she has one, and threaten to use it if money is not turned over. In some cases, the mugger will physically overpower the individual, using violence until the valuables are obtained. It generally does not pay to resist the mugger, since in too many cases the wrong response on the part of the victim has resulted in serious injury or death. While it is disturbing to be in a situation of surrender to a criminal, it is better than the possible consequences of resistance.

**Tips to help avoid muggings.** Again the element of opportunity plays a major role in whether or not one is mugged. The following suggestions should help reduce the opportunities:

- ☐ Do not exhibit large sums of money in stores or banks.
- ☐ Do not wear expensive jewelry or wristwatches when shopping.
- ☐ Maintain an account in a bank and have Social Security, pension, or other checks mailed there by direct deposit.
- ☐ If being followed, go to a neighborhood store or other place of business and call police. If no place is available, shout, scream, and call for help. Noise will bring assistance and scare off the would-be attacker.

## Rape

Although most women have a very great fear of being raped, the incidence of rape among older women is extremely low. In fact, it is estimated that for women over age sixty-five, the chance of rape is so remote as to compare with the chance of being struck by lightning.[22] Nevertheless, serious precautions must always be taken.

**Tips to prevent being raped**
- ☐ Follow general rules of safety on the street.
- ☐ Be alert.
- ☐ Have keys ready so that doors can be opened immediately.
- ☐ Do not get on elevators with a stranger. Wait for the elevator to return empty. If a suspicious-looking stranger gets on the elevator, get off at the next floor.
- ☐ When the elevator arrives on the ground floor, elderly women should be instructed not to enter it immediately but to reach inside and press the "B" button first, and then the button for the desired floor. If the elevator is empty when it returns to the floor, the individual can then enter it and go to the desired floor without the chance of being taken to the basement.
- ☐ Women who live alone should list only their last name and first initial in the telephone directories and on mailboxes. It might also be helpful to "invent" a husband's or roommate's name for display on the mailbox to create the impression that someone else also lives at the residence.

---

[22]Ibid.

## Elderly abuse

The scope of abuse against the elderly is not fully realized. In fact, only recently has the subject begun to come to light. Abuse can take many forms but generally implies that there has been some degree of intentional physical or emotional harm done to the individual. The problem ranges from neglect, abandonment, and exploitation of elderly individuals to outright physically violent attacks. Some abusive acts take the form of beatings or unlawfully restraining the person until he or she consents to turn over Social Security checks or portions of their life savings.

Many of the victims are reluctant to admit they are victims of such crimes, shameful that their children or other relatives could treat them in such a manner. They are also sometimes afraid to ask for help because the little security they have is provided by the abuser. Some abuse and neglect of the elderly take place in nursing homes, both by family members and some staff who are entrusted with the care of the elderly. In the past there have been numerous reports of nursing home closings as a result of inadequate care. Nursing homes receiving Medicare payments and those classified as skilled nursing homes must now comply with numerous federal, state, and local rules and regulations in order to be licensed and approved. Many of the elderly in nursing homes are victims of thefts of personal items, including valuable jewelry and money. Others have what little money they have rationed out to them by administrators who "don't want to see them spend it all at once on Cokes or cigarettes," while still others are overly sedated so they "won't make too much noise," or restrained so they "won't fall and injure themselves." While it is difficult to differentiate some of these actions as crimes or unethical behavior, many, such as restraint, could be considered torts unless specifically designated by the patient's physician as being necessary for the patient's welfare.

Connecticut instituted an Elderly Protective Services law in 1978 that mandates that all persons whose work brings them into contact with the elderly report instances of suspected abuse to the State Department on Aging Regional Ombudsmen.[23] Officials report that since the new law has been publicized they have been "absolutely inundated" with reports of elderly abuse from all over the state.

Unlike child abuse, research on elderly abuse is scarce. Statistics are difficult to obtain for reasons already cited, and data on the personality characteristics of the abuser are all but nonexistent. The State of Connecticut and several universities are now gathering data about this newly emerging social ill and, hopefully, many preventive measures will stem from this research.

---

[23]"Victims of Family Violence Include Elderly Relatives." *Criminal Justice and the Elderly*, Fall 1978, p. 12.

## PREVENTIVE MEASURES FOR COMMON NONVIOLENT CRIMES AGAINST THE ELDERLY

Many of the violent crimes have been addressed in the first portion of this chapter, but unfortunately there is a category of nonviolent crimes to which elderly persons are perhaps even more vulnerable. Aside from serious injury that can result from robberies, nonviolent crimes, such as fraud, can be much more devastating to the elderly. Fraud is defined as the obtaining of money or property by false pretenses. King has stated: "They [the elderly] are more vulnerable, I think, to the swindle than most members of the public, and a large number of fraud and swindle cases involve older persons."[24] Con artists see the aged American as easy prey and not infrequently rob them of their earnings.

The city of Chicago is home of the Senior Citizen Community Safety Program (SCCSP), designed to concentrate on the crime-related needs of all the city's senior citizens. This program has a special project known as the fraud avoidance program. The philosophy behind this program is that in 98% of cases crimes of fraud can be prevented. All it takes is the knowledge of the way con artists operate and a healthy dose of suspicion—both of which can be obtained through crime prevention programs.[25]

Various confidence games frequently used against elderly citizens are discussed in detail in the following pages. "Confidence game" is an accurate term since confidence is exactly what the swindlers gain from their elderly victims just before they take off with their money.

Most persons are not too concerned about becoming involved in a fraud, and take an it-can't-happen-to-me attitude. Another downfall is to believe that all con tricks are so preposterous that no one would fall for them. Nothing could be farther from the truth. Even the most intelligent, well-educated, and aware citizens can be taken in by the right operator, with the right scheme, at the right time. Con artists are smooth-talking criminals who aim to separate vulnerable individuals from their money through deceit and trickery. They can be women or men working alone, in pairs, or in groups. They may contact their intended victims on the street, by phone, or at the door. They can pose in any one of a multitude of disguises, such as repairmen or inspectors.

Unfortunately, con artists cannot be identified by their looks. If this were possible, they would not be very successful in their trade. Therefore, to avoid being victimized by this type of criminal, one should study what the person *says* and *does*, not what he or she looks like. Key words and phrases such as cash, contracts, contests, home improvements, secret plans, something for nothing, and get rich quick should alert one to be suspicious.

[24]King, op. cit., p. 19.
[25]*Criminal Justice and the Elderly.* National Council of Senior Citizens, Legal Research and Services for the Elderly, Spring 1979, p. 7.

**Cash**

Whenever sizable amounts of cash are requested, caution should take its rightful place. First of all, why is cash necessary? Why not a check? Transfers of large amounts of cash should always be avoided.

**Contracts**

It is not unheard of—and certainly is unfortunate—that homes have been lost as a result of signing a mere television repair contract. Signing anything, least of all a contract, is not a frivolous matter. Contracts may include provisions that permit judgments to be entered against individuals if, for example, they do not make payments on time, and the contract may be secured with a deed of trust on the victim's home.

**Contests**

Although many contests are legitimate, some may be just a come-on scheme where "everyone wins" something, the only catch being an entry fee to qualify for a super prize. The fee will never be seen again by the contestant, nor will he or she have won anything substantial.

**Home improvements**

This is another unfortunate situation in which the con artist may pose as a building inspector or repairman. Once he gets his foot in the door, he proceeds to check such things as the plumbing and wiring. He may, for example, exclaim that the hot water heater is in terrible shape and should be replaced at once. To make things easier for the homeowner he just happens to know a "reliable" plumber who is available to fix the problem right away. The plumber replaces the tank and charges an exorbitant price while the "inspector" cases the house for future use.

Another method is to approach the homeowner with "leftover" materials from a job just down the street. The "contractors" explain to the victim that they can repair or paint the home at a reduced cost because they have extra materials. Unfortunately, these types of home improvements usually consist of paint that will wash off with the first rain, siding that begins to peel in a very short time, or a driveway black-topped with oil that never dries. By the time these things are discovered, the "contractors" are a hundred miles away.

**"Secret" plans**

Any time an individual is asked to keep something a stranger tells him a secret, he or she should suspect something, particularly when asked to invest anything of value. Why must any plans be secret? Why has the stranger asked that no one be told? Clandestine plans may be the only clue to illegal activity.

### Something for nothing

It has been said that the reason this scheme works is that there is a bit of larceny in all of us. The temptation to get something for nothing often prompts even the most reserved individuals to take a chance. A good rule to remember when something for nothing is promised, "nothing" is usually what the individual gets.

### Get rich quick

Any scheme that promises quick wealth should not only be carefully scrutinized, but also discussed in detail with others before a decision is made. Not many legitimate get-rich schemes exist, and when they do, they are not readily offered to the public. Odds are that the only person who will get rich quick is the swindler.

More elaborate swindling schemes are discussed in detail below. Knowledge of these schemes can help older persons to avoid them.

### Pigeon drop

Also known as the pocketbook drop, the pigeon drop is one of the oldest schemes still in use today. Its method is hard to believe, but it works. The target of this scheme is older women in most cases. It employs two con artists, who are usually women. It occurs many times during the year and can be avoided if the intended victim (pigeon) recognizes this confidence game and refuses to participate. It may vary, but the modus operandi is as follows:

> One con artist strikes up a conversation with an intended victim in the street. Shortly after, a second con artist appears with an envelope containing a large sum of money that has been found. The victim does not get a chance to examine the money. There is no identification with the money, but there is a note stating that the money was illegally obtained, such as by gambling. The question of what to do is discussed and resolved when one con artist states she works for a lawyer nearby and will ask him what to do. She leaves and returns stating that since the money was found by all three, it must be shared equally three ways, but each must show that they have an equal amount of money of their own, known as "good faith" money. The first con artist states she has an insurance award with her, she leaves to show it to the lawyer, returns, and states he gave her one third of the money.
>
> They then instruct the victim to go to the bank and withdraw cash. The woman who supposedly works for the lawyer says she will take the victim's money to him. When this happens, the two con artists disappear, giving the victim a fake address. The victim has given her money away.

### Handkerchief switch

This is another hard-to-believe swindle that works. The modus operandi is as follows:

> A man who cannot read or write is looking for a hotel room. He spots an intended victim and asks for help. He pretends to be a visitor settling matters of a deceased relative. He shows a

large sum of money and offers to pay for assistance. Another man will approach and caution the visitor to put the money in a bank. The second man says the hotel sought has been demolished, but he knows of a room. The visitor does not trust banks and asks his intended victim to hold his money until he gets the room. The victim usually will suggest that he put the money in the bank, and the visitor agrees if he can be shown that withdrawals are possible. The victim goes to the bank and makes a withdrawal. The visitor insists that the victim hold the money. The money is tied in a kerchief and the second man suggests that the victim place his money in the same kerchief for safety. The visitor opens the kerchief and puts the victim's money in with his and ties it up. Then he demonstrates how to carry the money, under the arm or in the bosom. He may open his jacket or shirt and insert his hand with the kerchief, at this time switching the kerchief for another identical one. The strangers leave and the victim examines the kerchief only to find pieces of newspaper. He has given his money away.

## The bank examiner

This is another workable swindle usually directed at elderly women. The modus operandi is as follows:

The swindler will usually call a woman on the phone and use a title from a bank or a police department. He will tell his intended victim that some accounts at the bank, including the victim's, show large withdrawals and he suspects a dishonest teller. He requests the victim's cooperation to catch the thief. The phony examiner will ask the victim to go to the bank and withdraw money from a certain window. Then she is to put the money in an envelope and give it to the examiner when he approaches. The swindler explains that the money will be redeposited by them, and that the individual can return to the bank in a few days to have her books adjusted. The withdrawal is made and the money is given to the examiner who has identified himself in the bank. In a few days the victim returns to the bank and finds that there are no irregularities in any of the accounts. She has given her money away.

These stories sound preposterous, but to the victim they sound plausible at the time. It must be remembered that swindlers are intelligent people, rarely use force or even threaten physical harm, and can communicate in such a way as to make their victim feel secure, emotionally stimulated, and "in on something." All three of the aforementioned schemes are dramatic, person-to-person encounters. There are many other rackets that do not require personal contact, but may be just as effective. These are discussed below.

## Mail frauds

Mail frauds are directed against consumers of just about any product. Elderly people seeking business opportunities, medical help, and self-improvement methods are particularly vulnerable. Swindles that take advantage of the postal system are described below.

**Consumer frauds.** Mail frauds include chain-referral schemes, some debt consolidation plans and offers to sell retirement estates at fantastically low prices. All are designed with one goal in mind—to assist the promoter in making a big haul of other people's money.

In chain referral schemes the come-on is to induce individuals to buy an appliance by telling them that they will end up getting theirs for free, since they can sell so many others to friends. The trouble is that the appliances are overpriced and impossible to sell, so that the individual is stuck with them.

A related scheme is the chain letter. This type of operation usually directs the individual to send money or an item of value to one of the individuals named in the letter. The letter assures the individual that he or she will receive a large sum of money by adding names of friends to the chain. In addition to being illegal in most areas, there is not enough money available for everyone to reap a huge profit, and most persons wind up with nothing.

Debt consolidations are offers to make life simpler and care-free by consolidating the individual's debts with one easy finance charge. When an offer such as this comes through the mail, it should be thrown away. Legitimate banks and lending institutions do offer debt consolidation, but not through the mail. Any mail offer probably includes higher interest rates than the individual is presently paying.

"Retirement estates" have long been offered to a "few lucky individuals" for ridiculously low prices. Usually in offers such as these there is something dreadfully wrong. Many times the retirement estate is nothing but a piece of lifeless desert or muddy swamp inaccessible even with a four-wheel drive vehicle. The "estates" are often small squares of land that do not compare at all to the advertisements. Within the past ten years, several developers, particularly in the Southwest and Florida, took nearly 30,000 people for over $350 million in land fraud schemes.[26]

**Business frauds.** Many legitimate and lucrative business franchises exist, but honest ones with money-making potential usually have a price tag to match. Many fraudulent operations are advertised through the mail at absurdly low prices. The usual consequence of investing in one of these is to end up with a worthless name and nonexistent services from the "franchise operator."

Business frauds may also involve a "work-at-home" scheme, which is more within the average person's financial range. The victim is usually a woman who seeks additional income by working at home. Many work-at-home offers will ask for a small "registration fee" and a sample of work to demonstrate the individual's skill. Any such offer should be carefully scrutinized, and the old cliche, "let the buyer beware," certainly has its place in this situation. One such offer to knit baby booties at home drew hundreds of thousands of inquiries; no one qualified, and none of the money was returned.

---

[26]*AIM's Guide to Home and Personal Safety*, Action for Independent Maturity, 1977, p. 10.

Other types of mail frauds may include phony insurance claims (some related to health insurance), magazine subscription contracts, worthless stocks, bonds, oil and gas leases, book publishing schemes, and memberships in "discount clubs" where savings would be too good to be true.

## Other types of fraud

There are a variety of other ways the consumer may be bilked. Some may be extensions of legitimate business practices that become illegal, such as the bait-and-switch.

**Bait and switch.** This is the practice of advertising an item at a very low price (the bait) to attract customers to the place of business. Once inside the store, customers find that bargains do not exist, or that they have all been sold. Customers are then steered to a higher priced item, often an unknown brand (the switch).

When you are in the store ready to buy or at least very interested in buying, all the seller must do is change your mind on the price you want to pay and the qualities or features you want. To protect yourself from the bait-and-switch scheme, take the following steps:

*Plan ahead:* Think about what it is you really need and how much money you ought to pay for it.

*Take your time:* Do not be rushed or high-pressured into buying something you had not planned to buy.

*Assert yourself:* If the "bait" is not available, find out why. Ask the merchant for a raincheck if he or she still insists that the advertised item is not available. Ask the salesperson to write down on the raincheck the date you can come back and pick up the sale item and the sale price you will pay for it.

If you still need help, bring the problem to the attention of the home office, especially if the store is part of a chain. Also contact the local consumer protection office and send copies of your complaint letters to the Federal Trade Commission. The FTC cannot take action on behalf of individual consumers; however, from the complaint letters of consumers, the FTC may be able to detect a pattern of abuse by one or another company and start its own investigation.

**Advertising schemes.** Another come-on scheme is the "advertising campaign." In this case an individual is led to believe that he or she has been chosen to be featured in a series of advertisements because the individual is unique in some way—a model homemaker, or has some other special quality.

The objective of this scheme is to get the individual to sign a contract for some benefit. However, the terms of the contract could include relinquishing one's home if the individual cannot keep up payments or no longer wishes to participate. The victim usually stands to gain nothing and can legally be held to the terms of anything signed.

**Fear-sell techniques.** Another technique to bilk money from elderly individuals is to use fear coupled with rash statements, such as, "Your water heater is about to blow up!" "Your electrical wiring could burn your house down any minute!" "You have termites in your basement that must be tended to immediately!" Statements such as these produce high anxiety and pressure many persons to rush into something they do not need.

**Surveys.** Door-to-door surveys offer another opportunity for the con artist to take advantage of a seemingly innocent situation. This approach is often used by persons trying to sell unwanted merchandise. The stranger attempts to gain entry but should not be allowed in until his or her true identity is known. Legitimate door-to-door surveys can usually be done without the interviewer coming inside.

**Charities.** Many individuals are solicited to make a donation to an organization they have never heard of. The request is written in such a way that not giving becomes synonymous with being prejudiced against racial or religious minorities. Before guilt feelings make an individual contribute, the organization's validity should be checked with the local Better Business Bureau or Consumer Protection Agency.

**Automobile frauds.** There are many fraudulent acts that center around the automobile. Odometer rollbacks are a well-known but not readily recognized example of defrauding the unsuspecting car buyer. "Free estimate" inspections of automobile transmissions also present an opportunity for deceit, since older parts are often substituted for newer ones during the inspection. The ball joint swindle begins as an advertisement for an inexpensive wheel alignment. After the customer arrives, the mechanic informs him that he cannot align the wheels because he must first replace worn-out ball joints, at a cost of over $100. Obviously, the best advice here is to have the car checked by an independent auto mechanic before purchases or repairs—and, again, let the buyer beware.

**Dance studios.** Elderly individuals are often lonely and want to meet people. Therefore, they are particularly vulnerable to dance studios promising fun and companionship. A sales representative comes to the individual's home and persuades him or her to take, for example, five lessons at $10 per lesson. The salesperson then informs the individual that if he or she signs a long-term contract right away there is a considerable discount in cost. If the customer does this, six months later he or she is likely to be contacted again about a new special discount package. The problem lies in the fact that if the individual did not read the contract carefully, he or she may end up paying for twenty-five years' worth of lessons.

**Fortune tellers.** These people may call themselves readers, advisors, healers, or spiritualists. They may promise to help with any problem an individual may have, including serious illnesses, money problems, or courtship relations. Fortune tellers by whatever name are usually clever people who listen closely to whatever an individual tells them. They persuade the person to come again and again, each time spending more and more money. The problem, of course, is that fortune tellers can really help no one with serious problems—and their work is illegal. Fortune tellers are often transients for this reason. If they suspect they may be investigated, they simply pick up and move out, overnight if necessary. Serious problems should be left to the consultation of medical doctors, financial advisors, clergymen, lawyers, or trusted friends or relatives.

**Funeral chasers.** As portrayed in the movie *Paper Moon,* a "salesman" appears at the home of a recently bereaved victim with a Bible (or piece of jewelry) in hand, claiming that the deceased person made a down payment on the item and that the victim owes for the rest of the purchase price. The swindler can be very convincing by displaying knowledge of the victim and the deceased (gleaned from the obituary column) and by taking advantage of a very emotional situation.

**"The fence."** In this scheme an individual approaches a victim with a "good deal," usually a television, stereo, etc. He or she may advise that the merchandise is "hot" but cannot be traced. The swindler requires cash so he or she can pick up the merchandise. However, the individual goes away with the money and is never seen again.

**Gift delivery.** In this scheme, someone calls at the victim's home to check the address for delivery of a "gift" ordered by a "friend" of the victim. The victim unwittingly supplies the name of the friend when asked to guess who could have sent the gift. The caller then casually mentions the fact that he or she represents an out-of-town warehouse that is going out of business and offers to take an order for goods to be delivered at a later date when the so-called gift is delivered. A cash payment for the goods is, of course, required. The victim receives neither gift nor goods.

## How to avoid victimization by confidence artists

Because a senior citizen's money is particularly dear, nothing can be more vital than to protect what money he has. It is thought that attitudes play basic roles in whether or not a con artist is successful. For example, greed can bring out that bit of larceny hidden in most everyone. The temptation to try to get something for nothing is why the pigeon drop is such a successful con game. In addition, many con artists flatter and mislead their victims until they cannot see the light of day until they have been stung. Then it is too late.

The best defense seems to be an awareness of the various schemes and a refusal to participate, no matter what the temptation or how sincere the con artist seems to be. Ideally, all senior citizens should be aware of the following do's and don'ts:

### Do

- Ask for and check at least three personal references when having service or repair work done for the first time. Also contact people who have recently used these services to see if they experienced any problems.
- Keep a copy of any contract signed and file it in a safe location at home or in a safe-deposit box. Contact an attorney for all major or complex purchases or rentals (e.g., land purchases, etc.).
- Beware of false or misleading advertising regarding discounts, sales, free gifts, etc. Compare these so-called bargains with merchandise at other businesses. Remember that nothing is ever truly free.
- Become familiar with all sources of credit before considering a loan or major purchase. For example, when considering a bill payer consolidation loan, remember that although you may pay less per month, you probably will be required to make payments for a much longer period of time.
- Know what your charges will be when you buy on credit. The Truth in Lending Act requires that *both* finance charge and the annual percentage rate of interest be prominently displayed on the forms and statements used by creditors. Contact local authorities if suspicions of fraudulent activity arise. In addition to the police department, the district attorney's office or the consumer protection agency may be of help.
- Get medical treatment or advice only from a licensed health care practitioner: a medical doctor, osteopath, or community health clinic.
- Have home repairs done only by qualified workmen. A reputable firm will usually provide names of previous customers who can be contacted for references.
- Get a receipt for any kind of work payed for.
- Testify in court, if asked, to help stop this kind of crime.
- Beware of friendly strangers offering goods or services at low rates.
- Beware of friendly strangers who tell you they found money and want to share it with you.
- Be suspicious of telephone calls from persons claiming to be bank officials who ask you to withdraw money from your account *for any reason,* particularly if they ask you not to check at the bank because that would tip off the embezzler. Banks communicate in writing on business transactions.
- Be alert to any scheme that involves removing your savings or other valuables from safekeeping and turning them over to *anyone.*
- Be suspicious of fortune tellers, readers, advisors, etc. If you are asked to turn over money or valuables, notify the police.
- Demand everything in writing along with the date, name, and signature of the individual making the promises.
- Always remember that *you do not get something for nothing.*

**Do not**

☐ Hesitate to notify police of any suspicious circumstances.

☐ Discuss personal finances with strangers.

☐ Expect to get something for nothing, especially from strangers.

☐ Draw cash out of a bank at the suggestion of a stranger under any circumstances.

☐ Be too embarrassed to report the fact that you have been victimized or swindled.

☐ Buy an item of significant cost without comparing at least three brands at three different stores.

☐ Sign a contract before reading it.

☐ Sign a contract that does not have *all* the blanks filled in.

☐ Allow a salesperson to pressure or rush you into signing a contract. Think it over; take it home and reread it. If necessary, have your attorney read it. It is always better to delay at least one day.

☐ Accept a verbal commitment as a valid contract.

☐ Rely on the advertised or promoted reputation of a business or its products that you are unfamiliar with. Always check with your local Better Business Bureau, at least to determine the firm's true reliability.

☐ Spend money on mail orders without first checking on the reputation and reliability of the company.

☐ Buy any item through the mail only because it can be obtained free by selling additional items to friends. Pictured items can be very misleading unless it is a photograph with dimensions and material content clearly described.

☐ Rush into any get-rich schemes. When someone approaches with a get-rich scheme involving part or all of your savings, it is usually *his* get-rich scheme. If it is a legitimate investment, the opportunity will exist tomorrow.

☐ Rearrange finances for any reason without consulting an expert who has references that can be verified.

☐ Consider taking advantage of retirement real estate offered at ridiculously low prices through the mail.

☐ Send money through the mail for any kind of work-at-home or money-making plan, or self-improvement or training course.

☐ Sign any kind of contract without the advice of another trusted person, preferably a banker, lawyer, or minister. Even a magazine subscription may involve more than the initial cost if there are additional sums for late payments.

☐ Be pressured into having any kind of repair work done immediately on the grounds that something terrible will happen if the situation is not corrected at once.

☐ Order and pay cash for any merchandise until the goods are in hand and the quality of the items is satisfactory.

☐ Be fooled by talk of "low" monthly payments. Find out the total amount to be paid and subtract the cost of the item. The difference is interest, and will be fairly obvious if exorbitantly high.

☐ Pay for anything on the grounds that it has been ordered by a recently deceased spouse or other family member. No one is obligated to pay for anything ordered by another person. Do not allow emotions to be exploited in this manner.

## SPECIAL PREVENTION PROGRAMS

There are many government- and community-based crime prevention programs, some of which are discussed in Chapter 13. However, those that have special significance for the elderly are mentioned briefly below.

### Direct deposit of checks

Many criminals know exactly when government checks arrive each month and may decide to attack that particular day. Many elderly citizens have had the unfortunate experience of getting their Social Security checks stolen right out of their mailboxes. This could be avoided by using the voluntary government program of direct deposit. Monthly government payments are delivered directly to the financial organization of the individual's choice and are deposited directly into the individual's personal checking or savings account.

Individuals using direct deposit may choose the financial organization to which the payment is to be sent, choose the account it is to be deposited in, cancel direct deposit at any time, or change financial organizations at any time. Persons eligible for direct deposit include those persons receiving:

Social Security benefits

Supplemental Security Income

Railroad retirement

Civil service retirement

Veterans Administration compensation and pension

In order to sign up for direct deposit, eligible individuals should take their next check to their financial organization and request to sign up for direct deposit. Within 90 days, the individual can expect the checks to be deposited directly.

Over six million Americans are now participating in direct deposit. Other benefits, in addition to preventing thefts and forgeries, include no more standing in lines, uninterrupted deposits, and no more waiting for the mail. Direct deposit has proved to be a great improvement over mailing checks to homes.

### Federally sponsored programs

Several federal agencies, including the HEW's Administration on Aging, the Community Services Administration, and The Department of Housing and Urban Development, have all sponsored crime prevention programs with particular interest in serving the elderly population. In addition to crime prevention programs, special concerns are given to victims of crime and elderly public housing tenants. The National Council of Crime and Delinquency assists organizations of the elderly to get training, technical assistance, and information needed to mount crime prevention campaigns.

## Community projects

A program taking place in Washington, D.C., known as the Elderly Anti-Victimization Project, has as its goal to reduce crime within public housing complexes for the elderly in the inner city. It employs victim assistance counselors who visit victims of crime and often obtain more information from the victims than do the police. It also provides an escort service to many elderly persons for check cashing, shopping trips, and special events. There are about seventy elderly participants and it has proved to be a popular transportation service. In addition to these services, the staff performs security inspections of elderly people's homes, engraving their valuables with an identifying number and installing new door locks where needed. Although the project's primary emphasis is on service, it also attempts to educate the public through various crime prevention lectures in scores of Washington neighborhoods.

Many other major cities have similar programs. A program in New York City also provides personal escort and transportation services, in addition to the use of telephone alerts, CB radios, crime security systems for the home, and the experimental "Buddy Buzzer," which links elderly persons to their neighbors.

Statewide anticrime programs are now being developed following enactment of a federal statute (PL 94-503) that requires states to provide for the development of programs and projects specifically for prevention of crimes against the elderly. One excellent program, developed in Florida, holds public hearings throughout the state and conducts statewide victimization surveys.[27]

Another interesting program designed to prevent elderly victimization is administered by the Senior Citizen Community Safety Program of Chicago. This program utilizes a series of "intergenerational sessions" with the hope of "sensitizing" youngsters, even those not delinquency prone, to the facts of aged life. The three-part program takes place in public and parochial high schools across the city. The first session offers the children an overview of aging and includes statistics on the number of elderly today and in the future. The students are given a myths-of-aging quiz, which challenges many stereotyped views of older people. Volunteers from the class are given an opportunity to experience some of the problems associated with changes in hearing and sight that accompany old age by wearing earmuffs and goggles.

---

[27]Sunderland, op. cit., p. 34.

Others try to thread needles wearing mittens and some try to talk with ping-pong balls in their mouths. These activities simulate the frustration experienced by the elderly who are afflicted by arthritis or have suffered cerebral vascular accidents.

During the second session one week later, students are introduced to a group of vivacious senior citizens who give their insights into the "beauty of aging." These sessions allow direct interpersonal communication between generations, which helps to foster an understanding and an empathetic relationship between the elderly and the youngsters. The closeness that can develop during this session is surprising.

The final session deals with crime and the elderly, and utilizes the empathy and understanding the students hopefully gained in the first two sessions. The sponsors show the children what a garden and a tidy lawn mean to an older person and why vandalism is so distressing to them. In addition, the children learn that stolen purses or Social Security checks may mean the older person has to do without basic necessities for a month or more and that injuries sustained during the commission of crimes may have lasting effects.

The long-term impact of this program of crime against the elderly cannot be predicted, but it is recognized that these children are at an impressionable age. If they can be exposed to some of the dignities of old age at this time, then perhaps more respect for the elderly and their property will be the rule in the future.

The Technical Research Services Divisions of the International Association of Chiefs of Police have undertaken a model project on aging, funded by the Administration of Aging. The objectives of this project are to:

1. Increase safety of the elders' environment.
2. Assist senior citizens to participate in volunteer services of local law enforcement agencies.
3. Develop stronger links between the older citizen and the police officer.
4. Develop and implement programs intended to reduce the vulnerability of the older American to criminal victimization.[28]

Included in this project was a "Crime Safety and the Senior Citizen" survey of five hundred police departments. The purpose of the survey was to establish a base of information regarding law enforcement activities for the elderly. The survey has since been developed into a "Crime and the Senior Citizen" survey for use by individual law enforcement agencies to assist them in evaluating problems and attitudes of senior citizens, fears of crime, and the

---

[28]Gross, Phillip, "Crime, Safety and the Senior Citizen." *Police Chief*, Vol. 44, No. 2, Feb. 1977, p. 6.

effects of both crime and preventive measures on the life-style of the aged American. For further details of this survey, see the February, 1977 issue of *Police Chief*.

Omaha, Nebraska was one city that utilized the survey. Individuals throughout the entire city, representing various socioeconomic backgrounds, were surveyed. The purpose was to obtain data concerning the victimization of senior citizens, their fears about crime, how crime has affected their mobility, what type of crime prevention habits they currently practice, and to give them an opportunity to suggest what type of crime prevention programs they would be most interested in.[29] From the results of this survey it was determined that burglary is the most frequently committed crime, followed by larceny, robbery, purse snatch, misdemeanor assault, felonious assault, and sexual assault.[30] The most common crime prevention measures include extra caution while moving about the community; senior citizens tend to avoid going out alone and at night. They avoid certain streets and carry only minimal amounts of money. The next most common security practices dealt with home security, but these were employed to a lesser extent than those used on outings.

Miami Beach used the survey in cooperation with the International Association of Chiefs of Police. The survey results provided Miami police officials with statistics concerning demographic data of Miami residents, types of crimes committed against the elderly, profiles of offenders, and the potential effectiveness of a crime prevention program.[31] Several actions and recommendations were made based on the results of the survey, including additional on-site security inspections for senior citizens, the conversion of a departmental van to a crime prevention display vehicle, distribution of more printed crime prevention material to senior citizens, and the establishment of a victim follow-up program to evaluate services to elderly victims and the effect of the prevention program.

Data from a comprehensive research project in Multnomah County, Oregon, indicates that except for some particular types of crime, older citizens as a group are not victimized more than other segments of the population.[32] There is a high incidence of property crime among older persons, followed by fraud and harassment. Research also indicates that the fear of being vic-

---

[29]Wolf, Robert, "An Aid to Designing Prevention Programs." *Police Chief*, Vol. 44, No. 2, Feb. 1977, p. 27.

[30]Ibid, p. 28.

[31]Tighe, John H., "A Survey of Crime Against the Elderly." *Police Chief*, Vol. 44, No. 2, Feb. 1977, p. 30.

[32]Rifai, Marlene A. Young, "The Response of the Older Adult to Criminal Victimization." *Police Chief*, Vol. 44, No. 2, Feb. 1977, p. 48.

timized by crime is much greater than actual victimization rates. Measures employed by citizens to protect themselves include: (1) not carrying money, wallets, or purses, (2) not going out at night, (3) possessing a weapon, (4) adding locks to doors and windows, (5) identifying property, (6) attending crime prevention block meetings, (7) leaving lights on at home when gone, and (8) getting a dog or alarm system. Problems in the elderly's response to crime can be assessed from these results, as well as the effectiveness of current crime prevention programs. Eventually, from the efforts of all researchers across the country, more responsive and informative methods for meeting the needs of elderly citizens can be provided.

## ONE LAST WORD

We have seen how crime and the fear of crime create special problems for the elderly. Statistics show elderly victimization rates far lower than for other age groups, but these statistics fail to take into consideration the impact of crime upon the elderly. Senior citizens can least withstand the effects of crime, and many times are forced to do without basic necessities because of being a victim of criminal activity. Crime is devastating the lives of thousands of older citizens. Many live in a fearful environment even though they may not have yet experienced victimization.

In one sense, the anticrime precautions taken by the elderly have paid off. They are victimized at lower rates than other age groups, but the margin of security is still not high. They are vulnerable in many ways, and thus have made a great sacrifice in order to remain "safe." They sacrifice their community life, social activities, and other basic freedoms of American life. Many remain at home, under self-imposed house arrest, so that neither they nor their home is left unprotected. The key to crime prevention for the elderly, however, is not to lock them in their homes. As we have seen, crime is largely a matter of opportunity, and if the elderly are made aware of its many profiles, they are less likely to become its victim. A successful crime prevention program for senior citizens must be concerned with their fears, as well as the actual threats to their safety and well-being. There is much emphasis today on meeting the special needs of the elderly, both in law enforcement agencies and other social service departments. This is a positive change, which indicates that the elderly are no longer regarded as "throw-away" citizens but are an important segment of society whose wisdom and judgment are to be respected.

Medical quackery is also a major criminal offense affecting the elderly. Because of the broad scope of the problem, and also because it affects other segments of the population, health frauds are discussed in the following chapter.

Chapter 7

# Health fraud prevention

If it is true that treason represents the highest crime in the nation, then health fraud—medical quackery—must surely be the lowest, because it often preys on the desperation of people without hope. Quackery is a subtle but very frequent crime involving both people and products. It is not outright armed robbery but it might as well be since both quackery and robbery accomplish the same things—they endanger the lives of the victims and separate them from their money.

Persons who advertise "miracle" cures but who have no medical training are quacks. Drugs and food supplements that promote false health claims are quack products, and quack devices are contraptions or machines that at best are ineffective and at worst cause injury to their users. The financial impact of quackery has been estimated to be more than $2 billion annually in the United States.[1]

## HISTORY OF HEALTH FRAUDS

Quack schemes have been in existence almost as long as mankind. Before humans really understood illness and disease, attempts to heal the sick included the use of herbs and spices, crude medicines, ceremonies by medicine men, blood-letting, and other rituals designed to drive the evil out of the body so that healing could take place. Perhaps early man really believed in his powers to heal the sick by these methods, but from these ancient practices came home remedies that no doubt provided the basis for many of the quack products developed in more recent times. Those who sold them may have been well aware of their uselessness, but nevertheless traveled from town to town peddling their wares, claiming relief from everything from constipation to droughts. If an individual did recover from an illness after taking one of these products, all credit was usually given to the product, the treatment, or

---

[1]Consumers Union, *The Medicine Show*. Mt. Vernon, N.Y.: 1976, p. 170.

the quack himself. No one realized that perhaps nature had run its course and the individual would have recovered without any treatments. Thus quackery flourished and the quacks profited, until enough of the townspeople discovered they had been duped; then the quack was lucky if he or she was just merely run out of town.

As humans climbed the ladder to civilization, so did the quacks and their devices. Each new legitimate invention opened the gate for the invention of quack products. When Benjamin Franklin, for example, discovered electricity, he probably had no idea that his invention inspired the development of an infinite number of useless electrical gadgets and devices, all claiming to have medical significance. The invention of the radio and phonograph also spawned numerous useless devices and gadgets, such as the radioscope. This electric health gadget was developed in the 1920s by Albert Abrams, MD, who used the radioscope in his system of diagnosing and healing, which he termed "radionics." He enlisted the cooperation of over 3,000 practitioners, mainly chiropractors, who would send dried blood specimens from patients to be inserted into Abrams's radioscope. Abrams would then send back the diagnosis on a postcard, with recommended treatments, which entailed use of another of his contraptions.

After World War II many quacks exploited the interest in medical uses of atomic energy. The Zerret Applicator, claiming to produce Z-rays, which would expand the atoms of the body and thereby cure all diseases, is but one example.

The most vicious form of medical quackery involves so-called cures for incurable diseases, such as diabetes, cancer, and arthritis. The quacks prey on the desperation many people face with such chronic illnesses. In addition to the money and time wasted with useless treatments, the real danger is that many people will delay seeking or completely ignore proper medical care.

Examples of the grave dangers of medical quackery can be found when one examines the results of just a few of the "miracle cures" that have been advertised in this country. The Kaadt Diabetic Remedy, for example, was recommended and prescribed by its developers, Drs. Charles and Peter Kaadt. The remedy was to be taken orally in place of insulin. The treatment offered by these physicians consisted of a solution containing vinegar, saltpeter, resorcinol, and Taka-diastase.[2] In addition, patients received "digestive tablets" and laxative tablets that were to be taken with the vinegar solution. All diet restrictions were removed with this remedy, and patients were told they could eat anything they wished. The therapy was made to

[2]Schaller, Warren, and Carroll, Charles, *Health, Quackery, and the Consumer.* Philadelphia: W. B. Saunders, 1976, p. 191.

sound very attractive to the diabetic—no more injections or diet restrictions. People all over the country flocked to these physicians in hopes of finding a better treatment for diabetes than insulin and diet control. However, many of these patients later testified that they had suffered complications such as gangrenous infection, diabetic coma, and irreversible damage to eyesight, many of the same complications of uncontrolled diabetes. Experts in the treatment of diabetes testified that there is no known cure for diabetes and that the only recognized treatment is insulin and diet control. The Kaadt medicine was found to be of no value in the treatment of diabetes. It even contained an ingredient that could be dangerous if used to excess.[3] It was estimated that these doctors took in $6 million over a period of 10 years before their licenses were revoked and they were brought to trial and sentenced for violations of the Food, Drug, and Cosmetic Act.

Other examples of medical quackery are the Mill Rue Tonic and the Arthur Cox Cancer Cure. Mill Rue Tonic, a liquid solution labeled as an "iron tonic," was promoted for the treatment of cancer, arthritis, diabetes, ulcers, high blood pressure, and other serious diseases. The promoter of Mill Rue, Roy F. Paxton, had no medical training but nevertheless engaged in personal consultations during which time he would diagnose patients as having diseases such as cancer, diabetes, and arthritis.

Arthur Cox called himself an "Indian herb doctor." He gathered, dried, and ground many different herbs, and from these made 26 different "medical preparations." These preparations were promoted for treatment of internal cancer, diabetes, dropsy, arthritis, epileptic seizures, gallstones, and prostate and female troubles. Cox also prepared a salve for the treatment of external cancer. This salve became very popular during the 1940s. His recipe for the external cancer salve consisted of horse urine, a box of clay, a turkey feather, a jar of petroleum jelly, and a bottle of castor oil. The turkey feather was dipped in the horse urine and rubbed in the clay to produce a mud, which was then painted on the skin, using the turkey feather as a brush. The petroleum jelly was used as a coating over the mud to slow the rate of evaporation of the mud mixture, and the castor oil was used to keep the bowels open.[4]

This example, of course, is just one of hundreds of supposed remedies for cancer, and is not the only one advocating the use of animal excretions . Other popular "remedies" during this era included the use of red clover tea, salves made from zinc chloride and blood root, plant material sundried in pewter, and even live green frogs applied to skin cancers. Many different diets have also been promoted as cancer cures—the promoters usually claiming that

---

[3]Ibid.
[4]Ibid.

their diet would detoxify or unpoison the body, thus preventing or curing cancer.

The biggest cancer quack of the 1950s was the Hoxsey treatment for internal cancer. The Hoxsey concoction was sold in two parts: a pink formula comprised mainly of lactated pepsin and potassium iodide, and a black formula containing cascara (a common cathartic) mixed with extracts of prickly ash, buckthorn bark, red clover blossom, barberry, burdock, licorice roots, pokeweed, and alfalfa. The formula reportedly was adopted by Hoxsey after his great-grandfather's horse was supposedly cured of leg cancer after grazing in a pasture growing such botanical specimens. Like earlier so-called cancer cures the courts found the Hoxsey treatment for internal cancer to be worthless. In 1960, its sale was finally stopped in the United States (although production continued in Mexico) but the expenditure by victims for the worthless treatment was over $50 million.

## MODERN HEALTH FRAUD SCHEMES

Today Laetrile is by far the most controversial cancer drug. It has been promoted so effectively that it has become a national issue because of the large number of people backing its use and legalization.

While attempting to improve the flavor of bootleg whiskey, Dr. Ernst Krebs, a California physician, discovered Laetrile by accident. It is a chemical known as amygdalin, and occurs naturally in peach and apricot pits, bitter almonds, and other plant material. Krebs tried the substance as a cancer treatment in 1920 but found it to be highly toxic. Ernst Krebs, Jr., claimed to have purified the substance in 1952, and once again Laetrile was advocated as an effective cancer treatment. Its promoters came up with an interesting but wrong theory to explain how Laetrile worked. The younger Krebs claimed that Laetrile sought out an enzyme found in cancer cells but not in normal cells. The Laetrile then would release cyanide, which killed off the cancer cells. Normal cells were supposedly not affected by the cyanide because they were rich in another enzyme that detoxifies the cyanide. This theory has long been discredited; cancer cells do not have an enzyme that activates cyanide, nor do normal cells have a protective enzyme that detoxifies the cyanide in the Laetrile. Therefore, the destructive effects of cyanide would be equally distributed between normal and cancerous cells.

After this theory was disproved, Krebs offered a more complex theory. He claimed that Laetrile is vitamin $B_{17}$ and that cancer is caused by a deficiency of this vitamin. Laetrile the drug suddenly becomes Laetrile the vitamin. Valid basis for either theory cannot be found. There is no evidence that any of the more than one hundred forms of cancer results from a vitamin deficiency.

In fact, some of the most effective anticancer agents work by preventing tumors from getting the vitamins they need to survive.[5]

Neither the United States Food and Drug Administration, the Canadian Food and Drug Directorate, the National Cancer Institute, the American Cancer Society, nor any other reputable organization has found any evidence to support the use of Laetrile in the treatment or prevention of cancer.[6]

Most of the support for Laetrile comes from those promoting the substance and from testimonials. Testimonials do not offer scientific proof. Rather they are often emotionally charged statements by people who have used the substance. Many of those claiming to have been cured did not have cancer in the first place. Also, some cancer patients have a temporary remission that would have occurred in any case; however, if such a remission coincides with receiving the Laetrile treatments, the patient attributes the remission to the drug. Other testimonials come from patients using Laetrile along with recognized and accepted medical treatments for cancer, such as chemotherapy and radiation. Testimonials in favor of Laetrile also come from persons who sincerely believe they have been cured of cancer, but who later find that they still have the disease. Cancer treatments that cannot be supported by scientific evidence traditionally have been promoted by testimonials. This was true of the Arthur Cox cancer cure, the Hoxsey treatment for internal cancer, the Mill Rue tonic, and is true presently of Laetrile.

Quackery that exploits the pain and disabling effects of arthritis is also flourishing. The Arthritis Foundation, a nonprofit national health organization, estimates the annual bill for unproved or quack arthritis remedies to be around $95 million, and it is further estimated that for every dollar currently going toward scientific research in arthritic diseases, another $25 is spent on worthless nostrums and unproved or irrational cures.[7] Many mechanical devices and gimmicks are part of arthritis quackery. Many promise not only relief from arthritis but also from constipation, dandruff, and baldness as well. Among some of the most popular devices were vibrators. Many proved to be not only ineffective but also dangerous and have since been seized by the Food and Drug Administration. Mechanical devices are now fading from the market as a result of federal legislation regulating the marketing of medical devices. However, as one quack cure fades, it is often replaced by another.

---

[5]Lehmann, Phyllis, "Laetrile: The Fatal Cure," *FDA Consumer*, U.S. Department of Health, Education and Welfare, HEW pub. no. (FDA) 78-3061, Oct. 1977.

[6]"Laetrile: The Making of a Myth," *FDA Consumer*, U.S. Department of Health, Education and Welfare, HEW pub. no. (FDA) 77-3031, Dec. 1976-Jan. 1977.

[7]"The Mistreatment of Arthritis," *Consumer Reports* **44**(6):340, June 1979.

Arthritis cure promoters are now heavily into nutrition, even though there is no scientific evidence that any food or vitamin has any effect on the cause or cure of arthritis.[8] Various unproved remedies, balms, and irrational medications too numerous to mention are now flourishing in today's market.

In addition, questionable arthritis clinics have sprung up in various areas of the country. These are questionable because some offer diagnosis by mail, some claim to know the many causes of arthritis and rheumatism and to be able to remove them, and some even boast that they can cure almost every patient.

In addition to quackery's infiltration of the treatment of major diseases, examples of quackery can also be found in dentistry, ophthalmology, and otology. The aged are most often victims of these quacks, who exploit their need for dentures, eyeglasses, and hearing aids. The dental quack promises fast service, perfect fit, and cheap prices but in actuality has neither the education nor the motivation to understand the factors involved in diagnosing dental conditions; nor is he or she qualified to determine the proper design of dental prostheses, but will charge almost as much as a reputable dentist. Home denture repair kits also compromise the individual's chances of getting properly fitted dentures. Ill-fitting and painful dentures will likely result from dealing with an unlicensed and unqualified dental quack.

Quackery in the eye care field includes mail order eyeglasses, contact lenses that cannot be worn without damage to the eye, and food supplements guaranteed to restore sight to the blind or cure glaucoma. In addition, gimmicks such as the bait-and-switch are used to entice persons to visit a store to check out eyeglasses at greatly reduced prices. Once in the store they are convinced that their eyes are in such serious condition that they require a much more expensive pair of glasses. Many mail-order offers claim that lenses will be ground according to prescription, but this is more the exception than the rule. Likewise, a customer is not likely to get cheap sunglasses with nonglare, ground, and polished lenses.

Hearing aid sales represent another avenue of exploitation, particularly of the elderly. Presently, reputable clinical facilities can accommodate only about 10% of all persons buying hearing aids each year. This provides fertile ground for unscrupulous operators who collect anywhere from $300 to $600 for a useless hearing aid. In addition, because these hearing aids are rarely guaranteed, the customer receives no refund when the aid does not work.

Nutritional quackery in the form of vitamin and mineral supplements and so-called health foods is also flourishing . Almost every food has been promoted as curing or preventing something at one time or another. In the last few years the food faddists have concentrated their promotions on "natural"

---

[8]Ibid, p. 341.

foods, or foods without chemical additives and preservatives, which will supposedly prevent or cure arthritis and cancer. However, they do not promote the fact that prehistoric man also suffered from arthritis or that dinosaur bones have shown evidence of a type of benign tumor—and they certainly ate no preservatives or additives.

Many fad diets omit essential nutrients and encourage avoidance of proper medical care. Vitamin and mineral peddlers claim that American soil is depleted and cannot grow nutritious foods, or that chemical fertilizers and modern food processing deprive food of its nutritive value. To these people we can only say that Americans are the best fed people in the world; dietary deficiencies that used to kill many are no longer seen, except in very rare instances—and then the deficiency is apt to be minor. Any diet selected on the basis of the four food groups (meat, milk, bread and cereal, and fruit and vegetable) will provide the necessary amounts of vitamins. Vitamin supplements are not necessary for healthy persons.[9]

Today's consumers are also flooded with offers to melt away fat, gain 10 inches on their bustline in only one week, grow hair anywhere they want to in two days, or look 20 years younger in 10 minutes. With these kinds of remedies available, it is puzzling why there are still so many obese, bald, or aged persons.

## ROLE OF ADVERTISING IN HEALTH FRAUDS

Miracle cures are widely publicized in many magazines and newspapers, and the American public is constantly barraged with claims and advice on what to do for any particular ailment. Stories of miraculous medical discoveries and label claims of numerous products are all geared toward attracting the attention of as many prospective customers as possible. What many people do not realize is that legitimate cures have not been discovered for all diseases and if such cures did exist, they would neither be advertised in the back of a magazine nor boast of a secret formula. Legitimate physicians do not do business by mail order, nor do they keep scientific discoveries a secret.

The factor of human credulity, or the tendency to believe something to be true without sufficient evidence, is certainly a major factor in the success of these advertisements. Most of these advertisements are testimonials, such as "I lost twenty pounds in only seven days," or "I gained three inches on my bustline in just two weeks," or "I stopped smoking in just three days." Although testimonials are the backbone for these types of advertisements, there are also key phrases that are characteristic of quack advertisements. These include: "secret formulas," "doctor-tested," "hospital-tested," "clinically

---

[9]Robinson, Corinne, *Normal and Therapeutic Nutrition.* New York: The Macmillan Co., 1972, p. 146.

proven," "100 percent effective," "proved beyond a shadow of a doubt," "no need to suffer anymore," "instant relief," "a very simple plan," "miracle drug," "a new discovery," "studies at a leading university show . . . ," "amazing results," "revolutionary." Some advertisements even claim that the government is keeping a new remedy a secret! Advertisements that are filled with these types of statements should be disregarded, as should medical stories that appear in magazines or newspapers that feature a predominance of these kinds of advertisements.

The significant impact of false or fraudulent advertising in quackery was recognized as long ago as 1880, when Anthony Comstock stated:

> If people are deceived and robbed by advertisements in reputable papers, and the thief pays for the advertisement out of money so obtained by him, are the publishers "particeps criminis" and do not these respectable gentlemen at the head of the newspapers so advertising for the lawless plunderer, share with him in the spoils . . . ?[10]

## ENFORCING LAWS AGAINST HEALTH FRAUDS

Most of the responsibility of enforcing laws against health frauds and false advertising lies with the Food and Drug Administration, the Federal Trade Commission, and the United States Postal Service. The Federal Food, Drug, and Cosmetic Act of 1938 made it illegal to sell therapeutic devices that are dangerous or marketed with false claims. Unfortunately, devices did not need to be proved safe and effective before being allowed on the market. Not until 1976 was the Medical Device Amendment enacted, which improved the FDA's authority to require certain devices to receive approval before being marketed and to remove quack devices from the market. "Certain devices" is the key phrase in this amendment. All devices that are implanted in the body and all life-supporting devices now require premarket approval by the FDA. Devices or products promoted for weight loss, weight gain, hair growth, bust and muscle development, and the like are not apt to be either implanted in the body* or life supporting; therefore, premarket approval is still not required. The FDA may, however, ban devices that are deceptive, present a risk to health, or impair health, and products for which the manufacturer cannot substantiate claims, all without going to court. This is a major step in the elimination of quack devices and products, but because thousands are still advertised and marketed, and new ones appear regularly, it will be some time before this menace is actually eliminated. In addition, the FDA, FTC, and

---

[10]Comstock, Anthony, *Frauds Exposed.* New York: J. H. Brown, 1880.
*The exception is silicone injections for breast augmentation, but this use of silicone is now illegal.

Postal Service all have additional responsibilities other than health fraud control and only limited personnel to handle these responsibilities. Although government action against quacks must be more vigorous, we cannot expect the government to be the sole keepers of our health. Consumers must take action also by becoming informed, educated, and able to recognize the quack. This, in addition to enactment of laws, can help prevent victimization from quackery.

## RECOGNIZING THE QUACK

Just as most quack advertisements contain characteristic phrases, quacks themselves demonstrate several common behaviors. For example, they can usually be recognized by their talk of secret formulas or of a single device or system that either can cure several ailments at once or is promoted as a cure for a serious chronic disease. They will cite testimonials of supposedly satisfied customers. They promise a quick cure, usually painless or effortless, with 100% effectiveness. Blanket statements that other drugs, X-ray treatments, or surgery do more harm than good should be a dead giveaway. The quack may claim that the American Medical Association or other physicians are persecuting him or her because they are jealous or afraid of competition.

Many quacks are self-taught "health advisors" who promote their products through lectures from town to town or advertise their wares in sensational magazines or through faith healers' groups. They may give themselves impressive sounding titles, such as nutrition expert, nutrition consultant, or president of some nutrition society. Nutrition quacks will also claim that most diseases are the result of an inadequate diet and that most people are poorly nourished. They claim that everyone should use food supplements. A more subtle sign, which may be more difficult for the layman to recognize, is that quacks are more interested in their victim than in the disease or complaint; quacks cannot discuss any diseases except in superficial terms. They avoid teaching their victims anything about the ailment, but rather concentrate on discussing their treatment and all the benefits it will supposedly bring. Legitimate drugs and health products do not have to be sold in this manner, and legitimate practitioners concentrate on health teaching and healing.

In addition to recognizing the above telltale signs, a consumer can get further protection against quackery by doing the following:

- □ Adhere to prescribed medical treatments even if results are not readily recognized.
- □ Do not put any stake in testimonials. Such persons are usually not in a position to diagnose their own or anybody else's illness or to determine what, if anything, was responsible for a cure.

- □ Avoid fads of all kinds.
- □ Stick with products that have been approved for market or research.
- □ Do not believe that a single panacea will cure a wide range of illnesses.
- □ Stay away from contraptions, creams, pills, etc., promoted for weight reduction. Diet and proper exercise are the keys to weight reduction, not massagers, "effortless" exercise machines, or body wraps.
- □ Never assume that because a product is marketed and advertised that it is legitimate, safe, or effective. Be a skeptic when it comes to advertised health products.
- □ Do not participate in mail offers for eyeglasses, hearing aids, or free medical diagnosis.
- □ Before buying a hearing aid, check the product for clarity of sound. Compare noisy and quiet places. Check the cost and scrutinize the fine print of the guarantee very carefully.
- □ If confused about a particular illness and its treatment, seek additional information from several professionals such as nurses, dietitians, physical therapists, and physicians.

**Victims of quackery should:**
- □ Inform their county medical society.
- □ Contact the Food and Drug Administration at 5600 Fishers Lane, Rockville, Maryland 20852, or at district offices located throughout the country.
- □ Inform the local Post Office if the quack scheme was promoted or came through the mail.
- □ Check with the Better Business Bureau about the promoter's reputation.

## MEDICARE AND MEDICAID FRAUD

Medicare and Medicaid frauds are very big businesses that cheat the government and thus the people of the United States. Investigations have revealed fraudulent practices in just about every health-related profession. Although physicians have engaged in Medicare and Medicaid frauds, chiropractors, dentists, pharmacists, psychiatrists, podiatrists, optometrists, opticians, and those who run medical laboratories may be guilty as well. It is beyond the scope of this book to thoroughly describe the tangled web of Medicare and Medicaid frauds, but common abuses of the programs and the phenomenon of "Medicaid mills" will be described.

A Medicaid mill, which is neither a clinic nor private practice, is usually located in a rundown section of a city. Most are small offices in large buildings that have not been maintained. The interiors are drab and depressing with cramped waiting rooms and several small treatment rooms. Some are severely ill-equipped, lacking such basic equipment as thermometers and stethoscopes. The physicians who staff Medicaid mills tend to be young foreign medical graduates with no private practice. The clientele of such facilities are mainly welfare recipients. Patient visits are brief, as the trick in Medicaid mills is volume—to see as many patients as possible as quickly as possible.[11] Described below are the most common abuses in Medicaid mills.[12]

**ping-ponging** Referring patients from one practitioner to another within the facility even though there is no medical need.

**ganging** Billing for multiple services to members of the same family on the same day. The practitioner takes advantage of persons who accompany the patient to the office by treating them also even though they have no specific complaint; or the person is billed even though no treatment is given. This most commonly occurs when a woman brings her children to the clinic with her.

**upgrading** Billing for more services than were actually rendered, such as treating a patient for a minor cut but billing for suturing a deep laceration

**steering** Suggesting a particular pharmacy that the patient should do business with.

**billing for services not rendered** Adding services not rendered to a bill with legitimate billings, or sending completely falsified invoices in which the practitioner bills for patients who were never seen or for diseases that were not treated. Investigations have turned up billings for dead persons and persons in prison.

In addition to these common practices, false claims also include forging the patient's signature, soliciting signatures on invoices before the work is performed, billing for work performed by others, double and false billings by pharmacies for medications, and selling prescription drugs without a prescription. There is also the matter of kickbacks, which many fraudulent practitioners so conveniently provide to businessmen who own the buildings in which the Medicaid mill is located.

The problem of Medicare and Medicaid frauds results not only from the greed of a few in health-related professions, but also because there exists a massive amount of money and a system whereby the elderly and the economically disadvantaged are assisted with meeting their health care needs. Unfortunately, the temptation to take advantage of this system and its loopholes is all too great for many. Billing policies have made it all-too-easy for fraudulent practitioners to take more than their due. Efforts to audit hospitals, clinics, laboratories, nursing homes, and practitioners should be intensified, and special audits should be made of Medicaid mills.

## CONCLUSION

Health frauds have been around for centuries and probably will be with us for centuries more. The quack devices and the theories behind them will continue to become more involved as legitimate medical technology ad-

---

[11]*Fraud and Abuse Among Practitioners Participating in the Medicaid Program.* Special Committee on Aging, U.S. Senate, 94th Congress, Second Session, 1976.
[12]Ibid.

vances. Today no one would think of trying the Arthur Cox cancer cure or the Kaadt diabetic remedy, because we can see the fallacies behind them. But to the people who tried them years ago, the theories and propaganda explaining why they supposedly worked must have sounded reasonable enough, just as many people today believe the theories and propaganda behind our modern-day quack schemes, such as Laetrile and the many "cures" for arthritis. Presently, only a handful of quacks are brought to trial, and hundreds of others go on their devious ways to popularity and fortune. However, one big consolation is that we can protect ourselves by recognizing many characteristic behaviors that a quack generally demonstrates.

# Section III

# BUSINESS CRIME PREVENTION

# Chapter 8

# Business security

Businesses have a complex security problem in that they must be concerned with both external and internal security measures. They are vulnerable not only from the outside to robbers, burglars, vandals, and shoplifters, but also on the inside because of a major personnel problem that just about all businesses experience at one time or another—lack of integrity by employees. These factors make small and large businesses alike prone to just about any property crime imaginable.

The economic impact of crime upon business is not precisely known, and there are a few problems involved in gathering the data that would provide us with the answer. First of all, many crimes against business go unnoticed. Crimes such as employee pilferage, embezzlement, fraudulent checks, vandalism, and shoplifting are hard to detect at the time they occur and may not be noticed until much later. Secondly, even if these types of crimes are recognized, they are seldom reported to outside law enforcement agencies (with the exception of shoplifting and fraudulent checks). This may be because many businessmen do not like to admit their internal security weaknesses, or they do not realize the impact of crime upon their business. In addition, many businesses are unwilling to prosecute or take any legal action because of the time, costs, and publicity a court case might bring. They wish only to regain their merchandise or money with the least amount of trouble or effort on their part, and if reporting a crime does not serve to do this, then law enforcement authorities are not likely to be notified. Therefore, the extent of crimes against business is likely to be grossly underestimated if one relies on police reports for data.

Taking these factors into consideration, however, the impact of crime upon business, including attempts by businesses to protect themselves against it, has been estimated at an awesome $25 billion annually.[1] Other

---

[1]Bunn, Verne A., "Urban Design, Security, and Crime." Proceedings of NILECJ, Law Enforcement Assistance Administration Seminar, Small Business Security, April 12, 1972.

estimates have placed the cost of crime against businesses as high as $50 billion. The fact is that a specific dollar amount cannot be placed on the problem, but whatever the cost, it is tremendous and overwhelming.

Businesses generally refer to their losses from crime as "shrinkage" since the money lost to crime reduces profits. However, businesses rarely assume all the losses alone since at least part of the shrinkage costs are passed on to the customer in the form of higher prices. Therefore, everyone helps pay for the cost of crime to business, either directly or indirectly. It has been said that the cost of goods could be reduced 10% across the board if business shrinkage were to cease throughout the country.[2]

Crimes victimize all business, small or large, retail, wholesale, manufacturing, or service. For the purposes of distinction, small businesses are those that do less than $1 million in retail business each year or less than $5 million wholesale or employ fewer than 250 employees. Using these terms, about 95% of all businesses are small, and their impact on the economy is significant. There is no doubt that the small business suffers to a much greater extent from crime than does large business. A small business is more likely to be the victim of a much greater variety of crimes than is a large business, and it is least able to absorb the losses or afford the overhead required for extensive protective measures.

Crimes against business are usually referred to as ordinary and extraordinary crimes. Ordinary crimes include burglary, robbery, vandalism, shoplifting, employee theft, bad checks, credit card fraud, and arson. Extraordinary crimes are mainly white collar crimes and crimes perpetrated by the organized underworld such as bribery, extortion, embezzlement, security frauds, and computer-assisted crimes.

Businesses in all locations are vulnerable to many types of crimes, but depending upon the type of business, there are differences. Retail businesses, for example, are affected more by inventory shortages, mainly the result of shoplifting and employee theft, than any other type of crime. Wholesalers also suffer from inventory shortages but their losses are primarily caused by employee theft since customers are usually excluded from areas that contain the merchandise. Manufacturers suffer losses through pilferage of goods from storage racks and loading docks as well as hijackings of entire truckloads of merchandise. The service industries such as airlines, banks, brokerage firms, construction industries, and hotels and motels are victims of a variety of crimes such as hijacking, robbery, theft of security bonds, embezzlement, computer-assisted crimes, theft and vandalism of building materials,

---

[2]Cohen, Harold, *The Crime That No One Talks About*. New York: Progressive Grocer Association, 1974, p. 258.

and theft of hotel and motel equipment by both customers and employees. Common crimes against business are defined below:

**arson** The willful destruction or attempted destruction of property, real or personal, by fire.

**bribery** Giving or offering anything of material value to get a person to do something that he or she thinks is wrong or would ordinarily not do.

**burglary** The unlawful entry of a structure to commit a felony of theft.

**embezzlement** Misappropriation or misapplication of money or property entrusted to one's care, custody, or control.

**extortion** Obtaining money, material goods, or promises by threats, force, fraud, or illegal use of authority.

**fraud** Obtaining money or property by false pretenses including bad checks and confidence games.

**fraudulent checks** Theft by deception whereby an instrument is written with the intent to defraud.

**hijacking** The robbing or comandeering by force of a vehicle transporting goods.

**larceny, theft** The unlawful taking, carrying, leading, or riding away of property from the possession or constructive possession of another.

**pilferage** Theft of goods, usually in small quantities, by employees from employers.

**robbery** The taking or attempting to take anything of value from the care, custody, or control of a person or persons by force or threat of force or violence and/or putting the victim in fear.

**shoplifting** The theft by a person other than an employee of goods or merchandise exposed for sale.

**vandalism** Willful or malicious destruction, injury, disfiguration, or defacement of any public or priate property, real or personal, without consent of the owner or persons having custody or control.

The impact of the many crimes against business cannot be ignored, since losses or shrinkages of the magnitude described cannot be tolerated. Crime against business has reached such proportions that it has been recognized as a major contributing factor in some business closings and corporate bankruptcies. The business community must begin to emphasize aggressive policies and procedures that anticipate and fight criminal opportunities that are particularly common to the business world. In the remainder of the chapter, crimes common to business will be discussed further, along with specific countercrime measures.

## SHOPLIFTING

Shoplifting is a major contributor to the problem of inventory shortages, which occur when the value of the merchandise on the store's shelves is less than the book value of the inventory. Shoplifting is the most common type of ordinary crime affecting retail stores, as Table 8-1 depicts. About four million shoplifters are apprehended each year, but it is estimated that only one of

**Table 8-1.** Principal types of ordinary crime perpetrated against retail businesses

| Types | Percent |
|---|---|
| Shoplifting | 28 |
| Burglary | 23 |
| Vandalism | 20 |
| Employee theft | 13 |
| Bad checks | 13 |
| Robbery | 3 |

From *Crimes Against Small Business,* Small Business Administration, U.S. Department of Commerce, Washington, D.C.: U.S. Government Printing Office, 1976.

every thirty-five shoplifters is caught. Therefore, the estimated number of shoplifting instances is around 140 million a year. The nature of the merchandise on the shelves of a retail store has an effect on the level of inventory shortages experienced. Items that can easily be resold are major targets of shoplifters. In department stores costume and fine jewelry, watches, junior and subteen clothing are particularly hard hit as are sportswear, young men's clothing, small leather goods, cosmetics, men's casual wear, cameras, and records. Drug stores suffer high losses in cosmetics, costume jewelry, candy, drugs, toys, and records, while food stores suffer high losses from meat and cigarette thefts.

**Reasons for shoplifting**

Shoplifting occurs for a variety of reasons, including desperation, impulse, peer pressure, revenge, or (rarely) kleptomania. Persons who shoplift for these reasons are generally amateurs and represent a majority over professional shoplifters, amateurs comprising about 85% of all shoplifters.

Teenagers from middle-income families represent the largest group of shoplifters, and from these, the majority are female. Youthful shoplifters are usually under peer pressure to steal. They may enter stores in gangs after members have dared another member to steal something. Or they may just steal for the thrill of it. Sometimes they may even shoplift as a means of getting attention or as an outlet for deep-seated emotional problems. In this case shoplifting is only a symptom of more complex psychological problems with which the child needs help.

Impulse shoplifters are more likely to be first-offender housewives. They do not enter the store with the intention of stealing, but once inside succumb to the temptation of opportunities to steal. Attractive and creative displays of goods they would like to have but will not or cannot pay for provide the stimulus, or the person may think of shoplifting as a means of balancing the budget even though it is at the shopowner's expense.

Persons shoplifting out of desperation are likely to be drug or alcohol addicts, vagrants, or anyone else in dire need of money. They sell their stolen goods in order to support drug or alcohol addiction or to pay off loanshark commitments. They depend on opportunity, surprise, and speed to commit their crime, and can be very dangerous if confronted in the act.

Persons shoplifting for revenge usually have either a real or imagined grievance against the store or its employees, and choose shoplifting as the channel of getting even. In this case, before entering the store they have their mind set on stealing something and may have their crime well planned. All they require is the opportunity.

The true kleptomaniac (*kleptes*, thief) is an individual with an uncontrollable compulsion to steal. When a kleptomaniac shoplifts he or she usually does not need nor even necessarily want the items taken. Fortunately, persons with this kind of problem are rare and do not account for many instances of shoplifting.

Professional shoplifters, although comprising only 15% of the total number of shoplifters, easily match amateurs in dollar amounts of stolen merchandise. Professional shoplifters earn their living through frequent thefts. They prefer small expensive items that can be quickly resold for cash through "fences." Many professionals specialize in a particular type of store and a particular product. Their shoplifting schemes are well thought out, and their smooth and efficient techniques are difficult to spot. Under ordinary circumstances they can and do steal items right out from under the nose of store clerks without detection.

**Shoplifting methods**

Just as there are several types of shoplifters, so are there different methods used to shoplift. Familiarity with these methods is one of the best ways a shopowner can prevent potential thefts. It is best to remember, however, that the variety of shoplifting methods is limited only by the ingenuity of those who steal. Listed below are common examples of shoplifting practices:

- □ Using accessory articles such as packages, newspapers, coats, gloves, and other items carried in the hand that can aid in the concealment of stolen goods. Some shoplifters use open-bottomed boxes that they set over items to be stolen.
- □ Large purses, knitting bags, diaper bags, briefcases, paper sacks and even umbrellas are good receptacles for items that a shoplifter purposely knocks off the shelf.
- □ Wearing "shoplifting bloomers" or baggy pants tied above the knees. Shoplifters will wear the bloomers under a long skirt or full dress with an expandable waistband, drop items past the waist and into the bloomers.

- Trying on garments, placing outer garments over the stolen ones, and wearing them out of store.
- Wearing overcoats that have been altered to have pockets or hooks on the inside lining.
- Using baby carriages as a means of deception; few persons would think to look in a baby carriage for stolen property.
- Wearing a long overcoat and carrying articles between the legs. This method has been termed the "shoplifter shuffle" and is mainly used by women.
- Entering the store without jewelry or accessories, but leaving the store wearing items of this type.
- Entering the store during the winter months without a coat, but wearing one when leaving the store.
- Distracting clerks; usually a team of two or three persons in which one creates a commotion while others shoplift.
- Walking to an unattended section of the store, grabbing merchandise and hurriedly departing.
- Switching tickets of a less expensive item to a more expensive item. The shoplifter then takes the item to the cash register and knowingly underpays for it. This is mainly a trick of amateurs, but nevertheless is difficult to detect and prove.
- Thieves working in pairs concealing objects in places in the store for later pickup by an accomplice. Shoplifters have been known to hide jewelry and other small items underneath counters with chewing gum, to be picked up later by a different person.

Professional shoplifters may use any different number of methods. They make use of sophisticated schemes and often employ finesse and special devices to aid in stealing. They may pretend and convince a clerk they are looking for a very expensive gift for their spouse, thus gaining the trust of the salesclerks who believe that in a very short time they will be making a very big sale. Professional shoplifters have even been known to act as salesclerks and take customers' money.

**Shoplifter behavior**

Also important in recognizing a potential shoplifter and thus preventing loss is being able to recognize behaviors that shoplifters characteristically demonstrate. Most of these behaviors are nonverbal and can serve to alert the shopowner and employees to a possible shoplifting situation. Most are behaviors that innocent customers do not ordinarily demonstrate, but because there is always that possibility, they should only be regarded as telltale or suspicious signs rather than as definite proof of the customer's guilt. Behaviors that should cause suspicion are described below:

- Persons entering stores with heavy overcoats out of season.
- Persons wearing baggy pants, full, or pleated skirts (when current styles do not dictate the wearing of such apparel).

- Persons demonstrating darting eye movements, and who conspicuously stretch their neck in all directions. Many professional shoplifters often do not give any other clues other than eye movements.
- Persons who exit the store with undue hurriedness.
- Customers who do not seem interested in merchandise about which they have asked.
- Customers who do not seem to know what they want and change their mind frequently about merchandise.
- Individuals who leave the store with an unusual gait or who tie their shoes or pull up their socks frequently, or make any other unusual body movements that might assist them in concealing articles.
- Customers who walk behind or reach into display counters.
- A disinterested customer who waits for a friend or spouse to shop.
- Customers who constantly keep one hand in an outer coat pocket.
- Customers who make a scene to distract clerks, so that an accomplice can remove property without paying for it.

## Preventive actions for businesses

Knowing the behaviors listed above helps in recognizing a shoplifter when observing one, but more important are the practices and policies of the businesses themselves in preventing opportunities for shoplifters. This aspect of prevention includes not only practices and policies of the stores, but also measures to physically and structurally control vulnerabilities to shoplifting. This can range from placing alarms on the merchandise to properly displaying the merchandise so that it is not overly tempting to be stolen. Although even businesses with the best antishoplifting campaigns will still experience this crime, the practices described below will assist in keeping it to a minimum:

- A well-organized inventory control plan is essential to pinpoint losses. Once this can be done, extra precautions can be taken to minimize losses that previously might have been undetected, although heavy.
- All personnel, particularly sales employees, should be specially trained to recognize types of shoplifters, suspicious behavior, methods of shoplifting, as well as policies regarding the apprehension of offenders.
- Physical layouts of businesses should discourage shoplifting. Entrances and exits should be limited and merchandise near doorways, crowded aisles, and display counters that obstruct views should be avoided.
- Greetings to each customer should be given as soon as possible after they enter the store. Greetings such as "Hello," "May I help you?" or "I'll be with you in a minute," make the legitimate customer feel noticed and recognized while reminding the shoplifter that this is not the time or place to attempt a theft. Sharp-eyed, alert clerks are the shoplifter's worst enemy.
- Salespersons should never turn their back on the customer. This is an open invitation to shoplifting if the customer is so inclined.
- The business should never be left unattended.
- People loitering or wandering through the store should receive special attention from the salesclerk.

- Expensive merchandise with strong buyer appeal should be locked in a display case in a location visible by more than one employee.
- If display lock-up cases cannot be used on valuable items such as cameras, suits, leather goods, small appliances, etc., other measures can be used. These include the use of chains or plastic ties, placing these goods in highly traveled areas, hiring additional personnel, and using a roaming uniformed guard. The latter, however, may not be feasible for small businesses.
- Control of fitting rooms by a count of merchandise to and from the rooms and by the constant presence of a counting employee slows down theft of clothing.
- The store should be divided into sections and areas designated as the responsibility of certain employees. Clerks should be attentive and not easily distracted.
- A warning system should be developed so that employees can be alerted to the presence of a suspected thief.
- Employees should also know the procedures for notifying the office when they suspect a shoplifter. Walkie-talkies can be of value in this situation.
- Telephones should be placed so that employees can continue viewing the sales area when talking on the phone.
- Special attention should be given to out-of-the-way corners and doorways.
- Cash registers should not block employees' view of the store.
- A receipt for every purchase should be given and the bag stapled shut.
- Display only one-half of merchandise that comes in pairs.
- Counters and tables should be kept neatly arranged.
- Instruct cashiers to examine merchandise for torn tags and incorrect prices when making sales.
- Merchandise should be labeled with the store's name or identification number.
- Empty hangers and cartons should be removed from display racks.
- Large stores may benefit from uniformed guards and plainclothes personnel who serve to remind the customer that only "paid for" merchandise can be removed from the store.
- Convex wall mirrors can be helpful if extra personnel are not available. Store personnel can see around corners and keep several aisles under observation from one work station.
- Anti-shoplifting signs should be prominently displayed throughout the business. These serve as a warning and a deterrent.
- Many electronic devices ranging from sophisticated alarms to surveillance cameras to electronic tags can be used. Electronic tags are usually attached to expensive garments. These need to be removed with a special instrument by sales clerks before being taken out of the store; otherwise a signal is sent out.
- Prices should be put on price tags with a rubber stamp or pricing machine, rather than in pencil or ink. Also, tags should be secured to the merchandise by hard-to-break plastic string.
- If merchandise is priced by gummed labels, these should be the type that are easily torn if tampered with.
- Extra price tickets concealed in merchandise is particularly helpful in preventing ticket switches.
- Employees' working hours should be scheduled with floor coverage in mind. The store should be well staffed during its busiest periods.

- Some stores have started large-scale public education campaigns through advertising brochures and posters, radio and television talks, and school discussions. These programs serve to alert people to the seriousness of shoplifting.
- Many stores are prosecuting shoplifters to the fullest extent of the law. Many businesses may not desire to do this, but whatever is done, the problem should not be completely ignored.

## Apprehension of a shoplifter

Statutes regarding the apprehension of shoplifters may vary somewhat from state to state, but generally a merchant with probable cause is allowed to detain a person in a reasonable manner for a reasonable length of time if he or she believes merchandise has been unlawfully taken. The shopowner or employee must observe a shoplifting act and be reasonably sure that the individual with the merchandise has no intention of paying. If the shopowner or employee has not witnessed the shoplifting act, but a customer has, then the customer/witness must be willing to testify in court, or further shoplifting acts must be directly observed by the store's employees.

Most states have statutes that protect the shopowner and employees from false arrest providing any action taken was backed by probable cause. However, the safest rule to follow in this case is be certain or risk a false arrest suit. Strict guidelines should be followed by security personnel and other employees when observing a shoplifting case so that merchandise can be recovered and there is no cause for a false arrest lawsuit. The first of these guidelines is to observe the act of concealment since this implies that the individual has no intention of paying for the merchandise. The next step is to continue observation of the individual to make sure he or she does not discard the item elsewhere in the store. After the individual clearly indicates a desire to leave the store without paying for the merchandise, or has already left the store, he or she may be detained. Leaving the store clearly establishes intent not to pay for the merchandise.

Some states have laws permitting shopowners to detain shoplifters while still inside the building but it is best to apprehend shoplifters outside the store when possible. This strengthens a store's case against the shoplifter, and prevents interference with the store's operation in case the shoplifter makes a commotion. However, if there is the possibility that the individual might get away with the stolen goods if allowed to get beyond the premises, or if the stolen merchandise is particularly valuable, the shopowner may wish to detain the individual while still inside the building.

Shoplifters should always be approached courteously and salespersons should never accuse them of stealing. The individual should never be touched lest the action be construed as roughness. A tactful statement such as,

"I believe you have some merchandise on your person or in your purse that you have forgotten to pay for," is a good approach. Once the suspect is apprehended, another clerk should join the detaining clerk and the suspect in a private area of the store, and the police should be immediately called. Notes regarding the incident should be kept by the store for future reference.

Prosecuting offenders has been known to significantly deter others with the same idea, including professionals. A get-tough policy has allowed many small businesses to stay in business who otherwise might have gone bankrupt because of shoplifting losses. The days of a slap on the hands and a good strong lecture have all but disappeared from most businesses' policies regarding shoplifting. Certain guidelines should also be followed by stores when prosecuting shoplifters.

First of all, the store should reclaim everything that is stolen including price tags, wrappers, cartons, boxes, paper, etc. These items should be initialed, dated, and photographed. Written statements concerning the incident should be obtained by all parties involved. Evidence not given to police should be sealed in a container with the officer signing and dating the seal. Evidence given to police should be exchanged for a receipt of the goods turned over. Reviews of the incident should be done before any appearances in court.

The above practices should assist storeowners throughout the prosecuting ordeal, and the successful prosecution of shoplifters, accompanied by penalties of fines or imprisonment, has a strong deterrent effect upon future offenders, and thus is a major aspect in the prevention of shoplifting.

## ROBBERY

Armed robbery is, needless to say, a major and frightening problem. It has become so widespread that it threatens every city and town regardless of size or population. Retail stores are particularly susceptible to this crime. Robbery does, however, represent the smallest monetary loss to businesses when compared to losses from shoplifting, employee theft, fraudulent checks, and burglary. Unfortunately, robbery brings with it great personal danger and threats of violence; employees and even customers have been innocently victimized by this crime. Because of the violent nature of robberies, any antagonistic moves on the part of business owners and employees are contraindicated. They should fully cooperate with the robber's demands while attempting to concentrate on details of the robbery, which may aid in investigation later.

### Methods of robbery

There are several general methods of operation in use by robbers. "Walk-ins" are particularly frequent after money deliveries. The robber will walk in and confront the victim. "Hide-ins," whereby the robber hides in the building, often occur just before closing; the robber waits to approach the victim when the last customer leaves. Impersonations are also used whereby the robber identifies himself as a police officer or repairman and asks to speak to the manager. The robber will then confront the owner/manager in a closed office. Some robbers will claim they are customers wanting to make restitution on bad checks, apply for a job, or will call the manager/owner at home saying that something is wrong at the business.

### Preventive measures for robbery

Employees and owners alike, especially those handling large amounts of cash and/or high value items, should be aware of the possibility of robbery. Definite plans to be followed both before and after the robber arrives should be established and adhered to. Critical robbery prevention measures for businesses are described below:

- Keep all interior and exterior entrances, front and rear, well-lighted.
- Keep advertising and merchandise out of the windows as much as possible to avoid blocking the view of the inside of the store from the outside.
- Lock rear and lateral doors at all times.
- Check alarms to make sure they are in good working order at all times.
- Place alarm switches at more than one location. All employees should be familiar with their use and locations.
- Do not open the business before or after regular business hours unless absolutely necessary.
- Avoid routine procedures that can be observed and used to the advantage of would-be robbers.
- Notify authorities if requests are received to open the business after regular hours.
- If suspicious persons loiter around the business, notify police but do not use the alarm system to do it. Be particularly alert at opening and closing times.
- Be careful of the answers given in response to questions asked by strangers regarding the hours of operation, number of employees, or alarm systems.
- Employees working alone should leave a radio or television playing in a back room.
- When reporting for work in the morning, one employee should enter and inspect the premises.
- Keep a minimal amount of cash on the premises.
- Separate cash from checks, even when making bank deposits.
- Count cash in a private area away from public view.
- Persons acting as bank messengers should:
  Travel back and forth to the bank with someone else.
  Take irregular routes to and from the bank and go at unscheduled times.
  Discuss business only with tellers. The next person in line may be attempting to gain information about company finances and practices.
  Never approach a night depository while someone else is there; wait until they

leave. In the event suspicious appearing persons do not leave, authorities should be called so that their motives may be determined. If possible, make deposits in daylight hours.

Use armored car service if risk of robbery appears high.

☐ Do not leave money unattended in a car.

☐ Advertise good cash protection by displaying "burglar alarm" and "two key" signs at entrances. Use two-key money safes that require two people to open the door.

☐ Screen employees thoroughly.

☐ Consider the use of a robbery alarm system, such as a Buddy Alarm System, that silently signals a remote monitor during hold-ups.

☐ Place cash registers a safe distance from the door but not so far back that they cannot be viewed from the outside.

☐ Keep spare keys hidden in storerooms so that if employees are locked in these rooms by a robber the phone can be used quickly.

☐ Maintain a recorded amount of marked currency that can be held ready to be given to a robber.

☐ Consider placing a "bait pack" in the cash drawer. This is a fake bundle of bills that explode with a permanent dye and tear gas bomb within a certain number of minutes after it has been removed from the register.

☐ Practice observation with employees. Randomly ask them to describe the last customer in the store.

☐ Teach employees to be particularly careful of:

Persons shopping for prolonged periods.

Shoppers wearing hats, sunglasses, gloves, or any article of clothing that is obviously not in general conformity with the time of year or geographic location.

Customers loitering for a long period near the money room.

Questions regarding security, alarms, number of employees, hours of operation, etc.

☐ Install height markers around door frames to aid in describing a robber.

☐ Do not set off a holdup alarm for forgeries or petty crimes.

☐ If robbed, attempt to remain calm and memorize peculiarities of the robber such as tattoos or scars. Note the type of dress and weapon being used. If the robber touches anything, preserve it for evidence.

☐ Do not attempt to defend yourself with a firearm if the robber has a weapon.

☐ Activate the silent alarm if possible.

☐ Notify police as soon as possible after the robber leaves.

☐ Retain customers as witnesses.

☐ Attempt to observe the get-away vehicle and license number.

## BURGLARY

Burglars enter business premises through basements and roofs and all kinds of openings—delivery chutes, elevator shafts, air vents, side doors, rear windows, front windows, and even front doors. Some work with an inside accomplice who lets the burglar in after business hours after first disconnecting the alarm system. Business burglaries generally take place during nonworking hours, such as at night or on weekends, or occur in unattended storerooms where the offender is unlikely to meet the victim. The greatest incidence of burglary attempts are directed against businesses selling jewelry, men's and women's clothing, liquor, groceries, electrical and other appliances, furs, and drugs. Service stations are also frequent targets. Burglars, by the very nature of their crime, can be more selective in the goods they take and can usually take larger quantities than robbers or shoplifters. Therefore, business losses to burglaries are in the hundreds of millions of dollars. However, many measures to deter, to increase the burglar's risk of getting caught, and to limit the profit potential can be taken by the business community. These measures are described below.

**Burglary prevention**

There is no single way for businesses to protect themselves from the burglar. Each control and preventive device added to the operation will form an additional protective wall to increase security. In addition to basic, inexpensive, commonsense burglary prevention measures, the merchant should consider the degree of risk he or she faces and the financial practicality of expensive measures. Security measures should be tailored to each individual store for maximal effectiveness. Businesses located in high crime areas or economically depressed neighborhoods should establish maximal cost-effective security. Burglary prevention techniques businesses can take are described below:

- Illuminate the entire property at night. Do not rely on nearby municipal lighting.
- Lighting should also illuminate the roof. Lights should be wired to set off an alarm if tampering occurs.
- Lights should not shine into the eyes of passing police.
- Do not give the burglar a place to hide. Eliminate shadows, low-lying shrubbery, and rubbish.
- Utility poles should not be installed closer than forty to fifty feet from the outer perimeter of the building, if possible.
- Exterior doors should be made of steel or solid-core hardwood. Glass doors and windows should be burglar-resistant. Bars, grilles, grates, or heavy-duty wire screening provides optimal window security.
- All exterior door latches should be of the anti-shim, deadlocking type. Padlocks should be hardened steel. Door hinge pins should be on the inside of the door if not welded or pinned on the outside. Door frames should be sturdy.
- Skylights, ventilation shafts, air conditioning and heating ducts, and crawl spaces should be permanently secured by the installation of metal grilles or grates and/or protected by alarm systems.
- Exterior locks should be changed as often as necessary, for example whenever keys are lost or stolen, or employees "disappear" with them. Locks should also be installed on fuse boxes.

In addition to the many external security precautions, internal security precautions can also increase target hardening against burglaries. Internal security measures include the following:

- Establishment of a security room. This room should be void of windows with a solid door and a minimum one inch deadbolt. Door buzzers and alarms are highly recommended, as well as limiting the number of people having access to the room.
- Placing safes in well-lighted areas visible from the outside. Safes should also be bolted down to the premises.
- Combinations to safes should be changed frequently, especially upon termination or the changing of employees. Door locks should also be changed.
- Dials on combination safes should be twisted several times after closing.
- Owners should not set combinations to their birthday, address, or telephone number.
- Weapons should not be kept in safes. This may only provide an unarmed burglar with the opportunity to steal more property and possibly use it against a night watchman.
- The owner or manager should know what keys have been entrusted to whom. All keys should be stamped "Do Not Duplicate."
- Cash registers should be left empty and open after hours to prevent damage.
- Items of high value should be removed from windows at closing. Avoid high displays near windows that keep passersby from seeing in.
- Clothing stores should use the reverse hanger method to protect racks of clothing from being easily removed at once, and chains or locks should be used for more expensive items.
- Automatic cameras installed at strategic locations can do much to increase security.
- Power units to alarm systems should be concealed and protected.
- References of new employees should be thoroughly checked.
- All bathrooms, closets, and other hiding places should be thoroughly checked to prevent leaving a burglar inside.
- Stamp all checks "For Deposit Only" as soon as they are received.
- Cleaning window sills periodically will assure that fingerprints are more likely to be left by the burglar.
- Tools and portable equipment should be locked in drawers or cabinets at the end of each business day.
- Soliciting of any kind should not be allowed on business premises and signs should be posted indicating this policy.
- Personal valuables such as purses should not be left on desktops and personal cash should not be left in drawers.
- Reception rooms should always be staffed.
- Blank checks, check protector, and credit card machines should be locked in the safe at the end of each business day.

These suggestions should enable business people to successfully deter or at least delay the efforts of even the most determined burglar. Even if the burglar is successful, following many of the suggestions will decrease the profit potential. Hopefully, the burglar will decide the expected benefits are not worth the effort or risk of being apprehended, in which case the burglary has been successfully prevented. But if the overall number of successful or attempted burglaries against business is to decrease, then all businesses must take responsibility to see that as many feasible and practical precautions as possible are established.

## BAD CHECKS

Misuse of checks presents a serious problem for any business. The total cost of bad checks is estimated at nearly $1.5 billion. The average bad check is written for $30, and the cost of collecting averages $10. Fraudulent checks are everyone's problem and everyone's loss since the monetary losses are incorporated into the price of goods and services and add directly to inflation.

Seven types of checks are apt to be offered: (1) personal, (2) two-party, (3) payroll, (4) government, (5) blank, (6) counter, and (7) traveler's. Personal checks are those made out to the business and signed by the individual offering it. Two-party checks are those issued by one person to a second person, who endorses it so that it can be cashed by a third person. Payroll checks are issued to an employee for services performed. Government checks can either be issued by the federal, state, county, or local government. These checks cover salaries, tax refunds, pensions, welfare allotments, etc. Blank checks lack encoded characters and require special processing. They are no longer acceptable to most banks since they require special collection processes, which results in extra costs. A counter check is still used by a few banks and is issued to depositors when they are withdrawing funds from their accounts. A counter check is nonnegotiable, being void anywhere else. Traveler's checks with preprinted amounts are sold to travelers who do not want to carry cash. Traveler's checks should be countersigned only in the presence of the person who cashes them.

Each type of check is vulnerable to fraud. Many personal checks, for example, are returned because of insufficient funds. Frequently such checks are for amounts in excess of the purchase and the balance is received in cash. They may be postdated or prepared in pencil. Two-party checks are highly susceptible to fraud since the issuing party can stop payment at the bank. Sometimes the payee's endorsement signature is different from that on the face of the check. Payroll checks are usually printed by a checkwriting machine, and should not be accepted if handprinted, rubber-stamped, or typewritten unless company officials and employees are known personally. Government checks are subject to theft and forgery; limitations of blank checks and counter checks have previously been described. If traveler's checks are stolen, the counter-signature on each check except the top one may be carefully forged before asking a cashier to cash them. The forger signs the top check and then cups his or her hand in front of the checks; with the cashier's view blocked, the person fakes the countersignature on the balance of the checks. Another method involves countersigning a book of legitimately acquired checks, and then "accidentally" dropping them on the floor. The individual pockets these, and produces a second book of checks, which were stolen and countersigned in advance.

### Check fraud prevention

The simplest and surest method of preventing the passing of bad checks is for businesses to stop accepting checks. This, however, is not feasible because of the competitive nature of business and the importance of providing check cashing as a service to customers. Check cashing by businesses is more or less a courtesy extended by businesses to customers, but most customers do not see this as a privilege. They expect their checks to be accepted, or they will not return to a particular business. Therefore, different approaches to the solution of bad checks must be implemented. Policies that reduce the risks of accepting fraudulent checks but still make check cashing possible are described below.

- Do not accept checks without two proper forms of identification (current, instate driver's license, major credit cards, national retail credit cards, employee identification with photograph). Social Security cards, library cards, membership cards, etc., are not valid forms of identification.
- Examine checks carefully. Make sure identification forms provided compare to physical characteristics of the check casher. Compare signature on identification to that on the check.
- Do not cash checks for more than the amount of purchase, or at least limit it to a $5 or $10 minimum.
- Do not accept counter checks.
- Do not accept postdated checks.
- Do not accept two-party or payroll checks.
- Do not accept checks with alterations.
- Restrict check cashing to one specified area such as the business office or service desk.
- Require second endorsements on checks already signed.
- Set a limit on the dollar amount of checks cashed.
- Be more cautious when cashing checks numbered below 300 (lower numbered checks indicate the account has not been established very long).
- Do not accept checks over sixty days old.
- Large stores may photograph each person cashing a check along with his or her identification; film is developed only if the check is returned.
- Be alert for smudged checks, misspelled words, and poor spacing of letters or numbers.
- Advertise check cashing policies in more than one location.

- Train employees. Stress that there are to be no exceptions; alert them to methods and techniques bad check passers use, such as pretending to be in a hurry, hoping that check cashing procedures can be overlooked.
- Some businesses use employee accountability—employees who deviate from established check cashing procedures are responsible if a loss occurs.
- Alert other businesses to a bad check passer.
- Be particularly suspicious of individuals who request cashing large amounts of traveler's checks at once, since legitimate customers do not usually request this.
- Checks signed with felt-tip pens should be given careful scrutiny since it provides an easier method of forging checks.
- Legitimate checks, except for some government checks, will have at least one perforated edge. Photocopied or otherwise illegitimate checks will have all smooth edges.
- Be cautious of persons who become angry when asked for identification.
- Watch out for the "I'm an old customer" routine, and do not become misled if the check passer waves to someone, particularly another employee, during the check cashing procedure.
- Do not cash checks for intoxicated persons.
- Employees cashing the check should mark it with their initials.
- Report check law violators to proper local law enforcement authorities and follow through with prosecution. Forged government checks should be turned over to the United States Treasury.

## CREDIT CARD FRAUD

There are over 500 million credit cards in use today. Cash is becoming more obsolete as the trend in business transactions is toward the use of credit. As with check frauds, certain established policies will help reduce vulnerabilities to credit card frauds. These are described below:

- Issuers of credit cards: Take steps such as thorough application investigations, since a fair percentage of credit card frauds occur as the result of issuance of cards on the basis of false applications.
- Credit card users: Protect the card as you would cash, since 60% of losses involve cards that were lost or stolen from legitimate card holders.
- Do not accept expired cards.
- Use verification services provided by most major credit card companies before accepting any credit cards.
- Do not accept credit cards without proof of identity.
- Do not accept credit cards without signature verification.
- Make sure card imprint appears on all copies of the invoice.
- Keep cashier areas well-lighted to discourage fraudulent transactions.
- Prosecute customers or employees responsible for credit card fraud.
- Be aware of methods used by employees to accomplish credit card fraud, such as imprinting two charge slips; one for the current transaction, the other for filling out later and forging the customer's signature, or "forgetting" to return a card following a transaction.

## SECURITIES THEFT AND FRAUD

There is an alarming number of unaccounted for securities, the total value of which is in the billions. The lost, stolen, or otherwise missing security certificates are potentially available for a vast array of fraudulent uses. The majority of security thefts involve the cooperation of dishonest employees, although thefts have occurred by outsiders and well-organized rings who rob messengers and the mails. Many security theft and fraudulent schemes have been used, all seeming to keep one step ahead of many security precautions. These fraudulent tactics are described below.

- Placing certificates in envelopes and dropping them in mail chutes located on the premises.
- Certificates of one company may be stolen from the vault of one broker and substituted with a certificate of equal value from the same company but taken from the vault of another broker. The substitution is generally not detected even if the theft is discovered since auditors frequently only check the number of shares and/or certificates and compare these numbers with the amount listed on inventory records.
- Fictitious names will be given to transfer agents by house employees, thereby directing the securities into the hands of thieves.
- House burglaries may result in stolen securities.

Once securities are stolen, fraudulent schemes are put into play so that the thief or thieves can convert them to cash or valuable property. Fraudulent tactics include the following:

- Stolen certificates may be used as collateral for a loan from a foreign bank. When the loan is defaulted, the bank sells the stolen security, and the thief is long gone with the benefits of the loan.
- Buyers of certificates may direct their purchased stock to be delivered to a home address. After they receive the certificate, they tell the broker it did not arrive. The broker will usually send a replacement, and the buyer will then present the first certificate as collateral for a loan, sell the replacement, and then default on the loan.
- Same-name frauds are those in which a phony security bears a name almost identical to a legitimate company, implying that the security is from a subsidiary of that company. These securities are then tendered for sale.
- Stolen securities can be used to build up balance sheets of marginal companies so that they can qualify for loans, meet asset requirements of state regulatory agencies, or be used to establish an inflated selling price for a prospective buyer of a business. Many stolen securities are "rented" for this purpose.
- False securities have also been used to establish banks, insurance companies, and mutual funds.

Many other schemes for turning securities into cash are in existence. Efficient fencing operations by organized crime handle large quantities of stolen securities. Many securities are deposited in Swiss bank and brokerage accounts where "dirty" money is "laundered," and it is eventually funneled back into the United States and infused into the financial dealings of legitimate businesses. More detailed descriptions of fraudulent schemes can be found in the United States Government publication, *Conversion of Worthless Securities into Cash.*[3] The stolen securities themselves represent only the tip of the iceberg when one begins to examine the complex circle of conversion techniques.

### Recognizing security thefts and frauds

Recognizing thefts and frauds of this kind may depend upon noting slight irregularities of financial transactions or odd circumstances at the time a security is offered for sale. There will be no glaring discrepancies, particularly in the case of organized fencing operations. However, there may be certain tip-off signs that should alert individuals who are about to purchase securities or accept them as collateral that the securities may be stolen or phony. These are as follows:

- Securities offered as loan collateral that are not in the borrower's name; he or she may go to great lengths to explain why.
- Fake or stolen securities may be offered for private sale at greatly reduced prices.
- Previously poor credit risks may show sudden and substantial increases in securities listed as assets.
- Financial records of a company may contain highly questionable transactions.
- Phony securities may bear a name very similar to a large, legitimate company.
- Phony securities may also bear the address of a location unfamiliar to everyone but the "brokers." The address given may imply a bank, but may turn out to be a rented office building.
- Suspicion should be aroused when the number of shares on hand does not correspond to the number of shares listed on inventory records.
- The transaction may involve a numbered Swiss bank account; no name given with the account.
- The certificate may have indications of counterfeiting, such as one-color printing, muddy colors, poorly aligned borders, no "raised" feeling to corporate name, and blurred certificate numbers.

### Preventive measures for securities theft and fraud

Many securities thefts could be prevented if only buyers, whether they be banks, loan companies, or private individuals, would thoroughly search and cross-examine the authenticity of both the securities and those who tender them. All too frequently, however, this is not done, perhaps because of naive trust or greed, in which case the deal becomes too tempting and ques-

---

[3]*Conversion of Worthless Securities into Cash.* House Select Committee on Crime, Washington, D.C.: U.S. Government Printing Office, Stock no. 5271-00339, 1973.

tions that should be answered are never even asked. There is also some
protection afforded by the holder-in-due-course doctrine in which banks and
brokers are protected from claims of ownership by prior holders of securities,
as long as they were not aware of any problems associated with the security at
the time of transfer. Therefore, buyers are not obliged to check the authenticity of information provided by the sellers, even though that information may
be readily available from computerized master lists of stolen securities. Another factor that may contribute to negligence in determining the authenticity
of securities is the attitude that insurance coverage will replace theft and
fraud losses.

An attitude of skepticism should be maintained when purchasing securities, particularly those involving off-shore firms and little-known domestic
companies whose assets consist mainly of securities. In addition, financial
institutions and brokerage firms need to establish accountability and to
adhere to security-oriented procedures for handling and storage of securities.
Accountability will enable those directly and indirectly involved in securities
losses to be identified. Inventory counts should be compared with the number of shares on hand and also the identification number on each certificate.
Inventory checks should be both routine and on a random basis.

Lending institutions should reject loan applications in which securities
not in the name of the intended borrower have been put up as collateral.
Legitimate owners of securities should never keep them at home where they
could be stolen during a burglary. Safe-deposit boxes should be used and the
certificate numbers, denominations, and issuers should be recorded and kept
in a different but safe place.

## BANKRUPTCY FRAUDS

Bankruptcy frauds refer to the illegal practice of "planned" bankruptcies
in which an individual purchases large amounts of merchandise on credit
from many businesses, converts the goods to cash, conceals the cash, and then
claims bankruptcy when creditors appear to collect. Organized crime may be
involved in such a scheme in addition to confidence artists and previously
legitimate businessmen desperately attempting to get out of debt. Losses
resulting from bankruptcy fraud run close to $80 million annually and such
fraud is the sole reason many small struggling firms go out of business. Trust is
usually built up between the individual and the businesses he or she intends
to defraud by: (1) placing small orders and paying for them in cash, (2) de-
positing a moderate sum of money in an account to help obtain credit, and (3)
slowly increasing the amount of merchandise ordered while correspondingly
paying a smaller amount down. The individual then places even larger orders, sells the merchandise at discount prices, conceals the proceeds, closes

the bank account, and either disappears or claims bankruptcy. There may be many variations to the above steps, but that is basically what must take place in a bankruptcy fraud.

## Recognizing bankruptcy frauds

Like so many other types of frauds, the signs of bankruptcy frauds may be relatively discreet, but the ability to recognize them may be the only salvation for many businesses. Listed below are possible warning signs.

- Unusual or different types of merchandise ordered in increasing quantities by a customer.
- The customer's balance increases.
- Payments are increasingly smaller and may be in the form of IOU's or post-dated checks.
- Customers who had previously rejected buying opportunities are now placing substantial orders.
- Customers have past criminal records.
- Credit references cannot be located or do not materialize.

The above behaviors should arouse suspicion but by no means is the list conclusive of a customer's intent to commit bankruptcy fraud. Increased protection against bankruptcy fraud should be provided, however, by alerting the businesses to the need for further investigations of questionable situations or practices by the customer.

### Preventive measures for bankruptcy fraud

- Assign credit limits. Delay shipments of merchandise when a customer exceeds the limits.
- Establish credit rating checking procedures and do not bypass them even for rush orders.
- Instruct sales personnel concerning bankruptcy fraud schemes and indicators of impending frauds.
- Be cautious and exercise skepticism of easy sales, particularly of goods unrelated to the customer's usual orders.
- Investigate thoroughly changes in management of credit customers.

## INSURANCE FRAUD

Insurance frauds often involve the participation of organized crime, in addition to the claimants themselves, doctors, lawyers, corrupt law enforcement authorities, and insurance agents. All persons involved in the scheme divide the awards, with the largest amount usually going to the lawyers. Although the primary loss of insurance frauds is borne by the insurer, these frauds also indirectly affect policy-holders whose premiums increase, employers who pay sick leave benefits, and businesses or homeowners on whose premises the fraudulent scheme was staged. Phony insurance claims usually request payment for such things as doctor and hospital costs, automobile repairs, lost work time, and compensation for "injuries."

As stated previously, a successful insurance fraud requires collusion of many persons. With the collusion of a corrupt attorney, for example, a phony accident claimant is able to secure an inflated automobile repair estimate from a dishonest body shop, phony medical bills from corrupt physicians, and fraudulent lost-time-from-work statements. Indications of collusion obviously are not readily apparent, but as with most other frauds, there may be subtle hints. These include:

- Use of lawyer-physician combinations suspected of previous insurance frauds.
- Treatment of the "victim" at a hospital operated by the physician.
- All "victims" being treated by the same doctor.
- The physician will not honor requests to itemize bills.
- The "victim" seems to want an expedient settlement, perhaps claiming he or she has to go on a trip and would like things cleared before leaving.
- Attempts by attorneys to bribe insurance adjustors.
- Signatures on claim forms appear slightly different indicating possible forgery.
- Claimants seeming to have unusual awareness of the claim adjustment process.

**Preventing insurance fraud**

In the case of insurance fraud, one should guard against being pressured into a hasty settlement. Before any action is taken or anything is signed, the claimant should be able to fully document his or her case. There should be a sound, independent medical evaluation of all alleged injuries. Insurance companies should also check on the claimant's claim history to determine if there have been excessive claims and what physician and lawyer handled them.

**ARSON**

The incidence of arson, the willful and malicious burning of property, has increased dramatically in the last decade. It is a billion dollar crime just in property damage alone. Indeterminable costs in the form of death and injury to innocent citizens and firefighters, increased insurance premiums, loss of jobs at burned-out factories and businesses, loss of taxes to communities where businesses were destroyed, property tax increases to support increased police and fire department activities, and lost revenue to damaged stores and shops also result from arson. In terms of these combined losses, arson becomes one of the costliest crimes in America.

There are various motives for arson. In addition to the pyromaniac or juvenile who gets a thrill out of watching things burn, some arsonists are normally law-abiding citizens who are in financial trouble and see fire as a quick solution to their problems. Many financially insolvent businessmen will turn to arson as a means of avoiding bankruptcy. In some cases, the owner no longer wants the business and cannot sell it, wishes to liquidate the business quickly or dissolve a partnership, wishes to rid the business of obsolete stock, has a desire to move the business to a new location, or reacts to poor business conditions in general through arson.

Sometimes the motive for arson is revenge. Disgruntled employees have been known to "settle the score" with their employers by setting a fire. Destruction of a business has also occurred as a result of labor troubles, as a way to conceal embezzlement or burglary, or as an example of intimidation of the business owner by organized crime forces.

In addition to understanding the motives behind arson, there is still a pressing need to comprehend other behavioral characteristics of the firesetter. A recent study by the Center for Fire Research at the Commerce Department's National Bureau of Standards revealed some common characteristics of arsonists. Adult arsonists, for example, were found to have several maladaptive behavior patterns relating to social ineffectiveness, such as drinking, marital, occupational, and sexual problems, as well as other criminal and antisocial behaviors. Juvenile firesetters typically demonstrated a number of problems such as stealing, hyperactivity, truancy, and aggression.[4]

**Progress in arson prevention**

In the past arson was classified by the Federal Bureau of Investigation as a crime against property rather than a violent crime. That classification ranked arson with "lesser" crimes such as petty larceny, fraud, embezzlement, and vandalism, which meant that the investigation of arson received low priority, thus inhibiting prosecution and funding for training personnel. The seriousness of arson has now been recognized, not only because of the expensive nature of the crime but also because of the serious physical threat to citizens. Consequently, it is now classified as a class one felony, or crime of violence, which brings its classification in line with the actual severity of the problem. The new classification points out that an arsonist causes a threat to life when burning any sort of structure, because more than just property is at stake. The threat to life occurs not only if people live or work in the structure but also if there is reason to believe that people frequent the structure for whatever reason.

The new classification has resulted in increased effectiveness in arson investigation and prosecution, which is an essential factor in prevention. As more investigators are trained and stronger evidence for prosecution is pro-

---

[4]"Study Examines What Makes Arsonists Tick." *Security Management*, Vol. 23, No. 9, Sept., 1979, p. 84.

vided, there will undoubtedly be more convictions. Convictions for arson should be publicized as a warning to potential arsonists, so that the notion that arson is still an easy crime to get away with will be dispelled.

In addition to legislative changes, many federal agencies such as the Law Enforcement Assistance Administration (LEAA), the United States Fire Administration, the Federal Bureau of Investigation, and the Bureau of Alcohol, Tobacco, and Firearms are extensively involved in establishing arson prevention programs. Millions of dollars in LEAA funds have been earmarked to assist state and local efforts to reduce deaths, injury, and economic losses from arson, and to upgrade the collection and analysis of information about the incidence and control of arson. LEAA has also funded community-based anti-arson campaigns in several major cities that conducted public education programs in arson prevention and programs to help change conditions known to contribute to the incidence of arson. Research is also being sponsored by the National Institute of Law Enforcement and Criminal Justice to determine the most effective response to the growing arson threat. In addition to this, guidelines for public safety agencies on existing arson legislation, investigative techniques and evaluations of existing antiarson programs are published.

Local law enforcement agencies must cooperate with local fire departments to combat arson effectively. Few firemen are experienced enough in gathering and preserving evidence to meet court standards. Police, on the other hand, are not often experienced in determining the cause and origin of fires and to recognize circumstances requiring thorough investigations. Therefore, some cities have combined fire and police services to form arson squads. The arson squad firemen check the fire cause and origin and point out evidence that might be helpful. Police photograph, mark, and take possession of the evidence for later possible trial use. This combined effort has paid off in terms of adequate investigation and successful prosecution. Those investigating arson cases should receive proper training through seminars and workshops. This training should also extend to firemen and police who are at the scene of the fire so that they can recognize possible indications of arson that would be important to investigators. Local public safety agencies should also foster public awareness of the extent and problem of arson. Crime prevention or public safety displays should include arson as a means of facilitating this awareness.

Arson prevention is not just a task for governmental or local law enforcement agencies to handle. Individual citizens and business organizations must also assist these efforts by taking steps to prevent arson in their own neighborhoods. Individual efforts should include the following:

   □ Eliminate fuel that juveniles and arsonists with psychologic problems use, such as readily available papers, leaves, and other rubbish. By cleaning these up, it becomes more difficult for the arsonist to simply walk by and start a fire.

- □ Secure all windows and doors to keep the arsonist from entering the building.
- □ Increase fire warning and alarm systems, contract for security guard services if threatened by arsonists, and request increased police patrol during the night.
- □ Be alert. Report suspicious activities in the neighborhood to law enforcement agencies. Participate in and help organize antiarson community programs.

## LABOR RACKETEERING

Labor racketeering is a form of extortion resulting in threats of violence or damage to businesses if certain demands of the racketeer are not met. Local unions may be infiltrated or otherwise adversely influenced, usually through the effective control of organized crime. Many forms of labor racketeering require the assistance of dishonest employees. Huge union welfare and pension funds provide the main inducement for racketeers to penetrate labor organizations.

Racketeers gain control of unions through many methods. They may promise the employer good labor relations in return for cash payments or other goods or services for their own personal gain. Other methods include forcing companies to hire unnecessary personnel such as a relative of the racketeer or an organized crime family member; picketing other businesses who buy merchandise from the threatened business until they no longer place orders; instigating work slow-downs; providing loans from union pension funds to financially troubled employers in return for kickbacks and personal favors. "Sweetheart contracts" may be devised in which workers obtain far fewer benefits than they could through legitimate negotiations, but the racketeer receives a fee from the employer, or the employer permits gambling, loansharking, or pilferage on the premises. Employees, on the other hand, usually do not realize they belong to a union until the contract is signed and dues payments begin.

Once in control of a union, racketeers take advantage of their powers in a number of ways. They may, for example, invest pension fund money in the stock market, hire fellow racketeers at exorbitant salaries to administer "welfare" programs for union memberships, borrow welfare funds with no real definite plans of repaying the money, or loan money from the fund in return for kickbacks.

Signs of labor racketeering are usually difficult to detect and the responsibility of such usually falls upon corporate officials occupied with other company duties. This is why familiarization with racketeering schemes becomes all the more important in its prevention. In addition to these schemes, other early warning signs that may indicate the approach of a racketeer include:

- □ Occurrence of wildcat strikes with increasing frequency.
- □ Sudden change of power within a union without apparent cause.
- □ Hints made by union representatives to deal with particular suppliers.

- Employee salaries that are well below those of competitive firms in the same general area.
- Representatives of unions who have past arrest and/or conviction records.
- Union representatives who consistently delay discussion of their background and experience.
- Union officials who demand hiring of certain persons, especially when a position does not need to be filled.
- Businesses threatened with labor disputes if they continue to trade with another specified business.
- Increased frequency of gambling and loansharking.

In addition to these signs, a business owner can turn to several different sources to check the background of a union official. Prosecutors may or may not come forth with their knowledge of a particular union official, but often they can refer the employer to other sources, such as magazine or newpaper articles or files such as the Waterfront Commission of New York Harbor, which contains thousands of names of persons associated with labor officials connected with organized crime.

Because of the nature of this type of crime, businesses should not attempt to combat it alone. Various sources of governmental assistance beyond the local level, such as the Federal Bureau of Investigation, the Department of Justice, and the nearest United States Attorney, are available and should be immediately consulted if racketeering is suspected. These agencies will then decide which local investigative agencies, if any, should become involved. Methods of contact can vary from anonymous letters explaining the difficulty (this method should be used if businessmen or their families are likely to be in danger) to open explanations of full details of the situation. Requests for assistance can be relayed via professional associations, thereby relieving the business of some of the worries.

Many racketeers have succeeded in complete takeovers of legitimate businesses. They may purchase businesses using untaxed profits from various illegal activities, but many businesses are turned over to racketeers and organized crime through coercion. Many times a business owner is forced to turn over the business as repayment of gambling debts or loanshark financing, or because of other unfair business practices.

Several practices exercised by businesses can ward off approaches by racketeers. These include:

- Keeping abreast of the internal affairs of the local union through newspaper accounts or publications of the union.
- Demonstrating enlightened personnel policies and encouraging rapport between management and staff.
- Prohibiting the offering of gratuities to union offiicials.
- Becoming thoroughly aware of the legal limitations of unions.
- Encouraging pooling of resources of several businesses to fight crime.

### Cooperative action among businesses

Businesses can play a major role in the prevention of racketeering, takeovers, and many other organized crimes by uniting together in prevention efforts. Businesses can work together in establishing working relationships with law enforcement, developing organized crime departments, and obtaining information about known racketeers and racketeer organizations, plus monitoring activities of organized crime in other industries. The cost and responsibilities would be divided among all participating businesses and therefore should be affordable to small enterprises. Businessmen who have knowledge of organized crimes such as loansharking or corruption of officials would then be better prepared and more willing to come forward with this knowledge to appropriate authorities. Prevention also involves participation of business with community anticrime action groups, encouragement of news media to expose and publicize organized crime, and education of the general public regarding the implications of organized crime.

### GAMBLING

Gambling is a crime that can affect businesses both directly or indirectly in many ways. The economic impact of gambling on companies where it occurs is not good. The crime adversely affects businesses in several ways. First of all, employees who gamble are likely to be inefficient at least part of the time. They may be more concerned about the latest sporting news than their job performance. They are prone to waste time gabbing about odds with other employees or wandering around searching for the plant bet collector. Second, employees who lose (and they all do eventually) become worried, inattentive, and tense as debts mount. When an employee becomes unable to pay debts, he or she may turn to a loanshark, which, more often than not, compounds the problems. Intense pressure from a loanshark may result in stealing or embezzling goods from the company. Off-premises gambling by key personnel can also lead to these consequences.

Perhaps the most common form of in-plant gambling is bookmaking—the solicitation and acceptance of bets on the outcome of sports events. There are also lotteries where bettors pick a number and winners are determined by drawings or by coinciding numbers appearing in financial sections of many newspapers. Indications of in-plant gambling include the following:

- Routine appearance of nonemployees on the premises.
- Regular use of the telephone at the same time each day by the same employees.
- Paychecks of several employees endorsed over to one person.
- Complaints by spouses that employees' wages have declined or that all the salary is not being brought home.
- Regular visits by an employee to departments not connected with his or her job.

□ Apparent central location in the plant where employees casually visit at different times during the day.
□ Employees regularly requesting salary advances.

## Preventing gambling

Gambling, so very often under the thumb of organized crime, is difficult to prevent or to stop once it has started. Recognizing the above signs and acting upon them may be beneficial. Employees who regularly request salary advances or whose spouses call to complain of salary decreases, for example, may benefit from financial counseling. Some firms also have credit unions that make available low-interest, short-term loans, or are able to refer the employee to alternate financial resources other than loansharking. In addition, other preventive measures include: prohibiting regular visits of a non-employee into the plant, observing and taking disciplinary actions on employees who regularly make visits to other departments not required by their job, limiting outside phone calls to bona fide emergencies, limiting use of pay telephones to visitors, being cognizant of changes in employee behavior such as tenseness, inattentiveness, or other signs of inefficiency or stress, discharging and prosecuting employees caught taking bets, and, very importantly, screening employees carefully to prevent the planting of an organized crime bookie within the business.

## LOANSHARKING

Gambling and loansharking often go hand in hand. Loansharking, the lending of money at an exorbitant rate of interest, is a very lucrative activity for the underworld. This activity affects businesses in many ways. Gambling debts, as already discussed, often pressure employees into loansharking, and they may subsequently steal merchandise from the company, give away corporate secrets, leave stock doors unlocked, or hire racketeers in order to repay the loanshark. Many times business owners themselves are financially pressured to meet the payroll, for example, and will desperately turn to loansharks for assistance. They may end up turning the business partially or completely over to organized crime. In some cases the owner does not realize the loan was obtained through loansharks, having naively made the deal through a third party.

Signs of loansharking, like many other threats of organized crime, are not easy to detect. In fact, a major factor in detection is the willingness of corporate leaders to entertain the idea that it might exist. Indications that point to the possibility of loansharking include: excessive moonlighting by employees, more frequent requests for salary advances, and endorsing of paychecks over to one person. Gambling on the premises increases the likelihood that loansharking exists. Other indications include lenders who offer loans without credit references, interest rates for loans that are substantially above the legal maximum, and evidence of employee beatings either on or off the premises.

### Prevention of loansharking

☐ Small businesses should plan ahead financially to minimize chances of being pressured into requesting loanshark assistance during emergencies.
☐ Businesses should also maintain strict budgeting procedures including a cash flow projection.
☐ Loanshark opportunities are reduced by eliminating in-house gambling.
☐ Employees should be encouraged to bring personal financial problems to management. Employees should be provided with alternate sources of loans.
☐ Educational programs for employees dealing with money management, symptoms of loansharking, and the dangerous situations that can arise from loansharking should be provided.

## EMPLOYEE THEFT

Employee theft is one of the most serious crime problems affecting businesses. Employee pilferage results in huge inventory shortages. In many businesses this problem is much worse than the problem of shoplifting, even though some companies may not be ready to admit that employee theft exists within their own organizations. Businessmen mistakenly assume that most inventory losses are caused by shoplifters, when actually employees account for the major portion of inventory shrinkage.[5] Results of a recent large-scale study of employee theft by researchers at the University of Minnesota revealed that about one-half of the workers interviewed admitted to stealing from their employers.[6] The researchers surveyed almost 5,000 employees of thirty-five retail organizations, hospitals, and manufacturing companies and found that most of the employee thieves were young, white, unmarried, professional or skilled workers. The thefts rarely involved money, but most often consisted of material goods thought of as fringe benefits. Sixty percent of the employees of retail businesses admitted stealing at least once a year, mainly by misusing their discount cards to buy merchandise for friends and relatives. The second most common incidence of employee theft was taking merchandise home. Approximately 45% of hospital employees stated they stole at least once during the year, taking such things as thermometers, toilet tissue, and bandages. Younger employees and nurses dissatisfied with their career and financial status were most likely to steal, as were technologists who had ac-

[5]*The Cost of Crimes Against Business*, Small Business Administration, U.S. Department of Commerce, Washington, D.C.: Government Printing Office, Jan. 1976, p. V.
[6]"Employee Theft Hits Home." *Law Enforcement News*, Vol. 20, No. 19, Nov. 12, 1979, p. 5.

cess to supplies. About 40% of the employees of manufacturing firms admitted to stealing, usually taking small quantities of raw materials used in manufacturing products. Engineers, particularly those considering a job change, were the worst offenders, but technical workers and computer specialists at the professional and administrative levels were also frequent offenders.

Estimates that further dramatize the extent of employee theft credit this particular crime with causing 75% to 80% of inventory shrinkage while shoplifting accounts for the remainder. In addition, it is estimated that in discount stores, for every dollar lost to shoplifters, three are lost to employees, while other businesses estimate dollar losses to employee pilferage to be seven times greater than shoplifting. Therefore, even though Table 8-1 indicates shoplifting as the most common type of ordinary crime against retail businesses, many other businesses, such as wholesale and manufacturing firms, will have greater problems with employee theft. However, some retail businesses also experience more internal than external losses. Studies that make use of employee interviews rather than police records for data are apt to be more accurate since crimes of employee theft are not reported to outside authorities nearly as often as they occur. The apprehension of shoplifters outnumbers those of employees by ten to one, even though the dollar losses are greater from employee pilferage.

Employee theft presents a great challenge for law enforcement, in-house security programs, and the shopowner. Fortunately, in most businesses, the majority of employees are honest, and for those who may be potentially dishonest, a significant number will have no opportunity for theft. There will, however, be dishonest employees who do have the opportunity and will take advantage of it. In the following pages, methods used by employees to accomplish theft and methods that can be used to combat employee theft are described.

### Methods of employee theft
- Passage of merchandise across counters to accomplices.
- Hiding merchandise on one's person or in a handbag, and taking it out of the store at lunch break or at the end of the shift.
- Underringing the cash register as a favor to friends or relatives.
- Overcharging customers and pocketing the extra money later on.
- Switching tickets for "special" customers, giving them substantial markdowns.
- Pilferage of merchandise through unsupervised doors.
- Failing to register sales and taking money after the customer leaves.
- Writing false refunds and taking cash.
- Collusion with deliverymen and drivers.
- Stealing from the warehouse with the cooperation of warehouse employees.
- Stealing from the stockroom by concealing goods.
- Stealing from returned goods and layaway.

☐ Ringing up "No Sale" on the register, voiding the sales check after the customer has left, and pocketing the money.

☐ Cashing fraudulent checks for accomplices.

☐ Giving fraudulent refunds to accomplices.

☐ Failing to record returned purchases and stealing an equal amount of cash.

☐ Falsifying sales records to take cash.

☐ Concealing thefts by falsifying the store's records and books.

☐ Taking money from cash registers assigned to other employees.

☐ Giving employee discounts to friends.

☐ Concealing stolen goods in trash or other containers to get them out of the store with supervised exits.

☐ Shipping clerks mailing goods to their own address or post office box.

☐ Wearing store clothing and accessories home at the end of the shift.

☐ Intentionally damaging goods in order to buy them at discount prices.

☐ Buying damaged merchandise at discount prices then later substituting damaged goods for first-quality merchandise.

☐ Stealing checks made payable to cash.

☐ Picking up receipts discarded by customers, putting them with stolen goods, and later returning them for cash refunds.

☐ Stealing during early or late store hours.

☐ Stealing from the dock or other exit areas.

☐ Writing phony bottle returns.

☐ Manipulating computers (to be discussed more extensively in the next section).

☐ Duplicating keys and entering the business during closed hours.

☐ Forging checks and destroying them when returned by the bank.

☐ Keeping collections made on what were believed to be "uncollectable" accounts.

☐ Receiving kickbacks from suppliers for invoicing goods above the established price.

As can be seen from the above list, there are any number of ways in which internal theft can take place. Any employee with larceny on his mind could probably think of additional methods not yet recognized by those who wish to prevent internal theft. All the dishonest employee needs is the opportunity and motive, which, as previously mentioned, may result from such things as grievances or indebtedness. Therefore, the approach to internal theft has four major aspects: (1) reducing opportunities for theft, (2) providing job satisfaction, (3) establishing employee accountability, and (4) screening personnel before hiring in an attempt to differentiate employees who would be considered low risk from those considered high risk. All of these facets of prevention are very important and are discussed in greater detail in the following pages.

## Reducing opportunities

Many different policies and practices can be instituted that will reduce the basic temptation for theft or, if theft occurs, will help minimize losses and pinpoint the culprit.

- Restrict all employees to a single exit if possible.
- Change locks when custodial or other personnel change.
- Do not permit employees to make sales to themselves.
- Require all employee purchases to be checked in the package room.
- Perform spot checks of employees who arrive early or stay late when there is no need to do so.
- Allow only authorized employees to set prices and mark merchandise.
- Make unannounced spot checks to be sure actual prices agree with authorized prices.
- Price items by machine or stamp, not by hand and definitely not in pencil.
- When giving refunds, match items to the return receipts and then return the merchandise back into stock as quickly as possible.
- Number refunds and keep control over refund books.
- Have returned merchandise inspected by someone other than the person who made the sale.
- Make frequent inspections to make sure refund policies are being followed.
- Do not give sales employees free access to storerooms; storerooms should be kept locked.
- Give everyone an identification card.
- Control access to restricted areas to eliminate unauthorized passage.
- Consider guard services to patrol main entrances and parking lots.
- Make frequent spot checks at delivery platforms and loading docks to see if packages have correct shipping labels.
- Check and recheck all merchandise received at docks to make sure the merchandise paid for is there and to detect collusion between purchasing and delivery personnel, or inaccuracy of receiving personnel.
- Prohibit direct commissions or the acceptance of gratuities, no matter how small, by purchasing agents from vendors.
- When purchasing new or unusual merchandise, require a second person to approve the order.
- Require both invoice and receiving documents to be attached together before payment for the goods is made.
- Verify count and condition of merchandise before it is moved to the selling area.
- Prohibit employees from parking within fifty feet of the receiving door and keep this area free from visual obstruction.
- Check perimeter security such as fences, gates, lights, etc., regularly.
- Have a secondary check by a worker or salesperson on all incoming shipments.
- Flatten all trash cartons and boxes and spot check trash containers.
- Centralize purchasing operations so that there can be better supervision of control procedures.
- Use prenumbered order forms with copies of executed purchase orders filed in both the accounts payable department and the receiving department. In this way, it is unlikely that an order could be destroyed; if it were, it could not be done without causing suspicion.
- Keep receiving doors locked when not in use. They should not raise even a few inches when locked.
- A supervisor should remain in the area until the door is locked.

- □ Survey the warehouse platform during lunch break periods and at shift changes.
- □ Develop strong audit controls, and inventory all supplies, equipment, and merchandise regularly.
- □ If the value of the goods warrants it, additional security of the stockroom and receiving docks can be provided by closed circuit television cameras.
- □ Solicit bids from several vendors and rotate purchases from vendor to vendor periodically.
- □ Use locked display cases for high value, concealable items; the manager should be responsible for the key.
- □ Limit the amount of cash allowed to accumulate in the register; surprise cash counts on registers should be made.
- □ Limit one employee to each register drawer, but the employee should not be allowed to do the final total on his or her own cash register. Totals on cash registers should not be known to employees.
- □ Require the giving of register receipts to each customer.
- □ Undertake spot surveillance to detect underrings and items not charged by the sales clerk.
- □ Establish policies on "No Sale" register openings.
- □ Bond employees.
- □ Deposit cash receipts daily.
- □ Make all payments by prenumbered check, countersigned by the manager.
- □ Examine cancelled checks for authenticity.
- □ Stamp incoming checks for deposit before turning them over to the bookkeeper.
- □ Managers should personally audit the bank accounts each month, comparing all cash receipts with deposits shown on the bank statement.
- □ Managers should receive and open all incoming mail the first few days of each month, and someone other than the cash receivable bookkeeper should open it the rest of the time.
- □ Do not make bookkeepers responsible for shipping and receiving merchandise.
- □ Managers should review old list of receivables monthly and compare the total with accounts receivable control account.
- □ Investigate inventory shortages, even small ones, immediately. If employee thefts are discovered and can be documented, follow through with prosecution. If it is known beforehand that a firm will not prosecute a thief, the deterrence value of fear of arrest and conviction is lost. Even dismissal is not adequate punishment since it allows the dishonest employee to move from one company to the next.
- □ Apply security controls to all employees, with management setting good examples in honesty.
- □ Require that all employees take periodic vacations.

## Providing job satisfaction

Since grievances against employers are a major cause of employee theft, providing job satisfaction can be as important (or more important for some small businesses) as reducing opportunities for theft through rigid policies. Job satisfaction prevents the development of real or imagined grievances against the employer and thus removes a primary motivation for internal theft. Employee theft is a serious form of employee deviance. It may begin gradually, as when the employee cheats the employer out of a little time, does sloppy work, or commits minor acts of vandalism. As job dissatisfaction mounts and hostility toward the employer builds, the likely outcome is retaliation through theft.

Employee morale is a major factor in employee pilferage. Businesses have noted a decrease in losses when morale is up and vice versa. Employee morale, or lack of it, depends on several factors such as wages, privileges for management and staff, working relationship of supervisors, and channels of communication between staff and administration. Employees who perceive the company as not caring about them or their problems are likely to have lessened loyalty for that company, and will be less likely to resist the temptation to steal if the opportunity arises.

Wages that are not competitive for the same or similar jobs in the general area also play a major role in the practice of employee theft. The employee may see his or her behavior as making up for low wages, poor fringe benefits, or as a means of giving oneself a deserved raise. In other words, if employees feel they are not getting paid what they are worth, they may make up the difference themselves.

Privileges for administration and staff should also be comparable as far as job description will permit. If management personnel are allowed to use company cars, supplies, tools, etc., for personal use, then all employees should receive the same benefit. Disciplinary measures should also be fair with regard to management and staff, and when losses are experienced, the shopowner should never rule out the possibility of management employees, as well as staff, as being the possible offenders. Administrative employees also experience grievances and personal problems that may lead them to thievery.

Also important in preventing the build-up of grievances is the relationship between supervisors and staff. Supervisors should be competent and capable of exercising good judgment when relating to employees, and workers should feel free to come to them to discuss work-related and personal problems. Many large companies now have programs to help prevent and assist employees with problems such as alcoholism, financial indebtedness, marital discord, etc. Other channels of communication that allow employees to bring forth grievances are company newspapers, bulletin boards, and suggestion boxes.

Honesty can be inspired by supervisors if they do not practice favoritism or "overlook" losses. Even minor losses should be treated with concern. If the employees feel that the management has a liberal write-off policy for losses caused by pilferage, pilferage is likely to increase. Shrinkage control should be embedded in everyone's mind, even when losses drop. Owners and supervisors alike should set good examples and high standards for performance. Employees tend to copy behaviors of the superiors, and if an employee sees a supervisor in a dishonest act, he or she will be encouraged in the same direction.

Personnel policies should be realistic enough so that employees can meet the expectations of management. Putting employees in positions for which they are not capable or qualified to handle may only cause them to lie or cheat about their job performance. Employees should receive written job descriptions so that job responsibilities are clearly delineated. If employees are capable of handling the responsibilities of their position and know what is expected of them and others, job satisfaction should be promoted. Also important is having proper materials, supplies, manpower, etc., for the employees to do their job correctly. Morale is bound to decrease if employees are expected to do the amount of work that twice as many employees should rightfully do, or if they do not have the right equipment because the employer has skimped on supplies.

Finally, a good performance should be recognized and rewarded. An occasional pat on the back plus competitive merit raises provides the incentive for a job well done. On the other hand, an honest, hardworking employee will soon become discouraged if he or she receives the same recognition, salary, and respect as those who do less work and whose loyalty to the company is questionable.

Fair employee policies that foster job satisfaction will probably not reform employees determined to steal, but fair policies and a company that demonstrates concern for the welfare of the employee will certainly reduce the temptation for borderline employees who otherwise may have been headed toward deviancy. Companies with enlightened personnel policies still experiencing a pilferage problem should first scrutinize other areas such as opportunities for theft and employee screening procedures for the cause. In some cases there may be a small group of hard-core employee thieves taking advantage of security loopholes.

A third method of reducing employee theft is to establish employee accountability. This concept of holding employees directly responsible for the performance of their job is not new, but Carson has broadened the scope of the concept to include security accountability.[7] Accountability in this sense is

---

[7]Carson, Charles R., *Managing Employee Honesty.* Los Angeles: Security World Publishing, 1977, p. 91.

not concerned primarily with petty thefts that are limited to the size of an employee's lunch box or pocket, but with preventing large-scale thefts that have commercial value to employees. In thefts of this kind the goods are not used for personal use, but are sold for profit, thus what the employee gains is cash. Employees involved in large-scale thefts usually will not see or touch what they steal, but accomplish their crime through the manipulation or falsification of records. Therefore, in order for an established security program to deter crimes of this nature, a new dimension of responsibility must be added. First, the security program should begin with a detailed security survey of the company. This establishes points where opportunities and profit combine to tempt an employee to steal. Second, security should oversee the verification of all records, requisitions, invoices, and other order forms. Prenumbered forms should be used that require the signauture of the person preparing the form. Checking and rechecking of all business forms by security helps assure continuity of numerical files and discourages discrepancies between purchasing and receiving. This system should help maintain relatively honest employees and foster the accountability concept throughout other departments within the company. Another source of temptation should be removed through accountability since an employee's job performance will be frequently checked by the security department. Most employees will recognize the risk of detection when strict accountability procedures are utilized.

The fourth aspect of preventing employee theft deals with the practice of selective hiring so that potentially dishonest employees are not hired in the first place. A single hiring mistake could be financially devastating for some businesses. No matter how desperately a business needs to hire new employees, screening or hiring practices should never be relaxed. Although no one approach to business security is totally effective in itself, employee screening can be a more practical and effective approach for many businesses than sophisticated and elaborate security programs. Small businesses, for example, that cannot afford even a small-scale security program must rely heavily upon hiring honest employees, as must banks and other financial institutions who entrust large sums of cash to their employees. In addition, employees committed to thievery have been known to go out of their way to see if they can outwit ingenious and sophisticated security equipment. Therefore, the possibility of being detected or the crime being made more difficult to commit by security programs does not always act as a deterrent. Even harsh punishment for such crimes is not an effective deterrent since the majority of employee thieves are not caught and, therefore, do not expect to get punished. The end result of selective hiring should, however, include a more qualified staff, who have integrity and are honest and who deserve respect from management. This in turn lessens the possibility of internal theft resulting from hard-core employee thieves, and employees likely to deviate because of unreasonable grievances. Good screening procedures are therefore essential to a sound internal security program.

The most common ways to screen employees are background investigations, polygraph tests, and psychologic examinations designed to measure various personality characteristics, including tendencies toward delinquency. Screening procedures used should be based on the nature of the business, its resources for carrying out the procedures, and the security needs of the business. Banks, for example, should require more in-depth and extensive screening procedures than a department store specializing in low cost merchandise.

Background checks are the most widely used screening procedures, but they do have limitations. They are vulnerable to incorrect information, often are incomplete, and cannot identify individuals who may have committed previous crimes that have gone undetected. In addition, many factors regarding background investigations have come under close legal scrutiny in the last few years. Since 1973, the Equal Employment Opportunity Commission (EEOC) has jurisdiction over employers of fifteen or more individuals, as a result of Title VII of the Employment Opportunity Act. Describing the authorities of the Equal Employment Opportunity Commission in preventing job discrimination is beyond the scope of this book and the frequency with which regulations change makes it impractical to include them in a textbook. The most important purpose of Title VII, however, is to prevent discrimination in hiring or selecting applicants on the basis of race, color, religion, age, sex, or national origin. It should be the responsibility of at least one member of the personnel department or the owner/manager to be aware of minor regulation changes as they are issued from the EEOC. Most of the regulations do not hamper attempts by employers to determine the relative honesty of potential employees, but there are some exceptions and guidelines that must be followed. For example, an employer cannot refuse to hire someone solely because of arrest records. The individual must have been convicted within a recent period of time so that there is reasonable certainty that the applicant is still dishonest.

The main tool of the background investigation is the employment application. Information regarding the applicant's race, color, religion, sex, or national origin may not be obtained in compliance with the regulations of the Equal Employment Opportunity Act. Statistical information that may be obtained includes such things as the applicant's full name, address, phone number, date of birth, Social Security number, marital status, number of dependents, and number of income tax deductions desired. There may be additional statistical data required by state and local regulations. All applicants should receive the same statistical data worksheet and should complete this information before completing a separate job-related application. The application should explain the reasons for the required information and also warn the applicant that false statements are grounds for not hiring or for dismissal should the individual be hired. The data received from the statistical part of the application are enough to permit checks with local credit and criminal files and also can be checked against the company's former employee file of persons not recommended for rehiring.

Job related applications should vary for each job classification, but they should also ask the applicant for his or her full name, date of birth, Social Security number, and date of application. These answers should match identically with information given previously on the statistical information form. The remainder of the application should be concerned with specific information related to the applicant's qualifications for the position. In addition, the company should have the resources to verify the responses to the information requested. Honesty and qualifications for the job should be the two most important considerations in choosing an applicant for employment; therefore, information given on the employment form should be verified. However, most employers will accept answers about places and dates of previous employment without checking and, according to Carson,[8] these are the two things most often falsified on applications.

Therefore, an employer cannot rely on the individual's statements as being true and correct without having checked them out. Evidence indicating that an applicant has been dishonest or that the applicant is not qualified must be well documented, since the burden of proof that there was no discrimination against the applicant rests with the employer.

The application should have a place for the applicant's signature, certifying that the person has read the instructions, understands them, and has truthfully answered them to the best of his or her ability. Any other conditions of employment, such as examinations, special licenses, or passing a polygraph test, should also be included so that the applicant's signature indicates agreement to these contingencies as special requirements for employment.

Verification of information given on the application can come from several different sources. Telephone directories, credit files, voter registration records, driver's licenses, and Social Security cards can verify basic statistical information. Information given about credit ratings is being increasingly restricted, and a decision not to hire an applicant on the basis of a poor credit rating should be supported with written statements from the credit source or substantiated by evidence from other sources. Serious indications of financial instability, which could lead to employee dishonesty, include a history of

---

[8]Carson, op. cit., p. 106.

declared bankruptcies, defaults, and repossessions. Financial strains of this type may induce an employee to steal from the employer as a means of getting additional income, or could force the employee to take a second job, which could cause decreased proficiency in the first job.

In addition to basic statistical information and credit checks, work experience should be verified. The applicant's type and length of employment should preferably be verified by personal contact with former employers. Written requests for this type of information may be answered by a standard reply from the personnel department that would not reveal other pertinent or sensitive information. All nonwork intervals, as well as the circumstances under which the applicant left a former job, should be fully explained.

Verification of information provided regarding criminal records should first be accomplished through local law enforcement agencies. If an arrest record is uncovered, it is not grounds to refuse hiring, unless convictions followed the arrests. However, recent arrests may still be tied up in judicial proceedings and therefore may still result in conviction.

Ideally, background investigations should be carried out by the company's security personnel. Smaller businesses that do not have a security team can obtain assistance from local law enforcement agencies and private investigative firms. This may seem like a costly and time-consuming chore, but it will be more costly to replace what a dishonest employee might steal, to readvertise, and train a new employee for the position. Therefore, shortcuts should not be taken in this most crucial assessment of employee honesty.

Polygraph examinations are also used with a fair amount of frequency and have proved to be highly valid and reliable when properly administered and interpreted. Their use, however, is also coming under legal constraint, being ruled unconstitutional in eleven states. In addition, they are fairly expensive and somewhat impractical for a majority of small businesses to utilize, since the cost ranges from $20 to $100 per applicant, depending on the number of questions asked. Applicants for high-temptation positions, however, should be given a polygraph test since it represents the best index of current honesty levels. The applicant, by signing the application, agrees to the passing of the test as a requirement for employment, if such a condition is stated on the application form. Polygraph tests, where legally permitted, must be given uniformly to all acceptable job candidates for a particular job classification. The questions asked must be related to the job applied for, and all subjects must be asked the same questions. Some companies give employees regular polygraph tests as a deterrent, but the applicant should be aware of this policy as a further condition of employment beforehand.

The polygraph indicates conscious truth or falsehood. Questions asked the applicant should serve to determine if he or she has stolen anything within a given period of time, the value of anything stolen, whether the theft was from an employer, and whether the applicant intends to steal again if hired. Because of past misuse of the polygraph, such as the asking of unethical or non–job-related questions, its use in pre-employment testing has been severely restricted. A company planning to establish a polygraph testing program should first be thoroughly familiar with local, state, and federal regulations regarding its use.

A third aspect of employee screening involves the use of psychologic tests in an attempt to measure relative honesty. Several personality tests, such as the Minnesota Multiphasic Personality Inventory, Rorschach, the Glueck Prediction Table, and the Kvaraceus Delinquency Scale and Checklist, have been used for this purpose , even though tests such as these are designed to be a tool for broad personality assessment rather than specifically predicting proneness to delinquency. They have, however, predicted delinquency with a certain amount of success, while at the same time disguising the intent of the test.

There is one test, developed by John E. Reid, that does not disguise the intent of the test and is specifically designed to predict employee theft. This test is known as the Reid Report and consists of a three-part questionnaire. The first part is comprised of yes-or-no answers that reveal attitudes toward crime and punishment. Example questions include, "Are there special cases where a person has a right to steal from an employer?" "Did you ever think about committing a burglary?" The second section asks the applicant to provide biographical data concerning education, employment, and financial history, medical history, indebtedness, and any police contacts. The third section asks questions about the applicant's past thefts and financial insolvencies, such as frequently writing checks knowing there were not enough funds to cover them, or filing false insurance claims for personal gain. The validity and reliability of such a test would seem to be highly questionable since all one would have to do to get an acceptable score is to fake the answers. However, test results of the Reid Report have shown high correlations with results of polygraph tests, indicating that it is highly valid and reliable. This is thought to be partially because of the attitudes and perceptions of reality of dishonest persons. In other words, persons who have committed thefts seem to think that everyone else has also, and their responses are reflections of what they consider to be norms for theft behavior.

The Reid Report is not intended to eliminate applicants from employment, but is widely used by retail stores, trucking firms, vendors, and other businesses for the purpose of selective placement.

The ramifications resulting from employee theft are great but many approaches to this complex problem can be taken. There is no longer any doubt that internal security of all businesses must be increased. A minority of hard-core employees stealing on a regular basis, coupled with the occasional employee thief, equals huge dollar losses for employers. Fortunately, most employees are honest most of the time or dollar losses would be infinitely higher. Reducing tempting opportunities to commit theft, providing job satisfaction, establishing accountability, and screening employees are all successful methods for substantially strengthening internal security. Many security precautions involve more efficient use of existing personnel, changes in routines, or alterations of physical structures; the cost of such measures is minimal. Other security measures, such as guard services, electronic security equipment, and polygraph and psychological tests, will be expenditures for which businesses will need to measure the cost against expected benefits. One guard, for example, can be a substantial expense, particularly for a small company, but depending on the business' security weaknesses and needs, he can more than earn his salary by deterring pilferage of merchandise through exits or patrolling employee parking lots or supervising loading and unloading docks.

## EMBEZZLEMENT

Embezzlement results in the loss of cash, securities, tools, spare parts, raw materials, scrap, machinery, office supplies, and just about anything else of value that does not belong to the person taking it. It is a form of employee theft or dishonesty since embezzlers fraudulently appropriate money or property that has been entrusted to them for their own use or benefit. The embezzler is in a position of trust, which makes it possible to take a great deal of money before he or she is even suspected of embezzling. The typical embezzler considers himself cunning, clever, and smart enough to outwit the owner or manager. Therefore, it is essential that owners and managers alike become familiar with the methods that are so often used against them. Discussed below are common schemes or methods used by embezzlers.

### Methods of embezzlement

Perhaps the very simplest embezzling scheme involves the taking of cash for personal use without making a record of the transaction. This can occur when no entries in accounts receivable are required and a cash sale is made. Many other fairly simple techniques, such as underringing the cash register or overcharging customers and pocketing the difference, giving unauthorized discounts to friends and relatives, and using company property such as cars for personal use, are also examples of embezzlement. Embezzlement also includes the following:

- Pocketing unclaimed wages.
- Making phony advances to employees.

- Manipulating time cards.
- Overloading expense accounts.
- Altering cash sales tickets after giving the customer his or her copy.
- Pocketing funds from delinquent accounts and informing the owner or manager the debt was uncollectable.
- Forging company checks and then destroying the cancelled check after it is returned from the bank.
- Keeping ex-employees on the payroll and pocketing their checks.
- Using company personnel or equipment to provide personal services, such as using company copying machines, postage stamps, secretarial or maintenance personnel for home use.

In addition to these fairly simple embezzlement techniques, Moran has described more complicated schemes that may start with small amounts of money but can run into thousands of dollars before they are detected.[9] One of these schemes is known as "lapping." This involves the temporary withholding of receipts—usually payments on accounts receivable. This is accomplished by an employee who receives cash or checks, either by mail or in person, as payments on accounts. The embezzler holds out a portion or all of a payment, and to avoid arousing suspicion, covers the amount taken from the first customer by taking an equal amount from another customer's account, who has made a payment a few days later. The money taken from the second customer's account is sent to be credited to the first customer's account, while, in the meantime, the embezzler has temporarily but successfully covered his transgressions, even though the cash deficit has doubled, since two accounts have been altered. This "borrowing" procedure continues, generally leading to the involvement of larger amounts of money and more accounts. An embezzlement of this nature requires detailed recordkeeping by the embezzler so that he or she can keep track of shortages and the transfers that need to be made to avoid suspicion. This scheme can even become more complicated if the embezzler has access to accounts receivable and statements, since he or she is in a position to alter statements mailed to customers.

Another complicated embezzlement scheme is known as check-kiting. The embezzler in this case must be in a position to write checks and make deposits in two or more bank accounts. The check-kiter takes advantage of the time period between the time that a check is deposited and the time that funds are collected. There are usually at least three business days from the time a check is drawn on one bank, clears, and is deposited in another. The embezzler, therefore, can deposit money drawn from one bank into a second bank. A day later, he cashes a check payable to cash which is equal to the

---

[9]Moran, Christopher J., *Preventing Embezzlement.* Small Business Administration, Small Marketers Aids, no. 151, Oct. 1977, p. 3.

original deposit, and draws the money from the second bank. The original check will not be presented by the second bank to the first bank for payment for two more days, so the check-kiter will deposit a larger check in the first bank, but the check will be drawn from the second bank. The larger deposit ensures payment of the original check and also increases the amount of the kite. The scheme is repeated and as the checks become larger, more cash is withdrawn. The embezzler sometimes manages to cover the shortage and the process stops, or it is stopped by one of the banks when they refuse to honor a kited check.

Embezzlers are not the dregs of society. They have decent jobs, and often, to the envy of others, are considered very respectable, law-abiding citizens. In general, however, the embezzler is in some type of financial bind—living above his or her means, accumulating debts, maybe having gambling or alcohol problems. Often a person will be pressured by others to steal. Once the pattern of stealing develops, it will usually continue while the embezzler tries to rationalize the crime. There is no "typical" embezzler; in many cases the culprits are young female staff workers who cannot make ends meet, but the embezzler may also be the company president or vice president or a member of the board of directors.

Even though embezzlement has been found to be committed by all types of employees, and is committed by males and females alike, there are certain behaviors that are characteristic of those who may be embezzling or who are prone to commit this type of crime. Although in no way are these characteristic behaviors conclusive of one's guilt of embezzlement, they should serve as a warning or to arouse suspicion of superiors that something may be amiss. Of course, it should be mentioned that great care should be taken to document illegal practices, as with any crime, so that innocent employees are not wrongfully accused. Many problems affecting businesses such as declining profits and sales are legitimate and cannot be projected upon employees. However, recognizing signs and symptoms of embezzlement is crucial to detection and can in some cases prevent embezzlement or at least minimize losses. Therefore, an employee demonstrating any of the following behaviors, particularly in combination over an extended period of time, should be investigated, since these are possible danger signals of embezzlement.

- Placing personal checks or IOU's in petty cash funds.
- Rewriting records, allegedly for reasons of neatness.
- Borrowing small amounts of money from co-workers.
- Requesting others to hold checks or writing postdated checks.
- The appearance of collectors and creditors at the company.
- Persuading others in authority to accept IOU's for short-term loans.
- Constant criticizing of others in an effort to divert suspicion.

□ Demonstrating defensiveness at reasonable investigative questions.
□ Gambling in any form, if losses are such that an employee could not legitimately cover them.
□ Excessive drinking and association with disreputable persons.
□ Buying expensive automobiles, new clothes, or even a new house that would appear to be beyond the means of the employee's salary.
□ Rationalizing expensive possessions or maintenance of a high standard of living as being possible because of money left from an estate.
□ Constantly volunteering to work overtime.
□ Refusing to take vacations or lunch breaks for fear of detection during absences.
□ Large numbers of customer complaints about errors in statements that can be pinpointed to one employee.
□ Inability or negligence in keeping company records up to date.
□ Keeping detailed records of company transactions for personal use.

## Preventing embezzlement

All incidences of embezzlement cannot be prevented but a business should not operate as though none of them can. There are many counter-embezzlement measures that deter this crime altogether or make detection easier should the embezzler decide to take the risk. Preventing or detecting embezzlement is no easy task but neither is it impossible. A routine audit of a company's financial dealings will not uncover the clever embezzler. More thorough audits, such as an investigative operations audit by outside accounting firms, can act as deterrents. Accounting systems that provide monthly statements of the business's financial status is also effective in that unusual or unexplained month-to-month variations can pinpoint losses to a particular department and, many times, to a particular employee.

In addition to outside auditing systems (which should be used at least once a year) many other measures can be taken. These are described below:

□ Establish an attitude of accountability. Hold employees accountable for their actions.
□ Separate duties of employees. No one person should handle a transaction from beginning to end. Persons who receive payments should never be responsible for also entering the payments in the accounts receivable records.
□ Exercise tight control over invoices, receipts, purchase orders, checks, etc.
□ Require cosigning and cross-checking of all such documents by persons from different departments. If one person can write checks it is an open invitation to embezzlement. The cosigner should be a supervisory level person in a related but different department.
□ Do not approve any payments without sufficient documentation or if they have been hurriedly requested.
□ Perform thorough background checks of all employees. Get to know them well enough to be able to perceive financial or other personal problems.

- Check additions to payroll. Additions should be approved by someone in authority and the personnel department.
- Company mail should be opened by the owner or manager. Many companies have their mail, including bank statements, sent to a post office box rather than the place of business to prevent its being opened by dishonest employees.
- All checks and cash received through the mail should be recorded.
- Daily comparisons of deposits made by employees and records of cash and checks received should be made by the manager and/or owner.
- If daily bank deposits are made by other employees, spot checks should be performed to ensure compliance with company policies.
- Owners and managers should personally reconcile bank statements with company books and records and should carefully examine the authenticity of cancelled checks.
- Employees in high-risk positions should be bonded, but employers should be fully aware of the limitations of bonding and should not relax security precautions on this basis.
- Keep supplies of blank checks locked and delegate authority of who may use the key.

Corporate or outside legal counsel should be sought when an embezzlement scheme is suspected. As stated previously, the responsibility of providing accurate documentation rests with the employer, and appropriate legal steps must be followed so that innocent employees are not implicated. As with most other types of criminal activity, no single precautionary measure will be totally effective. Detecting and preventing embezzlement requires awareness of suspicious behaviors, knowledge of appropriate internal controls, and general business security precautions.

## COMPUTER CRIMES

Computer crimes may be considered just another variation of employee theft, and rightly so, since those having access to computers are generally employees. But the significance and scope of this newest white collar crime is so broad that it deserves separate consideration. Computers can be used as tools to commit embezzlement, blackmail, and many other types of frauds. Today, because of computers, many businesses are more vulnerable to white collar crime than they ever have been before. Computers are widely used by banks, public utilities, credit and financial companies, and governmental agencies, to mention only a few. The increasing use of computers has caused a parallel rise in the number of persons who work with them. This, along with their complicated operating procedures, makes their use nearly impossible to check by supervisors and business owners who may have only a slight knowledge of how they work.

Computers are also attractive to a potential thief in that they are rarely associated with physical violence, thus a crime can be accomplished without contact with another person; it also is a method of stealing money or goods without directly removing them from the warehouse or a cash register. The monetary gain is also usually much greater than in many blue collar crimes or crimes requiring hand-to-hand contact with the goods. In addition, there is a certain intellectual stimulation involved with trying to exploit a machine for one's own personal gain.

### Types of computer crimes

The many types of computer crimes fall into two broad categories: (1) vandalism and sabotage, and (2) theft, fraud, and embezzlement.[10] The first category of computer crimes is mainly a result of disgruntled employees who take out revenge against their employer through vandalism of the computer. In some cases a politically motivated employee will sabotage computer equipment and tapes. Some politically motivated attacks against computers occurred during the Vietnam War at colleges and universities and at chemical companies manufacturing products for use in the war. Some attacks result in erasure of tapes while others result in actual damage to the computer itself, but both cost businesses huge sums of money. In one instance, a small business went bankrupt after an unhappy employee programmed the company's computer to destroy all accounts receivable six months after he quit his job. This left no record of who owed the company money, thus no money could be collected. Unfortunately, employees without the expertise to manipulate records can also do great harm. No special knowledge of its functions is necessary to vandalize or sabotage a computer, since just about any household tool can damage or destroy vital information or disable the computer itself.

To make matters worse, most computer criminals have no prior criminal record and as a result often end up with light sentences. Many corporations do not even prosecute computer criminals for fear of generating unfavorable publicity. Banks, for example, are often concerned that depositors will lose confidence if they learn of the vulnerability of computers to crime. Some computer criminals are merely reprimanded. Others are fired but are not forced to make restitution. Even when prosecution has followed the discovery of computer crimes, prior to 1978 existing statutes were not prepared to specifically deal with them. In spite of long-term prison sentences and heavy fines now awaiting the convicted computer criminal, computers are still highly vulnerable to misuse or abuse in many ways.

The second broad category of computer crime involves criminal acts such as theft, fraud, and embezzlement. There can be many different kinds of theft, such as theft of data or information, theft of services, theft of property, and financial theft. Theft of data often occurs in the case of industrial espionage so

---

[10]*Crime and Justice.* Washington, D.C.: Congressional Quarterly, Inc., 1978, p. 49.

that one company can gain a competitive edge over another. Espionage becomes a threat when another company feels it can turn the stolen information into a profit of some kind. Theft of services often occurs when several companies make use of the same computer. This creates temptation for a dishonest computer employee to attach his or her own computer terminal to the line and join the group. In addition, the transmission lines can be tapped and the electronic communications of other businesses can be recorded.

Property thefts via computer may run into the millions of dollars, since large amounts of merchandise can be transferred into another account without anyone ever touching the goods. Financial theft can occur in various ways. A common method has been the "round down" technique, which is used in systems that handle large amounts of financial transactions or accounts. Most computers carry out arithmetic transactions to as many as eight decimal places so there are always units of currency smaller than a penny left over. These figures are infinitesimally small but the constant rounding down of thousands of figures adds up quickly. Usually the round down remainders are distributed among all the accounts in a bank, but the computer program can be altered so that the fragments are deposited into a separate account. The money then can be withdrawn, and the thief goes on his way.

Computers have also served as vehicles for blackmail or ransoms. Corporate secrets and even personal information have been obtained through the use of computers. The perpetrators then threaten to reveal this information unless ransom demands are met. Personal information such as poor college transcripts or history of mental breakdowns, criminal convictions, etc., could prove very damaging to persons acquiring prestigious careers within a corporation.

Perhaps the most common and most costly computer-assisted crime involves fraud and embezzlement. A huge fraudulent computer operation was uncovered in 1973 in which the now defunct Equity Funding Corporation of America established approximately 56,000 phony life insurance policies and sold them to other insurance companies. The total value of the fraudulent policies was estimated at $2.1 billion. This incident represents the largest computer-related financial fraud, but many other fraudulent schemes have resulted in losses of millions of dollars. Governmental agencies as well as private business are victims of computer-assisted crimes. Many instances of embezzlement occur when employees, having knowledge of their company's computers, transfer money from customer accounts into their own accounts.

### Profile of a computer criminal

The computer criminal could be almost anyone. New employees and long-time employees alike (and total strangers in the case of a politically motivated sabotage) could all be likely suspects. However, Parker has developed a list of attributes that are "typical" of computer criminals.[11] According to Parker, a computer criminal is likely to be a male between the ages of eighteen and thirty, employed in a position of trust. He has unique skills for data processing, has never demonstrated deviant employee behavior before (and probably never will again), and takes a great deal of care to avoid harming people. Overall the computer criminal's behavior does not deviate much from that of associates.

## Methods of computer crime

Operation of computers can be broken down into five main parts: (1) input, (2) programming, (3) central process, (4) output, and (5) communications. Because each of these five areas is prone to certain kinds of crime, vulnerabilities occur in many different ways.

Input refers to the information fed into the computer. The input process is prone to criminal activity in that false information can be fed into the computer and/or the computer's records can be altered by the removal of important information. Many fraudulent crimes have taken place when false data, such as phony accounts, for example, have been introduced in the input phase.

Programming refers to the detailed instructions given to the computer by the programmer. Banks and other financial institutions have experienced many incidences of computer program tampering, whereby employees with access to the computer have instructed it to take money from one set of accounts and transfer it to others. The round-down scheme also involves the manipulation of computer programs.

The central processing unit of a computer is, in effect, the computer's brain or memory bank where processing of information takes place. What the computer processes is based on the instructions of the program. During this phase the computer is vulnerable to such things as wiretapping and electromagnetic pickups. In other words, the secrets of corporate data or personal information are subject to being stolen during this phase and can then be sold to rival companies, held for ransom, or used for blackmail. It also affords the culprit the opportunity to set up sophisticated programs without planning and writing them.

Output refers to the processed information provided by the computer and may consist of secret information, mailing lists, or payroll checks. Material of this nature is obviously very valuable and is, therefore, subject to theft.

Communications involve the transfer of output information from computer to computer. This is generally done by telephone or teleprinter. During

---

[11]Parker, Donn B., *Crime By Computer*. New York: Charles Scribner and Sons, 1976, p. 12.

this phase, the output data are subject to electronic interception and can be either altered or stolen. The transference of large sums of money between banks via computer is now standard practice for many banks, but unfortunately, the money is still vulnerable to theft just as it would be vulnerable to robbery if it were hand-carried in a briefcase.

## Computer security

Since computers are vulnerable in various ways to criminal activity, a variety of security precautions are necessary. The number and sophistication of protective measures to counteract computer abuse depends on several factors, such as the type of computer system, the sensitivity of the data, the principal purpose of the computer, and the reliability of the users. International Business Machines, the leading manufacturer of computers, has recommended four measures to curb computer abuse.[12] These are: (1) rigid physical security, (2) new identification procedures for keyboard operators, (3) new internal auditing procedures to keep a more complete record of each computer transaction, and (4) cryptographic symbols to scramble information. Leibholz and Wilson state that important considerations of computer security should include: (1) preparing for disasters, including the use of backups, (2) controls and audits to make sure operations are being done according to established procedures, and (3) mechanisms and procedures to minimize loss, recover operations, and catch perpetrators in the event that the first two measures do not work.[13]

**Physical security.** Physical security should begin with a modern computing facility, preferably located in an area that is neither too busy nor too isolated. The building should be as fireproof and floodproof as possible and have two sources of power and automatic backup controls. Separate facilities for computer operations offer two advantages. First, control of access is easier and, second, there is less possibility of water and/or fire damage in the event an adjacent structure would be affected. Additional physical security considerations involving construction of the facility include the use of fire-resistant materials, securely protected windows, artificial ventilation, grilled duct systems, and two separate exits, one for personnel and the other for supplies.

Protection also includes the use and placement of alarms, access controls, perimeter lighting, and surveillance. Alarms should be placed at all exits, including emergency exits, with light panels at the security station. Alarms should also sound if the tape and disk library is opened for any reason during

---

[12]*Crime and Justice*, op. cit., p. 57.
[13]Leibholz, Stephen W., and Wilson, Louis D., *User's Guide to Computer Crime*. Radnor, Pa.: Chilton Books, 1974, p. 55.

nonworking hours. Access can also be controlled partially with the use of alarms, since they signal in the event of intrusion. Locks are also essential in access control. The computer room itself should have a single locked door, available to authorized personnel only. In addition, maintenance personnel should be allowed in only under the supervision of the manager, and company officials and other visitors requesting access to a computer room should be clearly identified and never left alone for even a short time. The identity and purpose of each visitor to the high security area should be logged. They should not be allowed into the computer room with overcoats, briefcases, packages, or other accessories at any time for any reason. Access to computer facilities should be on a need-to-know basis.

Lighting is another very important physical security measure. It should be bright, leaving no dark spots or shadows. In addition, the lighting system should not depend on any one source of power and should be arranged so that failure of one light does not leave that area totally dark. Fences are also security assets but should be at least eight feet high and topped with three strands of barbed wire.

Surveillance is also an important aspect of physical security. There are several methods of surveillance including eavesdropping and observing with the naked eye, but perhaps the term surveillance most commonly presents an image of electronic devices, mainly closed circuit television cameras, described in greater detail in Chapter 11. Other methods of surveillance include the use of one-way mirrors and long-range photography.

**Protection against unauthorized use of computers.** Identification measures for computer users have been in use for many years and do provide a fair degree of protection. Many identification measures available today go beyond the machine-readable cards or badges by which terminal operators can identify themselves to the system. Relatively new devices have been marketed that allow terminal users to identify themselves to the computer by recognition of fingerprints or hand dimensions. Devices and procedures are also available to limit a valid terminal user's access to certain files only and/or to allow him or her to read certain files but not to alter them. Less sophisticated but still effective identification procedures are the use of passwords and individual security codes. Lockwords also protect a user's file from being read by others, but to maintain their effectiveness they must be changed periodically. In addition, terminal users could be required to indicate when they will return to active status, or to program the computer to disconnect terminals after a specified period of inactivity by the terminal user. Any unsuccessful attempts to gain entry during these time periods could be recorded and should be considered the work of probable impersonators. Many security packages have also been developed that severely restrict access of users and can also produce access history of activity against protected information. This provides auditors with a long-awaited method for trailing illegal entry attempts. It also provides some degree of deterrence since actual computer abuse does not usually take place with the first attempted entry; therefore, security managers are alerted in time to investigate the incident and notify the master terminal operator before a second attempt is made.

Auditing operations are an essential component of an early warning system for the detection of potential frauds. Audits may be performed by an internal group, by an outside organization, or both. The auditors should be combination accountants-programmers and computer analysts. Audits should be scheduled at appropriate intervals, but on a random basis. Auditors should evaluate internal controls of the computer system and make recommendations, if any, on the basis of the effectiveness of the controls, and whether or not they conform to company policies. Many tricks of the trade are available to auditors and each company may have varied responsibilities assigned to in-house auditors. It should be mentioned that although auditors perform a very useful function to the company, their presence as a security precaution cannot stand alone since, in many cases, auditors come on the scene after the crime has been committed.

In addition to large-scale auditing procedures, periodic inventories should be made of all tapes, disk files, programs, and supporting documents. Strict accountability for responsibility and maintenance of the tape and disk library should be established. All documents sent to the computer room for input processing should be accounted for, and all important forms, such as payroll checks, should be prenumbered in sequence. Errors, unexplained stoppages, or interruptions and consequent actions taken should be logged. Documentation of programs should include written records of all changes, reasons, dates, and authorizations. Transactions that are listed as exceptions should be investigated and resolved promptly.

Cryptographics, the process of converting conventionally coded data into another coded form, is a reliable security measure since it serves to make sensitive information more secure. There are several encryption variations that serve to instruct the computer how to encode and decode data on a particular system. Drawbacks to encryption processes involve cost. Initial investments of encryption hardware require substantial amounts of money as well as expensive daily operating costs.

Computer security is a complex operation and cannot be used to its fullest potential through a single method or program. Security must involve a combination of locks, files, alarms, lights, identification measures, audits, cryptographics, and personal involvement. Security is a function of the care demonstrated by individuals involved in all phases of counter–computer abuse measures. A password, for example, written down where others can see it compromises any security system. Even the most complex security system can be broken by the dishonesty of someone involved in the security itself. In addition, the future of computer security for many businesses is at stake since the cost of security may be prohibitive. There may eventually be legislation requiring some sort of security package, but at this time some businesses have minimal security because the cost of a good security program may exceed possible losses from an actual computer crime. And since a foolproof method of protecting computers does not exist, a company may be victimized anyway. Unfortunately, this attitude will only add to the continuing increase in computer-assisted crimes, and the fact that computers cannot be protected completely is no excuse not to make them more difficult to penetrate.

## INDUSTRIAL ESPIONAGE

Estimates of losses to United States industry caused by industrial espionage run as high as $7 billion a year. Anything a company has that could be of benefit to a competitor is subject to industrial espionage. Many incidences of espionage occur through computer crimes, as discussed in the preceding section. Dishonest employees have sold entire programs to other companies in attempts to quiet a blackmailer, to repay a loanshark, or to prove unyielding loyalty to a former employer. However, all incidences of espionage do not require the use of a computer, nor do they require brilliant and sophisticated thinking. Industrial espionage has occurred through such simple means as going through office trash. In most large corporations, a variety of information can be found in executives' wastebaskets. A spy checking through the contents for only a few days can learn a lot about corporate as well as personal business. Therefore, in preventing industrial espionage, it is important to consider both simple and sophisticated techniques used by the perpetrators. First of all, the corporation should have a good, solid security program established. Measures to prevent employee theft, robbery, burglary, and computer crimes outlined previously will also aid in preventing valuable information from being stolen. Stringent office security is essential, as well as utilizing previously identified measures for safe or vault security.

Company policies for safeguarding valuable or secret information should be well established, and spot checks should be done to make sure employees are following the set regulations. Obsolete and incorrect data should be shredded, as should the contents of wastepaper baskets. Employees having access to secret information should be thoroughly screened before hiring and all previous employment verified. Competitive companies are not above planting new employees in a rival company as a means of obtaining data. Employees should also be subjected to periodic polygraph tests if feasible and if working in high security risk positions. In addition to these measures, frequent checks for monitoring devices both at the office and executives' homes should be performed.

## TRANSPORT SECURITY

The economic loss from transportation crimes is estimated between $2 and $3 billion annually. It imposes serious threats to the reliability, efficiency, and integrity of our nation's commerce. Security planning for cargo is a must to reduce claims, employee temptation to theft, and threats of hijack, and to increase profits and safety for those involved in transporting cargo.

There has been a great deal of interest in methods to reduce cargo losses for several years, but not until 1975 did the Department of Transportation develop a program to deal specifically with this problem. The program encompasses all modes of transportation—rail, truck, ship, and air—and is concerned not only with the actual transportation of goods but also preservation, packing, packaging, labeling, and handling. In addition to the Department of Transportation, the Treasury Department's Bureau of Customs and the Department of Justice are also concerned with increasing the effectiveness of the transportation cargo security program.

The National Cargo Security Program emphasizes voluntary industry cooperation; no mandatory controls have been imposed. Corporate enforcement of cargo accountability and the use of simple, basic security measures will prevent the largest proportion of theft losses. The official federal forum on cargo security is a fourteen-member Interagency Committee on Transportation Security. In addition to governmental efforts to increase cargo security, the Transportation Association of America of the private sector established the National Cargo Security Council. Combined governmental and industrial attempts to reduce transportation crimes have resulted in great progress in reducing the extent of this multibillion dollar crime problem.

Transport security must be concerned with protection of merchandise while it is being loaded and unloaded and during transit. The United States Department of Transportation has reported that 80% of stolen cargo is taken from the premises of shippers and receivers, not during the actual transit.[14] However, the less frequent crimes of hijacking or skyjacking result in huge and sometimes catastrophic losses for transport businesses. For example, average losses from cargo thefts from trucks en route are estimated at $32,000, but some losses reach into the hundreds of thousands or millions of dollars depending on the value of the cargo being transported.

---

[14]The New York City/Newark Cargo Security Symposium on Packaging, U.S. Department of Transportation, Mar. 28, 1977, p. 14.

## Trucking security

The trucking industry is vulnerable to four principal types of cargo theft. These are: (1) vehicle theft, (2) burglary, (3) hijackings, and (4) thefts occurring during receiving and shipping. Vehicle thefts occur in the absence of the driver; criminals steal the loaded truck or trailer or take away the trailer with a rented or stolen tractor. Burglaries occur when the truck is left in a garage. Often one truck of many in the same garage is singled out for the burglary, indicating the thieves have prior knowledge of the contents and the scheduled movements of the truck.

Hijackings, the commandeering of the truck and threatening the driver with violence, occur far less frequently, but as stated previously, losses from hijackings are tremendous. After commandeering the vehicle the hijackers will take the truck to a location where they can dispose of the merchandise. It may be switched to another truck or directly turned over to a receiver of stolen goods who then takes possession.

Thefts occurring during shipping and receiving are very frequent, as noted previously. The "nickel and dime" thefts and pilferages are not as bold as hijackings nor do they result in huge single losses. However, the repeated pilferage of one or two cartons of cargo by dishonest employees soon results in a continual drain of profits, and the amount lost soon equals or surpasses that of a single hijacking. This high percentage of cargo loss is attributed to employees in various capacities. They may be acting independently, taking the merchandise for personal use, or be in collusion with any number of outsiders or other employees. In some cases, drivers are implicated, either working alone or in collusion with dockworkers, who, for example, will deliberately overload the truck, enabling the driver to remove the excess cargo during transit while still arriving at the destination with the correct amount of cargo. There have also been instances of drivers selling their loads to thieves or fences and then reporting their truck stolen or hijacked.

## Prevention of trucking cargo theft

The general vulnerabilities of a trucking company depend on several factors, such as geographic location, activity of organized crime, and the type and volume of business. Each trucking company should identify and reevaluate its particular vulnerabilities and should then use them as the foundation on which to build its security program. The trucking industry in general relies heavily on physical plant security because of the increased vulnerability of cargo merchandise to theft and pilferage by employees and outsiders, particularly when the premises are inadequately protected.

The intensity and methods of plant security will vary from company to company depending on variables such as location, past incidence of cargo theft, value of cargo, threats from underworld involvement, and the amount of security the company can afford to provide. All companies should have basic security equipment, such as locks and alarms, adequate lighting, fences, and security guards or electronic surveillance, when conditions warrant.

In addition to these methods of protection, other suggestions are listed below:

- Accountability should be established so that audit trails are possible from the first point of contact with the cargo to the last.
- Supervisory personnel should be present at the loading and unloading of cargo.
- There should be clear visibility of garages and loading docks.
- Cargo should be transported in sealed containers so that detection of theft is possible upon cursory inspection of the package.
- Cartons should not be overpacked to prevent bursting of seams.
- Unissued seals should be kept in a locked container.
- Discrepancies in numbers on the seal and shipping documents upon delivery should alert the receiver to the necessity of a complete inventory.
- Stamping of products with identifying serial numbers and letter codes facilitates identification if the outer container is destroyed or mutilated, and also prevents substitution of similar but inferior products if the package is opened during transit, and facilitates recovery of merchandise.
- Movement of high value merchandise should be via container, even though it may not be shipped immediately.
- Items that are easily pilfered should have separate storage facilities.
- Employee parking should be located away from the terminal area, and ideally the lot should be a separately fenced area with only one exit.
- Trash containers should be removed from the general proximity of the cargo facility, as this method is a convenient way to remove bulky cargo from the premises.
- Irregular inspections of job performance of personnel should be performed.
- Trucks should be periodically recalled for recounting after they have left the premises.
- Undercover vehicles should be used to escort highly vulnerable cargo transports. Some companies even use cars and irregularly follow drivers to and from their destinations. Some have radar to check the speed of the driver, in addition to the route.
- Experimental electronic tagging, although not entirely feasible, enables the location of vehicles and containers tagged to be detected.
- If products are sold by weight, good weighing facilities are essential.
- External marking of packages and containers should not reveal the nature of the contents. Company advertising, particularly of well-known brand names and articles especially attractive to thieves (food, clothing, cigarettes, radios, televisions, records, automobile parts, and drugs) should be avoided.
- Use of secondhand cases and packaging equipment should be avoided. Marks of previous nails and straps make it difficult on inspection to determine whether pilferage has occurred en route.
- Packaging cartons should be large enough to avoid being lost but small enough to avoid malicious handling.
- Vehicles should be equipped with appropriate locks at all possible points of access.

☐ Alarm systems to cover the entire vehicle should be installed. Each cargo door should be wired separately.
☐ Vehicles should be distinctively marked on all sides, including the roof, which will facilitate identification by police helicopter.
☐ Unattended trucks should be parked with cargo doors safely blocked, such as parking back to back or against a wall.
☐ Complete records of license, serial, and company assigned vehicle numbers should be kept.
☐ Complete information of all goods shipped, such as valuations, serial numbers, manufacturer's identification, and other descriptive information, should be kept.
☐ Records should be kept of vehicles and drivers in transit, including points of stop, routes, destination, estimated time of arrival, and return.
☐ Hiring practices should include thorough background checks as described previously in this chapter.

## Airline and airport security

Security in the airline industry has made rapid progress. Plagued with a crime explosion after the exponential growth of air freight in the late 1960s, the industry now claims lower losses than other carriers. Theft-related claims have been significantly reduced since 1970. Because air cargo is high-value/low-volume cargo, these companies transport more in terms of value of goods but are smaller transporters in terms of volume. Air transport is also more expensive than trucking, rail, or maritime. This type of cargo is most vulnerable while the merchandise is in the terminal awaiting further shipment or final delivery pick-up by truck. Losses in transit have all but been eliminated by anti-skyjacking measures.

Theft and pilferage of cargo is usually committed by persons authorized to be on the premises, driving authorized automobiles. A study of New York metropolitan airports indicated that 76% of all losses were sustained in this manner and that 70% of these losses were thefts from terminals. This same study showed that armed robbery and skyjackings were rare, comprising only 1% of thefts, but the losses from those crimes accounted for 25% of losses.[15] Air cargo that is particularly vulnerable to theft are: currency, furs, wearing apparel, precious metals, precious stones, electrical equipment, jewelry, watches, and clocks.

## Prevention of air cargo loss

Security precautions for air cargo are becoming more and more important as it is becoming more evident that a shipper chooses a particular carrier at least partly on the reputation for claims prevention. The most progressive

[15]*Crime in Service Industries.* U.S. Department of Commerce, Domestic and International Business Administration, Sept. 1977, p. 27.

example of airport security is the formation in 1968 of the Airport Security Council at Kennedy, LaGuardia, and Newark airports. These innovations have been widely copied elsewhere. Security measures undertaken, in general terms, are oriented toward preventing employee theft through accountability, background checks, and identification systems limiting access of nonemployees to terminals and cargo storage, through restricting parking areas, and emphasizing the need for physical security measures such as alarms, locks, security guards, and policies for security equipment use.

### Railroad and maritime security

Railroad and maritime security open up new dimensions of transport security that are beyond the scope of this book to describe completely. It is known, however, that rail transport losses are on the rise, and maritime security has been challenged ever since the very early incidences of sea piracy.

Thefts from railroads are enormous and can occur through several vulnerabilities. Freight trains, like trucks and airlines, are subject to intrusion by unauthorized persons and dishonest employees. Boxcar thefts are common, and even the rerouting of entire trains is not unheard of. Railroads have traditionally retained their own special police force to deal with the problems facing railroad security.

The main responsibility of maritime security in United States waters falls with the Coast Guard. The responsibilities of the Coast Guard are too numerous to be described here. It should suffice to say, however, that maritime security should also be a concern of all who use the piers, docks, and the waters of the world. The importance of sound hiring practices, good pier security, and reporting suspicious activity to the Coast Guard cannot be overemphasized in preventing maritime cargo losses. It should also be mentioned that many private pleasure boats have been stolen for the purpose of transporting illegal drugs or are taken for resale, so that the private citizen should also be mindful of security precautions. Many of the previously described crime prevention measures for the trucking and airline industries are equally applicable to railroad and maritime transport security.

### Nuclear security

It is no secret that the production of atomic energy presents the potential for grave dangers to the very existence of life itself. Nuclear power plants and storage sites of nuclear waste products now dot the entire continent. The prevention of danger to the health and safety of all citizens must, under any circumstances, be the main concern of utility companies operating nuclear facilities as governmental agencies charged with determining standards and regulations for their operation. Dangers of nuclear power plants arise not only from improper design and construction of nuclear facilities, but also by acts of sabotage or diversion and misuse of dangerous radioactive materials. As additional power plants are constructed and put into operation, this promises to be a main concern of the general public as well as security-minded individuals who will be staffing such facilities.

There are several federal agencies presently regulating some aspect of nuclear power plant operations. The Atomic Energy Commission has imposed stringent quality assurance programs regarding design and construction of facilities, and it has also established requirements to be adhered to in the implementation of security systems designed to protect nuclear reactors and related equipment from industrial sabotage and from the diversion of nuclear material. Requirements also govern the transportation of nuclear materials. The American National Standards Institute has also set forth detailed measures for the protection of reactor facilities. The security system set forth is designed to detect penetration in the event it occurs, apprehend in a timely manner authorized and unauthorized persons acting in a manner constituting threat to sabotage, and provide for appropriate authorities to take custody of violators. This provides for dealing with coerced or uncoerced employees authorized to have access to the plant and who are familiar with the details of design, construction, and operation of the nuclear power plant; mentally deranged persons whose knowledge of the plant may range from zero to complete; and armed outsiders with no authorized access to the plant whose goal is to perpetrate acts of sabotage against the plant. The security system is also oriented to a large group of people involved in spontaneous violent activity resulting from acts of civil disorder.

Needless to say, the role of security in protecting nuclear power plants is both well-defined and extremely necessary. By the very nature of materials used in producing power more stringent and detailed security programs are required. The private sector should demand very elaborate security programs, which must be enforced by governmental agencies. The proliferation of nuclear power plants throughout the 1980s should continually challenge this area of security in helping protect not only utility companies as a business, but also the welfare of the entire population of the United States.

## EXECUTIVE PROTECTION

Executive protection, in response to increasing terrorist attacks against corporate executives and political leaders across the world, has now become one of the fastest growing aspects of security. More than $7 billion is now spent by United States companies on security, both at home and abroad. Security budgets are beginning to swell, with more and more money going toward sophisticated defenses such as armored cars, electronic devices to track executives, and metal detectors to identify bombs. The traditional minimum wage guard is being replaced in favor of highly qualified guards. Some executives now maintain security guard services at their homes and most have elaborate security alarm systems installed. Even evasive driving classes for chauffeurs, the executives themselves, and their families are becoming a highly desired or necessary component of executive protection. There are also courses available to teach executives everything from detecting car bombs to how to behave if taken hostage.

The major threats to executive security are terrorist acts such as kidnapping, bombings, sabotage, assassination, and extortion. Terrorists generally attack to persuade the population and the government that certain political and social changes must occur, or to make the public aware of their particular grievances. They use surprise, threats, harassment, coercion, and violence to create an atomsphere of fear. Their selection of victims or targets and methods of attack used are both based on gaining maximal press coverage or publicity with the minimal amount of danger to themselves.

The largest number of terrorist attacks have occurred in Latin America and European countries. These attacks very often involve American businessmen and their families or American governmental employees. However, we cannot be lulled into feeling safe and secure on United States soil since revolutionary groups such as the Symbionese Liberation Army have proved that such acts can just as easily occur in the United States. There has also been an increase in bombings and kidnapping of less famous, but nevertheless vulnerable, individuals. Bank officials and their families have proved to be prime targets for kidnappings, because, in the words of one bank robber, "that's where the dough is." This shows too that the motive behind terrorist acts in the United States is usually personal gain rather than attempts to rectify social injustices. Therefore, security precautions are vital for those at the heart of political influence as well as for those who are not.

### Security precautions for executives

The following discussion of security precautions does not attempt to be all inclusive. It is more a discussion of general crime and basic prevention measures that should be available to all executives, but each executive and his or her security staff must tailor them to the individual's specific circumstances.

### Protection during travel

It is estimated that 95% of all executive kidnappings occur while they are traveling by car to and from work. This usually takes place by forcing the executive's car off the road and overpowering chauffeurs and/or body guards, if any. For this reason, precautions while en route to and from home should include the following.

- ☐ Reduce travel time to and from work by living closer to working quarters.
- ☐ Vary times of travel and routes taken.
- ☐ Use two-way radio or telephone communications.
- ☐ Consider compact or ordinary cars in place of conspicuous limousines.
- ☐ Consider bullet-proof glass, armor plate, and escort service.
- ☐ Take training in evasive driving.
- ☐ Use security guards.
- ☐ Do not leave the vehicle unattended; consider automobile intrusion alarms.
- ☐ Do not use personalized parking spaces.
- ☐ Call home or work each time before leaving. Inform secretary or family member of estimated time of arrival.
- ☐ Keep gas tank at least one-half full.
- ☐ Keep doors locked and windows closed during travel.

### Precautions during aircraft travel

- ☐ Use commercial airlines rather than company aircraft since physical protective safeguards for the private aircraft, hangar, access controls, etc., are not as formidable to the terrorist as they are at protected commercial airfields.
- ☐ If company aircraft is used, aircraft access controls and intrusion and tamper alarm systems should be used.
- ☐ The aircraft must be protected while at other airfields and the plane should have no distinctive organizational markings.
- ☐ All travel plans should be kept confidential. Stoppage of regular deliveries should be avoided and cancellation of appointments such as hairdresser's or social activities should be done discreetly.

### Executive office security

- ☐ Offices should not be directly accessible to the public or located on the ground floor.
- ☐ Office windows facing public areas should be curtained and reinforced with bullet-resistant materials.
- ☐ Escorted visitor access into executive offices is essential.
- ☐ Direct access to executive offices should be monitored by a secretary or guard.
- ☐ All persons entering executive offices should be screened.
- ☐ Visitors should be positively identified and this information logged. Identifying badges should be given. Unidentified persons should be approached by a guard.
- ☐ Offices as well as desks should be equipped with a hidden and unobtrusive means of activating an emergency alarm.
- ☐ In high-risk areas visitors and packages should be screened with a metal detector.
- ☐ Policies for entering executive offices during nonworking hours should be established. Cleaning and maintenance personnel should be accompanied by a guard.
- ☐ Restrooms near the executive offices should be locked to restrict public access. This should apply to janitorial closets as well.

- Stringent lock-and-key control measures to executive office areas is of paramount importance.
- Automated card readers or pushbutton door locks are also beneficial in restricting access.
- Emergency supplies such as first aid equipment, bomb blankets, candles, transistor radios, food rations, etc., should be kept at the facility, with only key personnel knowing their location.
- Policies should be established for screening of incoming mail and appropriate employees should be trained in identifying suspicious letters and packages.
- Executives should keep a low profile. Interviews, photographs, and release of personal information should be kept at a minimum.
- Executives should be trained in recognizing techniques of surveillance so that they may be able to tell when they are being watched by strangers.

### Residential and family protection
- Train family members to be alert to suspicious activity.
- Do not list home telephone numbers.
- Adhere to basic home security precautions discussed in Chapter 5.
- Familiarize all family members with special procedures to be followed in the event of an emergency.

In addition to the above suggestions, the reader is referred to Chapter 4, Personal Security, for further discussion of terrorism, executive protection, and protection of children.

To ensure the maximal effectiveness of executive protection precautions, there must also be a willingness on the part of the executive to admit that he or she is a potential victim of terrorism and to cooperate in prescribed security precautions. Some executives are reluctant to cooperate with extensive security precautions apparently from concern of how these precautions appear to others, rather than denial of the risk or a low corporate security budget. However, executive protection is too important to succumb to the influence of peer pressure. Threats to executives are a most serious problem and must be dealt with in a serious manner. Executive protection covers many important aspects, none of which should be ruled out.

### Establishing corporate policies

Few corporations presently have established guidelines, procedures, or policies for handling a crisis situation, despite the significant number of kidnappings over the last decade. Corporations not equipped with such crisis management guidelines could be increasing the risk of harm to a hostage if a kidnapping did occur. Precious hours would be lost delegating responsibilities such as how and when to notify police, notifying families, paying ransoms and how, and obtaining the consultation of experienced negotiators. Time lost from negotiations could be particularly crucial since most executives are released if ransom demands are met. One solution to this problem would seem to be the establishment of corporate crisis management plans and teams made up of top management personnel. These personnel would have complete responsibility for the crisis management for the first few hours until a professional negotiator could be obtained. Another advantage the corporation may wish to consider is that the plans and teams could assure safety of the hostage first and apprehension of the terrorist second. The Federal Bureau of Investigation, of course, also operates this way, but many foreign police do not, and presently most kidnappings occur overseas.

The establishment of crisis management plans and teams will require a significant amount of corporate time and resources. An outside consultant who can assist the corporation with the many aspects of crisis management will also be required. Nevertheless, the potential benefits of being prepared and doing everything possible to react in the best interest of the hostage would seem to outweigh any financial investments required by the corporation.

### The role of private security programs

A discussion of the many aspects of business security would not be complete without consideration of the administrative responsibilities of the corporate security executive. In the classic management textbooks, the functions of management are usually broken down into the following acronym POSDCORB, which stands for planning, organizing, staffing, directing, coordinating, reporting, and budgeting. These are the classic functions of management. But for crime prevention and loss control—as well as increasing the profit margin—we should include yet another "S" for the function of security. Responsibilities of the corporate security director fall into three main broad categories. These are planning, developing, and implementing corporate protection programs. The director must see to it that such programs assure a reasonable level of protection of both property and employees, depending upon particular corporate vulnerabilities. During the planning stage of such programs, the director is charged with identifying vulnerabilities, determining appropriate countermeasures, and determining cost effectiveness of such measures. The developing phase includes the establishment of specific guidelines and procedures to be followed for each recommended plan of action. For example, if the security director had previously determined employee hiring practices to be a major threat to corporate security, he or she would now have the responsibility of developing specific guidelines and procedures for employee screening. The director would then implement these newly established guidelines (the third phase of responsibility) by making sure all other departments concerned with hiring are adhering to prescribed guidelines, or by assuming direct control over part of the hiring practices. Security should, for example, become directly involved in employee background investigations, polygraph screening, etc., and work in cooperation with the personnel department on other guidelines of hiring.

Establishing hiring policies is just one example of the many services a security director performs. He or she also assesses the need for physical property protection and types of protection to be used, methods of protecting proprietary and private information, and establishes cash handling and accountability policies. The director also develops and implements the following: executive protection guidelines, appropriate methods of internal and external investigative methods, complete emergency preparedness manuals, educational and training programs for security staff, and budgetary procedures and management of all security services.

The corporate security director should serve as the executive liaison in matters requiring cooperation with local, state, and federal law enforcement agencies, as well as arranging physical security for conventions, meetings, and social activities. All other management employees should work directly with the security director in regard to planning, developing, implementing, maintaining and reevaluating security policies directly affecting their particular departments. The corporate legal counsel should assist the security director regarding aspects of company-wide security policies. In addition, when new buildings or remodeling of existing structures is planned, there should be consultation among the security director, architects, engineers, and real estate agents to assure proper design and implementation of protective factors in new or-renovated facilities.

## CONCLUSION

The range of techniques and procedures for preventing and detecting business crimes is extensive and varied, but then so are the types of crimes perpetrated against business and the methods of committing them. The economic impact of crime upon the business community is staggering. Most of the dollar losses caused by specific crimes are estimates, which makes a true figure difficult to obtain. Nevertheless, billions of dollars are lost annually. Small firms are forced to close, employees lose jobs, cities lose tax revenue although they must spend more on increased public safety programs.

Crimes against business today go far beyond yesteryear's main concern of shoplifting. Even though this is still a major problem, employee dishonesty in the form of pilferage, embezzlement, and sophisticated computer crimes is a major contributor to crimes against business. Organized crime has also significantly contributed to the problem, perpetrating such crimes as racketeering, extortion, arson, gambling, and loansharking against businesses. Threats of terrorist activities such as kidnapping particularly affect large businesses and banks since executives and their families are all placed at a certain amount of risk.

Average citizens, employees, members of the underworld, emotionally disturbed individuals, drug addicts, and anyone else hard pressed for money or recognition, including business owners themselves, are perpetrators of the many crimes against business. Many reasons are given for the commission of crimes, such as money, revenge, and blackmail, but these reasons do not excuse the fact that they occur. Indications are that crimes against businesses will only continue with more frequency and the economic implications will be more severe. Only with a concerted preventive effort on the part of businesses and law enforcement officials alike can the problem be brought under control. Consequently, the most basic aspect in loss prevention for business is a determination to prevent losses.

# Chapter 9

# Corruption

Corruption is the attainment or attempted attainment of gain, whether it be monetary, material goods, or fulfillment of emotional or psychologic drives, by unscrupulous or illegal methods. Corruption often involves the misuse of a position of trust. The system of corruption is widespread and perverse. Not only does corruption occur in many business practices in which the individual consumer is the victim, but it also involves businesses against other businesses, businesses against government, government officials against businesses and individuals, government against individuals, individuals against government, and foreign governments against American businesses. For example, Gulf Oil was threatened with the closure of its $300 million operation in South Korea unless the company made a $10 million donation to the presidential campaign of that country's ruling party chairman. Gulf Oil Chairman, Bob Dorsey, was able to decrease the amount paid from $10 million, which he believed was "not in the interests of the company," to $3 million, which he said was.[1]

Sutherland and Cressey graphically describe the widespread influence of corruption:

> In many lines of business, ruthlessness in making money has become an important part of the business code. Trade unions have become involved in racketeering. Political graft and corruption are widespread. Evasion of taxes is commonplace. Thus, lying, cheating, fraud, exploitation, violation of trust, and graft are prevalent in the general society. The offender who becomes reformed must be superior to the society in which he lives.[2]

---

[1]Gwirtzman, Milton S., "Is Bribery Defensible," in *Crime at the Top*, John M. Johnson and Jack D. Douglas, editors. Philadelphia: J. B. Lippincott Co., 1978, p. 337.
[2]Sutherland, Edwin H., and Cressey, Donald R., *Criminology*. Philadelphia: J. B. Lippincott Co., 1974, p. 611.

**Table 9-1.** Annual cost of *some* white collar crimes

| Crime | | Cost (in billions) |
|---|---|---|
| Bankruptcy fraud | | $ 0.08 |
| Bribery, kickbacks, and payoffs | | 3.00 |
| Computer-related crime | | 0.10 |
| Consumer fraud, illegal competition, deceptive practices | | 21.00 |
|     Consumer victims | $ 5.5 | |
|     Business victims | 3.5 | |
|     Government revenue loss | 12.0 | |
| Credit card and check fraud | | 1.10 |
|     Credit card | 0.1 | |
|     Check | 1.0 | |
| Embezzlement and pilferage | | 7.00 |
|     Embezzlement (cash, goods, services) | 3.0 | |
|     Pilferage | 4.0 | |
| Insurance fraud | | 2.00 |
|     Insurer victims | 1.5 | |
|     Policyholder victims | 0.5 | |
| Receiving stolen property | | 3.50 |
| Securities thefts and frauds | | 4.00 |
| TOTAL | | $41.78 |

From *White Collar Crime.* Chamber of Commerce of the United States, 1974, p. 6.

Abrahamsen also points to the seriousness of corruption when he states, "Corruption is more dangerous than disease, the mind may die of it."[3] Corruption has many adverse effects upon its victims, the majority of which are economic. Many of the costs of corruption are passed on to the public in higher costs for merchandise and increased taxes. Other corruptive practices stifle competition of the free market, thus limiting trade to only a few companies. Different sources offer different statistics regarding the incidence and costs of corruption. According to the Chamber of Commerce of the United States:

1. The yearly cost of embezzlement and pilferage reportedly exceeds by several billion dollars the losses sustained throughout the nation from burglary and robbery.
2. Fraud was a major contributing factor in the forced closing of about one hundred banks during a twenty-year period.
3. An insurance company reported that at least 30% of all business failures each year are the result of employee dishonesty.
4. Dishonesty by corporate executives and employees has increased the

[3]Abrahamsen, David, *Who Are the Guilty: A Study of Education and Crime.* New York: Rinehart and Co., 1952, p. 9.

retail cost of some merchandise by up to 15% and in the case of one company, caused shareholders to suffer a paper loss of $300 million in just a few days.[4]

It has also been estimated that unreported income from corruption may cost the government another $40 billion dollars in tax revenue.[5] Table 9-1 refers to the annual cost of several types of corruption.[6]

## HISTORY OF CORRUPTION IN AMERICA

The first major recognized incident of corruption in this country appears to date back to President Madison's administration. This scandal, known in American history as the Yazoo land fraud, involved the interplay between money and political decision-making. As pointed out by Berg:

> Despite the efforts of the Founding Fathers to design political institutions that would serve as a barrier to the commission of corrupt acts, the temptations offered by land speculation in the new republic apparently were too strong for many politicians to resist.[7]

American politics has long been involved with corruption. The administration of President Ulysses S. Grant was particularly scandal ridden. In 1833, for example, when the renewal of the charter of the Second United States Bank came before Congress, Senator Daniel Webster wrote a letter to the bank's president containing a direct request for money: "I believe that my retainer has not been renewed or refreshed as usual. If it be wished that my relationship with the Bank should be continued, it may be well to send me the usual retainer."[8] Miller notes, "From Jamestown to Watergate, corruption runs through our history like a scarlet thread. Although we self-righteously congratulate ourselves on high moral standards, the grafting politician, corrupt business tycoon and crooked labor baron are prominent fixtures in American folklore."[9] The carpetbagger era during the Reconstruction of the South, the Teapot Dome affair, the ouster of Adam Clayton Powell, Jr., the disclosure of various sexual adventures by members of Congress in the 1970s, the resignation of Vice President Spiro T. Agnew, the immortal Watergate affair, and the recent Abscam investigations all attest to the fact that corruption has always existed in our history.

---

[4]*White Collar Crime.* New York, Chamber of Commerce of the United States, 1974.
[5]*Crime and its Impact—an Assessment.* Washington, D.C.: President's Commission on Law Enforcement and the Administration of Justice, Government Printing Office, 1967, pp. 42-59.
[6]*White Collar Crime,* op. cit., p. 6.
[7]Berg, Larry L., et al., *Corruption in the American Political System.* Morristown, N.J.: General Learning Press, 1976, p. 14.
[8]Willard, James, *The Growth of American Law.* Boston: Little, Brown, & Co., 1950, p. 367.
[9]Miller, Nathan, *The Foundling Finaglers.* New York: David McKay Co., Inc., 1976.

## GOVERNMENT AS A VICTIM OF CORRUPTION

The major victim of corruption in this country is the United States government. The government annually appropriates approximately $250 billion to assistance programs. Many government programs involving grants, contracts, and/or loans are exploited by any of the following means:[10]

- False claims for benefits or services
- False statements to induce contracts or secure goods or services
- Bribery or corruption of public employees and officials
- False payment claims for goods and services not delivered
- Collusion involving contractors

Specific and documented examples of defrauding Uncle Sam include:

- Fraudulently issuing and cashing checks against a federally funded training program account.
- Fraudulently executing on-the-job training contracts for nonexistent companies, forging names of actual companies to obtain funds through the program, and embezzling and converting federal money to personal use.
- Deliberately selling materials to the government that do not meet contract standards.
- Accepting bribes for processing a loan application knowing the application to be fraudulent.
- Conspiring to defraud the government in obtaining federal rent subsidies for tenants by filing applications with false names, understating incomes, and adding the names of fictitious dependents of residents occupying the apartment and/or housing complex.
- Filing false vouchers for work that was never performed.
- Altering and forging material facts to secure a guaranty on a loan.
- Embezzling federal funds by generating and altering payment vouchers.

### Reducing corruption against government

Because of the complexity of the United States government, reduction of corruption against it will have to take into account many difficult factors. A grassroots approach will have to be taken by concentrating responsibility for curbing corruption with each and every agency. Suggestions offered for preventing corruption against the government include:

- Developing management information systems aimed at providing information on the most likely types and methods of fraud, including the development of techniques for estimating the magnitude of fraud in agency programs.

---

[10]"Federal Agencies Can, and Should, Do More to Combat Fraud in Government Programs." Comptroller General's Report to the Congress, GGD-78-62. Washington, D.C.: Sept. 19, 1978, p. i.

□ Elevating fraud identification to a high agency priority.

□ Taking steps to make employees more aware of the potential for fraud and establishing controls to see that all irregularities are promptly referred to appropriate personnel.

□ Fixing organizational responsibility for identifying fraud.

□ Providing agency investigators with appropriate fraud training; in future hirings, concentrating on recruitment of personnel with backgrounds and education more suited to the financial complexities of fraud.

Federal agencies that work with frauds against the government include:

□ The Food and Drug Administration district offices, or the national office, Rockville, Maryland 20852

□ The Federal Trade Commission, Bureau of Consumer Protection, Washington, D.C. 20580

□ The United States Postal Service, 1200 Pennsylvania Avenue, N.W., Washington, D.C. 20260 (information and complaints about mail-order products)

□ The Consumer Product Safety Commission, Bethesda, Maryland 20016

□ The Federal Bureau of Investigation, United States Department of Justice, Washington, D.C. 20535

On the state level the state's attorney general should be notified of any suspected wrongdoing.

## CORRUPTION OF GOVERNMENT OFFICIALS

Is ours really a government for the people and by the people? The government was in operation for two hundred years before we had a sunshine law and the Freedom of Information Act, which allow the people to know what is taking place. But then it is said that change is slow. Senator Russell Long of Louisiana, an authority on the subject of corruption in government, has stated:

> The government pays out billions of dollars in unnecessarily high interest rates; it permits private monopoly patents on over $12 billion of government research annually; it permits billions of dollars to remain on deposit in banks without collecting interest; it permits overcharging by many concerns selling services to the government; it tolerates all sorts of tax favoritism; it fails to move to protect public health from a number of obvious hazards; it permits monopolies to victimize the public in a number of inexcusable ways; it provides for too much tariff protection to some industries and too little to others. Many of these evils are built-in effects of American government resulting from the way we finance our political campaigns.[11]

Government agencies, on the whole, take strong stands against official corruption and have instituted citizen action groups and numerous other pro-

---

[11]"Paying to Get Elected." *The New Republic*, Oct. 16, 1971, p. 7.

grams to deal with the problem. The National Advisory Commission on Criminal Justice Standards and Goals is one example. The Commission stated:

> Official corruption erodes the efficacy of our democratic form of government and undermines respect for law, whether a small compromise with integrity or a major violation of public trust, corruption creates a backlash that alienates large segments of the public from their government. This public alienation may range from apathy and cynicism to the violence of outrage . . . . In this sense, therefore, the preeminent anticrime activity appropriate for citizen action is the sustained pursuit of governmental integrity.[12]

Not only does government corruption ultimately result in apathy, alienation, and outrage, but "Political corruption violates and undermines the norms of the system of public order which is deemed indispensable for the maintenance of political democracy."[13] Justice Louis Brandeis stated, "Crime is contagious . . . if the government becomes a lawbreaker, it breeds contempt for the law."[14]

Because of the extensive amount of corruption in the government, there has been a dramatic loss of trust. A public opinion survey by Louis Harris, which was authorized by the Senate Subcommittee on Intergovernmental Relations in 1973, revealed a reduction of public confidence in government institutions and officials to the extent that the public displayed greater faith in the local trash collection operations than in people running the White House (53% expressed confidence in the garbage collectors, while only 18% expressed confidence in the White House staff).[15]

These are very serious complications of corruption, and unfortunately, they are not overstatements or overreactions to the problem. One must acknowledge the extremely adverse influence of corruption on our political democracy, since, for example, organized crime, corporate conglomerates, and members of foreign governments can literally buy some of our elected officials and candidates merely by naming the right price. There is no debating the fact that a democracy in which the leaders bow to the whims of these individuals cannot possibly be a government for all the people.

In spite of the very serious consequences—even to the extent of compromising a democratic society—few have realized the magnitude of the

---

[12]"A Call for Citizen Action: Crime Prevention and the Citizen." National Advisory Commission on Criminal Justice Standards and Goals, 1974, p. 11.
[13]Berg et al., op. cit., p. 3.
[14]Neier, Aryeh, *Crime and Punishment: A Radical Solution.* New York: Stein and Day Publishers, p. 76.
[15]Berg et al., op. cit., p. 60.

problem. As Clifford states, "Only very recently has attention been given to the importance of administrative dishonesty or bureaucratic deviance, to multinational circumvention of laws, and to the national and global significance of economic crime; but this has been unfamiliar territory for the economic and social planner and the criminologist alike."[16] While the Watergate revelation came as a shock to the average citizen, most political scientists have long been aware of this type of activity. Not only have there been a number of famous cases of national significance, but there have been a vast number of minor cases on the state and local levels as well.

The documentation of corruption within the government that has been exposed and prosecuted would be a massive historical project in itself, not to mention incidents that have gone undetected and unprosecuted. Such a project is well beyond the objectives of this book but we will cite a few fairly recent examples in an attempt to exemplify the scope of this subject.

Michael Dorman, in his book *Payoff,* gives several examples of mayoral corruption. A striking display was when West New Jersey City Mayor John R. Armellino pleaded guilty in 1971 to a conspiracy with Joseph Zicarelli to protect mob gambling activities. Armellino admitted taking payoffs of $1,000 per week from Zicarelli, the Mafia boss of Northern Hudson County. Zicarelli also was indicted with John B. Theurer, the Republican chairman of Hudson County, on conspiracy charges of attempting to gain the appointment of a county prosecutor who would protect organized crime's gambling interests.[17]

Dorman cites another case in which Jersey City Mayor Thomas J. Whelan and seven other public officials were convicted of conspiring to extort money from companies doing business with the city and county governments.

Konolige has reported that a former speaker of the Pennsylvania House of Representatives has been indicted for allegedly extorting a total of $56,000 from parents seeking his help in gaining admission to medical and veterinary schools for their children. In an unrelated incident, two other Pennsylvania state legislators from Philadelphia faced several counts of bribery and conspiracy in similar alleged schemes involving a dental school.[18]

Corrupt government officials commonly use extortion when exploiting their position and public trust, and very often the incident involves only one corrupt official and specific individuals, such as the corrupt representative and the parents who paid to have their children admitted to medical school. However, many incidences of governmental corruption can become quite

---

[16]Clifford, William, *Planning Crime Prevention.* Lexington, Mass.: Lexington Books, 1976, p. 3.
[17]Dorman, Michael, *Payoff.* New York: David McKay Co., Inc., 1972, p. 68.
[18]Konolige, Kit, "M.D. Degrees for Sale," in *Crime at the Top,* John M. Johnson and Jack D. Douglas, editors. Philadelphia: J. B. Lippincott Co., 1978, p. 242.

complex, and the results can directly and indirectly affect entire populations of states or nations. The following is one such example:

> The Mob was making a fortune on state control of liquor distribution. A Mobster was quoted as saying, "the governor of the state has the power to designate the brandname of every bottle of liquor sold in the state. The state operates the liquor stores. For a price, we get the state to handle brands bought from companies that we control. Hell, we've got a license to steal. You should see some of the half-assed brands we peddle down there at premium prices. The customer doesn't have any choice; it's a monopoly situation. The only place he can buy booze is at the state store, unless he goes to a bootlegger—and we control most of the bootlegging, anyway. The Governor of Alabama gets a salary of $25,000 a year, but in his four year term he can pick up at least a million dollars in liquor payoffs. If he's making that much, you can imagine what kind of dough we're making."[19]

Political payments such as the above are the main stimulus encouraging governmental corruption, and this factor is discussed below in greater detail.

## Political payments

A political payment has been defined by Jacoby and associates as "any transfer of money or anything of value made with the aim of influencing the behavior of politicians, political candidates, political parties, or government officials and employees in their legislative, administrative, and judicial actions."[20] A political payment can be made to United States politicians or to politicians in other countries. The Central Intelligence Agency, for example, gave at least $1 million to help prevent the election of the Marxist leader, Dr. Salvador Allende Gossens, as President of Chile.[21]

## Preventing government corruption

Prevention of corruption will depend on both strong internal controls within each agency and surveillance by independent citizens' groups. A number of current practices will have to be eliminated or limited. These practices are described below.

**Patronage.** A number of governmental positions are still based on the old patronage systems. Richard Nixon's personal lawyer, Herbert Kalmbach, entered a guilty plea for promising a more prestigious ambassadorship to J. Fife Symington in return for a $100,000 contribution. The Senate Watergate Committee found that more than $1.8 million was given in campaign funds by

---

[19]Dorman, op. cit., p. 72.

[20]Jacoby, Neil H., Nehemkis, Peter, and Eells, Richard, *Bribery and Extortion in World Business.* New York: Macmillan, Inc., 1977, p. 86.

[21]Ibid.

ambassadorial appointees. The practice of returning money or favors to politicians in return for appointments is not limited only to ambassadors, since federal judges, U.S. attorneys, and U.S. marshals are still appointed as a result of political connections. Appointments are made by the President with the influence of a practice known as "senatorial courtesy."

**Limiting campaign expenditures.** All election candidates should be limited to a specified amount of money that they could spend on their election campaign. Local officials should be limited the most while Congressmen and governors should be allowed to spend progressively larger amounts. The largest spending budgets should be given to presidential hopefuls. An election commission could increase the amounts as inflation warrants.

**Lobbying.** New guidelines should be written to greatly restrict the functions of lobbyists. While the private sector should be able to communicate its interest to law makers, the use of "contributions" by these same persons or groups should be curtailed.

**Disclosure of contributions.** Full and complete disclosures of campaign contributions should be thoroughly enforced. At the same time, the amount of money given to any one candidate by large corporations or conglomerates should be severely limited to a specified amount. Campaign contribution disclosure statements requiring names of individuals and/or corporations contributing, the amount contributed, and the date of the contribution have been in force for several years now and have prevented much secrecy. However, stricter limitations, such as on the amount of money that can be donated, still need to be adopted.

**Conflict of interest.** Any violation of conflict of interest should be dealt with in an uncompromising manner. Elected officials who use their position of trust to further their own personal welfare must be made aware of the severity of their crime through severe punishment.

**Public financing of campaigns.** The public financing of campaigns would go a long way toward ending the patronage system. While an exact approach would need to be worked out, the amount of money needed for campaigns could be decreased if candidates concentrated on the issues rather than rhetoric.

**Limiting the amount of advertising.** If the amount of advertising a candidate could buy was limited, the richest candidate would not be able to saturate the public airways and print media. Perhaps the number of television advertising spots could be limited to twenty-five, five-minute broadcasts. In these twenty-five spots, the candidate would have the opportunity to express a different aspect of his or her platform. The spots could be run on twenty-five consecutive nights before the election between 6:00 and 6:30 PM, with candidate A being first and candidate B second, alternating every day, and each candidate would address the same issue on a given night. The public could then choose the candidate on the basis of issues rather than rhetoric.

### Penalties for corruption

When a political or governmental official is proved in a court of law to be corrupt, the penalty should be as great as the crime. It should be made clear that the public will not tolerate a violation of its trust. Perhaps the penalties for white collar crimes in general need to be revised before a change can come in punishing elected officials for their crimes. It is traditional for those who fight for equality and fairness to meet with resistance. But today, even after fairness and equality have struggled through wars, riots, and various acts and amendments to the Constitution, inequality still exists in the administration of justice. There is no way that fairness in penalties exists for a young black from a slum who gets a twenty-year maximum security prison sentence for a burglary resulting in perhaps $200 worth of goods, and a county treasurer embezzling over $60,000 of public funds and receiving probation with restitution. Likewise, a pardon given to our nation's highest leader for conspiracy to cover up illegal entry and wiretap of a competitor's headquarters should have been accompanied by pardons for every other individual convicted of similar crimes—or all those convicted should serve equal penalties. No single individual is above the law. Our forefathers did not establish this country for that purpose. If they had, there would have been no need for the Revolutionary War. Therefore, we must re-establish our judicial process to prosecute individuals in high positions who betray public trust as we prosecute individuals convicted of the so-called blue-collar crimes.*

Those who argue against severe penalties for white-collar crime do so mainly because white-collar crimes are not violent as are murders, rapes, and robberies. But the danger to the public as a whole is nevertheless real, and the consequences of corruption are grave. The violent tactics of organized crime who so often corrupt our political leaders are comparable to any violence used in the commission of blue-collar crimes. Then again, corrupt leaders are very often excused for their act on the basis of their motivation for committing their offense. In other words, a trusted official who comes under the influence of the Mob or takes a kickback from a corporation in return for a political favor is merely acting out of greed or a drive for power, and this, for some reason, is more tolerable than blue-collar criminals who act on the basis of need, desperation, or revenge. Perhaps blue-collar criminals merely lack

---

*A special toll-free "fraud hotline" has been started to encourage persons to report any information they may have concerning wrongdoing by any federal agency or in any federally administered program. The number is 800-424-5454.

the political clout of the white-collar criminal and are unable to bribe, pay off, or otherwise cover up their offenses.

## CORRUPTION AMONG POLICE

The fact that some corruption exists in police departments is well documented.[22-24] Investigation into police corruption is also nothing new. In 1894, the Lexon Committee found patterns of police corruption.[25] Police corruption may be defined as any type of behavior by a law enforcement officer who receives or expects to receive money or any type of compensation for favors rendered.

Early police practices, particularly the treatment of prisoners, were not readily recognized as corrupt practices, and in some cases were regarded as normal and usual treatment of prisoners for that time period. For example, many prisoners were threatened, beaten, or otherwise tortured into confessing to the commission of certain crimes. These inhumane practices, however, did eventually come to light, which brought about much needed reforms in the police systems. One such case was the 1928 case of Fred Delgado, who at age fifteen was arrested by the Wichita police for an offense of sexual perversion.[26] The story of his ordeal and how it brought about much needed changes in the police department follows:

> After his arrest Delgado was taken into a small room of the Wichita police headquarters, which was reserved by police for the questioning of prisoners. Several police and Ku Klux Klan members and city commissioner of Wichita, C. C. Dehner, were present in this room when Delgado was brought for questioning. Once inside the room, someone inquired if Delgado was guilty or not guilty. The boy replied that he was not. He was then ordered upon a table and his clothes unfastened. He was informed that if he did not confess, a certain operation would be performed. One of the officers nearby began handling a large knife, but the boy still maintained his innocence. A reporter was standing nearby. Dehner, the city commissioner, looked at the reporter and said "Come here, Doctor, and perform this operation," but the reporter backed away.
>
> Meanwhile, Dehner called for some turpentine and someone brought him a liquid. He started to smear it on the boy's flesh. "Quit, quit," screamed the fifteen-year-old. "I'll confess to anything you want." The boy was let up and then recanted his confession. "You made me say it," he cried. Again, he was put through the ordeal of the knife and the liquid, and a second time he confessed. He was convicted in juvenile court on the basis of his confession and sent to a reform school for boys. His real age of fifteen was changed on the police blotter to read sixteen, since the law forbade the holding of fifteen-year-old children in jail.

[22]The Knapp Commission Hearing, 1971.
[23]Maas, Peter, *Serpico*. New York: The Viking Press, 1973.
[24]Murphy, Patrick V., and Plate, Thomas, *Commissioner*. New York: Simon & Schuster, Inc.
[25]Knapp Commission, op. cit., p. 61.
[26]Glassberg, Benjamin, et al., *Prisons or Crime Prevention?* Girard, Kan.: Haldeman-Julius Publications, 1928, pp. 60-61, Little Blue Book No. 1271.

This incident would have ordinarily been closed were it not for the reporter present in the room. Dehner was not on good terms with the *Wichita Beacon* since it had always fought the Klan and Dehner was a good Klansman. The reporter related what he had seen and the entire story was published on the front page of the *Beacon*, making the insignificant case of Fred Delgado influential and famous.

A group of Wichita lawyers then organized to fight the mistreatment of prisoners by police. Suspects were thrown in jail on suspicion and held incommunicado; women were forced to change their clothes while the policemen watched; prisoners were beaten if they so much as said a word to the arresting officer.

Because of such incidents, the citizens of Wichita wanted and got a new police chief, twenty-eight-year-old Orlando Winfield Wilson, better known as O. W. Wilson. He had received a Bachelor of Arts degree from the University of California, which was almost unheard of for a policeman during this time. He had majored in criminology in the Department of Political Science and studied under August Vollmer. While studying for his degree, Wilson worked his way through school as a police officer for the Berkeley Police Department. From there he went on to become chief of the Fullerton, California police department. A short time later, the city of Wichita appointed him as its new chief. Wilson received national attention for his successful efforts at reorganizing a police department that had many internal difficulties. He also developed a mobile crime laboratory, laid the foundation for the first women traffic matrons, promoted the use of the polygraph and other scientific aids, and hired officers with college training.*

The Fred Delgado incident is only one example of many similar incidents that took place in thousands of police departments across the country during the same era. It is only unfortunate that from time to time similar incidents still happen in police departments today.

In addition to the mistreatment of prisoners, there are many different situations in which police can become involved in corruption. By far the most serious situation occurs when police organizations are under the influence of politicians, who in turn may be in the control of larger organizations, such as organized crime or huge corporations. When this situation exists, the police are powerless to enforce laws that the corrupt politicians do not favor. However, examples of police corruption can be found within the department it-

---

*O. W. Wilson resigned his position at the Wichita Police Department in 1939 and returned to the University of California at Berkeley where he was appointed Professor of Police Administration, succeeding Vollmer who was retiring. He later was appointed Dean of the School of Criminology. Later Wilson was offered the position of Police Commissioner for the Chicago Police Department, which he accepted. His best known book is *Police Administration*, which has been translated into several foreign languages.

self. For example, the testimony of the former police chief of Seattle, Washington, revealed that policemen in the vice squad collected as much as $12,000 a month in payoffs from gamblers, operators of prostitution houses, and other racket figures.[27] The system of corruption was so well established and defined that it developed its own bureaucracy, with certain jobs designated as bigger payoffs than others. One-tenth of the police force was reportedly involved. Police corruption can also occur in very small towns, and in some cases the entire department may be corrupt. In one case, for example, all four members of a four-member police department were indicted on charges of taking payoffs from a Mafia boss in return for giving information about an investigation of his activities being conducted by another law enforcement agency.[28]

The Knapp Commission divided corrupt police officers into two basic categories: (1) "meat-eaters," and (2) "grass-eaters." "Meat-eaters" are those police officers who aggressively misuse their authority for personal gain. "Grass-eaters" are officers who, if offered, will accept a payoff. It should be mentioned that only a small percentage of police officers are corrupt and the vast majority of the officers who are corrupt are "grass-eaters." The majority of payoffs accepted are by officers in the narcotics and vice units. The Knapp Commission has differentiated five categories of payoffs, which are described below.

**extortion** Police officers actively and aggressively demanding money. Usually the "victim" is a narcotics dealer, gambling operator, or pimp.
**pads** Payments given to a police officer on a regular basis such as weekly, biweekly or monthly. Those who receive such payments are referred to as being "on the pad."
**score** A one-time payment.
**gratuities** Receiving free goods or services. This is an ethically borderline practice, and is usually prohibited by departmental regulations.
**court-related payoffs** Payoffs to police officers to change their testimony so that a case will be dismissed.

## Prevention of police corruption

To reform departments and significantly reduce the possibility or occurrence of police corruption, the Knapp Commission has recommended the following guidelines:

1. Corrupt activity must be curtailed by eliminating as many situations as possible which expose policemen to corruption, and by controlling exposure where corruption hazards are unavoidable. Local businesses, community agencies, and other groups should be warned by the police department that officers are not to be given tips, gratuities, or other benefits for the performance of their

[27]Dorman, op. cit., p. 25.
[28]Ibid, p. 69.

duty. Policies to arrest bribe takers as well as bribe givers should be encouraged.

2. Temptations to engage in corrupt activity on the part of the police must be reduced by subjecting both to significant risks of detection, apprehension, conviction, and penalties.
3. Incentives for meritorious police performance must be increased.
4. Police attitudes toward corruption must continue to change.
5. A climate of reform must be supported by the public.

It should be mentioned that it is a difficult task for a police administrator to completely control corruption of lower ranking officers, no matter who the administrator is. In 1973, for example, nineteen Chicago police officers were convicted for a series of tavern shakedowns reaching back into the days when O. W. Wilson was superintendent.[29]

## CORRUPTION IN BUSINESS

There are numerous documented examples of businesses making payoffs. In May 1975, for example, it was disclosed that Lockheed Aircraft paid $22 million over a 5½-year period to foreign officials and political parties to win sales contracts. In March 1976, Boeing disclosed that since 1970 it had paid nearly $70 million in commissions to foreign representatives to help sell its aircraft. Exxon admitted to approving $27 million in political payments, and Gulf Oil gave at least $3 million to the Democratic Republican party of South Korea. In the case of United States versus McDonough Company, one president and three vice-presidents of several comparatively small garden tool manufacturing firms received ninety-day jail sentences and a fine of $5,000 for deliberate price-fixing and market-rigging.[30]

In cases of corporate corruption in which the president or other high-ranking executive is convicted, sentences very rarely result in a jail term—or at most a term of thirty to ninety days. This is so even though the corruption has resulted in millions of dollars in losses to the public, the government, or the business itself. On the other hand, our prisons are full of persons from lower socioeconomic backgrounds who are sentenced to five to ten years for stealing a car, for example, valued at only a few thousand dollars. In 1931, Shaw made reference to this discrepancy:

> The thief who is in prison is not necessarily more dishonest than his fellows at large, but mostly only one who, through ignorance or stupidity, steals in a way that is not customary. He snatches a loaf from the baker's counter and is promptly run into gaol [jail]. Another man snatches bread from the tables of hundreds of

---

[29]Neier, op. cit., p. 73.
[30]Ball, Harry V., and Friedman, Lawrence M., "Criminal Sanctions in Enforcement of Economic Legislation," in *Crime at the Top*, John M. Johnson and Jack D. Douglas, editors. Philadelphia: J. B. Lippincott Co., 1978, p. 293.

widows and orphans and simple credulous souls who do not know the ways of company promoters; and, as likely as not, he is run into Parliament.[31]

The problem is still with us, as Hougan notes:

> If preliminary reports and investigations could be believed, Lockheed had invaded the treasuries of a dozen nations, helped to corrupt the political processes of both hemispheres, deceived the taxpayer, destabilized the governments of three allies, undermined NATO, subverted the marketplace, boosted inflation, and prompted a series of newspaper sensations that appeared to have resulted in suicides as far apart as Tokyo and L.A.[32]

Some heads of multinational companies have essentially unrestricted power, and with immediate access to millions of dollars to spend as they see fit, they are driven by one overriding goal—to improve the company's profits. Studies have shown that the multinational firm's ability to transfer large sums of money from one currency to another at a profit plays an important role in the devaluation or revaluation of each of the world's major currencies.[33] Recently there has been much attention given to corruption within the petroleum industry. This subject is discussed below in greater detail.

## Corruption in the oil industry

Corruption of oil company executives is nothing new. On June 25, 1928 Robert W. Stewart, president of Standard Oil of Indiana, was charged with giving false testimony to a Senate Committee.[34] Today, many persons believe that the energy "shortage" is a gigantic fraud against the American people. Because of the complexity of the issue as well as its enormous scope it will be very difficult to find a "smoking gun." However, as early as 1973 the Federal Trade Commission issued a complaint against Exxon, Texaco, Gulf, Mobil, Standard Oil of California, Standard Oil of Indiana, Shell, and Atlantic Richfield, charging them with violating Section 5 of the Federal Trade Commission Act (15 U.S.C., Section 45).

In its complaint, the FTC asserted:

> That respondents [the oil companies] have denied society the savings from cheap and plentiful crude oil by limiting the transportation capacity serving such pools and are at the same time responsible for society's resources not being allocated in the most efficient manner in that the higher prices caused by respondents have resulted in the utilization of inefficient stripper wells and wells and

---

[31] Shaw, Bernard, *Doctors' Delusions, Crude Criminology, and Sham Education.* London: Constable and Co., 1931 (reprinted 1950), p. 203.

[32] Hougan, Jim, "The Business of Buying Friends," in *Crime at the Top*, John M. Johnson and Jack D. Douglas, editors. Philadelphia: J. B. Lippincott Co., 1978, p. 196.

[33] Gwirtzman, Milton S., "Is Bribery Defensible?" in *Crime at the Top*, John M. Johnson and Jack D. Douglas, editors. Philadelphia: J. B. Lippincott Co., 1978, p. 337.

[34] *Wichita Eagle*, June 26, 1928, p. 1.

fields of high cost and low yield. This assertion appears to be in conflict with: 1) the concept that America does not have plentiful oil in terms of being self-sufficient, 2) the fact that cheap oil is not available from any source and 3) the proposed national policy espoused by many that high prices and profits should be allowed in order to encourage the development of relatively inefficient, high cost and low yield wells as a step toward self sufficiency.[35]

**Background.** In its complaint issued in July 1973, the Commission charged the nation's eight largest petroleum companies and described them as being vertically integrated companies operating at all of the following five basic levels of the petroleum industry: (1) exploration and production of crude oil, (2) transportation of crude oil, (3) refining of crude oil, (4) transportation of refined petroleum products, and (5) marketing of refined petroleum products. The companies were charged with having combined or agreed to monopolize, with having maintained monopoly power, and, individually and with each other, with having restrained trade and maintained and reinforced a noncompetitive market structure with respect to the refining of crude oil in the relevant market.[36] The FTC went on to charge that:

> Since at least 1950, respondents, individually and with each other, have maintained and reinforced a noncompetitive market structure in the refining of crude oil into petroleum products in the relevant market.
>
> In maintaining and reinforcing the aforesaid noncompetitive market structure, respondents, individually and with each other, have been and are engaged in, among others, the following acts and practices, some of which, *inter alia*, control and limit the supply of crude oil to independent refiners and potential entrants into refining:
>
> (a) Pursuing a common course of action to abuse and exploit the ownership and control of the means of gathering and transporting crude oil to refineries;
>
> (b) Pursuing a common course of action in participating in restrictive or exclusionary transfers of ownership of crude oil among themselves and with other petroleum companies;
>
> (c) Pursuing a common course of action of adhering to a system of posted prices leading to the maintenance of an artificial level for the price of crude oil;
>
> (d) Entering into numerous processing arrangements with independent refiners thereby expanding their control over refining capacity and limiting the availability of refined petroleum products to independent marketers, and potential entrants into marketing;
>
> (e) Pursuing a common course of action of accommodating the needs and goals of each other in the production, supply and transportation of crude oil to the exclusion or detriment of independent refiners and potential entrants into refining;
>
> (f) Pursuing a common course of action of using their vertical integration to

---

[35]Federal Trade Commission Docket No. 8934, In the Matter of Exxon Corporation, et al.
[36]Ibid.

keep profits at the crude level artificially high and profits at the refining level artificially low thereby raising entry barriers to refining;

(g) Pursuing a common course of action to abuse and exploit the ownership and control of the means of transporting refined petroleum products from refineries;

(h) Pursuing a common course of action of accommodating the needs and goals of each other in the transportation and marketing of refined petroleum products to the exclusion or detriment of independent marketers and potential entrants into marketing.

The companies have exercised monopoly power in the refining of petroleum products in the relevant markets by engaging in, among others, the following acts and practices:

(a) Pursuing a common course of action in refusing to sell gasoline and other refined petroleum products to independent marketers;

(b) Pursuing a common course of action in participating in restrictive or exclusionary exchanges and sales of gasoline and other refined petroleum products among themselves and with other petroleum companies;

(c) Pursuing a common course of action in their marketing practices thereby avoiding price competition in the marketing of refined petroleum products.

Respondents, individually and with each other, have followed and do follow common courses of action in accommodating the needs and goals of each other throughout the petroleum industry thereby increasing the interdependence of respondents and reducing respondents' incentive to behave competitively.

**Effects.** The oil companies' acts and practices have had, among others, the following effects:

(a) Respondents have established and maintained artificial price levels for the goods and services rendered at each level of the petroleum industry;

(b) Barriers to entry into the refining of petroleum products have been raised, strengthened and otherwise increased;

(c) Actual and potential competition at all levels of the petroleum industry has been hindered, lessened, eliminated and foreclosed;

(d) The normal response of supply to demand for refined petroleum products has been distorted. Shortages of petroleum products have fallen with particular severity on sections of the country where independent refiners and marketers are primarily located;

(e) The burden of shortages of petroleum products has been forced to fall with particular severity on those sections of the United States, east of the Rockies, where independent refiners and marketers are concentrated thereby eliminating the most significant source of price competition in the marketing of petroleum products and threatening the competitive viability and existence of the independent sector.

(f) Independent marketers have been forced to close retail outlets and significantly curtail retail operations because of their inability to obtain refined products.

(g) Respondents have obtained profits and returns on investment substantially in excess of those that they would have obtained in a competitively structured market.

(h) American consumers have been forced to pay substantially higher prices for petroleum and petroleum products than they would have had to pay in a competitively structured market.

**Violations.** The FTC further stated:

> The aforesaid acts and practices constitute a combination or agreement to monopolize refining of crude oil into petroleum products in the relevant markets in violation of Section 5 of the Federal Trade Commission Act;
>
> Through the aforesaid acts and practices, respondents have maintained monopoly power over the refining of crude oil into petroleum products in the relevant markets in violation of Section 5 of the Federal Trade Commission Act;
>
> Respondents, individually and with each other, have restrained trade and maintained a noncompetitive market structure in the refining of crude oil into petroleum products in the relevant markets in violation of Section 5 of the Federal Trade Commission Act.
>
> Because of THE PREMISES CONSIDERED, the Federal Trade Commission on the 18th day of July, 1973, issues this complaint against said respondents.[37]

The case against the oil companies is still in litigation even though it was begun over eight years ago. The official designation of the status of the case by the FTC is that it is "still pending."

A recent public hearing on energy fraud raised some very serious questions, including:

- □ The vertical integration of major oil companies
- □ The lack of consumer education to prevent energy fraud
- □ The suppression of technology of competing supplies of energy in order to maximize profits in oil and gas
- □ Whether or not current Department of Energy policies are themselves restraining the energy market[38]

Most readers of this report will find the Department of Energy's answers to these questions less than satisfactory.

## Corrupt practices

There are a number of different techniques that corrupt businesses employ to defraud the people.

**Deceptive advertising.** It is impossible to try to estimate the amount of

---

[37]Ibid.

[38]*Energy and Consumer Protection, Competition and Fraud.* Official Transcript of Public Briefing and Addendum, March 30, 1978, Washington, D.C.: U.S. Department of Energy, October, 1978. (Copies available from National Technical Information Services, U.S. Department of Commerce, 5285 Port Royal Road, Springfield, Va. 22161).

deceptive, and many times outright false, advertising we are subjected to. Every day we are told that using a certain brand of toothpaste will improve our sex life, or that one detergent is far superior to another, or that there is a significant difference among different brands of aspirin. Since we are constantly told these things over an authoritative source—electronic and print media—we may unthinkingly accept the claims the advertiser makes as fact.

**Price-fixing.** Price-fixing is the arbitrary setting of prices. For example, lawyers' and physicians' fees are set to exclude competition.

**Mergers.** Misuse of the merger to acquire smaller competitor companies results in control of the market of a certain product or service.

**Conspiracy.** A conspiracy in this case is an illegal plan among similar companies to change prices.

**Exclusive dealerships.** These dealerships prohibit the carrying of products of competitors.

**Franchising.** Franchising results in restraint of trade if the franchiser unreasonably limits the right of franchisees to make decisions regarding their own business.

**Reciprocal trading.** This can be described as "I'll scratch your back if you scratch mine." In other words, a buyer will agree to buy from a seller if the seller will also buy from him, thus limiting outside competition.

**Trade associations.** Groups, such as realtors, for example, may develop an association to promote "professionalism." Unfortunately, these groups tend to abuse the original purpose of the group and promote fee schedules or noncompetitive commission rates instead of professionalism.

**Set resale prices.** The principal example of this concerns a name-brand manufacturer setting a minimum price below which the product cannot be sold.

**Tying.** Tying is an illegal practice between manufacturers selling products and vendors buying products. In this relationship a manufacturer of floor wax, for example, will sell his product to vendors only if they also agree to purchase related products, such as mops, sponges, etc.

**Exclusive contract.** An example of this is the practice of a large producer contracting with a freight hauler to haul only his particular product and no similar products of a competitor.

### Restraint of trade

The most flagrant example of price-fixing and restraint of trade is conducted quite openly by the Organization of Petroleum Exporting Countries (OPEC). OPEC stifles the open market system of free competition by developing across-the-board price controls for exported oil. Also involved in restraint of trade practices are many lawyers, physicians, realtors, brokers, and mechanics. Some organizations for realtors, barbers, lawyers, physicians, etc., by limiting advertising, setting fee rates, and hindering competition, artificially increase the cost of these services, thus causing Americans to spend millions of unnecessary dollars because of excessive fees. A good example of restraint of trade was brought to light in a recent decision against the American Medical Association:

> In November 1978, a Judge for the Federal Trade Commission ruled that the AMA, the nation's largest association of physicians, has hindered, restricted, restrained, foreclosed and frustrated competition in the provision of physicians' services throughout the United States and caused substantial injury to the public.[39]

In his decision in the matter of the American Medical Association (AMA), Connecticut State Medical Society, and New Haven County Medical Association, Inc., FTC Administrative Law Judge Ernest G. Barnes found that the respondents (the Medical Association) have "conspired, combined and agreed to adopt, disseminate and enforce ethical standards which ban physician solicitation of business, severely restrict physician advertising and prohibit certain contractual arrangements between physicians and health care delivery organizations and between physicians and nonphysicians." These acts and practices, Barnes concluded, constitute unfair methods of competition and unfair acts and practices in violation of Section 5 of the FTC Act.

Barnes noted that the result of the challenged practices has been the:

> placement of a formidable impediment to competition in the delivery of health care services by physicians in this country. That barrier has served to deprive consumers of the free flow of information about the availability of health care services, to deter the offering of innovative forms of health care and to stifle the rise of almost every type of health care delivery that could potentially pose a threat to the income of fee-for-service physicians in private practice. The costs to the public in terms of less expensive, or even perhaps, more improved forms of medical services are great.[40]

This initial decision was based on the FTC's complaint issued against the associations on December 19, 1975. That complaint charged the associations with violations of Section 5 of the FTC Act by restricting the ability of their members to advertise for and solicit patients and to enter into various contractual arrangements in connection with the offering of their services to the public. Specifically, the complaint charges that respondents have agreed with others to prevent or hinder their physician members from:

---

[39]*FTC News*, Nov. 29, 1978.
[40]Ibid, p. 1.

    □ Soliciting business, by advertising or otherwise
    □ Engaging in price competition
    □ Otherwise engaging in competitive practices

The complaint further alleges that, as a result of those acts and practices:

    □ Prices of physician services have been stabilized, fixed, or otherwise interfered with
    □ Competition between medical doctors in the provision of such services has been hindered, restrained, foreclosed, and frustrated
    □ Consumers have been deprived of information pertinent to the selection of a physician and of the benefits of competition

The FTC's complaint and the initial decision deal with the associations' ethics restrictions. Those restrictions do not, according to Barnes, deal with the medical or therapeutic aspects of a physician's practice but with restrictions on economic activities.

Barnes noted that respondents challenged the FTC's jurisdiction over them. In dealing with the jurisdictional question, Barnes found that the respondents were a "company . . . or association . . . organized to carry on business for its own profit or that of its members," as required under Section 4 of the FTC Act. He further found that respondents' acts and practices were "in or affecting commerce," as required by Section 5 of the FTC Act. Thus, he concluded that the FTC has jurisdiction over the respondents.

Barnes noted that the main body of evidence against AMA consists of the Principles of Medical Ethics, official interpretations of the Principles, and letter after letter from AMA officials explaining the Principles and urging compliance with them.[41]

It was found that the ethical restrictions on advertising and solicitation seek to prevent any doctor from presenting his or her name or information about his or her practice to the public in any way that "sets him apart from other physicians." These restrictions, according to Barnes, "affect all facets of competition among physicians." Specifically cited in the initial decision were restrictive ethics actions taken by respondents against advertising and solicitation efforts of Health Maintenance Organizations (HMO) and their physicians.

Barnes further found that the ". . . organization of each of the respondents, their interrelationships and the mutuality manifest throughout their application and enforcement of ethics proscriptions attest to the logical conclusion that the respondents and others have acted in concert to restrain competition among physicians." The effect of the conspiracy, according to Barnes, has been to "deprive consumers of the free flow of commercial infor-

---

[41]Ibid, p. 2.

mation that is indispensable in making informed economic decisions, and to interfere with the freedom of physicians to make their own decisions as to their employment conditions." Further, the AMA's restrictions have discouraged, restricted, and in some instances eliminated new methods of health care. Barnes' order required that respondents:

- Cease and desist from engaging in the challenged practices
- Revoke and rescind any existing ethical principles or guidelines that restrict physicians' advertising, solicitation, or contractual relations
- Provide adequate notification to its members and affiliated societies of the terms of the order
- Deny affiliation to any society that engages in any practices that violate the terms of the order

Because of the power of the AMA as an organization and the far-reaching effects of this decision, it will prove to be an issue that will be debated and modified for some time to come. Crimes such as this, which affect millions of persons simultaneously and cost hundreds of millions of dollars, can only be prevented by alert citizens and the sending of complaint letters to the appropriate federal agency such as the FTC.

There are numerous other examples of unfair and deceptive practices by businesses that pose serious problems for consumers and federal, state, and local law enforcement officials. For example, many consumers are easy targets for abuses by vocational training schools. They may be persuaded by misleading advertisements and promises by salespeople that the school will provide adequate training and placement services needed to get jobs as medical assistants, insurance adjusters, models, truck drivers, etc. Many students, however, are unable to get jobs after graduating either because many employers consider the training unacceptable or the school's training or placement services are inadequate. The student's investment of both money and time may prove virtually useless.

People can also lose money on new business ventures, such as business "opportunities" that promise a chance to work at home. The advertisements are enticing, promising high salaries. Unfortunately, many people never see profits but instead sustain losses which, in some cases, exceed their original investments of thousands of dollars.

Other consumers, particularly retired persons, are victims of land sales schemes. A seller may carefully lead a consumer into buying underdeveloped land by misrepresenting facts. For example, the seller may say that recreational facilities will soon be available, that development potential of the area is good, that land is an excellent investment, or that interest rates will go up if the consumer waits too long to buy. If these representations prove false, the consumer seeking financial gain or a home with the facilities and amenities of a successful development may be left instead with largely underdeveloped land with a market value below cost.

Phony bargains are other examples of unfair and deceptive practices by businesses. Through the use of come-ons and false claims, such as phony clearance sales, "reduced" prices that are not reduced, and the ridiculous claim to sell merchandise under cost, many businesses persuade customers to buy merchandise they would not ordinarily have bought and probably did not need.

Some corruption also results when businesses knowingly sell misrepresented goods. An example is the selling of inferior goods as first quality merchandise. In a closely related scheme, consumers are misled by advertisements of a sale of a famous name-brand product at a ridiculously low price, such as a certain brand of blue jeans. However, in many cases, the name brand turns out to be a counterfeit or imitation of inferior quality, which may even bear a copy of the name brand's trademark.

Stock swindling is another form of corruption. Stock swindlers often acquire a company's capital stock selling for a few cents per share. Through letters, telephone calls, stock-market advisory services, and tipster sheets posing as conservative financial publications they advise their unsuspecting customers to buy. As the customers buy, the stock naturally soars; but once the swindlers have unloaded their shares, it drops back to its original figure. Some swindlers sell fraudulent stocks by setting up brokerage companies that go out of existence when the stocks have been unloaded. What is called a "boiler room" in this racket is a large, soundproof room lined with telephones manned by "dynamiters," or expert salesmen, who work on a commission basis trying to persuade potential customer/victims to buy.[42]

## THEORIES OF CORRUPTION

There are many competing theories of corruption. Several of these are described in the following pages.

### "Evil man" syndrome

This theory postulates that corruption is the result of an exceptionally evil man arising at different points in history. In many cases, the evil man does not appear to be anything more than an individual hungry for power. Striving to control, dominate, or manipulate more and more people or situations may drive the so-called evil man toward corrupt practices.

---

[42]Campbell, Samuel C., *Methods of Criminals*. Girard, Kan.: Haldeman-Julius Publications, 1945, pp. 22-23, Little Blue Book No. 1751.

However, placing the cause of corruption on a single source overlooks the fundamental institutional factors that make possible abuses of power. It also fails to acknowledge the necessity of objectively and rigorously assessing the performance of personnel and agencies that are trusted with the responsibility of protecting the integrity of the country's basic freedoms.

### Organized crime

Organized crime has been responsible for some degree of corruption, as has previously been documented. By offering large sums of money or by making threats of violence to high-ranking executives and officials or members of their families, the organized criminal is often able to heavily influence others. In fact, every Mafia family designates at least one high-ranking member as a corrupter. In many cases, the job is given to the consiglieri, or counselor to the family boss. It is the corrupter's job to make an offer that cannot be refused. The Mafia's ability to corrupt has been proved many times but perhaps the accomplishments of Antonio Corallo top them all. Within a time period of seven years, Corallo managed to involve not only himself, but a New York State Supreme Court judge, a federal prosecutor, a key aide to New York Mayor John V. Lindsay, and a Democratic party power broker in three bribery prosecutions. Those three prosecutions represented merely the cases in which Corallo was caught. There is no way of knowing how many additional political fixes he arranged.[43]

However, as much as we would like to put all of the blame on organized crime for corruption, we simply cannot. Most incidents of corruption involve ordinary citizens who simply abuse their positions of trust. However, a percentage of corruption in which ordinary citizens are involved can be attributed to factors within the system, or systemic corruption.

### Systemic corruption

Many current political scientists see the problem of corruption in America as being systemic in nature, or a result of established policies, guidelines, rules, or regulations. When this is the case, laws created to implement policy directly incite corruption. As one example, the Texas Youth Council (TYC) administered a program whose budget depended directly on the number of children sent to its reformatories. The budget was established at approximately $10,000 per child in 1969 and 1970. When newspaper revelations of the "agreed judgment" technique for sending children to schools operated by the Texas Youth Council caused an outcry in El Paso, the TYC revoked the paroles of a much higher number of children than usual to make up for the

---

[43]Dorman, op. cit., p. 72.

decrease in the number of those sent directly to the schools for the first time. Therefore, the budget was roughly maintained.[44]

There are numerous other examples in which laws have directly influenced corruptive practices. Armed forces recruiters, for example, have traditionally been expected to enlist a certain number of persons; however, with the present unpopularity of enlisting in the armed services, this task has become more difficult. Therefore, rather than failing to meet criteria, rules are bent, and those who ordinarily would not be eligible are recruited, or clandestine compensation is given to some enlistees.

Another example is the law that provides monetary reimbursements to social services agencies charged with the responsibility of protecting children who are wards of the courts. This serves to encourage keeping as many children in foster homes as possible rather than freeing them for adoption, since financial assistance is stopped when a child is adopted.

Another cause of systemic corruption is the unwillingness of persons in higher authority to support the efforts of those below them. For example, police officers who originally set out to enforce all laws may soon find out that their efforts are not appreciated. When superiors in the station house pretend not to notice what is going on around them, when a notorious underworld figure is convicted of a serious crime but is given a slap on the wrist for a sentence, or when some of the most influential persons in town want to continue an illegal practice, the officers who pursue these issues may soon find themselves transferred to another department, relieved of a case, or terminated. Therefore, the police officer who cannot "fight them" sometimes gives up and "joins them."

Another intrinsic factor that may stimulate police corruption is low salaries. Many highly qualified individuals with high moral standards and integrity do not apply to police forces for this reason. In addition, low salaries may cause police officers to perceive a real or imagined economic need, which increases their susceptibility to corruptive practices such as bribery. Some theorists believe that because the system contributes to corruptive practices, it would be almost impossible for public servants to resist the temptations of corruption.

Although there may be a variety of factors leading to corruption, underneath them all lie the two most important motivating factors of all: the love of money and/or power and the fulfillment of other self-interests. Any theories that give other causes for corruption are only attempting to camouflage the actual motivating factors of greed and self-fulfillment.

[44]Lieberman, Jethro K., "How the Government Breaks the Law," in *Crime: Emerging Issues*, James A. Inciardi and Harvey A. Siegal, editors. New York: Praeger Publishers, 1977, pp. 193-195.

## SYMPTOMS OF CORRUPTION

How to tell if something is wrong in city hall is the most strategic question in the issue of corruption in government. Corruption can take many forms including favoritism, graft, padded payrolls, bribes, conflict of interest, sweetheart contracts, and officials turning their heads to open violations of laws and ordinances. Unless some form of documentation can be obtained it will take someone on the inside stepping forward to reveal the truth, such as was the case of John Dean and Watergate. Or if officials are willing to entertain the idea that corruption might exist in their particular department or agency, then a list of eleven questions developed by the Internal Revenue Service should be of value. These eleven questions are designed to help determine if corruption is present or has ever been present in the past in various agencies. Among the information sought is:

1. Did the corporation, any of its employees, or a third party acting on behalf of the corporation make any bribes, kickbacks, or other payments of any kind, not necessarily money, to any representative of another company or organization for the purpose of obtaining favorable treatment in securing business or as payment for favorable treatment received in the past?
2. Did the corporation, employees, or any third party acting on behalf of the corporation make any bribes, kickbacks, or other payments regardless of form, to any government official or employee, domestic or foreign, whether on the national level or state, county or local level, including regulatory agencies, for the purpose of affecting the action of the government in order to obtain favorable treatment in securing business or to pay for business secured or special concessions obtained in the past?
3. Were corporate funds donated, loaned, or made available to any government, political party, candidate or committee, either domestic or foreign for the purpose of benefiting or opposing governments or candidates?
4. Was corporate property of any kind donated, loaned, or made available to any government, political party, candidate or committee for the purpose of benefiting or opposing same governments or candidates?
5. Was any corporate employee reimbursed by the corporation for time spent or expenses incurred in performing services for the benefit of or opposition to any government, political party, candidate or committee, either domestic or foreign?
6. Did the corporation make any loans, donations, or other disbursements, directly or indirectly, to corporate employees or others for the purpose of benefiting or opposing any government, political party, candidate or committee, either domestic or foreign?
7. Did the corporation make any loans, donations or other disbursements to corporate employees or others for the purpose of compensating such employees or others for contributions, for the purpose of benefiting or opposing any government, political party, candidate or committee, either domestic or foreign?
8. Did the corporation or does it presently maintain a bank account or any other

account of any kind, either domestic or foreign, which is or was not included on corporate books, records, balance sheets, or other financial statements?

9. Did any or presently does any corporate employee or other person acting on behalf of the corporation have authority and/or control over disbursements from foreign bank accounts?

10. Did the corporation or does it presently maintain a domestic or foreign numbered account or an account in a name other than the name of the corporation?

11. Which additional present or past corporate employees, or other persons acting on behalf of the corporation may have knowledge concerning any of the above questions?

In addition to these eleven questions, the National Advisory Commission on Criminal Justice Standards and Goals has developed a 74-item questionnaire on corruption in government (see box).

Based on the answers given in the questionnaires, an institution will be able to identify existing conditions that may encourage corruption or indicate that corruption is already taking place. These tools are therefore a preventive measure—a means of identifying necessary changes before corruption can develop, or as an after-the-fact aid in identifying needed changes in order to prevent or decrease further corruption.

**National Advisory Commission on Criminal Justice Standards and Goals**
## QUESTIONNAIRE ON CORRUPTION

1. Do respected and well-qualified companies refuse to do business with the city or State? Yes ☐  No ☐
2. Are municipal contracts let to a narrow group of firms? Yes ☐  No ☐
3. Is competitive bidding required? Yes ☐  No ☐
4. Are there numerous situations that justify the letting of contracts without competitive bidding? Yes ☐  No ☐ For example, are there frequent "emergency contracts" for which bids are not solicited? Yes ☐  No ☐
5. Have there been disclosures of companies that have submitted low bids but were disqualified for certain unspecified technical reasons? Yes ☐  No ☐
6. Do turnpike or port authorities or governmental departments operate with almost total autonomy, accountable only to themselves and not to the public or other government officials? Yes ☐  No ☐
7. Does the mayor or Governor have inadequate statutory authority and control over the various departments of the executive branch? Yes ☐  No ☐

Prepared by the National Advisory Commission on Criminal Justice Standards and Goals for its *Report on Community Crime Prevention.*

*Continued.*

QUESTIONNAIRE ON CORRUPTION—cont'd

8. Are certain government employees frozen into their jobs by an act of the city council or State legislature? Yes ☐ No ☐
9. Is there not an effective independent investigation agency to which citizens can direct complaints regarding official misconduct? Yes ☐ No ☐
10. Are kickbacks and reciprocity regarded by the business community as just another cost of doing business? Yes ☐ No ☐
11. Is it customary for citizens to tip sanitation workers, letter carriers, and other groups of government employees at Christmastime? Yes ☐ No ☐
12. Is double parking permitted in front of some restaurants or taverns but not in front of others? Yes ☐ No ☐
13. Do some contractors keep the street and sidewalks reasonably free from materials, debris, etc., while others show little concern about such matters despite ordinances prohibiting litter? Yes ☐ No ☐
14. Is it common knowledge that architects add a sum to their fees to cover "research" at the city's planning and building department? Yes ☐ No ☐
15. Is illegal gambling conducted without much interference from authorities? Yes ☐ No ☐
16. Do investigations of police corruption generally result in merely a few officers being transferred from one precinct to another? Yes ☐ No ☐
17. Is there no special State unit charged with investigating organized crime and the conduct of public employees? Yes ☐ No ☐
18. Does one encounter long delays when applying for a driver's license, for the issuance of a building permit, or for payment in connection with services rendered the city or State? Yes ☐ No ☐
19. Are government procedures so complicated that a middleman is often required to unravel the mystery and get through to the right people? Yes ☐ No ☐
20. With each new administration, does the police department undergo an upheaval—the former chief now walking a beat, and a former patrolman now chief, etc.? Yes ☐ No ☐
21. Are zoning variances granted that are generally considered detrimental to the community? Yes ☐ No ☐
22. Is there a wide gap between what the law declares illegal and the popular morality? Yes ☐ No ☐
23. Are officeseekers spending more of their personal funds campaigning for political positions than the cumulative salary they would receive as incumbents during their term in office? Yes ☐ No ☐
24. Do city or State officials have significant interests in firms doing business with the government? Yes ☐ No ☐
25. Would officials benefit financially from projects planned or under way? Yes ☐ No ☐
26. Is there a lack of qualified government personnel to supervise and monitor public works projects? Yes ☐ No ☐

27. Is there no merit system incorporated into civil service procedures? Yes ☐ No ☐
28. Are patronage appointments extensive? Yes ☐ No ☐
29. Do government salaries fail to approximate what could be earned in comparable private sector positions? Yes ☐ No ☐
30. Are vice operations in certain sections of the city more or less tolerated by authorities? Yes ☐ No ☐
31. Is moonlighting by government personnel not regulated? Yes ☐ No ☐
32. Is it common knowledge that jury duty can be avoided or a ticket fixed? Yes ☐ No ☐
33. Have public officials accepted high posts with companies having government contracts? Yes ☐ No ☐
34. Has a legislator or councilman introduced legislation by which he would benefit financially? Yes ☐ No ☐
35. Is there no effective bribery statute that embraces all government personnel, not just department heads? Yes ☐ No ☐
36. Do officials use government equipment or material for personal projects? Yes ☐ No ☐
37. Do the media fail to report the existence of organized crime within the community or State? Yes ☐ No ☐
38. Is there a high turnover rate within municipal departments? Yes ☐ No ☐
39. Do the police discourage citizens from making complaints or pressing charges? Yes ☐ No ☐
40. Have certain prisoners been known to receive special favors while in jail? Yes ☐ No ☐
41. Does the police department have no internal investigation unit? Yes ☐ No ☐
42. Are State police with statewide investigative authority not authorized to operate in municipalities if there is reasonable suspicion of corruption there? Yes ☐ No ☐
43. Are an extraordinary small percentage of arrested organized crime figures convicted, and, of those convicted, are sentences insignificant in relation to the crime and criminal? Yes ☐ No ☐
44. Are complainants in judicial proceedings frequently not notified of the date they are supposed to appear in court? Yes ☐ No ☐
45. Are court fines regarded as a source of revenue for the municipality? Yes ☐ No ☐
46. Are there part-time prosecutors? Yes ☐ No ☐
47. Are key public officials not required to disclose sources of income and the nature of their investments? Yes ☐ No ☐
48. Is the presence of organized crime repeatedly denied, even though no one has really looked for it? Yes ☐ No ☐

*Continued.*

**QUESTIONNAIRE ON CORRUPTION—cont'd**

49. Are records of official government agencies closed to public inspection? Yes ☐ No ☐
50. Are archaic laws still on the books? Yes ☐ No ☐
51. Are public employees not required to answer, under penalty of removal from office if they decline, questions pertaining to their official conduct? Yes ☐ No ☐
52. Are records of disciplinary action against government employees closed to inspection? Yes ☐ No ☐
53. Is it common knowledge that if the press prints unflattering, though truthful, stories about the police, delivery trucks are ticketed and sources of information for reporters within the department dry up? Yes ☐ No ☐
54. Is it common knowledge that candidates for judgeships and for police positions of lieutenant and above must be accepted by ward committeemen? Yes ☐ No ☐
55. Is morale among public servants low? Yes ☐ No ☐
56. Are citizens barred from public meetings and from access to what should be public records? Yes ☐ No ☐
57. Do laws protect from public scrutiny information that should be public, such as ownership of real estate? Yes ☐ No ☐
58. Do projects for which money has been authorized fail to materialize or remain only partially completed? Yes ☐ No ☐
59. Can city employees represent private interests before city boards? Yes ☐ No ☐
60. Do State workers have to contribute a percentage of their wages to the party's campaign chest? Yes ☐ No ☐
61. Are machine politics an inherent part of the system? Yes ☐ No ☐
62. Are bribegivers, as well as bribetakers, arrested and prosecuted? Yes ☐ No ☐

## PREVENTING CORRUPTON
### Efforts of the Federal Trade Commission

Several government agencies that serve to establish anticorruptive legislation, enforce anticorruptive laws, and prosecute offenders are now in existence. The Federal Trade Commission, however, is charged with most of the responsibility for executing these duties, assisted by small claims courts and strike forces. A discussion of the scope of the Federal Trade Commission and supporting efforts in preventing corruption is included in the following pages.

In 1889, President Benjamin Harrison labeled the big monopolies as "dangerous conspiracies that tended to crush out competition." His leadership led to the passage of the Sherman Antitrust Act in 1890. This was the

63. Do public officials attend conventions at the expense of private sector groups? Yes □ No □
64. Do civil service regulations inordinately impair the hiring, disciplinary, and firing latitude of public officials? Yes □ No □
65. Do large campaign contributions follow favorable government rulings? Yes □ No □
66. Are ethical codes not institutionalized to any significant degree? Yes □ No □
67. Are those arrested for narcotics and gambling violations primarily bottom rung violators (street pusher and numbers runner vs. wholesaler and numbers banker)? Yes □ No □
68. Do bail bondsmen flourish within the community? Yes □ No □
69. Are public positions filled when there is no need for such jobs, such as the post of swimming instructor at a location where there is no pool? Yes □ No □
70. Do business establishments give certain public employees free meals, passes, discounts, and the like? Yes □ No □
71. Are sheriffs permitted to pocket the difference between the sum they are authorized to spend on food for jail inmates and what they actually spend for this purpose? Yes □ No □
72. Is it well known that dedicated police personnel do not relish assignment to vice or plainclothes units? Yes □ No □
73. Is there no mechanism to monitor court testimony of building inspectors, liquor inspectors, and other enforcement personnel to determine whether their court testimony differs from their original reports to the extent that defendants are thereby freed? Yes □ No □
74. Can public employees who wish to retire receive their pensions despite pending charges of misconduct? Yes □ No □

basis for Congress passing an act in 1914 establishing the Federal Trade Commission. Further power was given to the FTC when a Supreme Court decision resulting from *United States versus Morton Salt Co.*, in which the Commission's visitation power, the power of subpoena, and authority to require annual and special reports from any corporation were upheld. The FTC is a very small bureaucracy by government standards, but it has successfully fought for the public and won against such giants as Sears Roebuck, Beech-Nut Packing Company, Standard Oil, Curtis Publishing Company, United States Steel, Procter and Gamble, and Morton Salt, among others. The Commission is comprised of five members appointed by the President and confirmed by the Senate for seven-year terms. The President designates one commissioner as Chairman.

The Commission has three major operating bureaus: (1) consumer protection, (2) competition, and (3) economics. Its basic objective is to maintain strongly competitive enterprises as the foundation of our economic system. Although the Commission has many duties, the public policy underlying them all is essentially to prevent the free enterprise system from being stifled, substantially lessened by monopoly or restraints on trade, or corrupted by unfair or deceptive trade practices.

The Commission's primary legislative authority stems from Section 5 of the FTC Act, which states that unfair methods of competition and unfair or deceptive acts or practices in commerce are unlawful. The Clayton Act and the Consumer Credit Protection Act identify specific unfair or deceptive acts or practices and provide authority for Commission enforcement activities.

The Commission uses a public interest standard to determine which marketplace activities it will pursue. It does not settle individual consumer complaints, but it pursues programs and cases with larger economic impact. In the past, the Commission has been criticized for concentrating too much of its resources on trivial cases, and therefore it has changed its priorities to emphasize larger issues that have national implications.

Broad investigative and adjudicative procedures that are separate from the regular court system are possessed by the FTC. The FTC Act and the Administrative Procedures Act specify how the Commission must proceed in prosecuting its cases.

An investigation of a business or industry may be initiated on the basis of consumer or industry complaints, referrals from the Congress or other government agencies, or the Commission's own monitoring activities. The Commission's investigation, essentially information-gathering and analysis, leads to a consent order, a complaint, a rule-making proceeding, or a decision to close the case. Most cases are settled when a business agrees to cease and desist from a challenged practice.

In many cases businesses charged with and found guilty of unfair and/or deceptive practices must reimburse consumers. This is known as redress—the providing of satisfaction for losses resulting from unfair or deceptive business practices. In many cases, however, the amount of redress is relatively small or available only to a few consumers. The Commission's ability to obtain consumer redress has been limited by:

□ Impracticality due to lengthy and time-consuming procedures
□ The weak financial position of many businesses that are investigated
□ Internal management problems
□ Company assets being unavailable for redress
□ Legally established limits of redress
□ Difficulties in locating eligible consumers
□ Reduced value of any refunds because of inflation

When taken advantage of by unfair practices, consumers should seek redress. Forms of redress include: (1) restitution (generally money), (2) specific performance (requiring the business to provide the promised goods and services), (3) rescission (unmaking or wiping out a contract), and (4) reformation (modifying the contract to make it conform to the original intent of the parties). Consumers who are economically damaged by unfair or deceptive business practices can seek redress through:

- Direct contact with the business
- Local consumer groups
- Better Business Bureaus which can help to settle disputes
- State agencies which investigate consumer complaints and file suits against businesses violating State consumer protection laws
- Small claims courts
- Suits in other courts, either individually or through class action suits brought by many consumers
- Federal agencies, such as the Federal Trade Commission

In order to become more effective in fighting for the rights of consumers, more power should be given to the FTC. This would include more legislative clout, and increased budget and staff for investigations and prosecutions. However, the FTC, which is made up of a high percentage of lawyers, should guard against becoming another Washington bureaucracy and strangling itself with red tape.

### Small claims courts

Small claims courts offer considerable potential for handling consumer problems, but there are indications that they do not function as efficiently as they can. Many courts are located only in downtown sections and are often open only during weekdays when most consumers also work. In some courts there are not enough staff to help consumers prepare complaints. Even when a consumer wins a case, problems in locating the defendant or ignorance of collection procedures hinders collecting on a judgment. Consumers can seek redress in other courts, but high legal fees often make this impractical. Class action suits can make the fees somewhat more affordable, but these are permitted in only a few states.

### Strike forces

One tool that seems fairly effective against organized corruption is the use of strike forces. Members of strike forces concentrate their efforts on major organized crime figures. Members are usually put on detached duty by their agencies to work exclusively on the assigned projects. They are generally federal employees under the supervision of the Justice Department's Organized Crime and Racketeering Section.

### Additional countercorruption measures

Public officials should be prohibited from receiving gifts, gratuities, or other compensation from individuals representing the private business sector. Therefore, the public servant does not become "indebted" to anyone and is not forced to exploit his or her position to return favors. A gift of a bottle of brandy, a free ticket, or discount can be construed as directed at the same ends as would be "gifts" of $5,000. Practices that are breaches of integrity in appearance as well as in fact must be halted, and these policies should be publicized to all government-related and private business customers.

General policies that businesses should follow in order to decrease the probability of corruption overseas include adhering to foreign laws, not giving payments to government officials or accepting them from foreign political organizations, and maintaining accurate corporate financial statements.

## CONCLUSION

Corruption is one of the largest forms of crime perpetrated against the public, but only recently has it been given the attention and recognition worthy of a major crime problem. It is neither as threatening as an armed robber with a gun nor as psychologically damaging as rape, but this almost invisible form of criminal activity costs the public more than many other types of crime combined.

There are several varieties of corrupt practices, which may involve private citizens, local police and governmental officials, business executives, and top-ranking national government figures. Many rationalizations for corruption have been put forth, such as the evil man syndrome, lust for power, organized crime influence, and many systemic causes. As yet, preventive measures for corruption still need further exploration. Recognizing the presence of policies or situations that encourage corruptive practices is a major step toward preventing them. In addition, strengthening penalties for white-collar crimes in general may increase deterrence, and preventive measures are also established by the FTC. At present, however, the major prevention tool lies in the ability of the majority of individuals to maintain their integrity and uphold high moral standards, which has traditionally generated anti-corruptive behaviors such as truth and honesty. In addition, the equalities afforded us by the Fathers of our country through the Constitution have guaranteed that no one person is above the law and that government officials as well as the general public are not excused from this type of activity. The responsibility to correct pervasive flaws in the political process must be shared by all of us.

# Chapter 10

# Security surveys

A security survey is a complete inspection and analysis of either residential or commercial facilities for the purpose of determining security flaws. Security surveys involve on-site evaluation by a trained security director, crime prevention officer, or private consultant. The security survey can take many forms, and because of the diversity of facilities and communities, no one standard checklist will totally suffice. Therefore, it is often necessary to devise a specific survey to suit a given situation.

## OBJECTIVES OF SURVEYS

Security surveys have three principal objectives leading to the ultimate goal of crime prevention. They are (1) to make an assessment of the facility's present security status, (2) to identify existing deficiencies in security, and (3) to suggest security improvements that would make it more difficult for the potential offender to commit an offense at the physical facility.[1]

The first two objectives are accomplished through a detailed analysis and examination of the present external and internal lines of defense of the facility. An in-depth inspection should be conducted of the facility's surrounding grounds, security lighting, doors, windows, locks, alarm systems, and structural and environmental design. In addition to an examination and analysis of physical characteristics, security surveys should also include an evaluation of operational policies. For example, in retail business security surveys, policies pertaining to refunds, exchanges, shipping, purchasing, receiving, delivery, inventories of merchandise, shoplifting, employee theft, and hiring practices should be carefully analyzed.

The third objective is achieved through providing specific security recommendations based on the results of the survey, the characteristics of the

---

[1]Doeren, Stephen, and O'Block, Robert L., "Crime Prevention: An Eclectic Approach," in *Criminal Justice: Theory and Practice*, Dae H. Chang, editor. Dubuque, Iowa: Kendall/Hunt Publishing Co., 1979.

area in which the structure is located, the degree of security required, and the individual's or organization's financial ability to adopt security recommendations.

## PLANNING THE SURVEY

Security surveys should be well thought out and planned before the actual evaluation commences. Planning will help ensure thoroughness of the inspection. In residential areas, advance public relations may be necessary on the part of the crime prevention officer. In a large industry, the security manager will need to prepare a list of key persons who are to be interviewed. Planning and forethought are the keys to a successful and comprehensive survey.

## ELEMENTS OF THE SURVEY

There are three major elements of a security survey.[2] They are: (1) physical security, (2) personal security, and (3) information security.

*Physical security* involves the inspection of all structural, physical, environmental, and architectural aspects of the facility to be surveyed. Included are such specifics as doors, windows, locks, lighting, fencing, alarms, and geographic location.

*Personal security* examines the threats an individual might reasonably expect to encounter. This ranges from evaluation of the security needs of a housewife and children who remain at home a large part of the day to staff employees and executives who could be the potential targets of a kidnapping for monetary gain or publicity by terrorist groups.

*Information security* is the control of all forms of printed matter or verbally communicated data. Information security involves all of the records, documents, correspondence, and new ideas or plans of a corporation. Obviously, one of the most vulnerable areas is the company's computers. In addition, information security must take into account all information passed verbally, particularly over the telephone.

## SURVEY INSTRUMENTS

A wide variety of security survey instruments exist and are available in several different styles. A police department may find it convenient to develop a standardized checklist for residential crime prevention purposes, while the survey conducted by a private consultant for a large industrial

---

[2]Kingsbury, Arthur A., *Introduction to Security and Crime Prevention Surveys*. Springfield, Ill.: Charles C Thomas, Publisher, 1973, p. 27.

complex may be a several-hundred-page report. Whatever the form, the survey should be considered a very confidential document since it will contain information that the criminally inclined would find very useful.

## CONDUCTING THE SURVEY

The security survey will only be as good as the person conducting it. The surveyor must possess certain innate qualities, such as a reasonable degree of suspicion, alertness, foresight, and deductive reasoning.

Security surveys are often conducted as a community service by local law enforcement agencies, but unfortunately, most law enforcement agencies are unable to conduct security surveys on a full-time basis because of a lack of manpower. Therefore, these services are provided only upon request. Furthermore, since considerable investment of time and manpower is required to conduct security surveys for large businesses and industrial plants, law enforcement agencies are usually limited to providing residential security surveys. Therefore, large organizations must retain the services of private security firms to develop the appropriate crime prevention measures. There now exist a number of reputable private security firms that perform security surveys on a contractual basis for industry.

It should be recognized that residential, industrial, commercial, and public-building security surveys, whether conducted by law enforcement agencies or private security firms, are effective as crime prevention mechanisms only to the extent to which the recommendations are adopted.

### Data collection

A wide variety of data must be collected during any security survey. In addition to the material included on the survey form, the surveyor must use observation and interviews to obtain pertinent information that may not have been required by the security survey form.

**Observation.** The power of observation is an important tool in the survey. The surveyor needs to be alert not only to the out of place, but also to the complacent. No written checklist can include all the possible variances and situations that might develop. Therefore, observation should be to the surveyor like an ax is to a woodsman—a tool that needs to be continually sharpened.

**Interviewing.** No security survey can be complete without interviews. When surveying a large factory it is generally not possible to interview everyone, but top management as well as other key personnel should be identified and interviewed. Interviews should begin with the president and work downward. While it is good to identify and interview the key people in an organization, the surveyor should not forget about the best source of information—the secretaries. Secretaries can provide much information regarding the daily operations of an organization. Although some information can be obtained during a formal interview, talking informally, perhaps at break time, may be more useful.

## Analysis

Once collected, the data that form the survey need to be rigorously analyzed. It is at this point that the surveyor needs to draw together all the information that has been obtained from the survey instrument, the interviews, and observations. Especially important is the identification of possible exposures of the company. Also, trends and potential scenarios need to be reviewed. After all data have been reviewed, the surveyor is ready to make recommendations.

## Recommendations

Recommendations are the end results of the security survey. Recommendations need to be clearly stated. The most important aspect of a recommendation is that it should state only one specific objective. It is important also that the recommendations stay within a reasonable cost-effective budget. If the cost of implementing a security measure is more than the anticipated loss, management will not likely consider it. If too many unrealistic recommendations are offered, the consultant will quickly lose credibility. Recommendations should be broken down and grouped into specific areas such as auditing, purchasing, credit department, etc. Fig. 10-1 illustrates the actual table of contents of a security survey conducted for an oil company. Notice that the recommendation section is clearly broken down and delineated.

## Implementation and follow-up

The crime prevention officer and the private consultant usually have very little or nothing to do with the implementation of security survey recommendations. However, one person whose job will depend on the implementation of security recommendations is the corporate director of security. No matter how thorough the surveyor has been, all the recommendations in the world will not have any effect unless they are implemented.

In most cases the actual implementation of the recommendations will be up to the person requesting the survey. Many times consultants find that they are thanked and paid for their efforts, and little or nothing more is done with the survey. Given this phenomenon, the recommendation must be so clearly

```
                              TABLE OF CONTENTS


        Section                                                     Page

          I.   INTRODUCTION.....................................      1

         II.   ANALYSIS OF THE SURVEY..........................       5

        III.   RECOMMENDATIONS..................................     10
               A.   Accounting..................................     11
               B.   Computer Security...........................     12
               C.   Computer Facility--Proposed Remodeling......     13
               D.   Corporate Security Supervision..............     15
                    a.   Basic Functions of Corporate Affairs Office.....   16
                    b.   Qualifications for Corporate Affairs Office.....   20
                    c.   Summary................................     21
               E.   Credit Cards................................     22
               F.   Elevators...................................     23
               G.   Executives..................................     24
               H.   Fire and Natural Disasters..................     25
               I.   Garage......................................     26
               J.   Information Security.........................    27
               K.   Key Control.................................     28
               L.   Legal.......................................     29
               M.   Office......................................     30
               N.   Printing....................................     31
               O.   Refinery....................................     32
               P.   Subsidiaries................................     33
               Q.   Recommendations for Eleventh Floor..........     34
               R.   Recommendations for Twelfth Floor...........     37

         IV.   COST-BENEFIT ANALYSIS............................     40
               A.   Savings Potential of Corporate Affairs Office....     41

          V.   MANAGEMENT SUMMARY...............................     44

         VI.   CONCLUSION......................................      47

        APPENDICES.............................................      48
               A.   The Survey Instruments......................     49
               B.   Documentation of Terroristic Activities.....     75
```

**Fig. 10-1.** Security survey for a petroleum corporation.

written that there is no confusion as to the method of implementation and the anticipated goal.

**Follow-up.** Between three and six months after implementation of the survey recommendations, a brief follow-up will be necessary in order to make necessary adjustments and to allow for new or unanticipated contingencies. The follow-up can be an informal inspection or it may involve a brief written report.

## EXAMPLES OF SECURITY SURVEYS

On the following pages are examples of security survey checklists developed by the author. They include personal, home, apartment, business, and fire prevention surveys.

# PERSONAL SECURITY SURVEY

| YES | NO | Do you . . . |
|-----|-----|--------------|
| ☐ | ☐ | 1. Have the names and identification numbers of all your credit cards written down and kept in a safe place? |
| ☐ | ☐ | 2. Maintain a no-fight policy if you were to be robbed at gun or knife point? |
| ☐ | ☐ | 3. Have a citizens band radio in your car? |
| ☐ | ☐ | 4. Have a mobile telephone in your car? |
| ☐ | ☐ | 5. Always lock your car when leaving? |
| ☐ | ☐ | 6. Park in only well-lighted areas? |
| ☐ | ☐ | 7. Check your car's safety equipment frequently and keep the gas tank one-fourth to one-half full? |
| ☐ | ☐ | 8. Always drive with the windows rolled up and the doors locked? |
| ☐ | ☐ | 9. Lock the door after leaving and entering? |
| ☐ | ☐ | 10. Look inside your car before entering? |
| ☐ | ☐ | 11. Check around your car before entering? |
| ☐ | ☐ | 12. Carry a travel lock for your hotel room? |
| ☐ | ☐ | 13. Avoid tourist traps and "seedy" nightclubs when out of town? |
| ☐ | ☐ | 14. Feel that you should quicken your pace or run if you suspect you are being followed? |
| ☐ | ☐ | 15. Avoid carrying keys that are attached to identification? |
| ☐ | ☐ | 16. Carry the minimum amount of cash that you expect you will need? |
| ☐ | ☐ | 17. Avoid being flashy and flamboyant? |
| ☐ | ☐ | 18. Usually go shopping with someone else? |
| ☐ | ☐ | 19. Have your keys ready when approaching your door? |
| ☐ | ☐ | 20. Avoid discussing your income and personal business with anyone? |
| ☐ | ☐ | 21. Avoid unnecessary trips at night? |
| ☐ | ☐ | 22. Refrain from taking shortcuts through deserted buildings, vacant lots, alleys, etc.? |
| ☐ | ☐ | 23. Refrain from picking up hitchhikers or stopping for stalled cars no matter what the circumstances? |
| ☐ | ☐ | 24. Refrain from hitchhiking? |
| ☐ | ☐ | 25. Know who your associates are and inform others when going out? |
| ☐ | ☐ | 26. Place packages in the trunk of the car after shopping? |
| ☐ | ☐ | 27. Screen and carefully check domestic employees' references? |
| ☐ | ☐ | 28. Inform babysitters of your location while away? |
| ☐ | ☐ | 29. Supervise workmen or servicemen while they are working within the house or on the grounds? |
| ☐ | ☐ | 30. Instruct your children in personal safety measures, particularly those that apply to children who walk to and from school alone? |
| ☐ | ☐ | 31. Know how to respond to obscene telephone callers? |
| ☐ | ☐ | 32. Use only your first initial and last name in telephone directories if single? |

O'Block, Robert L., *Security and Crime Prevention*. St. Louis: The C. V. Mosby Co., 1981.

## HOME SECURITY SURVEY

| YES | NO | |
|-----|-----|---|
| ☐ | ☐ | 1. Are entrance doors solid core? |
| ☐ | ☐ | 2. Do they have deadbolt locks? |
| ☐ | ☐ | 3. Do bolts extend at least three-fourths inch into the strike? |
| ☐ | ☐ | 4. Is there little or no "play" when you try to force door bolt out of strike by prying door away from frame? |
| ☐ | ☐ | 5. Are doors in good repair? |
| ☐ | ☐ | 6. Are locks in good repair? |
| ☐ | ☐ | 7. Are all locks firmly mounted? |
| ☐ | ☐ | 8. Are chain locks or heavy duty sliding deadbolts used on the doors as auxiliary locks? |
| ☐ | ☐ | 9. Can all of the doors be securely bolted? |
| ☐ | ☐ | 10. Can any of the door locks be opened by breaking out glass or a panel of light wood? |
| ☐ | ☐ | 11. Have all unused doors been permanently secured? |
| ☐ | ☐ | 12. Are roof hatches, trap doors, or roof doors properly secured? |
| ☐ | ☐ | 13. Are bedroom doors equipped with adequate locks? |
| ☐ | ☐ | 14. Are all exterior doors generally kept locked? |
| ☐ | ☐ | 15. Has an interview grille or oneway viewer been installed in your main door? |
| ☐ | ☐ | 16. Do you use the interview grille or peephole? |
| ☐ | ☐ | 17. Are visitors denied admittance until their identity and purposes for the visit are known? |
| ☐ | ☐ | 18. Are unsolicited callers checked and verified before admittance? |
| ☐ | ☐ | 19. Are patio doors equipped with impact-resistant glass? |
| ☐ | ☐ | 20. Are patio doors equipped with adequate locks? |
| ☐ | ☐ | 21. Are garage doors locked at all times, particularly at night and when you are away? |
| ☐ | ☐ | 22. Are automatic garage door openers utilized? |
| ☐ | ☐ | 23. Are swimming pools protected from unauthorized entry? |
| ☐ | ☐ | 24. Are tool sheds, greenhouses or other similar structures adequately secured? |
| ☐ | ☐ | 25. Do you avoid keeping a key "hidden" outside your home? |
| ☐ | ☐ | 26. Are windows usually locked at all times? |
| ☐ | ☐ | 27. Are window frames, key locks adequate? |
| ☐ | ☐ | 28. Are window and wall air conditioners and exhaust fans secured against removal? |
| ☐ | ☐ | 29. Can windows used for ventilation be locked in closed and partially open positions? |
| ☐ | ☐ | 30. Have ladders, trellises, or similar aids to climbing been removed to prevent entry into second story windows? |
| ☐ | ☐ | 31. Are trees and bushes around windows trimmed regularly? |

O'Block, Robert L., *Security and Crime Prevention*. St. Louis: The C. V. Mosby Co., 1981.

*Continued.*

| YES | NO | |
|---|---|---|
| ☐ | ☐ | 32. If iron window guards are used, are provisions for emergency exits available and known to all family members? |
| ☐ | ☐ | 33. Are the garage windows equipped with locks? |
| ☐ | ☐ | 34. Is indoor lighting functional? |
| ☐ | ☐ | 35. Is outside security lighting adequate? |
| ☐ | ☐ | 36. Are there lights to illuminate the sides of residence, garage area, garden area, etc.? |
| ☐ | ☐ | 37. Are lights left on during all hours of darkness? |
| ☐ | ☐ | 38. Do you turn on outside lights before you leave the house at night? |
| ☐ | ☐ | 39. Are neighbors encouraged to light their front property lines? |
| ☐ | ☐ | 40. Are broken street lights reported immediately? |
| ☐ | ☐ | 41. Is there adequate lighting for garages and parking areas? |
| ☐ | ☐ | 42. Do fences serve the purpose of protecting the property without providing a hiding place for the burglar? |
| ☐ | ☐ | 43. Are gates in good repair and lockable? |
| ☐ | ☐ | 44. Is there a watchdog? |
| ☐ | ☐ | 45. Is the dog left as protection when you are away from home? |
| ☐ | ☐ | 46. Do you belong to a Neighborhood Watch program? |
| ☐ | ☐ | 47. Have you engraved property and put up operation identification stickers? |
| ☐ | ☐ | 48. Is an inventory of valuables in the home maintained? |
| ☐ | ☐ | 49. Is the list kept in a safe-deposit box? |
| ☐ | ☐ | 50. Are very valuable items insured and kept in a safe-deposit box? |
| ☐ | ☐ | 51. Do you avoid displaying valuables where they might be seen from the street? |
| ☐ | ☐ | 52. Are draperies drawn at night? |
| ☐ | ☐ | 53. Do you avoid displaying valuables to strangers? |
| ☐ | ☐ | 54. Do you keep most of your cash in the bank? |
| ☐ | ☐ | 55. Are checkbooks adequately protected from theft? |
| ☐ | ☐ | 56. Are all family members alert in their observations of persons who may have them under surveillance or who may be "casing" their home? |
| ☐ | ☐ | 57. Can your mailbox be locked? |
| ☐ | ☐ | 58. Are bicycles, mowers, ladders, etc., kept inside? |
| ☐ | ☐ | 59. Are there adequate plans to avoid being lured away from the home, leaving it vulnerable to burglary? |
| ☐ | ☐ | 60. Is there a safe or security closet to protect valuables kept at home from fire or theft? |
| ☐ | ☐ | 61. Are there adequate plans in the event that a burglar is surprised in the home? |
| ☐ | ☐ | 62. Do you turn on lights and make noise if you are awakened during the night? |
| ☐ | ☐ | 63. Does the home require burglar alarms? |
| ☐ | ☐ | 64. Are there adequate burglar alarms? |

| YES | NO | |
|---|---|---|
| ☐ | ☐ | 65. If the home is equipped with alarms, is backup power available? |
| ☐ | ☐ | 66. Are panic buttons installed in the home? |
| ☐ | ☐ | 67. If you have a gun, is it kept in a secure place? |
| ☐ | ☐ | 68. Are firearms in the home equipped with lockable trigger guards? |
| ☐ | ☐ | 69. Has the fire-fighting equipment been inspected or recharged within the past year? |
| ☐ | ☐ | 70. In case of a fire at night, do you keep an extinguisher by your bed? |
| ☐ | ☐ | 71. Do you keep a flashlight by your bed? |
| ☐ | ☐ | 72. Is it a policy never to reveal information concerning finances or personal data to a telephone caller? |
| ☐ | ☐ | 73. Is a telephone answering service or answering device utilized? |
| ☐ | ☐ | 74. Are children instructed in correctly handling telephone calls from strangers? |
| ☐ | ☐ | 75. Is there a telephone in the bedroom? |
| ☐ | ☐ | 76. Do you have a list of all of your neighbors' telephone numbers? |
| ☐ | ☐ | 77. Do you have the numbers of police, fire, and ambulance by your phone? |
| ☐ | ☐ | 78. Do your neighbors have your phone number? |

**While on vacation**

| YES | NO | |
|---|---|---|
| ☐ | ☐ | 79. Are arrangements made to pick up papers and mail? |
| ☐ | ☐ | 80. Do you cancel such deliveries if the above is not practical? |
| ☐ | ☐ | 81. Is telephone service maintained when you are away? |
| ☐ | ☐ | 82. Are arrangements made for your dog to be fed and watered at home, so that it remains there for protective purposes? |
| ☐ | ☐ | 83. Do you keep valuables in your hotel room while out? |
| ☐ | ☐ | 84. Are valuables left at home placed in safe-deposit boxes or other storage facilities? |
| ☐ | ☐ | 85. Is the alarm system checked prior to your departure? |
| ☐ | ☐ | 86. Are automatic timers used while you are away from home? |
| ☐ | ☐ | 87. Are draperies left in an open position while you are away? |
| ☐ | ☐ | 88. Do you leave an itinerary with a friend or relative? |
| ☐ | ☐ | 89. Are you placed on the police vacation watch while away? |
| ☐ | ☐ | 90. Do you avoid publicity of your trip until after you have returned? |
| ☐ | ☐ | 91. Do you avoid packing your car the night before leaving? |

Comments _____

_____

_____

_____

_____

## APARTMENT SECURITY SURVEY

| YES | NO | |
|-----|-----|---|
| ☐ | ☐ | 1. Is there adequate interior and exterior lighting? |
| ☐ | ☐ | 2. Can measures be taken to prevent blind spots or hiding places around the apartment? |
| ☐ | ☐ | 3. Does your apartment have a doorman and/or security guard? |
| ☐ | ☐ | 4. Are visitors screened by doorman and/or guard? |
| ☐ | ☐ | 5. Are elevators monitored? |
| ☐ | ☐ | 6. Are apartment windows adequately protected? |
| ☐ | ☐ | 7. Do you know the names and phone numbers of your neighbors? |
| ☐ | ☐ | 8. Are locks changed when you move into the apartment? |
| ☐ | ☐ | 9. Are things that are out of order reported immediately? |
| ☐ | ☐ | 10. Would you remember to use the emergency button if threatened in an elevator? |
| ☐ | ☐ | 11. Do you avoid trips to the laundry room or mailbox at night? |
| ☐ | ☐ | 12. Do you avoid admitting persons into the building unless you know their identity and purpose? |
| ☐ | ☐ | 13. Do you use only your first initial and last name on mailbox and telephone listings if you are a female and living alone? |
| ☐ | ☐ | 14. Does the apartment have a supervised playground area for children? |

O'Block, Robert L., *Security and Crime Prevention.* St. Louis: The C. V. Mosby Co., 1981.

## BUSINESS SECURITY SURVEY

| YES | NO | **Access control** |
|-----|-----|---|
| ☐ | ☐ | 1. Are visitor passes required before visitors can enter? |
| ☐ | ☐ | 2. Are the visitor passes distinctive from those issued to employees? |
| ☐ | ☐ | 3. Is a record kept of when and to whom a pass was issued? |
| ☐ | ☐ | 4. Are passes collected when visitors depart? |
| ☐ | ☐ | 5. Are badges hard to copy? |
| ☐ | ☐ | 6. Are perimeter fences adequately illuminated? |
| ☐ | ☐ | 7. Is the roof illuminated? |

O'Block, Robert L., *Security and Crime Prevention.* St. Louis: The C. V. Mosby Co., 1981.

**BUSINESS SECURITY SURVEY—cont'd**

| YES | NO | Access control—cont'd |
|-----|-----|---|
| ☐ | ☐ | 8. Are the parking lots adequately illuminated? |
| ☐ | ☐ | 9. Are lights controlled by an automatic timing device? |
| ☐ | ☐ | 10. Are burnt-out bulbs replaced immediately? |
| ☐ | ☐ | 11. Are light fixtures protected against breakage? |
| ☐ | ☐ | 12. Are passageways and storage areas illuminated? |
| ☐ | ☐ | 13. Is the lighting at night adequate for security purposes? |
| ☐ | ☐ | 14. Is the night lighting sufficient for surveillance by the police department? |
| ☐ | ☐ | 15. Is the business protected on all sides by fences? |
| ☐ | ☐ | 16. Are they in good repair? |
| ☐ | ☐ | 17. Are trees, bushes, and tall grass kept clear of the fence? |
| ☐ | ☐ | 18. Are the locks checked regularly? |
| ☐ | ☐ | 19. Are the gates kept locked when not in use? |
| ☐ | ☐ | 20. Is it equipped with alarms? |
| ☐ | ☐ | 21. Does it have barbed wire overhangs? |
| ☐ | ☐ | 22. Is each door equipped with a secure locking device? |
| ☐ | ☐ | 23. Are doors constructed of a sturdy material? |
| ☐ | ☐ | 24. Is the number of doors limited to the essential minimum? |
| ☐ | ☐ | 25. Are door hinge pins spot-welded or bradded to prevent removal? |
| ☐ | ☐ | 26. Are hinges installed on the inward side of the door? |
| ☐ | ☐ | 27. Are time locks used to detect unauthorized entrances? |
| ☐ | ☐ | 28. If padlocks are used are they made of high-quality materials? |
| ☐ | ☐ | 29. Are the padlock hasps of the heavy-duty type? |
| ☐ | ☐ | 30. Are all fire doors protected by opening alarms? |
| ☐ | ☐ | 31. Are all doors connected to an alarm system? |
| ☐ | ☐ | 32. Is there a specific lockup procedure that is followed? |
| ☐ | ☐ | 33. Are windows equipped with locks? |
| ☐ | ☐ | 34. Are windows connected to an alarm system? |
| ☐ | ☐ | 35. Are windows protected with burglar-resistant material? |
| ☐ | ☐ | 36. Is someone responsible for checking all windows to make sure they are closed and locked every night? |
| ☐ | ☐ | 37. Are all alarms connected to a central control center? |
| ☐ | ☐ | 38. Is the station manned at all times? |
| ☐ | ☐ | 39. Are there periodic checks on response time to alarms? |
| ☐ | ☐ | 40. Are the alarms tested on a periodic basis? |
| ☐ | ☐ | 41. Is there a backup emergency power source for the alarm system? |
| ☐ | ☐ | 42. Are surveillance cameras used on exits and entrances? |
| ☐ | ☐ | 43. Are surveillance cameras used on parking lots? |

*Continued.*

| YES | NO | **Office security** |
|---|---|---|
| ☐ | ☐ | 1. Is proper vigilance used on elevators? |
| ☐ | ☐ | 2. Are strangers properly greeted? |
| ☐ | ☐ | 3. Are your billfold, purse, and other personal belongings protected while on the job? |
| ☐ | ☐ | 4. Are fellow employees reported when observed stealing? |
| ☐ | ☐ | 5. Is there only one person in charge of issuing all keys? |
| ☐ | ☐ | 6. Is a record kept of who has received what keys? |
| ☐ | ☐ | 7. Do all keys state "Do Not Duplicate"? |
| ☐ | ☐ | 8. Are maintenance personnel, visitors, etc., required to show identification to a receptionist? |
| ☐ | ☐ | 9. Is there a clear view from the receptionist's desk of entrance, stairs, and elevators? |
| ☐ | ☐ | 10. Can entrances be reduced without loss of efficiency? |
| ☐ | ☐ | 11. Are office doors locked when unattended for a long period of time? |
| ☐ | ☐ | 12. Are items of value secured in a locked file or desk drawer? |
| ☐ | ☐ | 13. Are desks and files locked when the office is left unattended? |
| ☐ | ☐ | 14. Has the supervisor in each office been briefed on security problems and procedures? |
| ☐ | ☐ | 15. Do all office employees receive some security education? |
| ☐ | ☐ | 16. Do office closing procedures require that all high value items be locked in desks at night? |
| ☐ | ☐ | 17. Is all office equipment permanently identified and registered? |
| ☐ | ☐ | 18. Are all typewriters and other valuable desk-top equipment secured to desks with office equipment locks? |
| ☐ | ☐ | 19. Are office entrance doors kept locked except during business hours? |
| ☐ | ☐ | 20. Are locking procedures for files containing proprietary information observed? |
| ☐ | ☐ | 21. Is proprietary information distributed only on a need-to-know basis? |
| ☐ | ☐ | 22. Is all confidential material shredded before being placed in the trash? |
| ☐ | ☐ | 23. Are all janitorial employees logged in and out? |
| ☐ | ☐ | 24. Is petty cash kept to a minimum? |
| ☐ | ☐ | 25. Is petty cash stored in an adequate security area? |
| ☐ | ☐ | 26. Are blank checks also properly stored? |
| ☐ | ☐ | 27. Is the accounting system adequate to prevent loss or pilferage of funds at all times? |
| ☐ | ☐ | 28. Is the plant protected by an adequate guard force? |
| ☐ | ☐ | 29. Are the guards provided with written orders outlining their duties and responsibilities? |
| ☐ | ☐ | 30. Do guards understand their role? |
| ☐ | ☐ | 31. Are guards prepared to act in case of emergency? |

| YES | NO | |
|-----|-----|---|
| | | **Office security—cont'd** |
| ☐ | ☐ | 32. Are guards legally armed? |
| ☐ | ☐ | 33. Are guards alert? |
| ☐ | ☐ | 34. Is there an effective security radio system? |
| ☐ | ☐ | 35. Is adequate security material on hand and used correctly? |
| | | **Vehicle control** |
| ☐ | ☐ | 36. Is there a separate area for employee parking? |
| ☐ | ☐ | 37. Is there a separate area for visitor parking? |
| ☐ | ☐ | 38. Are service vehicles verified? |
| ☐ | ☐ | 39. Is a log of service vehicles kept? |
| ☐ | ☐ | 40. Are parking areas fenced? |
| ☐ | ☐ | 41. Are parking areas illuminated? |
| ☐ | ☐ | 42. Are parking areas patrolled by guards? |
| | | **High security areas** |
| ☐ | ☐ | 43. Are high security areas locked at all times? |
| ☐ | ☐ | 44. Are high security areas under close supervision by security personnel? |
| ☐ | ☐ | 45. Are badges marked to designate those who may enter high security areas? |
| ☐ | ☐ | 46. Do employees have to verify their identity when entering security areas? |
| ☐ | ☐ | 47. Is access to high security areas controlled by guards or electronic devices? |
| | | **Warehouse** |
| ☐ | ☐ | 48. Are returned goods promptly accounted for, promptly re-stocked and posted to inventory control records? |
| ☐ | ☐ | 49. Are complete counts taken of all incoming material? |
| ☐ | ☐ | 50. Is all merchandise moved from dock to truck checked by an independent party other than the person filling or trucking the order? |
| ☐ | ☐ | 51. Are small and valuable items stored in safeguarded areas? |
| ☐ | ☐ | 52. Is warehouse access limited to authorized personnel? |
| ☐ | ☐ | 53. Are waste collection and trash containers spot checked? |
| ☐ | ☐ | 54. Do internal or independent audit practices include verification of shipping and receiving procedures? |
| ☐ | ☐ | 55. Are dock areas well lighted and under closed-circuit television surveillance? |
| ☐ | ☐ | 56. Are shipping and receiving areas geographically separated from each other? |
| ☐ | ☐ | 57. Do supervisors verify orders placed on trucks? |
| ☐ | ☐ | 58. Is there a separate waiting room for truck drivers? |
| ☐ | ☐ | 59. Is provision made for employee parking outside of a perimeter fence, away from shipping and receiving? |
| ☐ | ☐ | 60. Are trucks checked in and out? |

*Continued.*

**BUSINESS SECURITY SURVEY—cont'd**

| YES | NO | **Personnel** |
|:---:|:---:|---|
| ☐ | ☐ | 61. Are employees issued badges or identification cards? |
| ☐ | ☐ | 62. Are employees required to display badges before entering? |
| ☐ | ☐ | 63. Are all identification cards numbered? |
| ☐ | ☐ | 64. Do identification cards have photographs of employees? |
| ☐ | ☐ | 65. Is a record kept of all lost or stolen badges? |
| ☐ | ☐ | 66. Is a record kept of all badges issued? |
| ☐ | ☐ | 67. Are all employees appropriately screened before they are hired? |
| ☐ | ☐ | 68. Are all applicants fingerprinted? |
| ☐ | ☐ | 69. Are all applicants photographed? |
| ☐ | ☐ | 70. Are all applicants required to supply birth certificates? |
| ☐ | ☐ | 71. Are personnel files kept on all employees? |
| ☐ | ☐ | 72. Are references checked? |
| ☐ | ☐ | 73. Are employees required to provide past employers? |
| ☐ | ☐ | 74. Are past employers checked? |
| ☐ | ☐ | 75. Are employees required to provide other names used by them? |
| ☐ | ☐ | 76. Is a check made of the employee's past financial and credit history? |
| ☐ | ☐ | 77. If there have been any losses of company or personal property as a result of burglary, robbery, theft, arson, fraud, embezzlement, etc., were these losses reported immediately to security? |

| YES | NO | **Customer surveillance** |
|:---:|:---:|---|
| ☐ | ☐ | 78. Are customers greeted upon entering the business? |
| ☐ | ☐ | 79. Are clerks well trained in observing shoplifting behavior? |
| ☐ | ☐ | 80. Have appropriate internal preventive measures been taken to inhibit shoplifting? |
| ☐ | ☐ | 81. Are personnel assigned working hours according to the store's busiest hours? |
| ☐ | ☐ | 82. Are shoplifters prosecuted to the fullest extent? |

**Comments** _____

_____

_____

_____

_____

**TERRORISM SURVEY**

| YES | NO | |
|---|---|---|
| ☐ | ☐ | 1. Does the organization have a good understanding of the implications of a terrorist threat both locally and internationally? |
| ☐ | ☐ | 2. Do the organization and employees have a good understanding of the principles of protection? |
| ☐ | ☐ | 3. Is there a formal security program? |
| ☐ | ☐ | 4. Do all the employees understand the program? |
| ☐ | ☐ | 5. Is there a joint personnel evacuation plan developed within the different departments? |
| ☐ | ☐ | 6. Are biographical files kept on all VIP members and their families? |
| ☐ | ☐ | 7. Does a plan for preventing terrorist acts exist? |
| ☐ | ☐ | 8. Do the organization members know of and understand the plan? |
| ☐ | ☐ | 9. Is the plan adequate? |
| ☐ | ☐ | 10. Does everyone know what to do in case of a bomb threat? |
| ☐ | ☐ | 11. Do supervisors understand how to control panic if there is a bomb threat? |
| ☐ | ☐ | 12. Has a "bomb threat procedure" been established for the organization? |
| ☐ | ☐ | 13. Have inspection procedures for incoming packages been established? |
| ☐ | ☐ | 14. Is access to critical areas controlled? |
| ☐ | ☐ | 15. Have personnel been instructed regarding aspects of a bomb threat situation? |
| ☐ | ☐ | 16. Have personnel been instructed and trained in reacting properly in emergencies? |
| ☐ | ☐ | 17. Are leaders trained for emergency operations? |
| ☐ | ☐ | 18. Is there a plan for VIP protection? |
| ☐ | ☐ | 19. Is it adequate? |
| ☐ | ☐ | 20. Does everyone concerned understand who will handle all hostage negotiations? |
| ☐ | ☐ | 21. Is all mail screened for letter bombs? |
| ☐ | ☐ | 22. Are fire extinguishers available? |
| ☐ | ☐ | 23. Are emergency materials available? |
| ☐ | ☐ | 24. Is there a safe room? |
| ☐ | ☐ | 25. Does everyone know what to do in case of an incident? |
| ☐ | ☐ | 26. Are there adequate and marked emergency exits? |
| ☐ | ☐ | 27. Are employees cleared for security? |
| ☐ | ☐ | 28. Are other good security precautions habitually practiced? |

O'Block, Robert L., *Security and Crime Prevention.* St. Louis: The C. V. Mosby Co., 1981.

*Continued.*

**TERRORISM SURVEY—cont'd**

| YES | NO | Driving precautions |
|-----|-----|---------------------|
| ☐ | ☐ | 29. Are routes that could be observed by a terrorist routinely changed? |
| ☐ | ☐ | 30. Are vehicles adequately secured at all times? |
| ☐ | ☐ | 31. Are high-risk vehicles armored? |
| ☐ | ☐ | 32. Are radios provided to high-risk vehicles or to all vehicles in a high-risk area? |
| ☐ | ☐ | 33. Have a clandestine signal system and codes to reveal danger or to communicate other information been standardized? |
| ☐ | ☐ | 34. Are systems to inhibit tampering of vehicles used? |

Comments _____

_____

_____

_____

_____

**FIRE PREVENTION SURVEY**

| YES | NO | |
|-----|-----|---|
| ☐ | ☐ | 1. Are exit signs mounted? |
| ☐ | ☐ | 2. Are all fire doors kept closed? |
| ☐ | ☐ | 3. Are sprinkler heads dry? |
| ☐ | ☐ | 4. Are smoke detectors correctly placed and in working order? |
| ☐ | ☐ | 5. Are fire extinguishers serviced regularly? |
| ☐ | ☐ | 6. Are supplies kept out of the furnace room? |
| ☐ | ☐ | 7. Is trash kept from piling up? |
| ☐ | ☐ | 8. Are all fuses in electrical boxes the correct type? |
| ☐ | ☐ | 9. Is all electric wiring in good condition? |
| ☐ | ☐ | 10. Is the kitchen exhaust fan kept in working order? |
| ☐ | ☐ | 11. Are storage areas neat? |
| ☐ | ☐ | 12. Are escape ladders in place? |
| ☐ | ☐ | 13. Do all doors open outward? |
| ☐ | ☐ | 14. Does there exist any present fire hazard? |

Comments _____

_____

_____

_____

_____

O'Block, Robert L., *Security and Crime Prevention*. St. Louis: The C. V. Mosby Co., 1981.

## CONCLUSION

The preceding security surveys are only examples of properties that should be observed and evaluated by the surveyor. As stated previously, no one standardized instrument will adequately cover the many varieties of situations or security needs of residences or businesses. Each survey must be individually tailored to fit specific characteristics, which requires the use of observation and interviewing, as well as obtaining basic data listed in the survey. When conducted with these terms in mind, the survey provides a wealth of information that must be analyzed by the surveyor. From this analysis recommendations can then be drawn to neutralize any security flaws of the organization or residence. It will be up to the recipient of the survey to implement proposed recommendations, with appropriate follow-up assistance by the surveyor. Regardless of the intricacies and information gleaned from the survey, the benefits afforded by the survey will depend upon the implementation of recommendations.

# Chapter 11

# Target hardening

Target hardening implies making property, personal and real, less vulnerable to criminal activity by protecting it through a variety of physical security devices. Target hardening most commonly is accomplished through the use of locks, timing devices, various types of alarm systems, and surveillance methods. This chapter is devoted to a discussion of the role of these widely used physical security devices in crime prevention.

## LOCKS

Locks have always been the most commonly used security device. Almost anything of value that must be left unattended is secured with some type of locking mechanism. Locking devices generally fall into two categories, mechanical and electromechanical. In selecting types of locking devices used to protect valuable assets, there are many factors to be considered, such as availability of a power supply, frequency of door use, emergency exit requirements, and whether the area being protected must comply with government standards, company standards, or is a private residence that must meet local requirements. Many varieties of mechanical and electromechanical locking devices are available (Fig. 11-1).

### Mechanical locks

**Key-in-knob.** Key-in-knob locks are very commonly used. They are very popular with homebuilders attempting to cut costs of new houses. Key-in-knob locks are cylinder locks with the keyhole in the knob. They have a spring latch that is beveled on one side to allow the door to close. Key-in-knob locks are somewhat fragile locks because the knob can be easily forced and broken, exposing the locking mechanism. They offer privacy and convenience, but minimal security. Key-in-knob locks offer little challenge to anyone seriously interested in breaking in. An amateur burglar can simply hack away at the door knob with a heavy object or pry it loose with a sturdy tool.

270

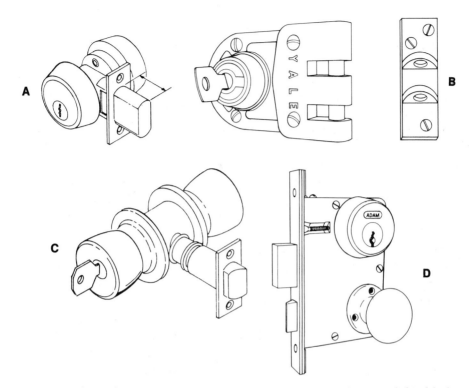

**Fig. 11-1. A,** Horizontal long-throw deadlock. **B,** Rim lock with vertical dead bolt. **C,** Key-in-knob lock. **D,** Mortise lock.

Since the keying mechanism is within the knob, entry becomes a simple matter once the knob is substantially damaged or removed.

Another liability of key-in-knob locks is the latch. The shorter the latch, the easier it is to jimmy the door open. On most key-in-knob models, the latch extends less than one half inch. Doors protected solely by a key-in-knob lock are extremely vulnerable and should be reinforced with a deadbolt lock.

**Mortise locks.** Mortise locks are set in a rectangular cavity cut into the door edge. They have both a spring latch and a deadbolt; the spring latch can be locked by buttons in the door edge. Most mortise locks are operated by a key from the outside and a turning knob on the inside, although models with keys on both the inside and outside can be purchased for use in doors with windows.

Because the bolts on mortise locks are not beveled, they cannot be opened with credit cards or the like. Further, the bolts are quite hefty and extend one half inch or more into the door jamb, offering good resistance to jimmying. But if there is excessive clearance between the door edge and jamb, a mortise lock becomes easy to jimmy. To correct the problem of poor door fit, some locks have face plates that can be angled to minimize the clearance between door and jamb.

Mortise locks must be used properly if maximum security is to be obtained. The beveled latch on most mortise locks is not intended to keep the door securely locked; that is the function of the accompanying deadbolt, but many times out of convenience or carelessness, the latch that locks the additional deadbolt is not turned. In this case, mortise locks are comparable to the minimum security offered by key-in-knob locks.

**Rim locks.** Rim locks are surface-mounted on the inside of the door. A cylinder extends through the door to the outside where the lock is opened by a key. According to locksmiths, the most secure lock is a vertical bolt mounted on a solid door.

Adding an auxiliary rim lock is the simplest way to bolster the security offered by a present primary door lock. A vertical-bolt lock is secured to its mating plate in the same way a door hinge is secured by its pin. As a result, vertical-bolt locks are virtually jimmy-proof. When properly installed, they cannot be disengaged from the mating plate unless the lock itself is physically destroyed, and that is a noisy, tough task.

A burglar may commonly try to dislodge the lock or mating plate from its moorings. But if properly installed with long, coarse-thread screws that secure the lock to the door, and if mating plates are solidly secured to the jamb, the lock becomes a formidable deterrent; it would be much easier to tear down the door.

These auxiliary locks use a lock cylinder mounted with a rim nearly flush with the outside surface of the door and an inside thumb-turn or lock cylinder. The double-cylinder arrangement provides added security for doors with glass panes or thin wooden panels that can be easily smashed. If there is an inside cylinder instead of a thumb turn, a burglar will not be able to reach through a broken pane and work the lock by hand.

However, an inside lock cylinder may be too secure in a fire or other emergency, since one cannot get out without a key. If such a lock is used, a key should be kept in plain sight near the lock but out of arm's reach of the door. All family members should know where the key is and how to use it.

**Deadbolt locks.** Deadbolt locks are bolts with squared ends, as opposed to spring latches which have beveled bolts. The beveled bolt can be opened ("carded") with a plastic card pushed between the door and the jamb, but a square deadbolt is not susceptible to this type of abuse.

With most deadbolt locks, a cylinder is set into the face of the door and only a key will throw the three-fourth or one inch bolt open or closed. Inside may be a turn knob, or if the door has glass windows, a second cylinder may be installed inside.

**Padlocks.** Padlocks are useful for securing outdoor sheds, gates, garages and even as supplemental locks to many businesses. There are five basic types of padlock mechanisms: (1) pin tumbler, (2) lever tumbler, (3) disc tumbler, (4) combination locks, and (5) warded locks. Pin tumblers with a hardened steel shackle and lever tumbler locks provide the best protection against picking, hack-sawing, and jimmying. Disc tumbler padlocks combine good security and low cost. Combination locks eliminate the inconvenience of carrying another key and offer excellent security, if stoutly constructed. Warded locks are the least expensive and give only limited protection. They are best suited for keeping inquisitive youngsters out of places they should not be.

**Time-recording locks.** Time-recording locks register the time of day a door is opened. They are primarily designed to reduce employee theft and are often used in cases where night crews work in stores or warehouses. However, time-recording locks are useful in preventing burglaries also since they force a manager to lock all doors when closing, avoiding the human characteristic of forgetfulness in locking some doors. Personnel cannot be locked into a structure or location by law since exiting the building in the event of an emergency must be possible. However, when doors are opened at a time that would be considered unusual, unnecessary, inappropriate, or suspicious, and there have been no emergencies, an investigation can be conducted since the time-recording lock sheets provide the necessary justification for such investigations. Surveillance of locations recording door openings at odd hours could prove very beneficial. Quality time-recording locking systems also are equipped with removable cores that can be changed at a moment's notice should any employee with "key responsibility" be terminated or resign.

**Key control.** The most elaborate locking mechanism will be of no value if it is not locked. Likewise, not knowing how many former employees have keys will render the system ineffective. Therefore, key control is of prime importance. In the establishment of key control one person and one person only should be designated in charge of the distribution, recording, and return of all keys. This person in most cases should be the office manager/owner or an assistant. Large organizations having security programs should delegate the responsibilities of key control to the security director.

## Electronic locks

**Card entry.** The use of plastic cards with a tamperproof, indecipherable magnetic code sandwiched between the two extension surfaces of the card is becoming a very popular means of access control. When inserted into the card reader at the secure location, this invisible code triggers the card-reading device. The card-reader can make individual access decisions based on the code or request a microprocessor-based central controller to check the corresponding access information that has been programmed into its memory. The programmed access information is completely customized to suit the application demands. It can limit certain employees to entry between specified hours only, or limit the number of entries allowed per day, or limit the number of doors available for a group of people to use. For further security, it can demand additional action or information, such as requiring that an employee call a supervisor or enter a memorized code on an integrated set of pushbuttons. Some card-readers have associated terminals that provide information to the card-holder. An employee, for example, can be advised of how many hours he or she has worked during the week.

**Cipher lock.** The operation of the cipher lock is based on a pushbutton panel that is mounted near the door, outside the protected area. There are ten numbered buttons on the panel. The user simply presses a four-digit combination and the door will unlock for a preselected period. Codes can be easily changed by authorized personnel. The cipher lock can activate all types of electric door strikes and door operators. If the buttons are not pressed in the correct sequence, entry cannot be made. With over 5000 possible code combinations and a built-in "time penalty" for incorrect combinations, the cipher lock becomes as safe as a bank vault.

Mechanical cipher locks have valid use in certain situations in which any of the following criteria apply: (1) low security access requirement, (2) a large number of entrances and exits, which must all be usable at all times, but budget constraints preclude electromechanical locks, and (3) no power supply is located in the building.

More sophisticated—and extremely expensive—high-security, controlled access, entry systems are now available. The geometry of a person's hand, for example, can be computer coded and serve as the basis for triggering an electronic door release switch.[1] Such systems undoubtedly point the way for future innovations in the field of access control systems.

## AUTOMATIC LIGHT TIMERS

Since many residential and commercial burglaries occur during the hours of darkness, and darkness is an intruder's best friend, a good protective measure has proved to be the use of automatic light timers. When the owner is away, the lights can be automatically turned on at any desired time, and can automatically be turned off according to a preset interval. Spring-driven mechanical timers can accomplish this function, but the electrical timers eliminate the need for winding and resetting. Persons desiring continuous security

---

[1]Thorsen, J. E., "Has Absolute Identity 'Come of Age'?" *Security World*, Vol. 15, No. 7, July 1978, p. 33.

over an extended period (days or weeks) should invest in the electric timers.

The automatic timers can be connected to a standard household line socket. A control knob on the timer's front panel permits programming of the desired timing sequence. These devices can also be used to automatically turn appliances on and off, such as radios and coffee pots. The added stimulus of a radio playing plus lights should make the average intruder less likely to enter the residence. Location of lights and times that lights are turned on and off should be varied.

## AUTOMATIC DIALERS

Automatic dialers are devices that silently dial and transmit emergency messages to preprogrammed telephone numbers, such as police, fire, paramedics, or neighbors. Many intrusion detector systems include this function as an added feature, but they can be manually operated by a "panic button," which is connected to the automatic dialer.

Some units have two sending channels. These can be used for a variety of purposes. Most often, the first channel is used to transmit a burglary message and the second channel is used to dispatch a fire alarm message. Other uses include sending emergency calls when a bedridden patient has an emergency, and monitoring freezer temperatures, water pressure, boiler pressure, or the operation of any other electrical or mechanical device capable of tripping a switch.

## ALARM SYSTEMS

One of the first questions one may ask about alarm systems is how much protection do they really offer, or why have an alarm? According to Distelhorst:

□ Premises protected by alarm systems are burglarized from one half to one sixth as often as those without alarms.
□ Burglar alarm systems currently protect about 1.4 million residences and about 2.2 million business establishments across the nation.
□ Police budgets have been reduced in most locales and frozen in others, while private investment in alarm security is growing yearly by about 10%.
□ Alarm systems in 1977 helped police capture from 25,000 to 30,000 criminals in the act, according to best estimates available to the National Burglar and Fire Alarm Association.
□ Criminals caught in the act are nearly always convicted and at costs substantially lower than the funds spent investigating and prosecuting those arrested away from the scene of the crime.[2]

---

[2]Distelhorst, Garis F., "Alarms Deter Crime." *The Police Chief,* June 1978.

The use of alarm systems is ancient. The Roman Empire reportedly was alerted by squawking geese to surprise attacks by the Gauls in 390 BC. Although a rather crude alarm system by our standards today, the squawking geese did provide a degree of security, and this is the prime objective of the modern sophisticated alarm systems only on an increased and more efficient basis. Our present alarm systems have become irreplaceable tools in crime prevention and are a significant part of both the private security system and business and industry. This is due in part to the fact that many American citizens and businesses are seeking more protection than our criminal justice system can provide, and in doing so, they have turned to alarm systems. This, of course, has resulted in an expansion of alarm industries and steep increases in sales of alarm products.

Statistics demonstrate that alarm systems do affect crime. In communities where alarm systems are used, the burglary rate is significantly reduced. Also, most insurance companies offer lower premiums to businesses that are protected by alarm systems. Numerous federally insured institutions, such as banks, are required by law to install alarm systems.

### Defining alarm systems

There are three fundamental parts of a modern intrusion alarm system:
1. *Sensor:* detects or senses a condition that exists or that changes the normal pattern. There are many different sensing devices.
2. *Control:* provides the power, receives the information from the sensors, and transmits it to the annunciation function.
3. *Annunciation:* alerts a human to respond to the sensor location. This alert is either in the form of a bell, buzzer, siren, or flashing light.

These three parts together make up an intrusion alarm system.

### Types of alarms

There are many types of alarm systems available on the market today. A user's choice of an alarm system is limited only by the cost. Naturally, the more sophisticated devices are used primarily in large industrial or business complexes, whereas simpler devices are used in residences or small businesses. Power to operate the alarm system can be supplied either by battery or public utility electricity, but a combination of both is necessary if the system is to function during power failures.

There are currently five systems: (1) the local alarm, (2) central station alarm, (3) proprietary alarm, (4) cable security system, and (5) police department alarm. There is only one system out of the five that does not function either directly or indirectly in connection with the police, and that is the local alarm.

**Local alarms.** Local alarms can be seen or heard only at the protected premises. Police must be notified separately. This type of alarm operates by activating a device (bell, gong, horn, siren, or flashing light) upon detection of an intruder. The noise or light alerts anyone within hearing or seeing distance. This alarm system is practical for homeowners who may not be willing to pay for or cannot afford a system that will automatically alert police. Many homeowners feel that merely being alerted to the presence of an intruder is sufficient, and this is the precise function of the local alarm. It will alert the resident when the intruder begins to enter, and in most cases, this alone is enough since most persons hearing an alarm will take responsibility to notify police. However, the local alarm also enables a burglar to know when his presence has been detected, and he knows he must leave as soon as possible or get caught. Thus many burglars are long gone before the police have arrived at the scene. This is good for the homeowner in that he did not have to confront the burglar, but it also makes apprehension and conviction of the intruder more difficult for authorities.

**Central station alarm.** This type of alarm system operates through independently owned and operated monitoring facilities. The alarm device is wired directly to the central station. When the alarm is received at the central station, it is interpreted and either maintenance, police, or fire personnel are notified. This type of alarm must always be monitored. Many central station alarm systems have audio monitors so that the monitoring guard can actually listen to what is happening when the alarm is received. This is beneficial in case the alarm is triggered by false alarm situations; the guard will know immediately whether or not to notify police. The connection to the remote location may be provided by a radio link, leased wires, or regular telephone lines.

**Proprietary alarm systems.** This system is very similar to the central alarm system. In the proprietary, or in-house, alarm system, the monitoring facility is maintained by the owner of the protected property. A private guard force monitors the system and responds to the alarms, then notifies the police if they are needed. This type of installation is used in industries and in institutions such as schools and manufacturing plants that have their own security police forces. When an intruder enters any of the protected areas, a signal is flashed to the central console that is being monitored, and one or more guards are immediately dispatched to the scene. With a properly designed installation of this type, one person can monitor the security status of an entire industrial plant.

**Cable security system.** A new and unrelated development that achieves the same objectives at a lower cost than central station and proprietary alarm systems is the cable security system. It functions via cable television's bidirectional coaxial cable network. Cable television can be set up to report emergencies detected through smoke and heat sensors, panic buttons, and intrusion alarms. These systems have proved successful in several planned communities and are currently being marketed in areas with cable television hookups. Most model homes built in planned communities are supplied with a minimum of one smoke detector, two television outlets, two medical alarms, and two police alarm buttons. Extra devices can be added by the buyer. Installation costs vary depending upon equipment used. In addition to basic equipment, intrusion wiring, alarm panels, standby power, roof sirens, and a manually operated special assistance button may be purchased.

Monitoring of a structure so protected is accomplished at a monitoring center where a computer monitors terminals installed on the protected property. The computer checks the terminals every six seconds, and displays the name, address, and telephone number of any subscriber whose alarm has been triggered. A technician calls the number to avoid false alarms. If the subscriber does not answer or if the alarm is confirmed, police, fire, or paramedic units are dispatched immediately. To help prevent malfunctions, a status light on the terminal tells the subscriber if the computer is monitoring that unit.

Now over five years old, the cable security system promises to be a highly reliable method of target hardening. Reports on the effectiveness of cable security reflect positive results in the form of significantly fewer successful burglaries of homes so protected, less structural damage to homes from fires, and decreased response time of emergency medical personnel.

**Police department alarm.** This type of alarm initiates direct police response. In some cases this type has an automatic telephone dialer. In such a system, the alarm is connected to a device that will automatically dial a number and transmit a recorded message. Separate telephone lines are run to the police department just to receive calls from automatic dialers.

### Common types of alarm sensors

As mentioned previously, various sensing devices are in existence, enabling an individual to protect property through any one method or a combination of several. These various types of alarm sensors are described below:

- ☐ Magnetic contacts protect doors, windows, skylights, and other openings. The magnet is attached to a door, for example, with a switch attached to the door frame. When the door opens, the two are separated and the switch triggers an alarm. This is one of the most widely used residential alarm sensor devices.
- ☐ A trip wire or break wire is a fine wire strung across an entrance being protected. If the wire is broken by an intruder, the break will open the circuit and activate the alarm.

- Metallic foil or tape carrying an electric current can be glued to glass doors or windows. Breaking the glass breaks the tape and the current, triggering the alarm. The most common problem with foil or tape is that it is not properly maintained. The foil will wear from normal window washing, become ragged, and break. This type of sensor is frequently seen around the perimeter of glass doors of many businesses. The tape is self-adhesive and easily installed.
- Glass breakage detectors are a recent development. They are sensitive to the sound of breaking glass. Once fastened to a window or glass door, the detector will trigger an alarm if the glass is broken.
- Door and window plungers throw an alarm switch in an open position when doors or windows are opened. Various mercury vibration and tilt switches also trigger alarms when an item is tilted.
- Sensing screens are made of brittle basswood or fiberglass mesh and have thin wires in them carrying an electric current. They are custom-made for the doors and windows they protect. When the screen is broken, the wires break also and trip an alarm.
- Pressure mats are flat switches embedded in plastic. Installed under carpeting, they trigger an alarm when stepped on.
- Photoelectric beams (electric eyes or broken beam detectors) use a light beam projected to an electronic photocell. An interruption in the beam—like that caused by a human body crossing its path—breaks the current and sets off an alarm. A major disadvantage is that it is difficult to apply to areas where there are no long or straight paths for the light beam. Laser light alarms must be limited to geographic locations with flat terrains and mild weather.
- Ultrasonic motion detectors emit high-frequency sound waves, usually inaudible to the human ear, which bounce off the solid surfaces in a room and return to a receiver. An intruder moving about the protected room alters the frequency of the waves; a control unit detects the difference and sounds an alarm. Noise discrimination circuits tune the system to its own wavelength, greatly reducing the possibility of an external ultrasonic source interfering with the field and setting off the alarm.
- Microwave detectors (radar), like ultrasonic sensors, trigger an alarm when an intruder disturbs an established microwave or electromagnetic field. Radar detectors use radio waves of a frequency higher than sound waves.
- Passive infrared detectors trip an alarm by sensing changes in infrared energy levels caused when a human body moves about the protected area.
- Capacitance (proximity) detectors protect safes and valuable objects by establishing an electrical field around the guarded object. A person approaching such an object changes this field and triggers the alarm.
- Vibration detectors and microphones are secured to the ceiling of a vault. Vibration or noise in the vault structure—such as that produced by a burglar trying to break through the wall—sets off an alarm.
- A panic button is a normally closed switch connected in series with the sensing devices. Its purpose is the instantaneous manual triggering of the alarm system. These switches can be placed in a bedroom enabling the homeowner to drive away intruders at night, or they may be placed in other parts of the house, such as the front or back door in case an intruder attempts to force his way in after the resident answers the door, or if he enters without setting off the alarm.

**Table 11-1.** Contact classification of intrusion detectors

| Noncontact | Indirect | Direct |
|---|---|---|
| Photoelectric beam | Magnetic contacts | Screens |
| Ultrasonic | Metallic foil | Pressure mats |
| Microwave | Glass breakage detectors | Trip wire |
| Infrared | Door and window plungers | Panic buttons |
| Capacitance | Vibration detectors | |
| Noise detectors | | |
| Heat sensors | | |

- Holdup devices are manually operated. Buttons, footrails, or alarm switches can be attached to money clips, enabling the victim to signal for help while the holdup is in progress. Some holdup devices engage a closed circuit television camera, which films the crime in progress.
- Ionization smoke detectors use a slight amount of radioactive material causing the air within a sensing chamber to conduct electricity. Combustion particles that enter the chamber interfere with this conductivity and trigger the alarm.
- Photoelectric smoke detectors are the so-called "electric eye" detectors that use a light beam and a photocell. When smoke enters the sensing chamber and reflects the light onto the photocell, the alarm is triggered.
- Heat sensors trigger an alarm when the room temperature exceeds a certain level or when the temperature rises at an abnormally fast rate. Mercury, air, and bimetallic disks are among substances used to measure temperature increases.
- Ultraviolet and infrared flame detectors trigger an alarm when they sense the lightwaves emitted by flames.
- Waterflow detectors monitor sprinkler systems, informing the subscriber or central station when the sprinkler system turns on, or when a valve is closed.
- Sound units (noise detection units) operate by detecting noise. They are generally limited to use where there is low ambient noise.

Some alarm systems companies divide the above sensing methods into three general categories of direct contact, indirect contact, and noncontact. Direct contact sensing devices must be touched, moved, or otherwise physically disturbed by the intruder, while indirect contact alarms need not be touched. The noncontact sensors are activated by the mere presence of the intruder. Table 11-1 summarizes the categories of various alarm sensors.

## Integrated/independent systems

The overall concept of integrated systems, or protection-in-depth, must be examined if alarm systems are to offer maximum protection. This concept is necessary because each personnel access control system should be individually tailored to the property it protects. One system may be adequate in some situations but generally combinations of systems are more desirable.

There is no single system that cannot be defeated, no lock that cannot be picked, because human ingenuity is almost limitless when faced with challenges. The problem fits the old adage "What one person can invent, another can circumvent." It is the role of the security professional to select the appropriate interlocking systems to delay the intruder until an appropriate response can be made and the intruder apprehended. When this is accomplished, protection-in-depth, or integration of systems, has been utilized.

An integrated system concept refers to a group of several individual components which, by themselves, may serve one purpose, but in conjunction serve to complement and supplement the weaknesses of their component parts. An example of an integrated system is an alarmed perimeter fence, a second "fence" comprised of ultrasonic detectors, and an inside mobile patrol of guards equipped with radios. The perimeter fence might be circumvented by pole-vaulting over it, but the second fence would be unseen and the resulting audible alarm would alert the guard force. Should someone parachute into the area beyond the ultrasonic detectors, the guards would be the final line of defense, complementing the first two.

There is a second type of system that may serve the same purpose. The independent systems method relies on the concept of failsafe. Instead of relying on an integrated system, which may have one common weakness (e.g., requires power supply), the independent systems are laid in parallel and are not interconnected. For example, the perimeter fence is alarmed with the signal going to point A guard shack. The ultrasonic detector alarm signal is transmitted to point B guard shack. Both alarm systems are tied into separate emergency generators to assure uninterrupted power. In addition, the building entrances are controlled by mechanical cipher locks. All three systems are independent and do not rely on each other.

The decision of which system to use is predicated upon many factors: (1) what is to be protected, (2) is there a contractual obligation to use a certain type of system, (3) is a proprietary guard force in existence, (4) does the area lend itself to one particular type of system, (5) how long must the item(s) be protected, and (6) how much money is available? The systems available commercially may seem expensive, but when their cost is compared to the cost of *x* number of guards, the price is always more reasonable. It should be noted, however, that guards are an essential part of either an integrated or independent system, for machines cannot make arrests, at least not yet. Therefore, the question is: What is the best balance for the price between guards and equipment?

In industry the location of the property to be protected will also influence the type of access controls used. Many items are too large to be stored in a single alarmed safe, thus the entire building must be protected by in-depth protective systems, such as alarm perimeter fencing and mechanical/electrical cipher locks on selected building entrance doors. Of course, cost may dictate that less expensive measures be taken.

Many buildings and the rooms within buildings must not only be protected from unauthorized entry, but also from unauthorized visual contact of the inside of the room. This can be accomplished by sight barriers, guards, alarmed fences, buried sensors, or intrusion detection devices. The degree of protection-in-depth given any structure, product, or other property should be directly related to the damage that would result from a breach of security.

An aspect of the integrated/independent systems concept not yet discussed is the use of environmental barriers—or manipulating nature so that the environment is less conducive to criminal activity. Environmental barriers may be either manmade or natural. Examples include the use of a thorn bush hedgerow around a building to discourage entry except at predesignated entry points; ornate, wrought-iron trellises on detention center windows for both aesthetic purposes and function; and the construction of corridors with curves instead of corners so that no one can hide and strike without warning. By designing such environmental barriers into new areas, both attractiveness and function are achieved. Environmental barriers to criminal activity are discussed in greater detail in Chapter 12.

Restricting access to certain areas is not a new concept. For over 3000 years the Chinese used authorization devices to control access at the Imperial Palace. During the Chou Dynasty, some 1000 years BC, rings were used as authorization devices. All workers at the palace wore rings with designs indicating the area in which they worked.[3]

Each company must decide what its own requirements are—and then commit the necessary resources. There should be an ongoing evaluation of combined factors, and it is very important to keep maintenance records of all equipment so that when replacements are required, the best replacement will be procured. It is also essential to purchase equipment with the foreknowledge that such equipment is compatible with existing systems. Costly adaptations can result from allowing the purchasing department to select the lowest bidder without checking compatibility with the systems already in use.

### Perimeter barriers

One of the earliest access control methods involved the erection of a perimeter barrier, to either keep animals and personnel inside a designated

---

[3]Bean, Charles H., and Prell, James A., "Personnel Access Control—Criteria and Testing." *Security Management*, Vol. 22, No. 6, June 1978, p. 6.

area or protect the area from outside influences. Crude barricades of wood, stone, or mud became a perimeter of first protection. Such barriers were often supplemented by inside patrols of either humans or dogs who would sound a warning when intruders were detected. Such protection-in-depth was effective.

In the more advanced societies, the area or property requiring protection may be extremely valuable and the perimeter fence must accordingly be much more sophisticated as the first-line defense. Because of high costs of providing guard services, the perimeter fence may be the only protection the structure has; therefore, any enhancement of the security aspects of the fence is desirable.

Industrial contractors with classified government contracts are required by their contractual commitments to provide certain minimum physical safeguards to protect classified material entrusted to their care. Although an encircling perimeter fence is not a specific requirement of the *Industrial Security Manual for Safeguarding Classified Information,* DoD 2200.22-M (revised August, 1978), most major defense contractors, such as Rockwell International, Lockheed, and the Boeing Company, use eight-foot high, chainlink fencing surmounted by three strands of barbed wire as perimeter protection. Many corporations and industries find it necessary to enhance the effectiveness of a perimeter fence in a variety of ways. The following case study is an example of the various techniques used by Boeing to increase and tighten the security provided by a perimeter fence enclosing a petroleum storage area.

> The storage area supervisor had noted that on several occasions some of the 55 gallon storage barrels had been tampered with and part of their contents drained into smaller containers. Upon examining the north perimeter fence, it was noted that someone had excavated a hole sufficiently deep and wide enough to squeeze under the fence. Also, an empty, one-gallon plastic milk carton was lying just outside the fence. Rather than fill in the hole a tripline (fine nylon string) was stretched across the opening and attached to an electronic pressure release switch carrying a constant charge of 18 volts. The switch, in turn, was wired into a specially designed (internally created within the Boeing Company) device. This device consisted of a single rocker arm activated by a solenoid. The rocker arm head would raise up one-half inch when electronically activated. A company telephone was placed under the rocker arm and the four-digit number of Security was dialed. As the last digit was dialed on the circular dial, the dial was frozen in place by inserting the head of the rocker arm in one of the dial holes. Thus, when the circuit was triggered, the last digit would be dialed and the security number called. The security dispatcher was advised to dispatch a guard patrol to the barrel storage area upon receiving such a call. With the aid of such a device, six juveniles were apprehended and turned over to local authorities on charges of trespassing and theft.[4]

[4]Terry, Dale. Unpublished independent study, Wichita State University, Spring 1979.

Of course, more sophisticated and permanent means are commercially available to detect unauthorized persons attempting to breach perimeter fencing. Some of the methods of enhancing fences include ultrasonic, infrared, and microwave intrusion detectors, buried pressure-sensors, metal detectors, and electrostatic fluctuation devices. In a study conducted by the Intrusion Detection Division, U.S. Army, at Fort Belvoir, Virginia, such systems were tested.[5] In the test, a college student ran, walked, and crawled to the test fence under varying weather and light conditions. The results of the study indicated the invisible detectors (ultrasonic, microwave, and infrared) were excellent in detecting the running or walking student, but were only fair to good in detecting him when he crawled. The same held true for the electrostatic and buried sensors, thus pointing to an overall weakness when dealing with a crawling intruder.

Electrostatic fences detect intruders by generating an electric current along the intertwined wires. Sensors set at predetermined intervals (according to manufacturer's suggestions) measure the change in conductivity and activate an alarm when the conductivity is changed beyond certain points. The length of fence normally protected by each electrostatic fence unit is 1000 feet.

It should be mentioned that the electrostatic field generated in any given section of fence is subject to false alarm activation by ground shrubs that are allowed to grow too close and touch the charged field, or by winds or small animals.

**E-Field perimeter detection.** An entirely new type of perimeter security is motion detection provided by E-field, developed by Stellar Systems, Santa Clara, California. The E-field technology is a result of three years of intensive research and testing by that company. It should not be confused with the conventional type of capacitance systems, which also use various arrangements of wire for detection. An E-field fence (EFF) by its very nature automatically overcomes most of the major problems associated with other types of outdoor sensors.

The system features single-end feed, with no trenching between the beginning and end of the fence, and there are no critical alignment problems. One other advantage of the system is that valuable objects can be placed next to the fence for protection, since once placed there, they are protected by the same field that protects the fence.

An E-field fence can follow the contour of the terrain, unlike line-of-sight systems, which require that the ground be graded flat. Also, unlike these

---

[5]Barnard, Robert L., "When Security Covers the Expanded Picture." *Security World*, Vol. 14, No. 9, Sept. 1977, pp. 34-35.

systems, it goes around corners simply and does not require additional equipment for each corner. There is also no loss of detection at the corners. An EFF is not triggered by birds, windblown paper and foil, or small animals. However, shrubs and tall grass must be removed or trimmed back from the protected area to prevent a false alarm.

### Proximity detectors

This type of detector is a device that will trigger an alarm whenever an intruder comes close to it. The intruder does not have to actually touch any part of the system. For example, a proximity detector will detect an intruder who tries to scale a fence without actually touching it. The case of the unit itself can easily be made part of the protected circuit. Thus safes, jewelry cases, and file cabinets can be protected so that an alarm will sound if anyone comes close to them, but normal business can be conducted close by. The main limitation to this type of system is that it is very sensitive, and there are apt to be frequent false alarms. The most common causes of false alarms in this type of system are changes in temperature and humidity. The sensing wire must also be strategically located where it will detect intruders but will not be influenced by small animals, bushes, or branches that sway in the wind.

**Capacitance proximity sensor.** Sylvania's Capacitance Proximity Sensor (CPS) is an electronic system that senses the approach of a human body to any metal object in the circuit. CPS generates an alarm signal when preset detection criteria are satisfied.

The protected object must be insulated from the ground. A discriminator circuit sensitive to capacitance then monitors the object-to-ground capacity and triggers an alarm when any change occurs, such as the presence of a human body. Sensitivity can be adjusted to the point where the system will trigger even before the object is actually contacted by a person. Typical applications for the CPS include: single or multiple safes, file cabinets, desks, metal storage sheds, small aircraft, vehicles, display cases, tool bins, windows, and doors.

### Intrusion detectors: volumetric sensors

Volumetric intrusion detectors detect movement by generating electronic energy to fill a certain area and then react to any changes in the area energy level. These detectors are divided into three separate types: (1) ultrasonic, (2) microwave, and (3) infrared. Each operates on different principles and has its own strengths and weaknesses.

**Ultrasonic.** This type of detector uses a beam of ultrasonic energy to detect the presence of an intruder. Ultrasonic energy is soundwaves that have a frequency too high to be detected by the human ear. Since the ultrasonic energy cannot be heard, seen, or felt, the system has the obvious advantage of not being easily detected by intruders. As long as there is nothing moving in the protected area, the signal at the receiver will be constant. The ultrasonic system has many advantages over other systems. One of the biggest advantages is that it is not easy to identify. All systems have limitations, however, and the ultrasonic is not excluded. It is not suitable for use in areas that contain equipment that makes high-pitched noises, such as telephones and factory whistles. Also, because the system depends on reflection for its operation, it is hard to adapt to areas that contain large amounts of sound-absorbing material. For this reason, this type of system is not suitable for completely open areas such as storage yards. Advantages and disadvantages are summarized below:

*Advantages*
1. Easy to install—simply set on solid nonmetallic base three to five feet above floor and plug into AC outlet not controlled by wall switch.
2. Portable—location can be changed or alarm system taken if businesses relocate or homeowners move.
3. Some models have automatic reset after thirty minutes of activation.

*Disadvantages*
1. False alarm more likely than with perimeter systems.
2. Intruder must be inside the dwelling before alarm sounds.
3. More than one unit needed for full protection of most structures.
4. Likely to be expensive.

**Microwave.** The microwave intrusion detector operates similarly to the ultrasonic detector. One difference, however, is that the ultrasonic system utilizes sound pressure waves in air, whereas the microwave system uses very short radio waves. The microwave system is often called a radar alarm system, because it is actually a form of radar. The main operation of the microwave intrusion detector is exactly the same principle by which a moving airplane causes the picture on a television screen to flutter. The movement changes the direct signal. As long as nothing moves, there will be a direct signal. When an intruder enters the area, however, the standing wave pattern is upset and the received signal varies at a rate that depends on how fast the intruder is moving.

The microwave intrusion detector ranks with the ultrasonic detector as one of the most effective systems. At times, if installed properly, two or more separate rooms can be protected by a single system. The problem with the system is that many outside walls contain large windows, which are easily penetrated by microwaves, leading to frequent false alarms in poorly engineered installations. Microwave beams pass through these substances and detect movement beyond the desired area of coverage. Also, in some geographic locations, microwave systems are subject to interference from high-powered radars, such as those used in air traffic control and defense establishments.

**Infrared.** The infrared intrusion detector is triggered by the heat from an intruder's body. The detectors are adjusted so that they are most sensitive to radiation from a source having a temperature of 98.6° F., the normal temperature of the human body. If the temperature of the entire room varies up or down, the detector would not respond to the change. But if an object such as an intruder having a temperature approximately equal to body temperature were to pass through the area, the device would detect the difference in radiation and initiate an alarm.

Osborne describes the tremendous advantage represented by the infrared detector's ability to sense body heat.[6] Osborne first demonstrated the detector in 1967 to a doubting New York Police Department detective. The detective felt he could "beat" the device by donning protective clothing to baffle the heat emanating from his body. In each instance, the detector sensed the detective, even at the extreme end of a 100 foot long corridor.

Perhaps the greatest advantage found in using intrusion detectors is the reliability of the systems in detecting motion or body heat, and the large dollar savings realized by not having to use a full-time guard. Thus the initial costs experienced in establishing alarm systems are more than offset with the passage of time, and additional guard services are not necessary.

### False alarms

The major problem with alarm systems is that of erroneous or false alarms. This problem is similar to the situation of the little boy who cried wolf. Nine out of ten alarms transmitted are false. Responding to several false alarms can cause relations between subscribers and the police, on whom effective alarm protection so vitally depends, to deteriorate. Poor relations will also develop between subscribers and alarm companies, resulting in service problems, not to mention fines that may be levied against subscribers and/or alarm companies for too many false alarms. Accepting blame for the problem must be shared equally by subscribers and alarm companies, since some false alarms are a result of subscriber error while others are a result of defective systems or improper installation by the companies.

Many alarm systems users are not fully aware of their responsibilities and

---

[6]Osborne, W. E., "All on the Same Wavelength." *Security World*, Jan. 1978, p. 33.

do not take sufficient steps to avoid false calls or to prevent further trouble. Often alarms are set off by users who fail to lock doors or windows or who enter a secured area when the system is engaged. Improper entry is such a big contributing factor in the incidence of false alarms that the National Burglar and Fire Alarm Association has identified several practices relating to improper entry which result in false alarms. These include:

- Returning to premises and entering without informing the central station. In some cases the proprietors have entered and left the premises before guards or police have arrived, and later deny ever having entered the premises.
- Failing to notify the alarm company prior to unscheduled early or late entries.
- Unscheduled entrances by custodial staff, or changing janitorial services without instructing the new personnel on the operation of the alarm system. Janitors then enter areas protected by the alarm.
- Failure to notify alarm company of changes in holiday and/or weekend work schedule.
- Leaving a customer inside after building is closed and alarm system is activated.
- Other individuals such as real estate salesmen, mail, milk, or dry cleaning deliveries, gardening or cleaning personnel having access to a home without being familiar with the operation of the alarm system.[7]

A second factor contributing to false alarms is the variety of environmental factors that may trigger a false alarm. All systems, to operate properly, must be maintained and installed correctly from the beginning. A system that is installed in an inappropriate environment or improperly positioned will produce false alarms. The National Burglar and Fire Alarm Association has identified common environmental situations that may elicit false alarms. These are described below.

- Temperature irregularities, such as those caused by leaving heating or air conditioning units on, result in disturbances of air, or the movement of objects such as curtains, which in turn cause motion detectors to sound.
- Windows or doors unlocked and/or slightly ajar, loose-fitting doors or windows, loose wall partitions, or open air holes can allow movement of air; as can taping of cracked glass where window foil has broken.
- Window foil can be damaged by window washings or by taping advertising signs to foil. When signs are removed, the tape breaks the foil, setting off alarms.
- Remodeling requires re-evaluation and modification of existing alarm system.
- Noises from other areas, such as telephones, door bells, or work break horns, may falsely activate sound-operated alarm systems.
- Electric or battery-operated animated displays may falsely activate space protection systems.

---

[7]"Twenty-five Ways to Cry Wolf." *Security Management*, Vol. 23, No. 12, Dec. 1979, p. 12.

□ Altering occupied air space with major changes in amounts or locations of inventory may activate space protection systems.

□ Pets or stray animals left in the building may come in the path of a photocell or in areas where space protection is used.[8]

A third common cause of false alarms involves the improper operation of alarm systems. The National Burglar and Fire Alarm Association has also recognized several practices that contribute to the improper utilization of alarm systems. These include:

□ Using the alarm for other than intended purposes. Some merchants have been known to use the alarm to summon police because of bad checks or suspicious persons.

□ Negligence—failing to test the alarm before activating it.

□ Forgetfulness—failure to deactivate alarms upon entering premises.

□ Improper storage of merchandise causing sound, motion, space, or photoelectric cell alarms to activate if merchandise falls.

□ Improper guard actions, such as rattling or shaking doors.

□ Accidental abuse or damage of alarm system by repairmen, such as electricians, carpenters, telephone or intercom repairmen.

□ Inadequately informing employees concerning the operation and purpose of program, resulting in possible misuse of system or operation of system by unqualified or unauthorized employees.

□ Turning power off to alarm system control panel, which in turn is hooked to a switch plug or circuit breaker that must be left "hot" at all times.

□ Intentional abuse of alarm systems by subscribers forced to install them for insurance purposes, or by employees hoping that a high incidence of false alarms will cause the employer to discontinue their use.[9]

Scotland Yard has also investigated the problem of false alarms, and concluded that the bulk of the problem stemmed from lack of user responsibility in operating the alarm system.[10] To help with this problem, devices to counter carelessness when alarm installations are being switched on (this is when a substantial number of false alarms occur) were recommended. These anti–false alarm setting devices are automatically included with new alarms and can be added at little cost to older installations. Recommendations also include the use of entry/exit buzzers to show that the alarm is in the correct mode before being set, provision by alarm companies of cards detailing procedures a user should follow when switching the alarm on and off, and reporting of all activations of installations to alarm companies since it was found that many false alarms were not reported to the manufacturers.

An important aspect of the false alarm problem concerns police attitudes

---

[8]Ibid.
[9]Ibid.
[10]*Crime Prevention News*, Home Office, Queen Anne's Gate, London, p. 1.

toward alarm systems in general. Because of repeated false alarms, the police sometimes tend to give alarms low priority. As a result, response delays reduce the likelihood of apprehension and limit the value of alarms. Also, some officers may not conduct thorough on-the-scene investigations or be alert to the risks of valid alarms because of this problem. It is a well-known fact that false alarms waste valuable police resources and often divert coverage from more important areas. However, it should also be noted that this is not any more costly than checking out any of the various other false calls that officers receive.

There is a more serious problem caused by false alarms, and that is the personal risks involved in answering the alarm. The high-speed response to false alarms endangers the welfare of policemen, as well as other drivers and innocent bystanders. False alarms often also bring to the scene alarm company personnel who are often armed, presenting a further threat to personal safety. Some local governments impose stiff fines upon users whose systems repeatedly produce false alarms.

However, alarm systems afford a valuable method of overall security. They aid businesses in offering protection at a cost lower than hiring salaried security personnel, and also contribute to lower insurance premiums. Alarm systems also benefit law enforcement officials and the general public by aiding in the apprehension of criminals and by enhancing the effectiveness of police patrol and surveillance.

If the problems of alarm systems are to be solved, there are several factors that need to be considered. First, alarm system manufacturers need to develop dependable equipment. Along with the manufacturers, the assistance of others is needed if that equipment is to be correctly and effectively used. Personnel on the sales level should be trained in the concepts and operation of alarms. Merchandise of this nature cannot be over- or undersold just so the sales personnel can make a sale.

Also, alarm system installers and servicing technicians need to possess adequate skills and knowledge for proper installation and maintenance of a system. Many localities have successfully reduced false alarms by requiring all their users to have a permit. Under this type of system, the user normally is assessed a fine after a given number of false alarms. However, the purpose of the permit should be to encourage user caution, not to penalize users for protecting their property.

### Installation and maintenance

**Certified training and instruction.** Certified training programs for alarm sales personnel and alarm service technicians would help assure that these persons meet minimum educational requirements, which should in turn result in more knowledgeable persons employed in the alarm systems industry. Presently, almost any individual can open an alarm systems business without demonstrating knowledge, past experience, or other qualifications in this area. The system that is sold may be reliable; however, there may be no one available with experience or knowledge concerning correct installation and servicing. Certification of alarm company personnel would also enable consumers to determine the more reliable companies before buying any particular alarm product. Finally, such a program would upgrade the industry's public image.

Equally as important, companies and others installing alarm systems should willingly accept the responsibility of instructing or training users in the proper operation of the systems and to provide continued guidance when needed. It is important to understand that the responsibilities in the use of an alarm system do not end with the proper selection and correct installation. The owner and/or user must understand the system's operation and factors contributing to false alarms, as well as the problems and dangers inherent in a false alarm. Unfortunately, when an individual or business decides to purchase an alarm system, the main concern is protection of the home or business without regard to understanding the intricacies of operation. Little thought may be given to the effects of a false alarm on police, alarm company personnel, and fellow citizens.

Certification requirements may be several years in the future since the alarm industry representatives believe that licensing and certification is already sufficient and that the cost of such a program could be a threat to the viability of alarm companies. Programs and requirements must therefore be implemented without placing undue hardships on the industry while still meeting the objective of providing qualified individuals to serve the alarm systems market.

**Annual alarm inspections.** In addition to certifying sales personnel and training users, alarm systems that result in a law enforcement response should be inspected at least once a year for proper maintenance and function. Some Underwriters' Laboratories standards presently require inspection more frequently than once a year. Underwriters' Laboratories standards require inspections of local burglar alarm units, burglar alarm units connected to the police station, central station burglar alarm units, bank burglar alarm systems, and proprietary burglar alarm system units. Even though the alarm industry, law enforcement agencies, and independent testing laboratories support annual alarm inspections, most users are in opposition to them since the expense of such inspections would be borne by them. Therefore, most local governments do not make this requirement as yet.

**Backup power for alarms.** It is very important that all alarm systems be equipped with a standby power source. This is especially true for those alarm users whose systems are wired directly into a law enforcement agency for monitoring service. These users should ensure that their alarm systems have the capability to function continuously, even under the most adverse power conditions. Even the best, most expensive system is no good in a power failure if there is no backup power source on standby.

### Features of a quality alarm system

From the discussion of the many types of sensor devices, the reader can now understand the necessity for assessing environmental conditions before selecting a particular alarm. This requires studying the environment carefully plus knowledge of strengths and weaknesses of all sensor devices being considered for use. An alarm system indiscriminately installed without regard to these factors could cause a frequent number of false alarms, resulting in an inefficient or useless system.

Summarized below are the many features that should be included on a quality alarm system.

- The system should have electronic circuitry delay. This built-in delay of twenty seconds permits the owners to leave the protected building after the alarm system is turned on. The alarm system is then automatically activated. A second twenty-second delay occurs when the building is re-entered. This gives the owner time to shut the alarm off but insufficient time for the intruder to find the alarm control box and deactivate it (if he has even realized he triggered an alarm). Concealment of the control box, however, is important since the intruder has the same amount of time to disable it as the owner has to turn it off. Ideally, the control box should be placed behind a bedroom door or inside a closet, and should never be visible from a window.
- Complete systems should operate on house current and/or backup battery-supplied current. (Self-contained, trickle-cell, battery-powered units are satisfactory if equipped with a reliable testing device.)
- The system should have some monitoring device to alert the homeowner if any malfunction exists prior to operation.
- The audible alarm features of the system should be heard in any part of the protected premise, and loud enough to alert neighbors and/or passersby.
- Temporary losses of power, such as blackouts, that cause the system to change over to battery power should not trigger an audible alarm.
- Any external components of the system should be made as inaccessible as possible so that intruders find it difficult to cut through wires or cables outside the home in an attempt to deactivate the system.
- Main components of the system should meet the electrical safety standards set by Underwriters' Laboratories, Inc.
- Internal wiring should be installed in conformity with the standards of the Electrical Code.

□ If there is a fire alarm installed with the burglary system, it should include a "test facility" for checking to see if it is functioning correctly.

□ Warning decals should be displayed, advertising to potential burglars that the home or business is protected by an alarm system.

□ Every alarm system using an audible annunciator should have a reset feature to turn the bell and/or siren off after sounding for a maximum of 15 minutes.

## CLOSED-CIRCUIT TELEVISION SYSTEMS

Within the past decade industrial and governmental complexes have converted from the concept of manned guard posts at selected entry/exit points in a perimeter fence to entry points controlled by closed circuit television (CCTV). The video images from these points are normally centralized in a bank of monitors, which are observed by a single guard who controls access at the remote entry points by activating an electronic strike release on a pedestrian turnstile, security booth, or sliding gate. Many companies have made this change because of the rising costs of guard personnel and to provide twenty-four hour access to plant employees at numerous entrances.

The concept of split-image cameras is afforded by the installation of closed circuit television systems. This type of camera allows two different views to be obtained from one camera. The split image is normally of the employee's head and face, while the second image is taken of the employee's badge. This allows for simultaneous comparison of two positive sources of identification.

Nighttime video image can be enhanced with infrared illumination capability on cameras. Wide angle and fisheye lenses are used inside turnstiles and booths. Vehicular entrances can be covered by cameras with pan-tilt, zoom lens, auto-iris capability. These all-weather cameras cost thousands of dollars each, but such capabilities are needed to identify drivers inside cars, plus identifying decals on car windshields.

The CCTV installations can serve dual purpose functions. As an example, during strikes, the CCTV cameras at major entrances can be oriented to scan picket lines and zero in on potential problem areas. A central command and control station can then direct company security forces to such spots to avert or minimize violence.

With an additional expenditure, a video tape recorder with time-lapse recording capability will allow permanent recording, for example, of picket lines, accident scenes, or specific employees entering through a certain gate for any period from one hour (real-time) to more than one hundred hours. There is some distortion experienced in the time-lapse mode, and if certain acts are committed during the off-pulse, they are not recorded. For this reason, the monitoring guard serves an important function and can switch the video deck from time-lapse to real-time mode to obtain continuous recording of critical events.

Garcia documented the peaceful influence of CCTV systems when pickets are advised of the CCTV coverage:

> Rock throwing by the strikers during the first thirty minutes of the strike resulted in broken windows. The plant manager then advised the line captain they were being videotaped and prosecutions would be sought on future infractions. That was the end of rock throwing and broken windows.[11]

When it is important to know specifically when an event occurs, a time-date generator should be tied into the CCTV system. The time and date are then recorded directly on the tape for later use in documenting an event in court or for company disciplinary proceedings.

There are definite drawbacks when using a motion picture camera versus a video recorder. For example, photographic film is not reusable. Because the iris in the camera only opens so far to admit area light, artificial illumination must be provided in areas covered by a motion picture camera, while the electronically enhanced CCTV system can provide usable pictures under bright moonlight conditions. The motion picture camera system also creates more noise than the CCTV system.

Some drawbacks to both systems include: difficult focusing at the scene because of concealment containers, therefore both must be prefocused over known distances. Video recorders require a 110 volt power supply, and the physical size of both systems (three-foot cubes weighing fifty pounds) makes movement difficult. The advantages, however, of documentary evidence for disciplinary actions or prosecution can far outweigh the disadvantages.

## CONCLUSION

The need to protect one's business and/or home and personal property is greater today than it has ever been in the past. Many people will continue to delegate this responsibility to public agencies who cannot conceivably meet the demands for their services. The importance of utilizing good locks cannot be overemphasized in regard to attainment of property protection. "Surelocked homes" is not an elementary matter, and homeowners and business owners alike must give this aspect of target hardening its due attention.

The use of an alarm system or systems is also a functional part of a good solid security program to supplement public law enforcement protection when used even in the smallest residence or business. Government agencies,

---

[11]Garcia, Romeo, "CCTV For Strike Security." *Security Management*, Vol. 22, No. 5, May 1978, p. 6.

the alarm industry, and the telephone companies should all work together to reduce the cost of alarm systems and improve the efficiency and reliability of operation and transmission. At the same time that crime is rising, the costs connected with the provision of alarm systems and services also are steadily increasing. If alarm systems become so costly that only the wealthy and large companies can afford them, the poor and the small businessman will suffer a serious injustice. A proper alarm system can become a functional part of any security program, but it is also essential that both the limitations and capabilities of alarm systems be understood as they apply to one's environment. An investment in an alarm system must be a prudent, knowledgeable decision. Otherwise the system may be anywhere from useless to inefficient, or cost more to implement than would be lost should a break-in occur. After all, systems are no better or worse than the people who manufacture, install, service, and use them.

In short, when used properly the security alarm will become another tool in the arsenal of weapons against rising costs and increasing crime rates. The alarm system is a tool designed to retain hard-earned profits and personal belongings, as well as to improve the community's criminal confrontation experience.

### RECOMMENDED FURTHER READING

Mims, Forrest M., *Security for Your Home.* Fort Worth, Texas: Radio Shack, 1974.

Sloane, Eugene A., *The Complete Book of Locks, Keys, Burglar and Smoke Alarms and Other Security Devices.* New York: William Morrow & Co., Inc., 1977.

Roper, C. A., *The Complete Handbook of Locks and Locksmithing.* Blue Ridge Summit, Pa.: Tab Books, 1976.

# COMMUNITY-BASED CRIME PREVENTION

Chapter 12

# Environmental design

Environmental design, or physical planning, is another approach to preventing crime. Its objective is to improve security in residential and commercial areas by limiting criminal opportunity through the use of physical barriers. It encompasses the consideration of building sites, quality of materials used in construction (particularly doors, windows, locks, and roofs), architectural design of structures, and the role of trees, shrubbery, lighting, and fencing in preventing crime. Environmental factors that are also relevant include careful planning of streets, walkways, and other arteries, as well as increased police technology through computerized dispatching and tracking of patrol cars.

The importance of manipulating one's environment to prevent crimes or attack was recognized long ago. Caves with only one entrance/exit and no windows provided good security for early man, and some caves were even located on high cliffs in which the tribes could isolate themselves with removable ladders. As civilization advanced, many other barriers, such as moats around castles and great walls surrounding cities, were utilized. The classic example is the Great Wall erected to protect China from the Mongols. Although providing a greater degree of protection, these barriers were not impervious to penetration, as exemplified by the Trojan Horse. According to legend, several thousand years ago the citizens of Troy developed a highly advanced system of environmental design, but determined Greeks managed to break their system by using a large hollow horse.

Throughout American history, the role of environmental design was not readily recognized as a significant factor in preventing crime. In fact, the recognition of crime prevention through environmental design (CPTED) did not really begin to take root until the early 1960s. Elizabeth Wood, with experience in Chicago's public housing, developed a "social design theory," which stresses the importance of physical design considerations in achieving social objectives. She recommended that public housing facilities be designed both interiorly and exteriorly with areas for exercise, play, and loitering that would be private and yet allow for observation by occupants. Jane Jacobs, a contemporary of Wood, was interested in making the streets a safe part of the environment and in 1961 published *The Death and Life of Great American Cities*. She advocated street play for children, hypothesizing that mothers watching the street provided added protection for the streets and that passersby would increase safety for the children. She outlined positive effects of short blocks and the need for clear delineation between public, semipublic, and private areas. In 1964 Oscar Newman and Roger Montgomery, two architects, met with members of the St. Louis Police Department and two sociologists, Lee Rainwater and Roger Walker, to discuss a housing project. From this meeting arose the concept of defensible space. This concept fosters territorial recognition through design, maximizes surveillance through hardware, design, and routing, reduces fear and crime, enhances safety of adjoining areas, and reduces the stigma of public housing. The defensible space concept was studied in 1970 when the Law Enforcement Assistance Administration (LEAA) funded a project to revitalize two New York housing projects. Since that time various LEAA-funded studies have resulted in specific recommendations for increasing security in existing structures and for design considerations for new structures. The result has been a growing body of knowledge on the effects of combined architectural and crime prevention concepts in preventing crime. In 1972 Newman published his classic book, *Defensible Space*, in which he presented ideas and applied strategies from the New York public housing project to aid in reducing the risk of being victimized and reducing fear of crime when on the streets. Although Wood and Jacobs recognized the need for changes in environmental design in the early 1960s, it was Newman's work that brought an awareness of the relationship between environmental design and crime. C. Ray Jeffery was also very instrumental in bringing the concept of environmental security through its embryonic stage of development to a well-defined science.[1] The efforts of researchers during the 1960s and early 1970s eventually culminated in the development of a conceptual model of environmental security, which is discussed below in greater detail.

## ENVIRONMENTAL SECURITY (E/S) CONCEPTUAL MODEL

Gardiner has defined environmental security (E/S) as an urban planning and design process that integrates crime prevention with neighborhood design and urban development.[2] This approach combines traditional techniques

---

[1]Jeffery, C. Ray, *Crime Prevention Through Environmental Design*. Beverly Hills: Sage Publications, Inc., 1977.

[2]Gardiner, Richard A., *Design for Safe Neighborhoods*. Washington, D.C.: National Institute of Law Enforcement and Criminal Justice, Law Enforcement Assistance Administration, U.S. Department of Justice, 1978.

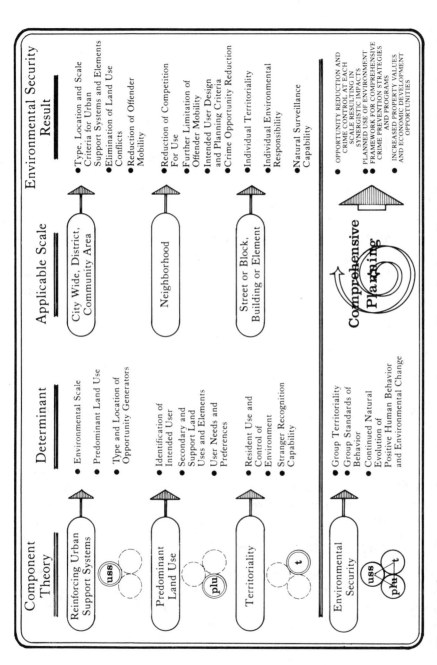

**Fig. 12-1.** The environmental security concept diagram. (From Gardiner, Richard A., *Design for Safe Neighborhoods*. Washington, D.C.: National Institute of Law Enforcement and Criminal Justice, Law Enforcement Assistance Administration, U.S. Department of Justice, 1978.)

of crime prevention with newly developed theories and techniques. It encompasses techniques and theories not only to reduce crime, but also to reduce fear of crime since this is equally serious and is a major contributor to the urban decay process. The basic premise of E/S, then, is that deterioration in the quality of urban life can be prevented or at least minimized through designing and redesigning urban environments so that opportunities for crime are reduced while correspondingly reducing the fear of crime.

Types of crimes that E/S is effective against are those generally referred to as street crimes, crimes of fear, or predatory crimes. The Federal Bureau of Investigation classifies them as violent crimes, or crimes against persons such as murder, forcible rape, aggravated assault, and robbery, and crimes against property such as burglary, larceny, and automobile theft. With this in mind, the reader should be able to recognize a significant limitation of E/S in preventing crime: the environmental approach will have little or no effect on offenses that are classified as white collar crimes such as embezzlement, computer-assisted crimes, gambling, loansharking, and various types of frauds. Nevertheless, the positive benefits of E/S as a deterrent of violent crime and salvation of urban areas are overwhelming. Gardiner's analysis of E/S is that it:

> ... is a comprehensive planning process which attempts to redirect that part of the neighborhood decay process that is caused by crime and fear of crime. The goals of E/S which initiate the positive process of preserving neighborhoods are straightforward: to reorganize and structure the larger environments (city districts and communities) to reduce competition, conflict, and opportunities for crime and fear of crime, which undermine the fabric of a neighborhood, and to design the neighborhood environment to allow residents to use, control and develop a sense of responsibility for it—resulting in territoriality.[3]

A diagram of the environmental security concept is presented in Fig. 12-1 illustrating the various components, applications, and results that can be anticipated when the environmental security concept module is employed in designing or redesigning particular environments.

## REDUCTION OF CRIME THROUGH E/S

Environmental security has as its primary goals the prevention of crime and reduction of fear of crime. The concept of environmental security provides several means by which these goals can be accomplished. The first of these is to maximize opportunities for apprehension. This is based on the theory that crime is at least partially deterred through a fear of apprehension

---

[3]Ibid.

rather than punishment, and that the greater the chance of apprehension, the less likely a criminal is to commit a crime. In this approach, the police attempt to maximize something known as omnipresence, that is, to project to the community the sense that the police are around every corner and that they may show up at any time. The detective force attempts to aid in this by apprehending offenders after crimes occur, thereby adding to the sense of certainty of apprehension. It is not known to what extent the apprehension strategy has on deterring crime, since, for example, only a small percentage of burglars are arrested. It is known, however, that since a real or perceived risk of apprehension is not always a deterrent, an actual ability to apprehend and arrest must be present. The effectiveness of the apprehension strategy is boosted through E/S in four ways. Environmental security serves to: (1) increase perpetration time, (2) increase detection time, (3) decrease reporting time, and (4) decrease police response time.

Perpetration time can be increased by making it more difficult for a crime to occur, which in turn also increases the time in which the criminal can be detected. Detection is enhanced by lighting, careful planning of buildings, entrances, landscaping, etc., which decreases reporting time since there is better observation of crimes in progress. A decrease in police response time is accomplished through better planning of streets, well-defined traffic lanes inside buildings, and clearly marked entrances and exits.

Many of these factors are related to what is known as "opportunity minimizing." This encompasses all aspects of target hardening, site inspection, liaison with builders, and design of model security codes. It also includes working with victims and citizen education, and delving into the possibility of identifying victim-prone individuals, just as industry has long recognized the existence of accident-prone individuals and has made concessions for them.

Specifically, environmental design, used as opportunity-minimizing strategies, includes making:

□ Access to the offender's target impossible, too difficult, or too time-consuming.
□ Detection or exposure on the premises too great by eliminating places where the criminal could conceal his presence.
□ Arrival of the police or armed guards likely while the offender is still on the premises or before he can make a clean getaway.
□ The risk of armed resistance by others, with possible death or injury to himself, too great.
□ Successful escape with stolen merchandise improbable because of poor escape routes and probable police interception.
□ It likely the offender will be identified through increased observation opportunities.

The main crime-reducing potential of E/S lies in various methods of reducing opportunities, which is also related to increasing the risk of detection and apprehension. Fig. 12-2 expresses the objectives of crime prevention through environmental design.

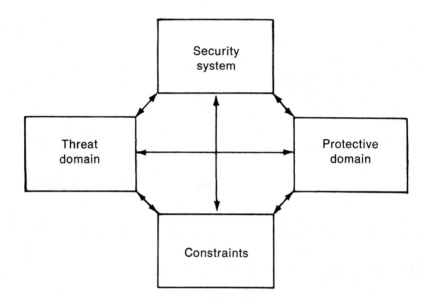

**Objectives and functions**

- Detect and discriminate the crime
- Actuate and transmit an alarm condition
- Annunciate and decode the alarm
- Command and control forces
- Transport forces to the crime area
- Search and examine the crime area
- Identify, locate, and arrest the criminal
- Provide evidence to aid in conviction
- Recover property and reduce morbidity and mortality

**Fig. 12-2.** Security system interaction and objectives. (From *Decision Aids and CPTED Evaluative Criteria*. Washington, D.C.: Law Enforcement Assistance Administration, U.S. Department of Justice. Technical Guideline No. 6, 1979.)

## INFLUENCE OF ARCHITECTURE

As has been stated previously in this chapter, architects are of extreme importance in designing and redesigning structures. However, they are also very influential from the very beginning of a project in coordinating building permits and codes between police and public housing authorities. Mutual influence among these three sources must be early enough so that drawings and specifications are not too fixed to permit needed or recommended changes.

The demand for a safer environment has resulted in a call for schools of architecture and urban design to include courses in crime prevention techniques in their curricula. The National Institute of Law Enforcement and Criminal Justice has recommended six points that should be included in the course of study:
1. Promoting opportunities for surveillance
2. Strengthening the differentiation of private from public space
3. Fostering territoriality
4. Controlling access
5. Separating incompatible activities
6. Providing alternate outlets for potentially delinquent and criminal energies[4]

Courses should also include a study of the effect of architecture on deterrence and displacement of crime. Course content for the study of crime deterrence should include aspects of target hardening such as fencing, alarm systems, lighting, and security patrols. However, crime displacement should be recognized as a possible adverse result of environmental security, since prevention of crime in one location may cause the same or a more serious crime to be committed in another. Will neighborhoods using E/S export crimes to other neighborhoods that do not effectively utilize E/S? Traditionally, this question has been left to criminologists, sociologists, and law enforcement officers to answer, but now it must also be faced by architects and urban planners.

## IDENTIFICATION OF POTENTIAL TARGETS

Identification of potential targets is a very important aspect of crime prevention. Any security program must be adapted and designed to the specific needs and special constraints of the target. After identifying potential targets, it must be determined if personnel or physical structures are the most likely target, whether the potential attack is likely to arise from external or internal

[4]"Crime Prevention Courses in Schools of Architecture and Urban Planning," *Private Security*. Washington, D.C.: National Advisory Committee on Criminal Justice Standards and Goals, Dec. 1976, p. 195.

activities, and whether the probable method of attack (burglary, robbery, kidnapping, arson, etc.) can be recognized. Persons, places, and organizations associated with controversial social and political issues, or organizations in which there are a high number of dissatisfied employees, for example, should be considered high-risk targets, as should persons of real or perceived wealth and influence.

Once this initial assessment of target risk has been undertaken, the individual, organization, or establishment can use environmental security as another approach in strengthening security measures. Through E/S, incorporation of security features in offices, plants, or residences can be accomplished. Factors to be considered should include:

- An evaluation of the locale or proposed locale of the structure
- Physical barriers to control access, including barriers for infrequently used entrances
- Determining the necessity, placement, and type of mechanical security devices (alarm systems, electronic surveillance instruments, locking systems) and incorporating them into the design and construction of the structure
- Utilization of door and window designs that provide maximum security while still allowing for observation of exteriors and the maintenance of privacy interiorly
- Design characteristics that promote quick searches of building interiors and the identification of unusual or suspicious persons, objects, or situations
- Design characteristics that foster observation of the structures, inhibit concealment, and cause the offender to spend an increased amount of time and effort in order to commit an offense, so that the possibility of reporting the crime and apprehending the offender is increased

It can be seen that in order to make the most of the potential benefits of E/S, many factors must be taken into consideration. Advanced planning is perhaps one of the most important of these, as are early cooperation among architects, law enforcement personnel, and public housing authorities, and the identification of targets. All of these factors should result in successful site selection, incorporation of physical security measures to protect both property and personnel, an established crime prevention attitude among occupants of the structure, and maintenance of security precautions once the building is complete.

## DEFENSIBLE SPACE

The chief proponent of the concept of defensible space, as previously mentioned, is Oscar Newman. His book of the same title clearly illustrates this concept.[5] Newman defines defensible space as a "surrogate term for the

---

[5]Newman, Oscar, *Defensible Space*. New York: The Macmillan Co., 1972, p. 3.

range of mechanisms—real and symbolic barriers, strongly defined areas of influence, and improved opportunities for surveillance that combine to bring an environment under the control of its residents.''[6] It is argued that the complexity of most large cities and the apathy of their citizens make this dream impossible by definition. However, in theory there is much to be said for the community action approach as a form of group cohesiveness. Newman further states, "A defensible space is a living residential environment which can be employed by inhabitants for the enhancement of their lives, while providing security for their families, neighbors, and friends." Areas lacking such characteristics increase both risk and fear of crime, which leads to a gradual deterioration of the general environment. When uncertainty of one's safety exists, even to the extent of being insecure when traveling to and from the housing unit, there is neither a cohesive neighborhood nor a sense of territoriality, and the result is further decay of the moral, spiritual, and physical conditions of the area. Recognition of these negative attributes of socially and physically dissolving environments brought to light the means by which combined efforts of law enforcement and architects could foster the development of the positive attributes of territoriality, cohesiveness, and effective policing measures that act as major deterrents to future offenders. Newman has demonstrated, through his work with New York housing projects, that the means to accomplish these positive results include grouping dwelling units to reinforce associations of mutual benefit, delineating paths of movement, defining areas of activity for particular users through their juxtaposition with internal living areas, and by providing for natural opportunities for visual surveillance.[7]

Within the area of environmental design, Newman suggests that the concept of defensible space be divided into four major categories: (1) territoriality, (2) natural surveillance, (3) image and milieu, and (4) safe areas.

*Territoriality* refers to an attitude of maintaining perceived boundaries. The residents of a given area feel a degree of closeness or cohesiveness and unite in orientating themselves toward protection of their territory, which they feel is theirs. Outsiders are readily recognized, observed, and approached if their actions indicate hostility or suspicious behavior. This principle can be likened to the behavior of a barking dog when another dog enters his territory.

*Natural surveillance* refers to the ability of the inhabitants of a particular territory to casually and continually observe public areas of their living area. Physical design of structures should promote optimum surveillance opportunities for the residents in order to reach maximum E/S potential.

---

[6]Ibid.
[7]Ibid.

*Image and milieu* involve the ability of design to counteract perceptions of a housing project being isolated and its occupants vulnerable to crime. Physical design of a housing project should strive to project uniqueness in an attempt to offset the stigma of living in public housing projects.

*Safe areas* are locales that allow for a high degree of observation and random surveillance by the police in which one could expect to be reasonably safe from crime. Location is one of the most important factors to consider when implementing the concept of environmental security.

## ROLE OF BARRIERS

A significant amount of environmental security is accomplished through the creation of barriers. Hall defines a barrier as a system of devices or characteristics constructed to withstand attack for a specified period of time.[8] The objective of barriers is to prevent or delay the unauthorized access to property. Hall further describes a barrier as being comprised of living and material elements. The living elements include watch or sentry dogs and guards who may be stationed on the premises, and local law enforcement officers and private security forces who are off-premises. Material components of barriers may be psychologic in nature, which are basically deterrent factors resulting from the material barriers, or they may be physical barriers that protect the premises against actual physical attacks. Doors, windows, walls, roofs, and locks are all examples of physical barriers. The effectiveness of material barriers primarily depends upon the amount of time they can withstand attack. The longer a barrier remains intact, the greater the chances of apprehension of the offender and prevention of the crime. All barriers can be defeated in time; therefore, logically the most successful barrier would be the one that could resist a threat for a sufficient amount of time until appropriate action could be taken by law enforcement officers after being notified by an alarm, a resident, or a passerby. The importance of apprehension in deterring crime has previously been alluded to, but it should be recognized that the critical factors in increasing apprehension are increasing perpetration time and reducing response time of authorities.

There are many types of barriers, and the type used depends on the environment and the property that is to be protected. The various barriers are discussed below and illustrated in Fig. 12-3.

### Fences

One of the most commonly used barriers is fencing. Fencing, or perimeter security, is considered the first line of defense. It is very important to the

---

[8]Hall, Gerald, *How to Completely Secure Your Home*. Blue Ridge Summit, Pa.: Tab Books, 1978, p. 12.

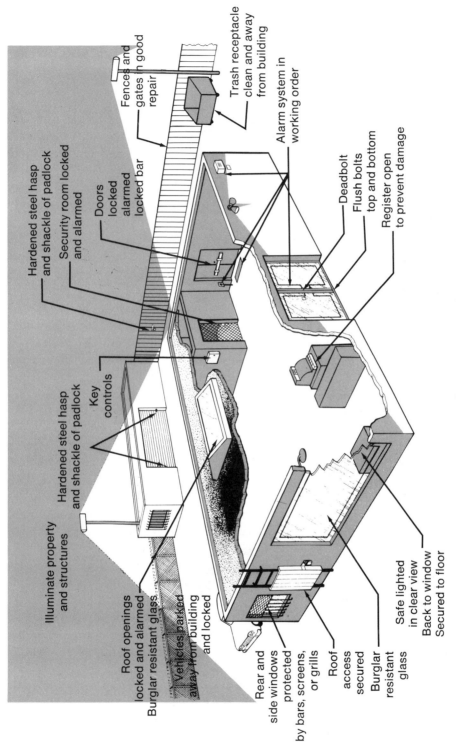

**Fig. 12-3.** Barriers for environmental security.

establishment of territoriality. Many fences are inconspicuous if properly constructed and installed, are fairly reasonable in cost, and are easy to maintain.

## Landscaping

Landscaping should be given particular attention when the grounds are checked for security. Large bushy plants or shrubs should be avoided as much as possible, particularly near entryways. Although attractive, removing them will eliminate ideal hiding places for potential intruders, rapists, or voyeurs. Large trees or plants that obstruct viewing of the structure from the street should also be avoided if feasible. Tall shrubbery and trees can provide camouflage for an intruder and, in many cases, it is best to eliminate or significantly reduce large amounts of foliage located near a structure. On the whole, foliage should be no more than two feet high, and trees and telephone poles ideally should be placed forty to fifty feet from the structure. Of course, this is not always possible.

Landscaping can also be used advantageously in that dense, thorny hedges and bushes serve as natural barriers and can add privacy if planted close to basement or ground-floor windows. Landscaping can also help cover an unsightly fence, but concern with aesthetics should never sacrifice security. Strict upkeep of the landscaping should be maintained year round, and inspections should be made to check for any attempts at breaking in behind the foliage-covered area.

## Windows and doors

The most frequent mode of criminal entry into a residence is forcing, breaking, or opening windows or doors that are inadequately protected. Windows and doors accessible to an intruder should be a primary concern for the security of any structure, since a majority of burglaries occur via these modes. Even though door and window security is an effective and simple method of increasing the security of a structure, builders continue to use low-quality, low-security hardware and materials, and manufacturers continue to produce locks that can be easily and quickly compromised.

**Window security.** Any window located less than eighteen feet above ground level or within ten feet of a fire escape should be considered accessible and therefore vulnerable. However, windows high off the ground should not be considered secure, just less vulnerable, since some high windows can be reached from adjacent buildings or from the roof using a grappling hook and rope. A number of precautions can be taken to protect such windows. Several options should be considered regarding the design, construction, and installation of windows, including specific requirements for window frames and glazing materials. Each window constructed and installed, for example, should be able to withstand a force of at least 300 pounds of pressure applied in any direction upon the nonglazed portions (in the locked position) without disengaging the lock or allowing the window to be opened or removed from its frame. Window frames should be constructed so that windows can be opened only from the inside. Frames should be solid so that glass, in resisting impacts of a sledgehammer, does not pop out of the frame. In addition, the frames should receive periodic painting, repair, replacement, or other maintenance as needed.

Considering hardware for windows is also a must in assuring security. Intruders prefer to enter windows by overcoming hardware, rather than by breaking glass, since the noise of breaking glass and the appearance of a broken window are likely to attract unwanted attention. When glass is broken, illegal entry is most often accomplished by reaching through a relatively small opening to release the window's lock or latch. Therefore, a quality key-operated window lock that cannot be released by reaching through a hole in the glass can offer substantial security against unauthorized entry.

A key-operated lock device should prevent the window from being opened or removed from its frame, while withstanding a force of 300 pounds applied in any direction to a nonglazed portion of the window. The key that operates the cylinder on a window lock should not be permanently kept in either the cylinder keyway or any location within three feet of any portion of the window. This strategy will prevent a criminal from breaking a small hole in the glass, reaching in, and using the key to unlock the window. It should be noted that for emergency exit purposes, the key should be placed in the general vicinity of the window and its location be known to all persons who use the room.

If a window is protected by metal bars (a grid or other configuration of sturdy metal permanently installed across a window in order to prevent entry), metal mesh grille (a sturdy grille of expanded metal or welded wires permanently installed across a window or other opening to prevent entry), or sliding metal gate (an assembly of sturdy metal bars joined together so that it can be moved to a locked position across a window to prevent entry) no special construction or hardware is necessary. Metal bars should be at least one-half inch in diameter and placed no more than five inches apart. Further, the bars should be secured in three inches of masonry or one-eighth inch steel wire mesh.

Various methods are available to make the glass itself more secure. Depending upon the amount of security desired, different materials can be utilized. Traditionally, the types of glass recommended by architects (sheet, plate, tempered, and wire) are relatively vulnerable to breakage. For highest resistance (unbreakable glass), vinyl-bonded laminated glass, one-half inch thickness or more, can be used. Acrylic plastic sheets of three-eighths inch thickness or more can also be used. The most important feature of vandal-resistant glazing materials is that although they eventually can be broken, the breaking process requires so much time, trouble, and noise that it provides substantial security in most instances. Display windows susceptible to hit-and-run tactics should be of burglary-resistant material and plainly labeled as such.

In order to increase surveillance of windows by neighbors, police officers, and other persons using public streets or sidewalks, plants and shrubs should not obstruct the view of any window visible from public areas. Natural obstructions or constructed visual barriers, such as fences, walls, and screens may promote concealment of intruders during a forcible entry of a private or commercial structure. Each publicly visible and accessible window should also be illuminated to allow for observation of the interior of the structure.

**Door security.** As with windows, there are many factors to consider if one wishes to install secure doors. Inadequate doors permit easy access to the premises by intruders. Fragile doors, improperly fitting doors, and inadequate locking mechanisms all contribute to the problem.

All exterior doors should be metal or solid hardwood, not hollow core. If solid wood, they should be at least two inches thick. Added security for solid or metal doors can be provided by the inclusion of an optical viewer; such a device should be mandatory. Double doors should be flush-locked with a long bolt. Other vulnerable points on a door that must be considered include the frame, hinges, door panels, and the lock.

Door frames should be sufficiently strong to withstand spreading under pressure. Two-inch thick wood or metal with a rabbeted jamb or hollow metal with a rabbeted jamb filled with solid material should assist in meeting this criterion. Burglars have been known to employ automobile bumper jacks between door frames to spread them enough to release door locks, thus easily opening the door. Certainly this is quite a tax placed upon the door frame; therefore, this is one area in which quality materials and construction cannot be overlooked. Crowbars are also used to pry the door out of the frame, usually placed at the level of the lock and pressure exerted to spread the frame. Frames not of sufficient strength, coupled with incorrect locks, usually will give enough to release the bolt in the lock. Hinges should be placed inside the doorway and all pins welded into place.

Glass panels on doors should be avoided if they are within reaching distance of the inside door handle. Glass panels in general invite intruders, thereby decreasing overall security of the door. Panels of any kind should be protected against being kicked or knocked out. This can be accomplished by installing bars or sheet metal on the inside of the door, which reinforces the panels.

Door locks should consist of deadbolts or deadlatches with a one-inch throw. Chain locks should not be relied upon as they offer very minimal security. The reader is referred to Chapter 11, Target Hardening, for a complete discussion of locks.

In general, it is best to limit exterior doors to the minimum while still complying with fire and building codes. Every door creates another possibility for unauthorized entry and, therefore, should be controlled as much as possible. Other varieties of doors such as sliding glass, garage, and loading dock doors must also be appropriately secured.

## Wall and hallway security

Walls are generally not considered to be points of entry because of their usual solid construction. However, for some years, the trend has been toward the construction of less secure curtain walls because of the increased costs of more secure materials. Intruders do break through walls using various methods. One method is to back a truck into an alley wall until it crumbles. A more sophisticated technique is using an instrument to burn through walls of almost any construction. Such an instrument is available for use in legitimate construction, primarily for burning holes in cement. (One can see the consequences when a legitimate tool gets in the hands of criminals.) Another problem in wall security is that cheap plaster wall separations are used in the construction of many shopping centers. Once any exterior openings or walls are illegally penetrated, the intruder can go from shop to shop through the cheap interior plaster walls. This is also true of insecure basement walls and floors; once inside, the intruder can work his way to the desired area. To counteract these problems, thick, solid walls should become a part of any construction and/or backup protective devices such as the various alarm systems, guards, or closed circuit surveillance systems should be utilized.

Hallways should always be considered early in the planning stage since many problems can arise when sensitive areas are placed in the path of high traffic areas. A frequent mistake is to locate restrooms in the stockrooms, which substantially increases the likelihood of pilferage. Therefore, it is essential that businesses determine which personnel will need to be in what location, and who will be using which access points. Management should see that needed security measures will not be ignored in the planning stages of building or remodeling solely because of objections of inconvenience on the part of employees. Although a compromise is often needed between security and convenience, neglecting security measures completely will only result in further loss to the business in the form of internal and external security problems, and increased costs of installing security measures after-the-fact.

## Other openings

Roof hatchways, skylights, manholes, coal delivery chutes, and ventilating ducts can all serve as potential entry points for an intruder, and may be overlooked when planning for security. They are generally not used and may be difficult to reach, but they should be locked, barred, bolted, and/or alarmed and continually inspected for signs of tampering. Roof openings, especially those not open to observation from occupied buildings, are particularly attractive to potential burglars since once on the roof, they are generally out of view from the ground level and can take their time in breaking in. Some imaginative intruders have been known to enter structures such as flat-roofed warehouses by cutting holes through the roof and ceiling, obviously neutralizing sophisticated perimeter alarm systems located at more obvious points of entry such as doors and windows. Entrances of this type are facilitated by roofing construction of light-weight, thin materials.

Skylights also present security problems in that their presence provides another source of entry. Skylights must be protected in much the same way as windows, preferably with bars and mesh installed on the inside of the opening so that it is not easily removed. The roofs of structures adjacent to accessible buildings can be additionally protected by chain link fences topped with barbed-wire, alarming, and/or surveying the roof.

## LIGHTING

Illumination is most important in discouraging criminal activity and enhancing public safety. Ample documentation of the effect of lighting on criminal activity is provided by a comparison of day and night crime rates and by the effects of an electrical blackout in a city. Lighting is one of the most effective deterrents to certain types of crime, such as vandalism, burglary, and muggings. Two ways that lighting can be used to prevent crime are: (1) to increase the probability of criminal activity being observed, and (2) to enable an empty structure to assume the semblance of being occupied. A person intending to commit a crime naturally desires to minimize the probability of being observed either by law enforcement officers or private citizens. This aversion to being seen includes the approach to and departure from the crime scene as well as the time required to commit the crime.

An increase in lighting levels, like most crime prevention methods, has costs. Lighting equipment, the labor to install and maintain it, and the electrical power to operate it, have become significantly more expensive in recent years and costs will probably continue to increase. Of the light sources suitable for exterior use, the common incandescent type is the least expensive to purchase and install. However, both the amount of light per watt of electrical energy used and bulb life are lower than for other types. Bulb life is of considerable importance, particularly in those areas where access to the fixture is difficult.

Exterior lighting is especially important in illuminating shrubbery, particularly that located at strategic points such as entryways and sidewalks. It is generally not necessary to illuminate each and every tree, shrub, or bush to have adequate lighting, but in addition to entrances and sidewalks, dark alleys and parking lots should be well lit. At least a 60-watt light shining at every point of potential entry (doors, windows, exhaust fans) should be considered for high-risk areas. Pathways from the house to a detached garage should also be illuminated. Placing lights should result in bringing the security of a structure close to that which can be expected during the day.

Each facility or residence will have varying factors that will require special attention when determining lighting requirements. However, it is generally recognized that major security problems in lighting concern exterior lighting requirements. Many plans for lighting call for lighting boundaries and approaches while others call for lighting certain areas and structures within the property boundaries. A combination of both is perhaps the best solution in deterring attempts at entry by intruders. In addition to providing security, lighting should also be used as a safety precaution to avoid accidents and possible lawsuits. This is an important consideration for both homeowners and business personnel.

Exterior lighting is generally divided into four broad categories: (1) standby lighting, (2) movable lighting, (3) continuous lighting, and (4) emergency lighting. Standby lighting is automatically or manually switched on and off as desired. Movable lighting is manually operated, can be moved from place to place, and is generally used as supplemental lighting. Continuous lighting is used for glare projection, which deters crime since security personnel can see out, but intruders cannot see in. It also is used when the width of the lighting strip is limited by adjoining property or buildings. Emergency lighting can be comprised of any of the other three types and used when the normal lighting system fails.

Floodlights and street lights are common examples of exterior lighting systems. Floodlights can provide adequate illumination for most exterior security lighting requirements. A floodlight forms a beam that can be projected to a distant point or used to illuminate a particular area. The beam widths of floodlights vary and are differentiated into narrow, medium, and wide. Floodlights located in high-crime rate areas should be protected by a vandal-resistant plastic cover. The placement of floodlights should be done with planning and skill so that maximum potential of their effectiveness can be realized. When properly used, floodlights have proved to be invaluable in the illumination of property that is vulnerable to vandalism.

Although statistical data on the effectiveness of street lights in reducing crime are inconclusive, if given a choice, the average intruder will usually choose a darkened street over a well-lighted one. Perhaps for this reason, street lighting has been blamed for displacing crime rather than reducing the overall level of crime. However, street lighting does serve to reduce the fear of crime, which is an essential factor in the survival of many urban neighborhoods. Street lighting makes an environment less strange, thereby reducing fear, but it cannot completely eliminate the fear of being victimized, since crimes frequently occur during the day. Whether or not it prevents or displaces crime, there are many other positive functions of street lighting. It serves to: prevent or reduce vehicular and pedestrian accidents, provide visual information for vehicular and pedestrian traffic, facilitate and direct vehicular and pedestrian flow traffic, promote social interaction, promote business and industry, contribute to a positive nighttime visual image, provide a pleasing daytime appearance, and provide inspiration for community spirit and growth.[9]

Burned out or broken street lights should be reported to the appropriate public safety department as soon as possible. Residents of neighborhoods in which there are not enough street lights should organize and petition for needed improvements. Businesses can also take advantage of municipal lighting although it should not be solely relied upon for providing adequate lighting.

Private residences as well as businesses should be equipped with an auxiliary lighting system. This consists of battery operated lights, which are normally kept plugged into an electrical outlet and the battery is kept charged by the household current. If power is halted, the device automatically turns on the light using battery power. Exterior lighting cables should also be encased to prevent cutting, and the lighting system should be connected to an alarm system so that if lights are turned off or if tampering occurs, authorities can be notified. Another highly recommended security measure for homeowners is to have a master switch for the entire property installed in the main bedroom. This allows for all lights to be quickly switched on if a suspicious noise is heard outside the house or if an intruder is suspected.

---

[9]*Street Lighting Projects,* National Evaluation Program, Phase 1 Report, Series A, No. 21. Washington, D.C.: National Institute of Law Enforcement and Criminal Justice, Law Enforcement Assistance Administration, U.S. Department of Justice.

The importance of automatic light timers has been mentioned in various sections of this book, and their importance in creating a deception of occupancy and averting a burglary should not be underestimated. This is perhaps the most important aspect of interior lighting in providing security. Timers with twenty-four hour dials allow users to set an on and off schedule of lighting that coincides with their normal light usage. Lamps turned on and off by the timers should be varied, and for maximum security several lamps should be used. Timers can also be used to turn appliances on and off.

## WARNING SIGNS

Antiburglary devices should be advertised to the general public. Warning signs can be effectively displayed at the perimeter of such defenses so that would-be burglars will possibly be deterred after finding out what they are up against. These warning signs mainly serve to indicate to the criminal that there are security measures in existence, that criminals will be prosecuted, and that the property is being watched after. Most warning signs will not deter the "hard-core" or professional burglar, but will serve to turn away vandals, mischievous juveniles, and some amateur burglars.

Messages provided through the use of signs vary. Commonly used ones include: "Property Protected by Alarm Systems," "Night Watchman on Duty," "No Loitering Allowed," "Beware of Police Dog," or "No Trespassing." Signs should strategically be placed at entryways and other vulnerable locations on the outside grounds. Signs can also be used on the inside of structures to promote security and, in effect, to control access.

## PARKING SECURITY

Parking for visitors, personnel, and residents must be given careful consideration in the design of a business, public facility, or housing complex. A well-designed parking area should provide safe, easy, and convenient parking to all motorists while efficiently utilizing available space. Individual factors that must be considered are entrances, exits, physical design of aisles, paving, lighting, and pedestrian walks.

The aisles should be large enough to accommodate automobiles, yet maximize the potential use that can be made of the area. Entrances and exits must be clearly differentiated, and as few in number as necessary to provide efficient operation. Also, adequate signs and directional arrows should be provided. Ninety-degree parking, where feasible, seems to be the most space-efficient, but if not feasible, sixty-degree parking angles should be used. The parking site should be located outside the inner perimeter of the facility so that guard control is facilitated. In this way, employees and visitors must all walk through a guarded gate, provided a guard is employed. If outer perimeter parking cannot be provided, some method of physical division separating the building from parked automobiles should be constructed. Chain link fences can often be used for this purpose while at the same time increasing security for the vehicles. Lighting is very important in the parking area. It helps to deter vandalism, pilfering, and attacks on personnel, and reduce the fear of victimization. Generally, floodlights or street lights are employed for this purpose.

## SECURITY OF PUBLIC FACILITIES

It is the responsibility of civil authorities to take charge of overseeing the establishment or improvement of security of public buildings. This responsibility includes antiterrorist measures, preventing destruction of the premises, and protecting personnel working in such structures, since public buildings are very often targets of terrorist attacks. Prime targets or high-risk public buildings include courthouses, administrative buildings, civic centers, and buildings of architectural merit or historic value. Each facility should have tailored anticrime measures incorporated into the design and construction of the facility, according to indications of security assessments. In addition to individual necessities for security, other measures that should be taken include:

1. Access restrictions and identification requirements for personnel and/or visitors requesting access to certain areas
2. Electronic screening of individuals and property within or near the facility
3. Installation of surveillance devices and sensors combined with special alarm systems
4. Emergency barrier doors and special locks activated manually or by remote control
5. Removal of dangerous objects or obstructions that could conceal or interfere with rapid and effective emergency responses
6. Provision of special lighting[10]

Interagency cooperation is again of prime importance in the execution of these requirements. Appropriate law enforcement agencies and fire departments should have opportunities to approve all design and construction plans well in advance of construction.

Routine inspections should also be conducted and security systems evaluated particularly before special events likely to attract large public gather-

---

[10]*Report on the Task Force on Disorders and Terrorism.* Washington, D.C.: National Advisory Committee on Criminal Justice Standards and Goals, U.S. Government Printing Office, 1976, p. 58.

ings or gatherings of persons likely to demonstrate militant behavior. In addition, it should be realized that security systems are only as good as those who implement and maintain them. For this reason, inspections should include checks on security personnel as well as equipment and overall security procedures. Searches should be conducted by properly trained and alert personnel capable of foreseeing unusual circumstances that might contribute to vulnerabilities. All possible steps within reasonable cost-effectiveness should be taken to protect the safety of persons using the building and the physical structure itself. Consequences of neglecting such responsibilities could be grave.

### Parks

Parks as public facilities deserve special consideration since they must be designed not only with security in mind, but also recreation and pleasant environmental characteristics as well. Parks have proved to be fertile grounds for criminals in the past and to counteract such situations, parks must be planned to promote easy accessibility for police patrol, observation by the private sector, and, very importantly, an attitude of territoriality. Parks should be located in "safe areas" and possess other desirable environmental characteristics, such as adequate lighting and methods to quickly report criminal activity.

### PHYSICAL SECURITY FOR ANTITERRORISM

Many incidents of terrorism are dependent upon the existence of architectural structures that encourage or do not resist terrorist behavior. Examples of such structures are those with multiple uncontrollable access doors, or those with floor plans that do not foster searches of the interior. In the case of serious bomb threats this could prove to be a real detriment. The responsibility for preventing such design errors is often left to public law enforcement officials. In many cases, public law enforcement agencies constitute the sole source of expertise regarding matters of security, not only for public facilities but also for many businesses and organizations. Therefore, the effectiveness of police countermeasures against incidents of terrorism can correspond directly to the incidence of such crimes within the community. This situation results in the necessity of police developing a high degree of expertise in this area of crime prevention. Authorities involved in such advisory capacities should be capable of distinguishing currently needed security designs or equipment and security devices that may be needed or desired in the future. This requires an individual with foresight, knowledge of sophisticated criminal tactics, and the ability to anticipate future vulnerabilities of a particular organization. In addition, law enforcement agencies should request the assistance of architects, contractors, and local fire departments when developing recommendations.

Structures that minimize opportunities for terrorist attacks have limited points of public access while still allowing for nonpublic access and exit routes enabling police to be quickly dispatched in an emergency and occupants to be quickly evacuated. Limiting access points allows for better identification procedures and better inspection procedures of bags and packages. Maximizing window space also lessens the potential for terrorist attacks. Visibility is increased, which reduces the desirability of the structure for occupation since authorities can more easily observe what takes place inside. Other extreme physical security measures, such as portal metal detectors, should be used only when the threat of violence becomes reasonably certain and the expense of employing them can be justified.

## SITE SELECTION

When constructing a facility for security, the first factor that must be considered is the building site itself. The main criterion that should guide the selection process is a maximum security site at a minimum or reasonable cost. A decision to build at a particular site should be made only after an in-depth study of the proposed locations. The study of the proposed locale should include interviews with security executives of other facilities in the area concerning their experience and rate of crime problems in each area. Area crime statistics should also be obtained from local law enforcement agencies, coupled with an on-site evaluation by persons with expertise in determining the area's crime potential. When deciding to locate at a particular site one should also consider requirements of the company or business, in which case there may have to be some degree of compromise. If, for example, a certain location is desired because of the potential manpower available but the site is also in an area prone to civil disturbances, both priorities must be evaluated. Of course, if there are no overbearing company priorities, then a site with a low potential for crime can be chosen without conflict.

After a decision has been made regarding the selection of a particular site, the security consultant can then recommend specific perimeter barriers and internal security measures based on the present and potential vulnerabilities of the locale. Specific factors (in addition to crime statistics) that will be useful in making an informed and intelligent decision of site selection include:

- Distance from public transportation facilities (the closer the better)
- Distance from public safety agencies
- Status of municipal lighting systems in the general area

□ Amount of travel on streets, including nighttime travel
□ Presence of other businesses in the area
□ Store hours of other businesses in the neighborhood
□ Sophistication or intensity of security measures taken by adjacent businesses
□ Location of the proposed site within a block; for example, corner lots increase security compared to lots in the middle of a block
□ Existence of potential fire hazards near the proposed site
□ Labor relations in the general area
□ General economic conditions of surrounding neighborhoods as evidenced by housing conditions, unemployment ratios, etc.
□ Likelihood of natural disasters or "acts of God," such as floods, hurricanes, etc.

## Planning the facility

Site selection is perhaps the single most important factor in determining the relative security of a structure. After the building site has been selected, the next step in assuring maximum security is conferring with the architect and designing the overall plan for the structure. Early communication with the architect is essential if he or she is to be provided with advance security requirements to be incorporated into the design. This will prevent the need for more expensive measures after construction is complete and will also prevent undesirable revisions of the design as a result of after-the-fact changes. Clients cannot assume that architects will automatically include the necessary security controls since, at the present time, security training is neither mandatory nor always included in the curricula of schools of architecture. In fact, most architects expect their clients to be aware of security problems and bring them to their attention when drafting the original plan of the structure.

Factors to consider in planning include recommendations made as a result of on-site evaluations, provisions for basic exterior security measures, provisions for internal security measures, and special provisions for high-risk merchandise handled by the business. As Strobl points out, the planner must attempt to anticipate problems and find means to incorporate the program into the overall operational procedures of the facility so that it is reasonably acceptable to the majority of the population affected by it.[11] Changes or measures likely to cause inconvenience to a majority of persons are not likely to be acceptable and must be minimized as much as possible during the planning stage. If security requirements are not incorporated in the initial plans and subsequent measures cause undue inconvenience to the occupants of the building, crime and the fear of crime will remain potential threats.

---

[11]Strobl, Walter M., *Crime Prevention Through Physical Security.* New York: Marcel Dekker, Inc., 1978, p. 1.

## MODEL SECURITY CODES

Although physical and architectural features of residential and commercial structures have been recognized as important variables affecting crime rates, all too frequently insufficient consideration is given to security factors before and during construction; security protection is too often added as an afterthought, if at all. The basic nature of our present society seems to be that people want things done for them and crime prevention is no different. If it were left up to the general public to make their homes and businesses more crime resistant, a large percentage of them would neglect this responsibility. There appear to be only a few rugged individualists left who will take care of problems themselves. That is why model security codes must be established and built into all new construction. Otherwise, it simply will not get done and we shall continue to have excessively high crime rates for homes and businesses and a continued demand for police attention that could be directed toward other types of criminal activity. Insurance premiums will also continue to soar, resulting in unnecessary expenses for everyone.

For this reason, many states are either conducting studies or have already enacted laws to improve building security standards for the purpose of inhibiting criminal activity. Building codes for this purpose have arrived rather late on the scene considering that for many years there have been building codes to assure electrical and plumbing standards, zoning ordinances, and fire prevention regulations. Therefore, the establishment of a set of uniform security building codes to promote crime prevention will be a substantial step forward for the field of criminal justice and related sciences. The objective of such codes should be to provide minimum standards to safeguard property and public welfare through the regulation and control of the design, construction, materials, use, location, and maintenance of all new or remodeled structures within a municipality. The National Institute of Law Enforcement and Criminal Justice of the LEAA has recommended security codes for commercial buildings that should be followed. The security codes developed by this agency include guidelines for the use and installation of doors, locks, windows, roof openings, and alarm systems.

Security codes have also been established for residential dwellings. The use of metal or solid hardwood doors, deadbolt locks, sturdy door frames, adequate window security, lighting, and landscaping are all essential factors that must be included in security codes for residences. At this time mandatory alarm systems should be avoided. Requiring alarms would only invite the misuse of these devices. Law enforcement agencies, municipal planning and building code enforcement officials, builders, realtors, and consumer protection groups should all work together in instituting appropriate security codes for residences. Special attention should be given to the exterior doors and locks, sliding doors, and window locking devices a builder proposes to use. In addition, all exterior doors should have an outside light.

It is important that all neighborhoods and municipalities institute model security codes for both residential and commercial establishments so that crime is actually reduced rather than displaced. Additional information can be obtained from the National Criminal Justice Reference Service or the National Sheriffs Association.

It should be mentioned also that the recommendations for security codes are a result of extensive research and laboratory testing of materials by the Law Enforcement Standards Laboratory (LESL) at the National Bureau of Standards. This agency has conducted research that has assisted law enforcement and criminal justice agencies in the selection and procurement of quality equipment. In addition to subjecting existing equipment to laboratory testing, a priority of LESL is to conduct research that will lead to the development of several series of documents, national voluntary equipment standards, user guidelines, and surveys. One such document is the "NILECJ Standard for the Physical Security of Door Assemblies and Components."[12]

## ENVIRONMENTAL FACTORS IN RURAL CRIME

Up to this point the concept of E/S has been directed mainly to urban areas. However, rural areas, becoming increasingly victimized by crime, may also need to experiment with E/S concepts. Many questions have been raised regarding the problem of rural crimes. Such variables as low visibility and relative isolation of farm property, decreased police patrols in rural areas, and vulnerability of farm equipment and outbuildings have all been assumed to contribute to an overall vulnerability of rural residents and property to crime. One study, however, found that many of these physical and spatial aspects of rural areas were not related to property crime victimization.[13] The size of the tract in acres, distance one lives from the nearest town, distance from one's neighbors, visibility of one's buildings to the neighbors, the number and condition of buildings, and fencing on one's property were not found to be related to property crimes. This might be explained by the fact that most properties are accessible to potential criminals. Results of the study did seem to suggest that property located behind the residence rather than between the residence and the public road was less vulnerable in that this location increased the risk to perpetrators.

---

[12]NILECJ Standard for the Physical Security of Door Assemblies and Components, National Institute of Law Enforcement and Criminal Justice, Washington, D.C.: U.S. Department of Justice, Dec. 1974.

[13]Phillips, Howard, et al., *Environmental Factors in Rural Crime.* Wooster, Ohio: Ohio Agricultural Research and Development Center, Research Circular 224, Nov. 1976, p. 5.

This is clearly an area that requires more research, since the effects of applications of E/S concepts to rural areas are yet unclear. It may be that rural crime will not be as receptive to the E/S concepts, but perhaps there are some aspects of rural crime that can be dramatically affected through physical design.

## CONCLUSION

The concept of environmental security is becoming a well-defined science that demands attention from architects, law enforcement authorities, city planners, business owners, and private citizens, all of whom should be concerned with measures to control crime. Clearly, E/S has been shown by several researchers and studies to effectively reduce crime and the fear of crime by reducing opportunities for crime and increasing the risk for the perpetrator. E/S should be a part of comprehensive planning from the design phase to the completion of construction projects. At the present time, however, model security codes are only encouraged, not mandatory, in most locales, as is true for the inclusion of E/S courses in architectural schools. It is important, therefore, to see that steps are taken to implement E/S measures as mandatory requirements so that all municipalities will benefit from the concept. This also will reduce the possibility of crime displacement.

Crime prevention through environmental security has most effectively been applied to high density urban areas and much research must be done on the applications of its concepts to rural areas. The most important factor in utilizing it effectively is to evaluate existing and planned structures, determine how they relate to present and potential crime patterns, and then recommend the inclusion of design measures in cooperation with architects, fire departments, and zoning and planning agencies to counteract criminal opportunities. This new area of crime prevention promises to be a most challenging and rewarding field for criminal justice, architecture, and urban planning.

# Chapter 13

# Community-based programs

Attempting to prevent crime entirely through the use of environmental design, alarms, and physical measures is absurd and totally self-defeating. To do so is to completely ignore the vast reams of psychologic and sociologic research that relate to the causation of crime. The use of community-based programs in addition to various other preventive measures is an integral component of crime control. Indeed, many a sociologist would argue that community involvement is the only approach. This may be because the community-based approach is directed toward treating the root of the problem of crime while many other programs provide only symptomatic treatment. For example, the use of environmental design in crime prevention may be effective, but it is valueless in regard to preventing the motivation behind a particular criminal act. In other words, environmental design becomes an effective treatment only in regard to an individual's inability to penetrate physical barriers and gain unauthorized entry; it neither delves into psychosocial factors to determine why an individual wants to become an intruder, nor prevents the individual's desire or need to break in. Therefore, the use of physical measures becomes nothing more than treating symptoms of the "crime disease" and is more individualistic than a community approach.

The premise of many social scientists is that the roots of criminal behavior are closely connected to the social, political, and economic conditions of society. What is required, therefore, if long-range crime prevention is to occur are basic alterations or modifications in the social structure or organization of society.

Social scientists differ in their approach to crime prevention with respect to the societal reforms that are suggested in order to prevent crime. The specific alterations suggested include changes in family structures and child-rearing practices, reduction of social class differentials, and elimination of all forms of social, racial, and economic discrimination. Of primary importance have been those macrosociologic programs, or efforts at large-scale social change, that have been organized to provide opportunities for more people to achieve the culturally approved goals of the society without having to resort

**325**

to illegal means. These programs include increased access to education, training, and employment for all members of the society, including those in the lowest socioeconomic categories.[1] Sandhu reiterates this position when he states, "Citizens can prevent crime by focusing their attention on social factors that lead to crime, for example, unemployment, poor education, and lack of recreational opportunities."[2] Similarly, the President's Commission on Law Enforcement and Administration of Justice noted that, "Making legitimate opportunities available to all people in society, principally in the areas of employment, education, and housing may turn out to be the most effective deterrent to crime and delinquency."[3] In addition, Sykes has stated that income, education, and occupation form a set of closely interrelated factors highly correlated with human conduct in a variety of areas, and the field of criminal behavior is no exception.[4] Waldron et al. aptly summarize the complex conditions associated with criminal behavior:

> Crime flourishes where unemployment is high and where the inhabitants do not have the skills and training needed to make an honest living. Crime flourishes where education is poorest, where schools are least equipped to teach youngsters, and where most drop out before graduation. Crime flourishes in those areas in which the average life expectance is ten years lower than in the city as a whole.[5]

In essence, society itself must be reformed if we are to have a realistic opportunity of reducing and preventing crime. Therefore, provision of relevant educational and employment programs, especially for the poor, are of paramount significance in the prevention of crime and delinquency. MacIver notes the importance of programs designed to provide work opportunities for underprivileged youth:

> Work opportunity is a primary requisite. But this implies realistic training, new contacts and associations, the removal of educational deficiencies, some instruction in manners and in modes of speech, recreational facilities for their free time, not infrequently better living conditions, temporary support, work-training programs, and aid in placement. Work opportunity becomes the focus of a comprehensive program.[6]

Romig also discusses the role of vocational training and work programs in delinquency prevention, and after reviewing several relevant studies, has

---

[1]Haskell, M. R., and Yablonsky, L., *Crime and Delinquency.* Chicago: Rand McNally & Company, 1970, p. 436.
[2]Sandhu, H. S., *Juvenile Delinquency: Causes, Control and Prevention.* New York: McGraw-Hill Book Co., 1977, p. 276.
[3]*The Challenge of Crime in a Free Society.* Washington, D.C.: President's Commission on Law Enforcement and the Administration of Justice, Government Printing Office, 1967, p. 213.
[4]Sykes, G. M., *Crime and Society.* New York: Random House, 1967, p. 96.
[5]Waldron, R. J., et al., *The Criminal Justice System: An Introduction.* Boston: Houghton Mifflin Co., 1976, p. 402.
[6]MacIver, R. M., *The Prevention and Control of Delinquency.* New York, Atherton Press, 1966, p. 126.

concluded that vocational training and work programs must also be accompanied by placement in jobs in which the individual can hope for advancement. Romig found that those vocational training and work programs that successfully contributed to delinquency prevention had certain essential ingredients, such as teaching job advancement skills, providing support learning skills, providing educational programs that culminate in earning a GED or other diploma, and furnishing follow-up assistance. Vocational training and work programs that incorporate these ingredients have the greatest promise as crime and delinquency prevention tools.[7]

Many other researchers have also found significant relationships between employment and participation in criminal behavior.[8-11] Correlations between delinquency rates and low educational achievement have also been found by a number of researchers.[12-14]

According to the President's Commission on Law Enforcement and Administration of Justice:

> Educational success is an avenue to occupational success and these successes have been considerably more difficult for the children of the poor to attain. The child who is successful at school sees an array of legitimate opportunities open for him, and research has indicated that for the lower class child this serves as a powerful insulator against delinquent involvement. It is therefore important to stress the goal of equal educational achievement as a matter of national priority . . .[15]

Much attention has also been given to the role of recreational programs in delinquency and crime prevention efforts. Considerable confusion exists regarding correlations between recreation and the prevention of crime and delinquency. After analyzing the results of several research projects, the President's Commission on Crime concluded that "these studies neither demonstrated in any conclusive fashion that recreation prevented delinquency nor were they able to demonstrate conclusively that recreation was without value in delinquency prevention." The Commission also stated: "It

---

[7]Romig, D. A., *Justice for Our Children: An Examination of Juvenile Delinquent Rehabilitation Programs.* Lexington, Mass.: Lexington Books, 1978, p. 52.

[8]Phillips, L., Votey, H. L., and Maxwell, D., "Crime, Youth, and the Labor Market." *Journal of Political Economy*, May-June 1972, pp. 491-504.

[9]Fleisher, B., *The Economics of Delinquency.* Chicago: Quadrangle Books, 1966.

[10]Singell, L., "Economic Opportunity and Juvenile Delinquency." Unpublished doctoral dissertation, Wayne State University, 1965.

[11]"A National Strategy to Reduce Crime." Washington, D.C.: National Advisory Commission on Criminal Justice Standards and Goals, Government Printing Office, 1973, p. 55.

[12]Kvaraceus, W. C., *Juvenile Delinquency and the Schools.* Yonkers, N.Y.: World Book Co., 1954.

[13]Zimring, F., and Hawkins, G., "Deterrence and Marginal Groups." *Journal of Research and Delinquency*, Vol. 5, July 1968, pp. 100-114.

[14]Wolfgang, Marvin, Figlio, R. M., and Sillin, T., *Delinquency in a Birth Cohort.* Chicago: University of Chicago Press, 1972.

[15]*Challenge of Crime in a Free Society*, op. cit., p. 214.

would appear that certain types of recreational opportunities may deter youngsters from delinquency, but this effect is largely dependent on the nature of the activity and cannot be attributed to recreation as an entity."[16]

Recreation cannot be considered to be a panacea for all varieties of delinquency, but certain types of recreational activities might possibly be of help in crime prevention efforts if utilized properly. The National Advisory Commission on Criminal Justice Standards and Goals maintains that recreation should be considered as a vital component of an intervention strategy designed to prevent delinquency; it should not be relegated to a position of minor importance.[17] The value of recreational programs may be in the fact that they can provide youths with acceptable and effective alternative behaviors for frustration, energy, and excitement, thus diverting them from participating in deviant behavior.

The significance of providing all members of society, especially the economically disadvantaged, with adequate educational, vocational, and recreational opportunities should not be underestimated in crime prevention efforts. In addition, the opportunity for job advancement and adequate housing also play a role in the effectiveness of any crime prevention program. Even though programs are primarily targeted for members of the lower socioeconomic strata of our society, crime is not restricted to this segment of society. The higher socioeconomic groups also demonstrate criminal behaviors. Crime may also occur among those people who are educationally and occupationally successful as measured by objective societal standards. However, they may perceive themselves as relatively deprived or disadvantaged compared to others who are even more successful. They may then become involved in criminal activity to improve their social status. Therefore, the inclusion of such programs, although necessary, will at best reduce crime and delinquency, not entirely prevent it.

## EDUCATIONAL PROGRAMS

Many government-sponsored and community-based programs have been instituted with the objective of reducing school failure. These programs center upon many areas of educational development, such as appropriate preparation, relevant curriculum, remedial services, and career orientation. Many of these diverse programs are described in the following pages.

### Head Start

Head Start is a federally funded program designed to provide educational, nutritional, and social services to preschool children of economically

---

[16]Ibid, p. 334.
[17]"A National Strategy to Reduce Crime," op. cit.

disadvantaged families so that they will enter school at a developmental level comparable to that of less deprived classmates. Ninety percent of those receiving this service must come from families whose income is below the poverty guidelines. Full-year Head Start programs are primarily for children aged three and above until the child enters a regular school, but younger children may be accepted under special circumstances. Summer Head Start programs exist for children who will be attending kindergarten or elementary school for the first time in the fall.

The program has increased these children's chances of getting as much from the first few years of school as children coming from more stimulating environments. In addition, social and psychologic help given to disadvantaged families helps to improve the quality of life for both child and family.

## Follow Through

Follow Through is designed to sustain and augment gains that children from low-income families make in Head Start and other quality preschool programs.[18] Follow Through provides special programs of instruction as well as health, nutrition, and other education-related services in primary grades, which will aid in the continued development of children to their full potential. Active participation of parents is stressed. Funds are available for project activities not included in services provided by the school system. These activities include providing specialized and remedial teachers, teacher aides, and materials; physical and mental health services; social service workers and programs; nutritional improvement; and parent activities. Public and private school children from low-income families are eligible for participation.

## Talent Search

Talent Search offers alternatives for continuing education to those young people who for some reason cannot benefit from conventional methods of education. Financial aid is given to institutions and agencies for the purpose of assisting financially or culturally deprived youths, who possess an exceptional potential for postsecondary education. The youths are encouraged to complete high school and undertake additional educational training from institutions that have existing forms of student aid. All young people from seventh grade on who are in financial or cultural need and who have exceptional potential for postsecondary education, including high school and college dropouts, are eligible for participation.

---

[18]Doeren, Steve, and O'Block, Robert L., "Crime Prevention: An Eclectic Approach," in *Introduction to Criminal Justice: Theory and Practice*, Dae H. Chang, editor. Dubuque, Iowa: Kendall/Hunt Publishing Co., 1979, p. 319.

## Upward Bound

Upward Bound is a precollege preparatory program designed to generate the skill and motivation necessary for success in education beyond high school among young people from low-income families who have inadequate secondary school preparation.[19] Students must meet income criteria and be characterized as academic risks for college education. Lack of educational preparation and/or underachievement in high school would ordinarily compromise these youths' chances of being considered for college admission and enrollment. Upward Bound is designed to increase the students' chances of being admitted to and graduating from college. The program consists of a summer program lasting six to eight weeks and continues through the academic year with programs on Saturdays, tutorial sessions during the week, and periodic cultural enhancement programs.

## Project 70,001

Project 70,001, in existence since 1969 in Wilmington, Delaware, represents a significant community approach to career education. Instruction is related to work experiences, and opportunities are provided to explore or receive training in a career. The program provides on-the-job work experience and related classroom instruction to students unable to participate in or benefit from regular programs of education and training. The Wilmington project is a cooperative education program developed from the efforts and resources of a large shoe manufacturer, the Distributive Education Clubs of America, the Delaware Department of Public Instruction, and the Wilmington public schools. Similar programs have been implemented in several other communities throughout the country.

## OCCUPATIONAL PROGRAMS

As mentioned previously, research indicates a high correlation between unemployment and crime. A substantial portion of convicted offenders do not have salable job skills, and in some penal institutions as many as 40% of the inmates are without previous sustained work experience.[20] Thus the importance of employment in crime prevention cannot be overemphasized. Many community- and government-sponsored programs have been implemented with the main goal of providing employment opportunities for the disadvantaged and hard-core unemployed. Several representative programs are discussed in the following pages.

---

[19]Ibid.

[20]"A Call for Citizen Action: Crime Prevention and the Citizen." Washington, D.C.: National Advisory Commission on Criminal Justice Standards and Goals, U.S. Government Printing Office, 1974, p. 4.

## Occupational Task Force

This prototype career education program offers occupational information to students at all grade levels, from kindergarten to grade 12, and integrates materials into every subject of the curriculum. The Occupational Task Force is administered by the Seattle public school system.

## National Alliance of Businessmen's JOBS Program

Businessmen and others are working to place disadvantaged youths in summer and part-time jobs. Businessmen's JOBS Program is the largest of this type, having placed almost one million youths in summer and part-time jobs provided by private business and industry.[21] Some companies have agreed to fill a certain percentage of new jobs with the hard-core unemployed and to set new eligibility standards in this regard. The Job Opportunities Council, founded in Riverside, California, promotes recruitment of hard-core unemployed individuals, and many other citizen groups are promoting the "hire first, train later" programs whereby the applicant undergoes a two-week orientation program prior to being placed with an employer who agrees to provide on-the-job training and other support. Many citizens' organizations provide job counseling and training, such as Project Bread of Salem, Oregon, which trains ex-addicts to earn a living as cooks.

## Neighborhood Youth Corps

The Neighborhood Youth Corps (NYC) is another large program to deal with labor market problems of youth. It offers paid work experience to youths, ages sixteen to twenty-one, to enable them to remain in school, to return to school, or to improve their employability. This program has three components:

1. The out-of-school program provides paid work experience and counseling to low-income high school dropouts. The following are goals of the out-of-school program: (a) to enable the enrollees to return to school, (b) to enable them to attain a high school equivalency certificate (GED), (c) to provide skilled training to prepare the enrollee for an appropriate job, and/or (d) to prepare the enrollee and place him in the best unskilled or semiskilled entry level job for which he can qualify. At least 90% of the enrollees must be seventeen or eighteen years old. Enrollment periods are indefinite and should end in placement in full-time employment or entry into another training program.
2. The in-school program provides part-time work experience and income for youths still in school who are in need of money to remain in

[21] Ibid.

school. It can also offer remedial education, skill development, counseling, and placement.

3. The summer program is designed to offer training, work experience, and income to help disadvantaged youths return to school in the fall.[22]

The Neighborhood Youth Corps is administered by the Manpower Administration, Department of Labor.

## Job Corps

The Job Corps program is a full-service manpower training program for low-income, underachieving young men and women between the ages of sixteen and twenty-one. Its purpose is to assist young persons who need and can benefit from an unusually intensive program, operated in a group setting. The objective of this program is to assist young persons to become more responsible, employable, productive citizens. At residential and nonresidential centers, enrollees receive an intensive, well-organized, and fully supervised program of education, vocational training, work experience. Room and board, medical and dental care, clothing, and allowances are also provided. These centers also provide vocational and recreational activities and counseling, with emphasis on supporting and motivating enrollees to accomplish their educational and vocational objectives. Preparing enrollees to cope with the responsibilities and frustrations of society, motivating alienated or discouraged enrollees, and enhancing an understanding of peer group influences among enrollees is a prime objective. Most centers also provide drug education and drug counseling to all enrollees, with primary attention given to those who experiment with drugs. In addition, it also provides job placement assistance upon termination of training. The Job Corps program places primary emphasis on preparation for work, acquisition of skills, and movement into meaningful jobs. The Department of Labor views the Job Corps as an effective counterforce to the development of dependency and inactivity frequently associated with delinquency. The Job Corps is administered by the Manpower Administration, Department of Labor.

## Apprenticeship Outreach

The Apprenticeship Outreach program seeks qualified applicants from minority groups to assist them in entering apprenticeship programs, primarily in the construction trades. Tradesmen specialists are employed by the sponsor to assist in developing material for prospective candidates and for coaching candidates.

The Apprenticeship Outreach program is administered by the Manpower Administration, Department of Labor.

---

[22]Doeren and O'Block, op. cit., p. 319.

## Work Experience and Career Exploration Program (WECEP)

This school-supervised work experience and career exploration program is designed for selected youth fourteen and fifteen years of age who are considered to be potential dropouts. While accumulating credits toward graduation, these youths, under carefully structured circumstances, may work in a variety of jobs, ranging from sales and retail to aides or professionals in the areas of health and social services. The theory behind this program is that part-time work as an integral part of an educational program could make education more relevant to alienated and disoriented youth.

The Work Experience and Career Exploration Program is administered by the Employment Standards Administration, Wages and Hours Division, U.S. Department of Labor.

## Work Incentives Program

The Work Incentives Program is designed to provide men, women, and out-of-school youth on welfare with meaningful, permanent, productive employment through appropriate training, job placement, and other services.[23] This program is directed to welfare recipients who are required to register for work or training. Services offered include the following: (1) placement or on-the-job training and follow-through supportive services; (2) work orientation, basic education, skill training, work experience, and follow-through supportive services to improve employability of individuals who lack job readiness; and (3) hiring of individuals participating in the program by employers who are then eligible to receive a 20% tax credit on the first twelve months' wages or salary paid to the individuals.

The Work Incentives Program is administered by the Manpower Administration, Department of Labor.

## RECREATIONAL PROGRAMS

Many diverse programs are now in existence that have the objective of providing socially acceptable opportunities for recreational activity for youths and young adults. In addition to the actual provision of recreational and physical activities, many of these programs emphasize the interpersonal contact between the participants with appropriate role models.

## Big Brothers and Big Sisters

Founded in 1904, the development of Big Brothers of America (BBA) was based on the theory that frequent interpersonal contact between a disadvantaged youth and an adult male role model could help prevent juvenile delinquency, by providing a more stimulating environment and a more complete

---

[23]Ibid.

and satisfying life for fatherless boys. Participants in BBA are drawn from all socioeconomic groups, although a large percentage come from lower socioeconomic groups. "Little brothers" are usually between six and eighteen years of age. Some have police contacts, some have been previously institutionalized, and many have inadequate family resources and/or are in continuous dissension with their families.

The referrals of youths to Big Brothers agencies are frequently made by parents or guardians, school counselors, juvenile courts and probation offices, welfare offices, and by the youths themselves. The Big Brothers agencies in turn recruit and screen adult volunteers for assignment to a youngster.

A similar program for girls, Big Sisters, has gained momentum in past years. Big Sisters provides services to girls and young women in need of a relationship with an adult. Girls from motherless homes are paired with an emotionally mature woman capable of developing a supporting relationship with the girl or young woman. Big Brothers and Big Sisters visit or participate in activities with their assigned child an average of once per week. Activities are usually of mutual interest and include sports, arts and crafts, field trips, or other recreation-oriented activities.

**Operation "Get Down"**

Operation "Get Down" is a semi-survival camping program designed for the underprivileged and disadvantaged youth of Wichita, Kansas. The program is jointly sponsored by the Wichita Police Department, Wichita Community Action Agency, Boy Scouts of America, Emergency Medical Services, and several other independent community programs and businesses.[24]

The combined efforts of volunteers from these organizations enabled approximately 150 underprivileged youth to participate in the program in 1978. The youths, who must qualify within established economic guidelines, are referred to the program by the Community Action Agency centers and the Juvenile Court counseling program.

**Scouting**

Although not thought of primarily as a crime prevention program, Boy Scouts of America has long been concerned with the problems of youth. This largest and most extensive program for boys has had a long tradition of providing positive role models and instilling values into the Scouts. Girl Scouts provides many of the same opportunities and activities for girls.

---

[24]Ibid.

### Boys Clubs of America (BCA)

Boys Clubs of America have achieved the reputation of being leaders in the area of juvenile delinquency prevention and recently were awarded $756,000 by the Department of Justice for the purpose of developing nine program models for the prevention of juvenile delinquency. Today, there are over 1000 Boys Clubs serving more than 1 million youths ages six to eighteen.

Although each of the Boys Clubs develops its own goals, all are organized to provide core services in the following areas: social recreation, health and physical education, outdoor and environmental education, cultural enrichment, citizen and leadership development, and personal adjustment. In essence, they are concerned with a youth's physical, social, educational, vocational, and character development.

### GOVERNMENT AND COMMUNITY-BASED CRIME PREVENTION PROGRAMS

The previously described educational, occupational, and recreational programs represent just a few of the many diverse efforts to control crime at its roots. These programs are primarily directed toward assisting certain underprivileged community segments enrich their lives, help themselves, and thus lessen a need or desire to indulge in criminal activity. They are designed not only to prevent crime but also to deal with myriad other social problems such as poverty, unemployment, illiteracy, and the accompanying unrest caused by these environmental conditions.

There is another broad spectrum of government and community-based crime prevention programs that take a different approach. These programs, several of which will be discussed in detail in the following pages, take the form of increasing community protection and citizen awareness and education regarding specific crime prevention techniques.

### Federally funded programs

Many crime prevention programs, whether national or local, have received federal funding through the Office of Community Crime Prevention under the Department of Justice. Although specific priorities of this program change from year to year, at this time the major programs are: community anticrime programs, comprehensive crime prevention programs, and family violence programs.[25]

**Community anticrime programs.** The objectives of these programs are to assist community organizations, neighborhood groups, and individual citizens to become involved in activities designed to prevent crime, reduce the fear of

---

[25]"Guide for Discretionary Grant Programs." Guideline Manual, Law Enforcement Assistance Administration, U.S. Department of Justice, Sept. 30, 1978.

crime, and contribute to neighborhood revitalization. Specific goals to accomplish these objectives include:

1. Establishing new community and neighborhood-based anticrime organizations and groups that can mobilize neighborhood residents to conduct crime prevention activities.
2. Strengthening and/or expanding existing community and neighborhood-based anticrime organizations and assisting existing organizations involved in community improvement efforts to develop anticrime programs.
3. Developing improved understanding and cooperation of crime prevention activities among criminal justice officials and neighborhood residents.
4. Integrating neighborhood anticrime efforts with appropriate community development activities.

**Comprehensive crime prevention program.** The purpose of this program is to test the effect of establishing well-planned, comprehensive, multifaceted crime prevention programs in medium-sized local jurisdictions by:

1. Demonstrating the efficacy of controlling crime problems in a specific locality by identifying problems, developing coordination mechanisms and commitment, developing a wide range of programs to respond to identified problems, and implementing the programs throughout the local government jurisdiction.
2. Gaining increased knowledge about the management of crime prevention strategies and implementation techniques.
3. Promoting and effecting improved coordination program planning and implementation among federal agencies having an interest or responsibility in crime prevention.

**Family violence program.** The objective of this program is to provide support for several comprehensive program models designed to test appropriate and effective responses to family violence. The results that are sought by this program are:

1. A reduction in community acceptance of intrafamily violence.
2. Increased reporting of incidents of intrafamily violence and documentation of the extent, nature, and interrelationship of these crimes.
3. The demonstration of an effective mechanism for institutional coordination among police, prosecutor, protective services, welfare, hospitals, community mental health, and other relevant public and private agencies and community organizations to respond to family violence situations.
4. Documentation of the needs of these families and the development of methods to address these needs, including a reallocation of existing services as well as creation of new services.

5. Improved knowledge, skills, and cooperation of medical and social service agency personnel in the collection and transmission of evidence and information to the legal system in cases of intrafamily violence.
6. Reduction in the number of repeat calls to the police related to family disturbances.
7. An increase in the prosecution of cases involving repeated violence of a severe nature.
8. The establishment of community corrections, pretrial diversion, and other programs specifically designed to improve the criminal justice system's handling of these cases.
9. Reduction in the number of intrafamily homicides and serious assaults.[26]

### Identifying community crime exposure

Before describing specific programs, a word should be said about citizen involvement, police-community relations, and factors that should be kept in mind when developing a community-based program.

It is important to recognize that any community approach must create a sense of belonging and cohesiveness among members of various neighborhoods. This can range from simply getting to know one's neighbors to large-scale programs that organize members of the community and establish common goals.

It is also necessary to identify community crime exposures for a particular neighborhood. Factors to be considered in the identification process include:

◻ Geographic location: Crime rates vary on the basis of location alone. For example, street crimes such as muggings or purse snatchings are more apt to occur on the streets of a large inner city than on the streets of a suburb of the same city.
◻ Nature and method of business and relationship to geographic location: Many businesses such as all night convenience stores and liquor stores are more susceptible than others to certain types of crimes, such as robbery and shoplifting. If these businesses are in a susceptible geographic location, such as between a school and a low income housing development, the problem is compounded.
◻ Analysis of law enforcement capability to suppress crime: Police departments should be assessed in terms of sufficiency of manpower and resources to meet their objectives of crime prevention. If a severe manpower or financial shortage exists, community crime prevention programs may be hampered from the very outset.
◻ Analysis of commercial protection resources and vendors: This is an assessment of private security resources, such as alarm companies, guard services,

---

[26]Ibid.

and other available devices for use, as well as the cost of these services, and feasibility of implementing any of the preventive measures on a community-wide basis.

▫ Analysis of community capability: This is an assessment of what resources already exist in the community that can be utilized, and what additional organizations can be developed.

## Government-citizen cooperation

Also germane to the success of community-based programs is cooperation between government and the citizenry. Community-based crime prevention will only become a reality when a sense of trust and mutual cooperation exists between citizens and government. In order for the government to achieve a sense of trust among the citizens it will be necessary that the government:

1. Be able and willing to provide necessary services to all citizens equitably, and in a manner that preserves the recipient's sense of dignity and self-respect.
2. Seek to make its services accessible and to operate humanely so that citizens can receive a variety of services close to their homes, with a minimum of bureaucratic red tape. Government should also seek the support and confidence of the citizens through policies of openness in its deliberative and programmatic procedures.
3. Correct administrative indifference toward or abuse of citizens by providing mechanisms through which citizens can make their complaints known and can obtain speedy, fair solutions to their problems.
4. Recognize the valuable contributions citizens can make to the governing process. Certain decision-making can therefore take place at the neighborhood level.[27]

In addition, police have a responsibility to provide types of services that enable citizens to become aware of and involved in crime prevention programs. The police should take responsibility for informing residents of their crime risk, coordinating campaigns to increase awareness about all types of crimes, and offering free security surveys so that citizens and businessmen alike can benefit from such an evaluation.

Government responsibilities have been identified and described but even the most conscientious government cannot provide successful programs without dedicated community involvement and leadership. Citizens have the responsibility of selecting both issues of genuine importance to a large number of residents and realistic strategies with which to deal with those issues. This is true whether the community is organizing with block clubs for street

---

[27]*Community Crime Prevention.* National Advisory Commission on Criminal Justice Standards and Goals, 1973, p. 33.

repairs or determining the allocation of city housing funds. Failure to consider these factors results in loss of credibility for the organization and disinterest in its goals by the citizenry.

Public credibility is the most important element in establishing and continuing an effective community organization. As mentioned previously, credibility can be earned for an organization through leadership and selecting issues of great importance to a significant number of people.

It is neither necessary nor desirable for an organization to gain credibility through endorsement by the wealthy and the powerful. Although this method is effective in achieving some goals, it is also detrimental to the organization because it stifles its independence in dealing with issues, developing leadership, involving different people, and making basic changes in the community and within the organization itself. Representative organizations are necessary in order to serve the interests of the residents, and this representation must be independent of powerful public and private decision-makers who control the planning process as well as public service bureaucracies. Community organizations without the influence of the rich and powerful residents tend to attain more control through public opinion, which can eventually extend throughout the entire city.

Local crime prevention agencies need the support of the community to determine priorities. Often police administrators and political leaders have passed off crime prevention as another public relations gimmick when actually it offers the most justifiable crime-stopping opportunity possible. Police and citizens have long existed in separate spheres, ignoring their shared responsibilities. But the time has come to realize that police cannot be held solely responsible for rising crime rates and citizens cannot expect too much of their police while ignoring their own role in crime prevention.

For the most part, community groups cooperate well with police, carry no weapons, and act mainly as eyes and ears for sworn officials. Citizens may engage in projects that are preventive and peaceful, but vigilantism is not tolerated. Citizen participation could include crime prevention surveillance in the form of patrolling, picture-taking of offenders, and using whistles, horns, and sometimes verbosity to scare off potential criminals. Participants should also be active lobbyists for crime prevention legislation and improved services.

A survey by the office of Community Anti-Crime Program revealed what community organizations consider to be major crime issues.[28] Table 13-1 pre-

---

[28]*Who's Organizing the Neighborhood?* Washington, D.C.: Office of Community Crime Prevention, Law Enforcement Assistance Administration, U.S. Department of Justice, Government Printing Office, 1979, p. 19.

**Table 13-1.** Major crime problems*

| Crime or problem | Percent |
| --- | --- |
| Breaking and entering | 16.3 |
| Burglary | 14.4 |
| Vandalism | 13.3 |
| Juvenile crime | 12.0 |
| Assaults | 10.3 |
| Drug abuse | 7.7 |
| Police-community conflicts | 4.8 |
| Crime against elderly | 3.6 |
| Auto theft | 3.5 |
| Street gangs | 2.9 |
| Rape | 2.7 |
| All others | 8.5 |

*From *Who's Organizing the Neighborhood?* Washington, D.C.: Office of Community Crime Prevention, Law Enforcement Assistance Administration, Department of Justice, Government Printing Office, 1979, p. 19.

sents these issues in order of perceived importance. Breaking and entering, burglary, vandalism, juvenile crime, and assaults comprise two-thirds of what are considered to be major crime issues. Police-community conflicts, although not in the first five, rank as more important than crime against the elderly, auto theft, street gangs, and rape. This would indicate that many citizens feel alienated from law enforcement systems and that changes within the police-community relationship need to take place. Emphasizing better police-community relations has been known to evoke a sense of community pride by decreasing feelings of social apathy, increasing feelings of self-identity, and promoting organizations for purposes of social control.

In addition to selecting relevant issues and the importance of government-citizen cooperation, the organizations should reflect the existing characteristics of the neighborhood. For example, community crime prevention programs are not restricted to the middle- or high-income groups, nor are they restricted to whites. In many areas the poor are involved, and in many neighborhoods blacks suffer a higher rate of crime and are just as concerned about crime prevention as whites, if not more so. Communities should make strong efforts for ethnic and racial mix in participation.

Another factor to be considered in organization development is economics. It appears easier to organize and maintain membership of middle-income groups than lower- and higher-income groups.[29] This is possibly because

[29]Washnis, George, *Citizen Involvement in Crime Prevention.* Lexington, Mass.: Lexington Books, 1976, p. 3.

middle-income groups are generally homeowners who have motivation to protect their possessions, while also having a high degree of community pride. Many lower-income groups, on the other hand, do not possess as much concern for property values. Many do not own their own homes and are not particularly motivated to protect someone else's property. Higher-income group members usually have been successful in demanding and getting better police protection, and they are also likely to live in neighborhoods that are relatively distant from the major or more violent criminal acts. This is not to say that the poor and the rich are completely disinterested in crime prevention; successful crime prevention programs are being formed in both wealthy sections and low-income and public housing neighborhoods. However, the economic status of a particular neighborhood or area must be considered in organization development.

Although many factors are important in the development and success or failure of a particular community organization, community crime prevention programs are springing up all over the country. Many are enjoying great success because of the magnitude of the crime problem and the significant number of interested persons. Also these organizations offer practical and realistic approaches to prevent potential problems associated with becoming a victim of crime.

### Community-based programs

There have been many strategies and programs adopted by organizations to deal with crime problems, the most common of which are listed in order of frequency in Table 13-2. Several community organizations are discussed in detail in the following pages.

**Neighborhood Watch or Block Watch.** Neighborhood Watch programs have been implemented in over 2,000 counties and municipalities. The programs are usually administered by the sheriff's or police department. It may be a highly organized effort or just an informal method of getting neighbors acquainted and agreeing to watch each other's property.

When neighbors know each other personally they are more aware of each other's habits and routines. This awareness in turn makes them cognizant of peculiarities and unusual events, such as strange cars or persons in the neighborhood. Neighborhood acquaintance is also a factor in the neighbors' willingness to get involved in reporting a crime if they suspect one is taking place.

Residents receive help in establishing a neighborhood watch program from law enforcement officers or civic organizations, and in return promise to cooperate with authorities in reporting criminal and suspicious activity. As a result of this mutual cooperation among neighbors, and between neighbors

**Table 13-2.** Most common methods employed by neighborhoods in the control of crime*

| Method | Percent |
|---|---|
| Community organization | 25.0 |
| Block/neighborhood crime watch | 11.0 |
| Citizen patrols | 8.7 |
| Recreation programs | 8.0 |
| Whistlestop projects | 7.3 |
| Community education | 6.5 |
| Special youth services | 5.8 |
| Home/commercial building security | 5.1 |
| Drug/alcohol abuse projects | 3.7 |
| Monitoring the courts | 2.9 |
| Property identification projects | 2.9 |
| Direct communication systems | 2.9 |
| Personal identification projects | 2.2 |
| Escort services | 2.2 |
| Bail fund | 0.7 |
| Monitoring of police | 0.7 |
| Filing of charges | 0.7 |

*From *Who's Organizing the Neighborhood?* Washington, D.C.: Office of Community Crime Prevention, Law Enforcement Assistance Administration, Department of Justice, Government Printing Office, 1979, p. 22.

and law enforcement authorities, it has become extremely difficult for a suspicious-looking character to enter a neighborhood on foot or by car without being observed. Extremely low burglary rates characterize neighborhoods in which people are truly concerned with each other and their mutual safety.

The primary objectives of watch groups are to:

1. Maintain a cooperative system of surveillance over one another's property, children, etc.
2. Report suspicious activity or persons or crimes in progress to the police accurately and immediately.
3. Mutually assist and encourage the accomplishment of home security inspections, target hardening, and property-marking activities by all neighborhood residents.
4. Maintain a continuing system for the dissemination of educational materials relative to self-protection and criminal awareness and adjust program emphasis in accordance with the most current information.
5. Assist the victims of crime and assist in their readjustment to normalcy.
6. Encourage citizens to come forward as witnesses.

7. Help both elderly or debilitated citizens and children to protect themselves against criminal victimization, and advocate and push for additional projects to protect these special groups of persons whenever
   necessary.[30]

Neighborhood Watch has been particularly effective in reducing the
number of burglaries in neighborhoods where it has been implemented and
citizens are participating. A 1975 evaluation of the program concluded that:

> Where Neighborhood Watch is being implemented a large percentage of
> citizens [households] have, in fact, been exposed to the Neighborhood Watch
> literature which is being distributed by the law enforcement agencies in large
> quantities, in relatively short periods of time for the most part. This evaluation
> study has determined that where Neighborhood Watch is implemented and citi-
> zens are participating, the program is a positive success in increasing the number
> of citizen reports—a positive success in substantially decreasing the number of
> attempted residential B & E's [breaking and entering]—a positive success in
> lowering the number of successfully completed residential burglaries.[31]

A decrease in the number of attempts to commit burglaries and the actual
number of successful burglaries is expected because of the well-publicized
program of crime prevention and target hardening along with citizen concern
for the safety and security of one's own and one's neighbor's property.

Next to having good locks, concerned neighbors can be the single most
effective security system. Concerned neighbors can benefit crime prevention
efforts in three ways[32]:

1. When neighbors join together and make a cooperative effort to watch
   for unusual and suspicious activities in the neighborhood, the word
   gets around and, according to recent studies, burglary rates are extremely low in such neighborhoods. Since most burglaries are of the
   spur-of-the-moment type and are committed by persons living within
   the same general area as the victim, it would be relatively easy for a
   neighborhood to acquire a reputation for alertness and for that area to
   be avoided by the average burglar.
2. As a deterrent, the presence of an observing neighbor could make the
   burglar change his mind about breaking into a residence and go
   elsewhere. Or a neighbor could make enough noise to scare a burglar
   even after he had broken in but before he could take anything. However, extreme caution should be used if a suspicious-looking person is

---

[30]*National Neighborhood Watch.* Program manual, National Sheriffs Association, p. 12.
[31]Ibid, p. 3.
[32]*Crime Prevention Handbook For Senior Citizens.* Washington, D.C.: National Institute of Law
Enforcement and Criminal Justice, Law Enforcement Assistance Administration, U.S. Department of Justice, 1977, p. 29.

The Crime Control and Public Safety Department of North Carolina has recommended ten steps for the establishment of a successful neighborhood Watch Program. These ten steps are included below.

**First step**

Call a meeting in a local home, church, community building or volunteer fire department and personally invite every resident in the community. Invite everyone regardless of race or income level. Everyone is hit by crime. Ask a member of the local law enforcement agency to come to the first meeting.

**Second step**

Get a complete list of names, addresses and phone numbers of everyone taking part in the program and elect a chairman to take charge of the meeting.

**Third step**

Ask the law enforcement officer to explain the limits of a citizen's role in community watch and to give residents suggestions on what to watch for in their homes and in the community. Ask the officer's advice on reporting suspicious activities and crimes.

**Fourth step**

Select the type of signs and bumper and window stickers necessary for high visibility in the community. Establish a cost for each household, collect the funds, and order the materials. The local sheriff's department or police department can supply free material from national associations or security lock companies.

**Fifth step**

Mark all valuable items in your homes and businesses with your driver's license number, and improve locks and security systems.

**Sixth step**

Put up signs at the entrance to your neighborhood and in every member's yard on the same day for maximum impact on residents and criminals.

**Seventh step**

Appoint block captains to pass information received from your crime prevention officer to members on their streets.

**Eighth step**

Schedule monthly meetings of the entire community for additional training sessions. Schedule meetings as needed to keep community cooperation alive, to keep high visibility, and to plan monthly programs.

**Ninth step**

Inform your state crime prevention agency of your community watch program in order to receive newsletters, including ideas from other communities and suggestions for monthly programs.

**Tenth step**

Keep in touch with the crime prevention officer.

Source: *Community Watch in North Carolina*, North Carolina Department of Crime Control and Public Safety, Raleigh, North Carolina, pp. 2-3.

seen entering a neighbor's house or apartment or if any kind of questionable activity is taking place in the neighborhood. If an intruder is inside a neighbor's residence, a telephone call to the house might be enough to scare the burglar away. In any event, citizens should not check on strangers; under no circumstances should they expose them-

## CASE STUDY OF NEIGHBORHOOD WATCH

Two years ago a tidal wave of crime crashed over Whispering Oaks, a middle-class subdivision in Austin, Texas. "There were as many as 35 class-1 offenses a month," recalls policeman George Vanderhule. "Mostly burglaries and vandalism, but also sexual assaults on adults and kids." Some Whispering Oaks residents were selling their months-old homes out of fear. Yet surrounding neighborhoods were almost free of crime. What was wrong in Whispering Oaks?

Officer Vanderhule saw too many bushy trees and high privacy fences, too many access roads. Far more serious, he found a neighborhood of strangers. "Nobody knew anybody else," he said, "so anybody could amble in, pick out hiding places, vulnerable properties, escape routes."

Vanderhule got at least one person from every Whispering Oaks block into a "Neighborhood Watch." His object was to teach crime awareness not to vigilantes but to concerned people. In five meetings he explained how neighborhood criminals can usually be repelled with things residents have in their garages and workshops. "You're buying time," he explained. "If your neighborhood criminal can't enter your home in four minutes, he'll try somebody else's." Lights and noise can be cheap, effective weapons, Vanderhule said, while costly alarm systems are not always necessary.

Vanderhule lent engravers to mark valuables—"with quickly traceable drivers' license numbers, not Social Security ones that take months to run down." He detailed ways to defeat muggers, rapists, con artists. Most important, he urged Whispering Oaks people to meet and to look out for each other. To recognize and report anything suspicious. As crime awareness grew, the subdivision's crime rate fell. In just one month it dropped 50 percent, halved again the following month. Very soon Whispering Oaks was both crime free and a lot more neighborly. Now its homes sell for more than comparable ones nearby—sometimes $6000 to $8000 more. The police—Austin's crime prevention officers—got no medals. Nor do thousands of other such officers elsewhere get enough notice. Yet a top official in the Justice Department's Law Enforcement Assistance Administration (LEAA) says: "Theirs is the way of the future. Not only to restore law and order in our communities and make policing more efficient, less expensive, but a way to give our whole lives a new quality."

Source: "Watch Out, There's A Thief About," by David Lampe. *Parade*, March 11, 1979, p. 4. Wichita Eagle and Beacon. Reprinted by permission.

selves to the fury of a frustrated burglar. They should call the police to investigate suspicious circumstances even though they may have some lingering doubts as to the stranger's legitimacy. The police will respond and politely check out the person.

3. Watch hours are assigned to different people, at which times it is their responsibility to keep an eye on neighborhood activities in a casual-appearing manner. If they see a suspicious-looking character, it is their responsibility to note descriptions, both of the person and the vehicle, if any. This becomes valuable information that can aid law enforcement authorities in apprehension if it is later found that a crime was committed.

Ideally, neighborhood or block watch programs should be comprised of ten to fifteen neighbors who are interested in mutual protection against crime, particularly burglary. Seattle, Washington, to name just one example, has a very successful block watch program. Participants are provided crime statistics for their particular area, which include the number of burglaries within a given time period, inventory of items stolen, method of entry, and specific locations of burglaries. Block watch maps are distributed to all members for use in tracking crimes and in making telephone calls regarding suspicious persons or activities. Other services provided include the demonstration and lending of engraving tools; demonstrations of various locks, reinforcement techniques, and security weaknesses of certain doors and windows; and home security inspections.

Another successful watch program is Crime Watch, sponsored by the Fort Lauderdale Police Department.[33] This program, using the slogan, "The Force is With You," stresses the importance of neighborhood awareness along with active citizen participation. Crime watchers are networks of neighbors trained by crime prevention officers in home and self-protection, suspect identification, and how to serve effectively as eyes and ears for law enforcement agencies. A telephone chain is established that enables neighbors to keep one another informed of any criminal activity and to receive information from the police concerning descriptions of suspected criminals or other pertinent information. When a member of a network sees a suspicious character or vehicle, identifies a suspect, or witnesses a crime in progress, they call the police hotline to report. This is the crime watchers' job, and it is stressed that they should *never* attempt to apprehend a suspect. As with all neighborhood watch programs, citizen participation is the backbone of the program.

Members of Crime Watch are instructed in accurate and rapid reporting of suspect and vehicle description. It is recognized that these two factors are

---

[33]*Crime Watch, Manual of Instruction.* Fort Lauderdale Police Department.

critical in apprehending a suspect. To aid police in making an arrest the following information should be provided to police by Crime Watchers:

1. The exact nature of the crime.
2. The location of the crime itself and location of where the Crime Watcher made the call.
3. As complete as possible, a description of the culprit involved, including any associates also observed, and information regarding any weapons that might also be involved.
4. As complete as possible, any description of a vehicle that might have been used by the culprit in the commission of the crime being reported, including cars, motorcycles, bicycles, etc.
5. The last known direction of the culprit(s) involved.

Fig. 13-1 illustrates the physical characteristics and attire that ideally

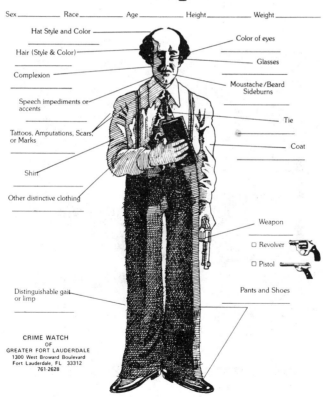

# Describe the suspect.

Sex _____ Race_____ Age _____ Height _____ Weight _____

Hat Style and Color _____

Hair (Style & Color) _____

Complexion _____

Speech impediments or accents _____

Tattoos, Amputations, Scars, or Marks _____

Shirt _____

Other distinctive clothing _____

Distinguishable gait or limp _____

Color of eyes _____

Glasses _____

Moustache/Beard Sideburns _____

Tie _____

Coat _____

Weapon _____
□ Revolver
□ Pistol

Pants and Shoes _____

CRIME WATCH
OF
GREATER FORT LAUDERDALE
1300 West Broward Boulevard
Fort Lauderdale, FL 33312
761-2628

**Fig. 13-1.** Physical characteristics of a suspect.

should be noted about a suspect. It is rare and often impossible for witnesses to provide police with such a detailed description of a suspect as in this illustration, but watch members do receive training and should strive to provide as thorough a description as possible. Most major cities have implemented similar programs with equal success.

Advantages of neighborhood or block watch programs as a means of crime prevention are:

1. They are not complicated programs and can be implemented in a short time.
2. They are fairly inexpensive to implement because there are no overhead costs and expensive equipment is not necessary.
3. They are flexible and can be adapted to meet the needs of any particular neighborhood.
4. These programs will usually generate a spirit of mutual concern and enthusiasm among citizens.
5. They do not require large investments of time or money by citizens.

**Operation identification.** Operation Identification has been an ongoing and successful nationwide program for several years. In these programs citi-

**Fig. 13-2.** An effective deterrent against unauthorized entry, Operation Identification decals make the potential benefits of a burglary less attractive.

zens are loaned electric engraving tools at no cost so that they may mark their valuables. The person's Social Security or driver's license number is used, prefixed with two letters used to abbreviate the state of residence. In the event valuables are lost or stolen and later recovered, identification and return of the property to its rightful owner is facilitated. In addition, identification numbers make fencing of stolen items difficult and increases the culprit's chances of discovery and ultimate conviction. The greatest benefit, however, appears to be a result of Operation Identification decals, which citizens place throughout their homes in doors and windows (Fig. 13-2). These decals warn the would-be burglar that possessions have been marked, thus making the burglary target less attractive. Specific household and outdoor items that should be engraved include: television sets, stereo equipment, radios, cameras, binoculars, guns, vacuum cleaners, kitchen appliances (toasters, mixers, etc.), typewriters, watches and clocks, fishing rods, car tape decks, hub caps, mag wheels, lawn mowers, bicycles, golf clubs, outboard motors, and hand and power tools.

Engraving tools can usually be obtained at the sheriff's department, police department, or public library. In many areas law enforcement agencies advertise the availability of engraving tools, offer door-to-door engraving services, and keep up-to-date records of participants' identification numbers.

Neighborhood and block watch programs provide excellent opportunities to initiate Operation ID, and engraving services are usually incorporated into the services of the watch program. Any community that does not have an Operation Identification program can get additional information from the National Sheriffs Association.

**Citizen patrols.** Many neighborhoods and communities have citizen patrol programs in which citizens patrol the streets in their own cars equipped with citizen band radios. This has proved to be another useful method in which law enforcement authorities have extended their eyes and ears with citizen involvement. The increased use of CB radios together with police monitoring of Channel 9 has made this type of program possible. The patrols have the advantage of speedy communications directly to the police department to report crimes in progress, suspicious activity, or emergencies.

Guidelines recommended by the National Sheriffs Association in establishing citizen patrols include[34]:

□ Patrol members should be at least eighteen years of age.
□ Patrol members should be issued identification cards.
□ Patrol members using radio equipment should possess an FCC license.

---

[34]*National Neighborhood Watch.* Program manual, National Sheriffs Association, p. 20.

- □ Automobiles used by citizen patrols should be identifiable to all regular police and other private citizen patrols operating in the same vicinity.
- □ Patrol members should not be permitted to work in excess of four hours per shift.
- □ Patrol members should not be permitted to carry weapons of any type.
- □ Citizen patrol vehicles should not be equipped with sirens or emergency lighting, except for spotlights for security checking.
- □ Each citizen patrol member should receive some fundamental training in law and ordinance.

**Citizen crime-reporting projects (CCRP).** Many citizen organizations in cooperation with law enforcement agencies sponsor areawide programs to educate and encourage the public to report crimes in progress, information that would help police solve crimes, and suspicious persons or events. Campaigns such as Crime Check, Citizen Alert, Crime Stop, Project Alert, Chec-Mate, and Home Alert are examples of such programs. Because they encourage citizen surveillance, crime reporting projects are a logical component of neighborhood watch programs, and tie in closely with the functions of citizen patrol.

Crime reporting provisions made by various communities include special telephone numbers and creation of radio watch programs wherein businesses with vehicles equipped with two-way radios are briefed on how to report crimes in progress and suspicious activity.

It is thought that citizen crime-reporting projects contribute to:

- □ A reduction of fear of crime
- □ An improvement in police-community relations
- □ An improvement in citizen cooperation with law enforcement agencies
- □ An increase in community cohesiveness
- □ The obtaining of more accurate crime statistics
- □ An increase in the number of apprehensions

If the quality of crime reports increases, it is expected that:

- □ Police will receive more reports of crimes in progress
- □ Better descriptions of suspects and more accurate locations of the crimes will be given
- □ Reports will be made with greater speed and clarity
- □ Police will arrive on the scene sooner and more often at the correct location
- □ Police will be better able to aid the victim
- □ Police will have access to better witness performance, which will lead to an increase in convictions
- □ An increase in apprehensions and convictions will lead to an increase in deterrence

Fig. 13-3 is a diagram of the CCRP framework. CCRPs represent a witness-oriented, community-based approach to crime prevention. Crime reporting and neighborhood surveillance activities can result in protecting strangers on the street as well as residents.

The effectiveness of many individual crime-reporting programs has been studied by the National Evaluation Program of the National Institute of Law Enforcement and Criminal Justice. Some of these programs are described in further detail in the following pages.

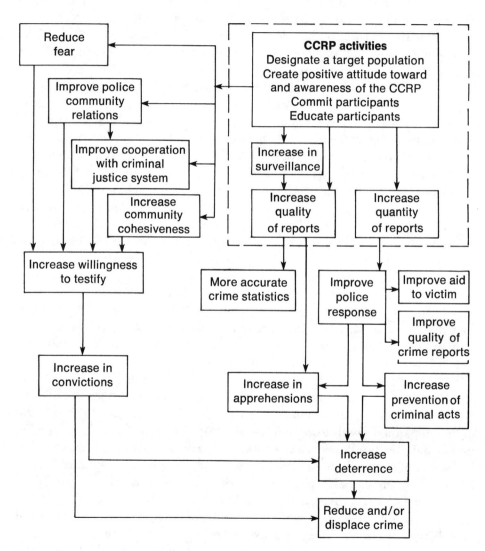

**Fig. 13-3.** Generalized CCRP framework. (From *Citizens Crime Reporting Projects.* Washington, D.C.: National Evaluation Program, Phase 1 Report, Series A, No. 14, Law Enforcement Assistance Administration, U.S. Department of Justice, 1979.)

**Whistlestop projects.** Whistlestop projects facilitate the reporting of in-progress street crimes by witnesses and victims through a whistle alert system that signals residents in their homes to call the police. The sound of the whistle also signals persons walking in the area that someone is in need of help. In Chicago, for example, Whistlestop projects are sponsored by volunteer community organizations and block clubs. Persons wishing to participate in the project purchase Whistlestop packets from storefront community organizations or from local shopkeepers. The packets include information on how to use the whistle and how to report a whistle incident to the police. The instructions stress that persons who witness a street crime should not intervene personally in the situation, but should use the whistle to alert persons near a telephone to call the police. The awareness of Whistlestop in the target community would ideally be such that persons hearing the sound of the whistle would know they should call the police immediately. It is estimated that more than 100,000 whistles have been purchased by Chicago residents.

**Radio Watch projects.** Participation in Radio Watch is usually limited to citizens whose occupations give them access to taxis or trucks with two-way radios but may also include individuals who have citizen band or ham radios in their cars. Crime reporting by these persons, who are normally isolated from direct contact with police, is facilitated by communication with the two-way radio dispatcher, who calls the police for the driver. Participants in the project are asked to report suspicious criminal activities and public hazards such as fire or traffic accidents.

Most Radio Watch projects are a relatively low-cost and low-effort venture for the implementing agency. They usually involve a training program for drivers and dispatchers, and participants often meet with project staff on a regular basis. Radio Watch projects are frequently cooperative efforts between business and law enforcement agencies.

**Project Legs.** Project Legs is sponsored by the National Exchange Club. This is a very simple program for citizen involvement that does not involve confrontation or apprehension. The purpose of the program is to supply the police department with extra hands—and legs. For example, after receiving proper training, the Project Legs volunteers go door to door in an area that has had a rash of burglaries to inform residents and prescribe precautions. Project Legs volunteers can also perform security surveys of dwellings and make recommendations, particularly for elderly residents. The volunteer might also be able to supply the manpower and the material to improve the security of an elderly person's home. These are just two possible services that Project Legs volunteers could provide, since police do not normally have the time or the manpower for many of these preventive measures.

**Volunteers in Prevention.** Volunteers in Prevention is a relatively new approach originating at Temple University within the Department of Criminal Justice. The project's goal is to train volunteers and supervisors to work in law enforcement agencies, prisons, probation programs for both adult and juvenile offenders, and other institutions concerned with offenders and ex-offenders. The objective of citizen involvement is to reduce, prevent, and control crime, and make neighborhoods more secure.

**Counseling and treatment programs.** Many citizen groups counsel and advise youths and adults with a variety of problems and within a variety of organizational frameworks. Hotlines may be established especially for persons with drug-related problems, or the local YMCA may offer counseling with referral of persons with serious problems to community health clinics or mental health clinics, drug abuse rehabilitation centers, planned parenthood organizations, juvenile aid services, and legal services. The Listening Post in Bethesda, Maryland, is a fine example of a telephone hotline and center to which young people can go for advice and help. Volunteers at the center try to create a warm environment where young people will find acceptance and to provide constructive alternatives for youths in trouble.

Citizens also volunteer at counseling centers designed to better parent-child relationships. Others assist trained personnel who treat drug- or alcohol-related cases. Many detoxification clinics are now in operation throughout the country. Volunteers offer telephone counseling and crisis intervention services, and anti–drug abuse educational campaigns are often maintained and conducted by citizen groups.

**National Council of Crime and Delinquency.** The National Crime Prevention Campaign is a prevention program that seeks to involve citizens from all walks of life. The campaign is sponsored jointly by the National Council of Crime and Delinquency (NCCD), which provides training, technical assistance and public information; the Department of Justice, which provides funding and evaluations; and the Advertising Council, Inc., which is promoting crime prevention efforts via television, radio, and billboard advertising. Among the participating organizations are: The International Association of Chiefs of Police, The National Sheriffs Association, The National Crime Prevention Institute, The Texas Crime Prevention Institute, the Federal Bureau of Investigation, U.S. Jaycees, General Federation of Women's Clubs, National Conference of Parents and Teachers, American Association of Retired Persons, National Retired Teachers Association, National Urban League, AFL-CIO, National Council of La Raza, National League of Cities, and the U.S. Conference of Mayors.

The goal of this large-scale campaign is to persuade citizens that most crimes can be prevented by learning how to avoid becoming a victim. The campaign also publicizes the need for and the ways that citizens can become involved so that crime prevention programs will eventually be established as necessary and normal community activities.

The National Council of Crime and Delinquency helps organizations develop or expand existing crime prevention programs. The NCCD will train volunteers of local, state, and national organizations in crime prevention techniques, give assistance in analyzing crime problems, disseminate information, and publicize successful crime prevention activities.

**Minnesota Crime Prevention Center.** The Minnesota Crime Prevention Center (MCPC) is a nonprofit organization, which, since 1975, has given technical assistance to cities on forming comprehensive crime prevention programs using physical design, law enforcement, administrative strategies, and community action.[35]

The process that MCPC has found to work in developing comprehensive crime prevention programs begins with a detailed crime analysis that provides a block-by-block picture. They review police crime reports and code them by type of crime, premise, location, type of entry, victim, and offender characteristics. They analyze these data in conjunction with city census information and come up with a "rate of crime opportunity" for the neighborhood. Police offense data are combined with perceptions of the crime problem by those who live and work in the community. This is a more sophisticated planning tool than is used by most community crime prevention programs.

The second planning aid is a "resource analysis." Community organizations, individuals, and representatives of various departments or agencies that can contribute to the effort are identified, and task forces are formed to further identify the problems and develop solutions. These task forces are meant to include all segments of the community, such as landlords, school and housing officials, building inspectors, city planners, businessmen, elected officials, and homeowner association members.

**Women's Crusade Against Crime.** The Women's Crusade Against Crime, started in St. Louis, seeks to improve the quality of life for citizens in participating cities as it is affected by crime and the criminal justice system. It is an organization well worth close examination. The following objectives characterize this organization:

1. To stimulate citizen involvement in the criminal justice system.
2. To educate the public about the criminal justice system.
3. To identify strengths and weaknesses in the criminal justice system.
4. To get all areas of the criminal justice system working together.
5. To implement various programs and reforms.

---

[35]"Planning Key to Crime Prevention in Minnesota." *Criminal Justice and the Elderly Newsletter*, Washington, D.C.: National Council of Senior Citizens, Winter 1978-1979, p. 4.

The Crusade is a nonpartisan, volunteer, interracial organization with approximately 3,000 members (including some men). Its programs and concepts have established a pattern for other citizens' groups across the country.

The Crusade is unique in that it embraces all segments of the criminal justice system—police, courts, corrections, youth problems, and education of the public. Each area has its distinct concerns and projects. Volunteers on the police committee remain in constant contact with local police officers, and also operate several auxiliary programs, such as Operation Identification, Crime Blockers, and Secret Witness programs.

The court committee maintains a desk in the St. Louis Municipal Courts Building, which serves to disseminate information concerning court cases, and also implements the famous "court watchers" program. For additional information on court watching, see Chapter 14.

The corrections committee maintains informal surveillance over the state's correctional institutions. Members make periodic visits to the Missouri Penitentiary and the workhouse, and on Saturday mornings volunteers provide opportunities for women prisoners to participate in educational and recreational programs.

The youth committee supports neighborhood youth centers, detention centers, and counseling projects. Members of this committee hold outings for youths in parks, which provide them with an opportunity to meet law enforcement officers. Several "fuzz festivals" have been staged in area parks to help promote better rapport between police and young people.

The education committee is responsible for the preparation and distribution of publications related to crime prevention, and for organizing annual crime prevention seminars. Subjects such as gun control, shoplifting, bail bonds, drugs, court reform, police training, criminal personalities, and rape have been subjects of such seminars.

The Women's Crusade has operated with funds provided through grants from the Law Enforcement Assistance Administration and individual donations. Several other crusades, modeled after the St. Louis program have been formed in cities such as Baltimore, Savannah, Salt Lake City, New Orleans, and New York. The "woman's touch" in the fight against crime is continually making its presence known as the Crusaders' efforts make positive advances in all areas of the administration of justice. The impact of this program in the community is made possible through the support of its many volunteers and backing from cooperating organizations, leading officials, and the media.*

**National Alliance for Safer Cities.** The National Alliance for Safer Cities was initiated in 1970 by the American Jewish Committee, with the cosponsor-

---

*Note:* For additional information concerning the Women's Crusade Against Crime, write to 1221 Locust Street, St. Louis, Mo. 63103.

ship of twelve other organizations whose memberships cut across racial, occupation, political, and religious lines.[36] The Alliance has expanded to include sixty-eight national and regional organizations, including the AFL-CIO urban affairs department, Americans for Democratic Action, Fortune Society, National Association for the Advancement of Colored People, National Businessmen's Council, National Council on Crime and Delinquency, and the National Urban League.

The diverse groups that comprise the National Alliance have a common goal: to reduce crime and the fear of crime throughout America. It is hoped that this goal can be accomplished through the establishment of educational programs and related crime prevention activities. Twenty-two specific steps to safer neighborhoods have been recommended by the National Alliance for Safer Cities, many of which are discussed below.[37]

- Neighborhood centers: These are designed to provide a place where teenagers can rap with adults about a wide range of problems. Some offer a high school equivalency program, daycare centers, and after-school programs for children of working mothers. Volunteers from the community act as counselors and help youngsters with their schoolwork. There are many other neighborhood centers oriented toward giving senior citizens a place to gather.
- Urban architecture: A new concept called "defensible space" has developed from a fear for personal safety in many cities. The objective of this idea is to reduce opportunities for crime by proper building design (see Chapter 12).
- Improved street lights: It is no secret that poorly lighted streets invite criminals into the neighborhood. Many cities that have improved their lighting show a marked decrease in the amount of criminal activity.
- Buzzer systems: These systems constitute a very inexpensive and successful method of alerting storeowners that a crime is in progress next door. The police department can then be called immediately. Buzzers can also be hooked up between apartments or private homes.
- Escort patrols. Citizen patrols can be used as escorts to help protect more vulnerable citizens from crime. This has been used effectively in many cities, both on streets and in apartment buildings.
- Public housing patrols. This is a program whereby tenants volunteer to sit in lobbies of public housing units and act as eyes and ears for the police department. The volunteers do not attempt to perform the role of the police but rather telephone the police from a phone in the lobby if suspicious circumstances arise.
- Parents League child safety campaign: This campaign utilizes parents walking in pairs to patrol the streets during the time children are going and returning from school. These patrols also check to see that police call boxes, public

---

[36]"A Call for Citizen Action: Crime Prevention and the Citizen." National Advisory Commission on Criminal Justice Standards and Goals, 1974, p. 34.

[37]"Cues for Action." New York: National Alliance for Safer Cities and Alliance for a Safer New York, 1979, p. 1.

telephones, and traffic lights are working properly. In addition, they make daily routine reports to the police.

- Auto theft protection: Organizations such as the American Association of Federated Women's Clubs and the National Auto Theft Bureau have conducted auto theft prevention campaigns in several cities by leaving pamphlets in unlocked cars and by attaching warnings to parking meters on the dangers of leaving keys in the ignition. Another effort includes the use of decals in the car windows indicating the owner's age, sex, and residence. If an officer spots a car owned by an elderly woman, for example, but driven by a young man, the officer can pull the driver over for questioning.
- Protection of Social Security checks: Theft of Social Security or supplemental income checks before and after delivery causes great hardships to recipients. The Treasury Department's direct deposit program, whereby checks can be deposited directly into the recipient's account, prevents such thefts. (For more information, see Chapter 6.)
- Block Mothers: Also known as the "helping hands" program, its participants consist of responsible women who have been trained by social welfare and police officials to care for and supervise children and to interview adolescents. It is designed to prevent child molestation, provide emergency babysitting, and to provide a refuge for any child who is threatened, frightened, or has run away. Participating mothers display "clasped hand" decals in the front window of their homes.
- Security guards: Many tenants of apartment buildings have joined together and hired uniformed unarmed guards to patrol their block during certain hours of the day. Most are equipped with walkie-talkies and have a tie-in with the police precinct.
- Auxiliary police: Volunteer candidates for law enforcement services now exist in almost every city. The auxiliary police perform certain police chores, such as locating lost children, responding to natural disasters, or accompanying a commissioned officer on patrol. They are not substitutes for regular police, but act as extra eyes and ears. Some cities allow auxiliary police to use firearms and work in crowd and traffic control, but they must receive specialized training for these responsibilities.

The National Alliance for Safer Cities is a strong and growing organization that has long recognized the need for community involvement.*

## Prototype community-based programs

Many different model programs have been established throughout the country, the results being an increase in community involvement in crime prevention efforts from coast to coast in both small and large cities. Several of these programs are discussed in greater detail in the following pages.

**Mobile Crime Prevention Unit: Brea, California.** The city of Brea, Califor-

---

*Note:* For additional information concerning the services of the National Alliance for Safer Cities, the reader may contact the National Alliance for Safer Cities, 165 East 56th Street, New York, N.Y., 10022.

nia purchased a twenty-five foot motorcoach with a federal grant from the Law Enforcement Assistance Administration. The coach was converted into a mobile crime prevention information center designed to bring crime prevention information directly to the residents of the community. The mobile unit is strategically located at popular public gathering places, such as shopping centers, parks, and schools, in addition to residential neighborhoods. The unit is equipped with interior seating, display counters to exhibit crime maps, charts, literature, security devices, and an audiovisual system for films and slide presentations. The attendant officers explain the crime prevention program to citizens, conduct tours of the unit, offer home safety inspection services, and provide residents with pertinent crime prevention literature.

**Security patrol of vacation homes: Tillamook County, Oregon.** Tillamook County, west of Portland on the Oregon coast, encountered a problem of burglarized or vandalized vacation homes. Since the vacationers occupied their homes only on weekends at best, the vacation home burglars were busy during the week. Tillamook County had only fifteen sheriff's department employees and an area state police force of twelve, who mainly were concerned with enforcing traffic ordinances and pursuing game violations. Hundreds of these homes, being remotely located, became prime targets for burglars who could easily break in during the middle of the night, ransack the homes, and be out of the county the next morning.

One of the first solutions to this problem was to increase manpower. This was done by developing a fifteen-person reserve force made up of interested persons in the community who wanted to learn about law enforcement and at the same time be able to serve their community.[38] These "reserve deputies" were given extensive training and then paired with the regular deputies at night to provide extra eyes and support. It soon became apparent that the number of break-ins and burglaries was reduced. After additional training and experience, the reserve deputies were allowed to make their own patrols, but were required to go with a partner. In addition, twenty-five high school boys were recruited as "law enforcement explorers" who concentrated on search and rescue work. The reserve deputies and explorer scouts were eventually paired and made security checks on the vacation homes. The homeowners began sending in money to support the project, making it apparent they were in favor of this type of assistance. The main function of this patrol was not to catch burglars, but to discover break-ins and find storm damage and vandalism. Even so, the vacation home burglary rate has decreased approximately 25% since the founding of the explorer program; complaints from

---

[38]Walpole, Delbert, "The Utilization of Explorer Scouts for Security Patrol of Vacation Homes." *FBI Law Enforcement Bulletin*, Oct. 1967, p. 4.

homeowners are practically nil, and the cost of protecting their property has been low.

**Dade County Public Safety Department.** The Dade County Public Safety Department has long recognized the value of citizen and community involvement with the police and police activities. In 1967, the department activated a police reserve unit with the following stipulations:[39]

- The reserve unit not be an honorary group of "police buffs"
- The reserve unit not be a social organization
- Each reservist to be selected, screened, and given the same kind of background check as regularly appointed recruit officers in accordance with the State of Florida minimum standard law
- Each reservist to complete at least 340 hours of training and, after appointment, continue to attend training sessions a minimum of four hours per month
- Each reservist to be assigned to the police division in a district operation where he would contribute at least sixteen hours of police duty per month and would be carefully supervised by a permanently appointed officer at all times
- Reservists to be governed by the same police rules, regulations, and departmental directives as full-time officers

Upon graduation from basic training, police reserve officers are assigned to the various district operations as uniformed officers. Their duty responsibilities are the same as their full-time counterparts, which are patrol, traffic, report writing, and other general law enforcement duties.

The Dade County Public Safety Department has found its police reserve unit to be an effective method of enlisting the help of citizens in combating crime and will encourage the continued development and growth of the unit. Police reserve officers interact directly with the community, not only as law enforcement officers, but also through occupational associations and professional relationships not readily accessible to the average police officer. Through these contacts, an attitude of community concern is generated toward law enforcement. Most other cities and townships across the country have similar police reserve units, which have also proved to be a highly successful asset to their public safety departments.

**Sun City, Arizona: the posse rides again.** Sun City, a retirement community located about twenty miles northwest of Phoenix, faced special problems when crimes such as burglary, larceny, auto theft, and strongarm robbery began increasing at faster rates in suburban areas than in large cities. Sun City depended upon the Maricopa County Sheriff's Department for protection, but what they could provide was not enough. Maricopa County is larger than the states of Connecticut, Rhode Island, and Delaware combined.

[39]Bohardt, Paul, "A Viable Police Reserve." *FBI Law Enforcement Bulletin*, Feb. 1977.

Scarcity of manpower and resources to protect this vast area made Sun City residents easy targets for many types of violent and nonviolent crimes. Today, Sun City is home of a 250-member volunteer posse. There are thirty-five other posses in Maricopa County, and the sheriff's department boasts the combined posses membership of 2,500, which is one of the biggest law enforcement programs in the nation.[40] The mission is protection, and all members are willing to devote their time, cars, and gas to protect Sun City.

The posse is not a band of "gun-totin' vigilantes." Members may wear a uniform that looks like that of a regular deputy, but they may not carry a gun unless they have taken a firearms training course. They have no powers of arrest unless specifically authorized by the sheriff. Each posse of Maricopa County screens its own members, holds its own meetings, and writes its own bylaws, but it must follow sheriff's department guidelines concerning rules and orders.

A variety of training courses are open to posse members, including first aid, map and compass, desert survival techniques, search coordination, tracking, firearms, and traffic control. Those who qualify may join the volunteer reserve program and study to become certified (by the Arizona Law Enforcement Advisory Council) law enforcement officers.

Sun Citians also have an extensive neighborhood watch program. Participating homeowners keep a careful watch on neighboring houses, especially when occupants are absent. If they see any suspicious activity, a call to the Sun City Crime Stop brings sheriff's deputies to the scene within minutes. Crime rates in Maricopa County have dropped since the development of these actions, which demonstrates again that involvement of private citizens is a necessary ingredient in the recipe for crime prevention.

### Problems encountered with community participation

Although it is clear that citizen participation is necessary and the benefits in crime prevention efforts are almost innumerable, certain disadvantages can exist in certain situations. In the first place, some neighborhoods may be very difficult to organize—and once organized cooperation may be short-lived. Many neighborhood programs are more easily organized when problems with crime are particularly intense, and this intense concern may be difficult to sustain over a long period of time. Residents may tire of assuming the responsibilities that neighborhood organizations entail. Successful programs may also have difficulty, since as the crime problem diminishes, the duties of each program can become duller and duller, and the necessity of the program becomes less apparent. Thus the enthusiasm and diligence that characterize

---

[40]White, Glenn, "Where Citizens Help Control Crime." *Dynamic Maturity*, Vol. 10, No. 4, July 1975, p. 11.

citizen participation in the formative phase of a program may be replaced by boredom, with citizen participation gradually deteriorating.

Another disadvantage of community programs is that their deterrence function is difficult to maintain. The appropriate role of most programs is to observe for crime and suspicious activity and then report it to police, but this restriction is often difficult to enforce. The tendency to challenge strangers and to intervene in disputes is difficult to suppress particularly when hearth and home are threatened. Self-assumed authority implied by the establishment of community programs may reinforce aggressive tendencies, particularly when a police-like role is involved, and simply observing and reporting may not be enough for some people. A citizen may be much more likely to intervene rather than simply report should he or she observe a real or apparent threat.

If the citizen's intervention is successful, the action may become an accepted function of the programs, thus dramatically altering the original philosophy and goals of the program. Potential for conflict will exist, and there may be pressure for members to carry weapons. More aggressive behavior may, in fact, be encouraged by the program's leader, so that he or she can maintain a position of leadership if other members are also advocating more aggressive functions. Escalating citizen aggressiveness can result from dissatisfaction with police functions. As long as emotions flare, it is more difficult to create a stable organization, and the tendency will be to increase aggressiveness within the organization.

Another factor that must be considered as a disadvantage in the development of many community programs is that police may not always cooperate with a particular program and may even oppose it. Police opposition to many programs is based on concern about vigilantism and interference with effective law enforcement. A citizen attempting to stop one crime may commit others, particularly if he or she is untrained. Therefore, this particular police concern is a legitimate one, since vigilantism could very well lead to more serious problems for the community than those caused by no citizen participation at all. Fortunately, the incidence of vigilantism arising from community-based programs is small.

Another disadvantage of community programs is that consciously or not, police decrease their level of effort in neighborhoods that have successful programs. Thus residents give up professional protection and replace it with ad hoc self-protection. In addition, if community programs were formed particularly as a result of dissatisfaction with the effectiveness of police, there may be a tendency for the police to regard the program as an adversary. This animosity may result in slowness to respond to requests for police assistance and further dissatisfaction expressed by the citizenry.

A final disadvantage of certain community programs arises from the fact that not all citizens are appreciative of the crime prevention efforts of other citizens. Some residents may be extremely upset about the intrusion on their privacy and the implied arrogance of some organizations. Thus a neighborhood watch program, for example, may be regarded by some as "nosy neighbors." The popularity of the many community programs, however, testifies to the fact that the majority of citizens do not take this attitude.

It is important to realize that the aforementioned disadvantages are not characteristic of most community crime prevention programs. Citizen participation is vital to the function of police, and in most programs advantages outweigh disadvantages. Never should any particular disadvantage be considered a legitimate excuse for the lack of community involvement. Police officials, however, should be aware that certain undesirable characteristics of a community program could develop, and they should actively work to overcome any potential obstacles.

## CONCLUSION

Citizen involvement in crime prevention efforts is not merely desirable but necessary. If each citizen looks out only for himself, there is no community and no strength in numbers. Fragmentation will develop, which will encourage burglars because they know that they need not contend with the eyes and ears of an entire neighborhood.

Residences that are transformed into fortresses only make for a self-centered approach to crime and increases social isolation, which in turn makes the development of community or neighborhood crime prevention programs almost impossible. As a result, there may be citizen involvement in crime prevention but not community involvement. Without a sense of community, the crime prevention potential of mutual aid and mutual responsibility is unfulfilled.

# Chapter 14

# The role of criminal justice agencies

The question of exactly what role criminal justice agencies should play in crime prevention has been debated for many years. Some oldliners argue that criminal justice agencies should have nothing to do with crime prevention activities, while others believe these agencies should be totally involved in prevention. One group argues that it is not the role of criminal justice—law enforcement agencies in particular, with their limited manpower and small budgets—to engage in time-consuming preventive efforts, some of which may be untried. It is also maintained by some that because crime is a complex social problem, its prevention lies well beyond the domain of criminal justice agencies. Leonard summarizes what often happens: "After the home has failed and after the church, neighborhood and community have failed, the police are called in to make the arrest and somehow, in a punitive scheme of things, to effect a dramatic change in the direction of a life pattern."[1] Early involvement of many influential variables, including criminal justice, is necessary, since after a life pattern of crime has been established it is fruitless to expect a change merely on the basis of after-the-fact punishments through arrests.

The role of criminal justice agencies in preventing crime is much broader than merely making arrests; there is also more involved than conviction and confinement of the guilty. And regardless of opposition, criminal justice agencies do attempt to deter crime in several ways. Law enforcement or police agencies have various crime prevention programs; the courts impose punitive sanctions, and correctional facilities attempt to prevent further criminal activity by convicts through rehabilitation. Arthur Woods, former Police Commissioner of New York, recognized that criminal justice must do more than arrest, convict, and confine criminals:

> The process of arresting a burglar, convicting him, sending him to jail for a few months or years, and then letting him out, still a burglar, probably a more

---

[1]Leonard, V. A., *Police Crime Prevention*. Springfield, Ill.: Charles C Thomas, Publisher, 1972, p. 39.

skillful one, free to go to work and break into our homes again, until we happen to catch him again and send him to jail again—we delude ourselves if we feel that this constitutes any real effort to stamp out crime in a community.[2]

The reduction of crime lies in a more in-depth orientation of police, courts, and corrections, so that a lasting control over the commission of crimes is established rather than merely establishing a temporary control over criminals. The efforts of police, courts, and corrections in establishing this control (or in some cases, failing at this task) are discussed in the following pages. However, it should first be emphasized that any attempts by these agencies to prevent crime must be accompanied by the willing participation and cooperation of the citizens. Criminal justice cannot stand alone in this regard. Just as the horse can be led to water but not forced to drink, various agencies can lead the way but the people must make the response. Therefore, the responsibility of preventing crime can in no way rest solely with official agencies. As Agarwal has stated, "The prevention and control of crime cannot be achieved without an honest, well-trained and efficient law enforcement agency operating with the cooperation and support of the masses it serves."[3] It will be necessary to develop a dialogue between citizens and the police so that citizens can have the opportunity to know police officers as individuals. Police officers then can express their concern for the welfare of citizens, rather than appearing as repressive servants of the establishment.

## HISTORY OF POLICE INVOLVEMENT IN CRIME PREVENTION

The involvement of the police in crime prevention is certainly not a new phenomenon.[4] England has a long history of official involvement in crime prevention. In 1655, Cromwell, the Lord Protector, was rebuffed in his efforts to set up a police system.[5] In 1729 Thomas de Veil was appointed to the Commission of the Peace for the county of Middlesex and the city of Westminster where he utilized "thief takers" and "informers" in an effort to prevent and detect crime.

In 1748 Henry Fielding was appointed magistrate at Bow Street. He was the first person to actively encourage citizens to report to the police when they were victimized. Up to that time people did not think about reporting crimes to authorities. Although Fielding is recognized in police work for the

---

[2]Woods, Arthur, *Crime Prevention*. Reprinted by Arno Press and the *New York Times*, New York, 1971, pp. 30-31.
[3]Agarwal, R. S., *Prevention of Crime*. New Delhi: Radiant Publishers, 1977, p. 62.
[4]Adams, Gary, "Crime Prevention: An Evolutionary Analysis." *Police Chief*, Dec. 1971, p. 52.
[5]*History and Principles of Crime Prevention* (mimeograph). Stafford, England: Home Office Crime Prevention Centre, Feb. 1976.

establishment of the Bow Street Runners, he is better known as the novelist who wrote *Tom Jones* and *The Life of Jonathan Wild the Great.* (The latter contains information useful to crime prevention officers.) After Fielding's death in 1754, his blind half-brother, John Fielding, succeeded him. In a pamphlet on crime he noted, "It is much better to prevent even one man from being a rogue than apprehending and bringing forty to justice."

Although the Fieldings are credited with initiating the concept of crime prevention, it was Sir Robert Peel who made the concept operational. With the Metropolitan Police Act of 1829[6] Peel made many innovations to the then prevailing system of British criminal justice. For example, Peel tried to predicate decision and policy setting and implementation upon detailed factual knowledge.[7] The first written instructions ever to be given to police were given to the Metropolitan Police in 1829:

> *It should be understood at the outset, that the principal object to be attained is the prevention of crime.* To this great end every effort of the police is to be directed. The security of persons and property, the preservation of the public tranquility, and all the other objects of a police establishment, will thus be better effected, than by the detection and punishment of the offender, after he has succeeded in committing the crime. This should constantly be kept in mind by every member of the police force, as the guide for his own conduct. Officers and police constables should endeavor to distinguish themselves by such vigilance and activity, as may render it extremely difficult for anyone to commit a crime within that portion of the town under their charge.[8]

Recognizing the significant influence that public citizens have on police prevention efforts, Peel also stated:

> The cooperation of the public that can be secured diminishes proportionately the necessity for the use of physical force and compulsion in achieving police objectives. The police at all times should maintain a relationship with the public that gives reality to the historic tradition that the police are only members of the public who are paid to give full-time attention to duties which are incumbent on every citizen in the interest of community welfare.[9]

In America in 1916, summer-session courses in crime prevention were established at the University of California in Berkeley and were conducted

---

[6]Shanahan, Donald T., *Patrol Administration: Management by Objectives.* Boston: Holbrook Press, Inc., 1978, p. 437.

[7]Manning, Peter K., *Police Work.* Cambridge, Mass.: The MIT Press, 1977, p. 76.

[8]Woods, op. cit.

[9]Adamson, Harold, "Citizen Participation in Crime Reduction," in *The Police Yearbook.* Gaithersburg, Md.: International Association of Chiefs of Police, 1978.

with the advice and assistance of members of the police department.[10] In 1918, Commissioner Woods wrote:

> The preventive policeman is the policeman of the future. However faithfully he does it he can no longer fully justify himself by simply "pounding the beat." The public will look to him to prevent crime, and to prevent from falling into crime those who may be under temptation, be they children, or drug users, or defectives, or normal human beings who already bear the convict mark, or who are pushed to the wall in the battle of life. Police forces must try to keep crime from claiming its victims as Boards of Health try to keep plague and pestilence away.[11]

The crime prevention division of the Berkeley Police Department was established in 1925 as a result of the efforts of Chief August Vollmer. Vollmer was determined to attack the complicated problem of juvenile delinquency. Another early effort directed at preventing crime in America was the establishment of the Crime Prevention Bureau in the New York City Police Department in 1930. Several officers, both women and men who were already working within the department, were designated as crime prevention officers. A few months later twenty-five experienced, trained social workers were appointed crime prevention officers.[12]

Even though the importance of crime prevention was recognized in the early 1700s and several programs promoting crime prevention were established, most of the emphasis today is still on arrests and investigations to solve crimes, rather than preventing them. Gray pointed out in 1972 that, "Prevention is a police function which, though discussed extensively, has gotten little priority in police activities until the last five years; and community groups and individual citizen efforts can be better developed and utilized (not controlled) by police than has typically been done."[13] Some departments are just beginning to put more emphasis on crime prevention. Haire reports the top twenty management principles of the Los Angeles Police Department; crime prevention priorities are second only to reverence for the law in importance (Table 14-1).[14]

Today, in addition to police departments and universities, private organizations such as the Police Foundation have been leaders in research into police crime prevention activities. For example, the Foundation's research has shown that police response time is not nearly as critical as citizen report-

[10]Glueck, Sheldon, and Glueck, Eleanor, *Preventing Crime*. New York: McGraw-Hill Book Co., 1936, p. 238.
[11]Woods, op. cit., p. 123.
[12]Glueck and Glueck, op. cit., p. 216.
[13]Gray, B. M., II, "Citizen Participation: Organized Groups to Combat Crime," in *The Police Yearbook*. Gaithersburg, Md.: International Association of Chiefs of Police, 1977, p. 160.
[14]Haire, Thomas D., "Community Mobilization: A Strategy to Reduce Crime." *The Police Chief*, Mar. 1978, p. 31.

**Table 14-1.** Los Angeles Police Department's twenty management principles*

| | |
|---|---|
| 1. Reverence for the law | 11. People working with police |
| 2. Crime prevention top priority | 12. People working with people |
| 3. Public approbation of police | 13. Managers working with police |
| 4. Voluntary law observance | 14. Police working with police |
| 5. Public cooperation | 15. Police working with criminal justice system |
| 6. Impartial friendly enforcement | 16. Management by objectives |
| 7. Minimum use of force | 17. Management by participation |
| 8. Public are the police | 18. Territorial imperative |
| 9. Police power | 19. Openness and honesty |
| 10. Test of police effectiveness | 20. Police/press relationships |

*From Haire, Thomas D., "Community Mobilization: A Strategy to Reduce Crime." *The Police Chief*, Mar. 1978, p. 31.

ing time, and that "Saturday night specials" play no dominant role in the incidence of violent crime. According to this study, high-priced, brand-name firearms are used just as frequently as cheaper weapons.[15]

## CRIME PREVENTION IN BRITAIN AND AMERICA

The early efforts of Englishmen such as the Fieldings and Peel in emphasizing crime prevention has perhaps resulted in a more positive and earlier reception of crime prevention concepts throughout history by English police agencies than their American counterparts have demonstrated. A comparison of present-day operations of American and British police agencies reveals some differences in orientation or emphasis of crime prevention functions.[16] For example, crime prevention, as opposed to detection, is a natural part of the British system because their police agencies were initially set up to prevent crimes. Organized crime in Britain is neither as prevalent nor as strong as in America, drug trafficking is negligible, and brutal crimes seem to be the exception rather than the rule. The police in Britain do a lot of intelligence-gathering; and a lot more plainclothes work is done than in America. Also, Britain does not have a national police force and each county is autonomous. Local forces can get help from Scotland Yard (which is merely the headquarters of the London Metropolitan Police, not a national body), since it runs the central record system and assists local forces, particularly in murder investigations. Generally, all police officers in Britain receive the same training, and because all forces are undermanned, a lot of informal poaching of personnel goes on. The British police routinely use informers,

[15]Murphy, Patrick V., and Plate, Thomas, *Commissioner.* New York: Simon & Schuster, Inc., 1977, p. 262.
[16]Lampe, David, Personal Correspondence, Austin, Texas, Nov. 14, 1979.

who are paid a small amount; the informers are usually people at least on the fringes of crime, willing to cooperate with the police to strengthen their own positions.

In character, crime prevention in Britain is somewhat different from that in America. First and foremost, the British shy away from neighborhood watch groups or anything else sparking of vigilantism. However, they do try to heavily involve insurance companies in crime prevention activities, and they also make a strong effort to protect especially vulnerable citizens. Although many businesses cooperate fully with crime prevention officers, the banks, which are vast national institutions, prefer to have their own security staff, usually made up of retired senior police officers.

Much crime prevention at the local level in Britain is based on the tradition of the friendliness of the local bobby and his position in the community. In the country and in small towns the individual constables have always been encouraged to involve themselves in the community, and in such places most citizens know and respect their local police officers. In London, of course, people do not as often know individual local officers, and senior officers at Scotland Yard have long been trying to do something about this. Among other things, they advocate a "village bobby" scheme, in which the homes of the beat officers who work in high-density, potentially high-crime areas are made into individual station houses. Officers in this scheme are all young extroverts, encouraged to organize playground sports for children and otherwise get involved in positive neighborhood activities. Although not so designated, this is a very obvious form of crime prevention.

## TOOLS OF PREVENTION USED BY POLICE

Presently in America there are now many major efforts directed at crime prevention by police agencies throughout the country. Many of these have been in use for decades, and may or may not have been recognized as preventive efforts when they were instituted. Some are the direct result of prevention efforts on the part of early scholars, researchers, and pioneers in criminal justice who recognized the need for more than the arrest and conviction of criminals. Still others are relatively new approaches spawned as a result of the latent interest in crime prevention. The various services of police and how they promote crime prevention are described in the following pages.

### Patrol

Many types of patrol are utilized by police in efforts to deter, control, or prevent crime. Patrol is the most used approach that police take in protecting property and citizens. A discussion of the various patrols is included below.

**Foot patrol.** Random foot patrol is the oldest type of patrol to be used by police officers. It is perhaps one of the best methods of getting to know the people in the area, and to become aware of potential problems through personal contacts with citizens living in the area being patrolled. Private citizens seem to welcome the opportunity to talk with an officer on a one-to-one basis, and therefore positive public relations between the police department and citizens is promoted. The officer can also go many places where potentials for crime exist that a patrol car cannot go. Many areas are now implementing random foot patrol programs in residential areas as well as business districts.

**Bicycle patrol.** Bicycles also afford officers an opportunity to go places where patrol cars cannot and have an advantage over foot patrol in that officers can cover more ground and are less likely to be outrun if chasing a fleeing felon. Bicycles are also quiet in operation and maintenance costs are low. Bicycle patrols also promote good public relations, and cycling is good exercise for the officer. There is, however, an increased amount of risk to the officers from lack of physical protection and, therefore, participating officers should preferably be volunteers who are in good physical condition.

Many bicycle patrol officers work undercover and in pairs as a team, riding at an easy pace while at the same time observing for crimes such as purse snatch, armed robbery, burglary, assault, etc. Officers should be equipped with flashlights, handcuffs, a gun and holster, a small transistor radio with a converter to monitor police calls, and their badge.

**Motorized patrol.** It did not take long after the initial popularity of the automobile for police departments to realize the utility of the "horseless carriage." Besides decreasing response time, the automobile also allows for increased protection for the officer, increased surveillance, and the immediate transport of persons taken into custody. Many departments also find motorcycles useful in several different situations, including the patrolling of parks and alleyways.

**Helicopter patrol.** Helicopters are used by many larger police departments as a means of increasing police presence. Because a helicopter would be seen by more people than would a patrol car, deterrence is increased. However, the effectiveness of helicopters in actually discovering crimes and pinpointing specific perpetrators without ground level assistance is questioned. The primary use of helicopters, at least in urban areas, appears to be the coordination of ground patrol activities and pursuit of suspects once they have been designated as such by ground patrol officers. Aerial distance makes it too difficult for the helicopter crew to identify suspects with reasonable accuracy. What appears to be a robbery suspect to the helicopter crew may in actuality only be an individual in a hurry. However, this particular inefficiency or weak spot of helicopter patrols is generally not recognized by criminals and, therefore, helicopters provide some degree of deterrence. In addition, helicopters are useful in discovering traffic accidents and pursuing fleeing vehicles in rural areas.

**Mounted patrol.** Should horses be used for police work? Members of the Royal Canadian Mounted Police (RCMP) obviously think they should. Horses have a long history of service to law officers. From the frontier days of the Old West to present-day big cities, horses have been of invaluable assistance to police agencies. Today they are especially valuable in the patrol of rough terrain such as public parks, and because of their height they offer the officer a better vantage point for observation. Because of their great speed they have rapid response time. They also are totally unaffected by gasoline shortages and can be especially effective in crowd control. If used properly the horse can also be an excellent public relations tool.

**Canine patrol.** It is difficult to measure the effectiveness of the use of police dogs purely by statistical means since there are other variables involved. However, several examples provide strong evidence that dogs can be of invaluable service in police work.[17-22] Examples of the different situations in which dogs can be utilized are:[23]

1. *As a psychological deterrent:* Stowe[24] evaluated the police dog's greatest service as a major deterrent to crime. Their mere presence on the street, even the knowledge that they may be lurking nearby, exerts a powerful restraint upon lawbreakers.

2. *To search buildings or areas:* The dog's keen senses of smell and hearing are very useful in searching buildings or large areas for burglars, prowlers, or other criminals. In Topeka, Kansas, police officers had searched for a half hour for a criminal who was hidden in a large building. A K-9 unit was then called in to assist and discovered the criminal in less than three minutes.

3. *To defend their handler against attack:* The handler usually encoun-

[17]Gourley, Douglas G., and Bristow, Allen P., *Patrol Administration.* Springfield, Ill.: Charles C Thomas, Publisher, 1971, p. 57.

[18]Leonard, V. A., *Police Patrol Organization.* Springfield, Ill.: Charles C Thomas, Publisher, 1970, p. 77.

[19]Ibid, p. 77.

[20]Chapman, Samuel G., *Dogs in Police Work: A Summary of Experience in Great Britain and the United States.* Chicago: Public Administration Service, 1960, p. 38.

[21]Stowe, Leland, "How K-9's Catch Crooks: Use of German Shepherds." *Reader's Digest,* Vol. 105, Nov. 1974, p. 174.

[22]"Dogs Earning Milkbones with Narcotics Seizures." *Narcotics Control Digest,* Vol. 7, No. 25, Dec. 7, 1977, pp. 6-7.

[23]O'Block, Robert L., Doeren, Stephen E., and True, Nancy, "The Benefits of Canine Squads." *The Journal of Police Science and Administration,* Vol. 7, No. 2, June 1979, p. 155.

[24]Stowe, op. cit., p. 175.

ters little or no resistance from criminals or suspects since even the out-stretched hand can be interpreted by the dog as an attack against the handler. In many instances, the dog has stood guard over his handler and by doing so, saved him from further harm at the hands of criminals.

4. *To track down criminals or lost persons:* Tracking is taught imme-diately following obedience training by having the dog follow a fresh scent on a short track, the time and distance factors being progressively increased. The dogs are taught to track by night and day, in open country, in wooded areas, and along roadways. A dog's sense of smell is 100,000 times stronger than a human's, and this keen sense of smell enables the dog to pick up scents of a suspect's personal items, such as clothing, several hours after it has been in contact with the suspect. Many times the dogs are able to pick up a scent from nonpersonal items, such as automobiles, and from crime scenes, etc., if the items are not contaminated. For police departments that do not own K-9 dogs, bloodhounds can be borrowed from the National Police Bloodhound Asso-ciation. This organization loans their highly trained and skilled dogs to agen-cies throughout the country in need of a tracking dog.

5. *To control unruly crowds and gatherings:* There is some disagree-ment as to whether or not police dogs should be used to control crowds or mobs. Momboisse believes that dogs are advantageous but points out that they can also be detrimental in mob control because of their tendency to be the "spark" that could ignite a riot.[25] George and Esther Eastman are con-cerned about the use of police dogs in crowd control: "If a department chooses to direct the patrol of doghandler teams against specific crime prob-lems, it must be certain that dogs are viewed by people as protecting rather than controlling them."[26] However, many police departments are using ca-nine teams to discourage unorganized crowd behavior and place the dogs in situations where rowdyism is likely but not yet apparent. In addition, dogs are also employed in many correctional facilities to deter riotlike behavior among inmates. Regarding the use of canine patrols, Shanahan states, "The use of the canine team should depend upon the need of the protected locality. Positive and negative aspects should be considered and the decision based on the best method of patrol for the solution of the problem and the attainment of the objective."[27]

6. *To detect marijuana and narcotics:* According to Acree, dogs have proved extremely effective in sniffing out drugs hidden in vehicles, aircraft,

---

[25]Momboisse, Robert M., *Riots, Revolts, and Insurrections*. Springfield, Ill.: Charles C Thomas, Publisher, 1967.

[26]Eastman, George D., and Eastman, Esther M., *Municipal Police Administration*. Washington, D.C.: International City Management Association, 1971, p. 91.

[27]Shanahan, op. cit., p. 197.

vessels, cargo, and mail.[28] Usually after three months of training the dog is able to detect tiny traces of the drugs whether they are buried underground, sealed inside a container, or even hidden under water. Stowe also notes the ability of the dogs to detect drugs even when the scent is masked by other strong odors such as ammonia, formaldehyde, perfume, or freshly sliced onions.[29] The dogs are trained to seek out samples of heroin, which registers a very faint odor, ranging from 86% (the purest form normally obtainable on the streets) to the smaller 6% and 4% samples.[30]

7. *To detect hidden explosives:* According to Stowe[31] this latest detector-dog specialization posed problems at first because the dogs had to completely suppress their instinctive scratching and snatching urges. It takes five months to train one dog at explosive detection. However, the canines acquire recognition of basic explosive ingredients in up to ten different odors, and their accuracy averages better than 95%. The expense of the canine patrol is also much less than that of sophisticated bomb detecting machines, which cost thousands of dollars.

8. *For general patrol:* The use of police dogs in high crime areas for routine patrol and hazardous situations is being accepted throughout the country.[32] Dogs are being used to accompany officers into areas where cars cannot go, and because of their keen sensory perception, they can warn the officer of danger long before the human eye or ear is able to do so. By giving quick warning, the dog often places the officer in the position of having the initiative, an advantage that he or she otherwise might not have. In most departments, the dogs patrol the "hot spot" crime areas where crime is most prevalent—areas where muggings, robberies, assaults, and burglaries are most common. Although these are the main trouble spots, the dogs are ready to respond to any calls wherever they might be of service.

Many different breeds of dogs have been experimented with for police work, including bloodhounds, Airedales, Labradors, boxers, and the two most popular breeds in America, the German Shepherd and Doberman pinscher. Shepherds are the most commonly used because of their widespread availability, obedience, and even temperament. However, Dobermans with good bloodlines should not be overlooked because of the myths and their image of being mankillers that Hollywood has given them. Dobermans are one of the

---

[28]Acree, Vernon D., "U.S. Customs Service, First Line of Defense Against Drug Smuggling." *The Police Chief*, Vol. 44, No. 3, Mar. 1977, pp. 22-23.

[29]Stowe, op. cit., p. 174.

[30]Savage, Mary, "Drug Detector Dogs." *All Hands*, Aug. 1973, p. 47.

[31]Stowe, op. cit., p. 174.

[32]Wilson, O. W., and McLaren, Roy C., *Police Administration*. New York: McGraw-Hill Book Co., 1972, p. 437.

most intelligent of all animals and if they are found to be mean, it is usually because their owners have purposely mistreated them to make them more aggressive. Dobermans are naturally protective of their families and their "territory," but they are not naturally mean.

Dogs may either be donated by citizens to the police department or the department may purchase them. In either case, something should be known of the dog's genetic background. Dogs selected for police work are usually no younger than ten months and no older than two years.

### Information systems

Presently, the area of criminal justice information systems is expanding and becoming more sophisticated through the utilization of computers. Police departments must be careful when deciding upon the use of information systems to avoid duplication of services and waste of funds and personnel time. There must not be separate repositories for identical records unless there are documented and legitimate reasons as to why such duplication would contribute to efficiency. Information systems and how they can contribute to the prevention of crime are discussed below.

**Rap sheets.** Criminal history information reports are confidential files that persons outside law enforcement seldom see. Sometimes referred to as rap sheets, these files list the history of arrest of an individual. In Fig. 14-1, an actual rap sheet is presented (the name of the offender has of course been changed). This particular rap sheet is presented not because it is unusual but because it is typical of a career criminal. It indicates a criminal history spanning thirty-five years, a strong association with alcohol, and the failure of the courts and correctional systems. Note that in some cases there was no formal disposition. Also notice that on April 6, 1971, this individual was sentenced to one to ten years, but four months later was already out and re-arrested. Most authorities would further point out that for every arrest listed there are probably ten undetected crimes the individual committed. As is indicated by this rap sheet, the police performed their job, but the courts, correctional facilities, and other social agencies that may have been involved were the obvious failures; possible reasons for this will be discussed later in this chapter.

**Crime analysis.** Novelists wrote about scientific detective work long before it was an actual practice. One of these authors was Sir Arthur Conan Doyle, whose fictitious character, Sherlock Holmes, used scientific methods. Holmes is known as "the world's first consulting detective."[33]

After the Civil War, Thomas Barnes, a nonfictitious chief of detectives,

---

[33]Saferstein, Richard, *Criminalistics: An Introduction to Forensic Science.* Englewood Cliffs, N.J.: Prentice-Hall, Inc., 1977.

| Contributor of fingerprint | Arrested or received | Charge | Disposition |
|---|---|---|---|
| SO Girard, Kansas | 9-3-44 | Drunkenness | Released on own recognizance |
| PD Kansas City, Missouri | 1-17-45 | Protective custody | |
| PD Kansas City, Missouri | 7-26-45 | Drunkenness | Released on O.R. |
| PD Pittsburg, Kansas | 4-16-51 | Driving while intoxicated (DWI) | Bond $153.00, forfeited |
| PD Fort Scott, Kansas | 6-5-53 | Theft by deception | 30 days' probation |
| PD Fort Scott, Kansas | 11-21-59 | Acts against nature | |
| PD Pittsburg, Kansas | 1-15-60 | Drunkenness | |
| SO Girard, Kansas | 10-4-61 | Strong armed robbery | Dismissed--lack of evidence |
| PD Lansing, Kansas | 12-13-61 | Robbery--third degree | One to five years state penitentiary |
| PD Kansas City, Missouri | 11-20-63 | Crimes against nature | One to ten years (conditional release) |
| SO Independence, Kansas | 3-1-66 | Fraud, auto theft | Two years' probation |
| PD Barton, Florida | 3-1-69 | Obtaining lodging with intent to defraud | Ten days--given credit for eight |
| SO Tampa, Florida | 8-2-70 | DWI | Held overnight |
| PD Plainfield, Indiana | 4-6-72 | Offense against property act | One to ten years |
| PD Dayton, Ohio | 9-10-72 | Falsification to mislead officials | Dismissed |
| PD Pittsburg, Kansas | 2-11-74 | Theft by deception | |
| PD Cincinnati, Ohio | 7-11-74 | Robbery | Two to five years reduced |
| SO Girard, Kansas | 6-3-75 | DWI | |
| SO Girard, Kansas | 8-4-75 | DWI | Six months |
| PD Pittsburg, Kansas | 9-5-76 | Acts against nature (children) | 90-day state diagnostic center |
| PD Pittsburg, Kansas | 1-6-77 | DWI | Held overnight |
| SO Girard, Kansas | 2-10-78 | DWI | Driver's license revoked |
| PD Pittsburg, Kansas | 1-5-78 | Reckless driving; driving without a license | 90 days |
| PD Tampa, Florida | 6-3-79 | Attempt to defraud | Dismissed |
| PD Tampa, Florida | 10-10-79 | Vehicular homicide | Two years' suspended sentence--committed to state diagnostic center --released 1-19-80 |

**Fig. 14-1.** Criminal history of John Q. Felon. (From Crawford County Sheriff's Office, Girard, Kansas.)

developed a theory of crime analysis utilizing the methods of operation of thieves. This "thief MO" became as well-known as Barnes himself. MO actually means *modus operandi,* or method of operation. Criminals can often be identified by analyzing their methods of operation as recorded in reports of prior crimes.[34] Barnes utilized the MO in the following ways:[35]

1. Detectives were trained in criminal techniques.
2. Theft records were recorded allowing the detectives to keep track of previous offenders.
3. Detectives could use these records for identification and have information on the types of crimes and methods the thief utilized and whether he was a professional or amateur.

Other early pioneers contributing to crime analysis include August Vollmer, and O. W. Wilson. Vollmer modified and developed the theories of crime analysis through his studies of traffic. Vollmer's traffic study related traffic crime incidents, using pin maps, graphs, and summaries. Wilson viewed crime analysis from another point of view, maintaining that crime analysis was a valuable tool in management and planning for a police agency. Wilson further stressed that scrupulous attention should be given to the nature and form of statistical data.[36] He implemented crime analysis in the areas of planning and management.

At present, crime analysis is neither well understood nor precisely defined. It is generally interpreted to be the extension of useful information from the study of historical crime. To date, no one technique has proved completely satisfactory although occasional successes have been encouraging.[37] Since 1973, a renewed interest has developed in crime analysis. According to Larson some of the reasons for this new interest are:[38]

1. Nationwide, there has been a rise in crime rates.
2. Because costs have risen for police operations, services that have often been taken for granted are being cut or reduced.
3. Administrators are trying to develop more effective allocation of resources.
4. Many police agencies or departments have received funding of anticrime programs by the Law Enforcement Assistance Administration (LEAA).

---

[34]Weston, Paul B., and Wells, Kenneth M., *Law Enforcement and Criminal Justice: Introduction.* Pacific Palisade, Calif.: Goodyear Publishing, Inc., 1972.
[35]Ibid.
[36]Wilson, O. W., *Police Planning.* Springfield, Ill.: Charles C Thomas, Publisher, 1957.
[37]Cox, Lyle A., Kolender, William, and others, "Crime Analysis and Manpower Allocation Through Computer Pattern Recognition." *The Police Chief*, Vol. 44, No. 10, Oct. 1977.
[38]Larson, Richard C., *Urban Police Analysis.* Cambridge, Mass.: The M.I.T. Press, 1972.

**Purpose.** One of the main purposes of crime analysis is to help agencies organize, analyze, and assemble information more effectively so that it is useful to the agency. The crime analysis unit can be utilized when making arrests as well as after the suspect is in custody. For example, the crime analysis unit may study specific crimes or crime patterns and trends that suspects in custody are accused of or are alleged to have committed. Also, the crime analysis unit can take the modus operandi (MO) of an offender and the characteristics of the offender's crime pattern and establish a complete analysis of the methods the suspect employs. The crime analysis unit can also be utilized to prevent crimes by assignment and deployment of patrol officers.

The MO and the offender classification made available by the crime analysis unit is also important to criminologists who may receive information indirectly from the crime analysis unit. Recognizing the need to consider this information in greater depth, Wolfgang et al. stated: "Age, sex, race, socio-economic status, and offender status (first offender, recidivist, chronic) may be assumed to be common attributes studied by criminologists or contributors to criminological literature. It appears that many of the works that have been examined for this content analysis did not discuss criminal offenders as such, but instead describe or analyze the crime problem in a more generic sense."[39] Therefore, crime analysis can be used not only by a particular police agency, but by persons in related fields of criminal justice for purposes of research.

**Basic elements.** In order for a crime analysis unit to be effective in crime prevention, it must be a coordinated effort, supported by top administration. The purpose of the unit and how it can be of benefit should be understood by all officers. The organizational placement is also another important element in crime analysis.[40] Goals and objectives should be clearly set with priority on problem areas. An objective is a concise written statement of a goal that is supposed to be accomplished. Each objective should be written in terms of a single result area. All objectives need to be clear, concise, and specific enough so that a plan of action can be followed to achieve the expected results.[41]

**Functions.** The main function of crime analysis is to identify crime trends and predictively project criminal activity. Crime analysis is best suited to those offenses with a high probability of recurrence and is directed toward

---

[39]Wolfgang, Marvin, Figlio, Robert M., and Thornberry, Terence P., *Evaluating Criminology.* New York: Elsevier North-Holland, Inc., 1978.

[40]Buck, George A., Project Director, *Police Crime Analysis Unit Handbook.* Washington, D.C.: Law Enforcement Assistance Administration, National Institute of Law Enforcement and Criminal Justice, Nov. 1973.

[41]O'Block, Robert L., "Management by Objectives (MBO)—a New Tool in the Fight Against Crime." *Journal of Police Science and Administration,* Vol. 5, No. 4, Dec. 1977, p. 413.

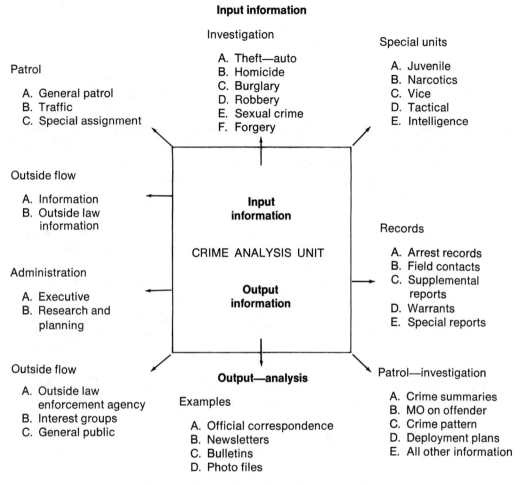

Input information

Investigation

A. Theft—auto
B. Homicide
C. Burglary
D. Robbery
E. Sexual crime
F. Forgery

Special units

A. Juvenile
B. Narcotics
C. Vice
D. Tactical
E. Intelligence

Patrol

A. General patrol
B. Traffic
C. Special assignment

Outside flow

A. Information
B. Outside law
   information

Administration

A. Executive
B. Research and
   planning

Outside flow

A. Outside law
   enforcement agency
B. Interest groups
C. General public

Input
information

CRIME ANALYSIS UNIT

Output
information

Records

A. Arrest records
B. Field contacts
C. Supplemental
   reports
D. Warrants
E. Special reports

Output—analysis

Examples

A. Official correspondence
B. Newsletters
C. Bulletins
D. Photo files

Patrol—investigation

A. Crime summaries
B. MO on offender
C. Crime pattern
D. Deployment plans
E. All other information

**Fig. 14-2.** Interrelationship of crime analysis.

those criminal offenses the police are most capable of suppressing or those offenses in which the perpetrator can be apprehended.[42] Crime analysis also serves to collect, present, and interpret data related to crime incidents.

**Crime analysis unit (input).** The usefulness of the crime analysis unit is directly related to the quality of the information received. Information is received into the unit from outside information sources and from records, patrol units, investigative units, and special divisions within the agency. The information received by the crime analysis unit is often analyzed using methodology of statistical components such as multivariate data analysis. Output of

---

[42]Buck, op. cit.

this information will be in the form of inferences, patterns, and trends based on the crime data input. This information is then disseminated to the appropriate personnel. A diagrammatic representation of this informational input-output process is presented in Fig. 14-2.

**Methods.** The following are various methods of crime analysis.

*Specialized unit.* Examples of specialized units are antimugging or vice units. The crime analysis unit compiles and compares data from areas of a city and this information is transferred to a large map of the city. The area with the highest crime rate becomes a crime target area. Therefore, the crime analysis unit assists in assignment and deployment of officers to the crime target area. These assignments may include trained individuals who can blend in with the environment of the city and help obtain an arrest.

*Mapping burglary and robbery.* Many cities have their crime analysis unit concentrate on burglary and robbery target areas. The city is usually divided into quadrants, or sections, and the crime analysis unit keeps track of the location, frequency of crimes, and times of occurrence. The crime target areas are soon defined and the crime analysis unit assists in stationing patrol units in the sections with the high robbery and burglary crime rates.

*Crime analysis comparison for communities.* Some cities use crime analysis units for comparing and contrasting criminal activities throughout the city. Many cities have established a "norm" of criminal activity. When the crime analysis unit discovers the criminal activity in a particular area has gone beyond the established norm, special attention is given to that area. The crime analysis unit in this instance serves as a method of problem identification and does not focus on any particular crime.

*Beat analysis on the street.* The beat analysis unit concentrates on the frequency of crimes of certain beats, at certain times, and certain days of the week, then develops the standards for solving the problem.

*Pattern analysis.* In pattern analysis pin maps may be employed. The pins may be of different colors to identify locations, times, percentages, and crime rate. A certain criminal pattern may become evident from the pattern of colors on the pin map. However, the crime analysis unit must utilize skills of individuals who have expert knowledge in levels of crime rates and can identify deviations from the norm.

*Pin map for patrol.* Some crime analysis units compile and compare information from patrol logs. The unit will also utilize information from its own source as well as from the patrol log sheets. The pin maps are used to see if patterns can be established. Information about any pattern of activity is communicated between the patrol division and the crime analysis unit.

*Computer systems.* Many crime analysis units have become computerized. The crime analysis unit stores information regarding location, methods of operation, times of occurrence, etc., of criminal activity, which can later be referred to for assistance in making arrests or when projecting and predicting crime trends.

*Traffic analysis.* Because traffic problems can cause major problems for cities, some cities have used the crime analysis unit to pinpoint trouble traffic areas. The crime analysis unit may use the classical pin maps or other methods of identification. The unit can help the city determine the proper placement of traffic lights and stop signs.

**Staffing.** One of the most important factors in a crime analysis unit is the staff that operate the unit or system. Informal crime analysis has been in use for many years in police agencies, but this type of crime analysis has often been limited to officers and detectives, in which case analysis is dependent upon the officer's or detective's experiences, memory, and time on duty. Modern crime analysis can best be served by individuals who are trained and have advanced degrees with emphasis on criminal justice or related fields and research methodology.

A $200,000 grant was awarded to the American Association of Retired Persons by the LEAA to help train elderly volunteers in crime analysis techniques. The San Diego Police Department has used more than a dozen older persons in its crime analysis for the past three years. This is a model program claiming much success; similar programs will be instituted in other communities. Programs of this type should be particularly useful in efforts to apprehend "career criminals."

**Management by objectives.** Management by objectives (MBO) is not a new management technique by any means, but its application to administration of justice and related fields is fairly recent. MBO involves identifying the major areas of responsibility of each department and each individual within the department and defining specific standards of job performance or objectives to be met by each. At a later specified date, actual results are measured against the stated objectives to see if the desired objectives have been obtained. There are several goals that could assist police departments in preventing crime. For example, the department's goal could be to cut down the response time to a request for emergency help; the field sergeant's goal might be to increase the number of cars that are in service at any particular time.[43]

### Educating the public

The Boston Police Department is one of many departments across the country that have been educating the community on what citizens can do to protect their property and themselves. In Boston the Informational Services

---

[43]O'Block, op. cit., p. 415.

Crime Prevention Unit is charged with this responsibility. A major emphasis of this unit involves methods to prevent commercial burglary. Victims of these burglaries are provided with options and alternatives by specialists of the unit, which should prevent recurrences of such crimes. The crime prevention unit also makes security suggestions to prevent initial burglaries from occurring. Statistics point to a significant decline in burglary rates in establishments that have instituted recommended security measures. Most police departments will also survey residences for security vulnerabilities upon request from the homeowner.

Other methods of educating the public include providing speakers for crime prevention on panels, television talk shows, workshops, radio programs, debates, luncheons, and meetings. Most larger departments have established speakers bureaus especially for this purpose. The speakers are generally eager to talk to groups of twenty or more concerning problems of security and to introduce various crime prevention techniques, such as Operation Identification, Neighborhood Watch, and numerous home and personal security measures.

### Specialized police units

There are many specialized units within police departments designed to promote crime prevention. Various methods are utilized and each subunit has its own goals and objectives in order to prevent crime. Some are based on education of the public and working with citizens on a more personal level while others may be specifically designed to increase the chances of apprehension and arrest of offenders by police. Various specialized programs now in use by police departments across the country are described below.

**Police crisis intervention units.** Police crisis intervention units certainly have a place within any department as a potential tool for preventing crime. The responsibility for handling domestic disputes without further violence is mainly delegated to police because they are in a position to respond promptly twenty-four hours a day, and to counteract violence, which is usually part of domestic disputes. There are other counseling agencies and mental health centers that a family in turmoil may be referred to, but this is generally done after an initial encounter with members of the police department. This is in sharp contrast to the extended families of the past in which relatives living in the same household would usually be available to mediate family disputes. However, with present-day family structures, the police are usually called upon first to handle family crisis situations.

**Juvenile specialists.** Juvenile specialists are often employed to work with youthful offenders and to visit schools, churches, civic meetings, and business groups. They bring many aspects of police work to the attention of the general public. The juvenile specialists employ a nonpunitive approach when working with juveniles, recognizing that first offenders could only be reinforced in their criminal behavior if sentenced to correctional systems. The juvenile specialist can teach inexperienced and experienced officers alike in the proper and acceptable methods of handling juveniles and methods to discourage youthful criminal activity. The thrust of preventive efforts by the juvenile specialist is centered on preventive patrols in which regular visits are made to locales in which there are likely to be large numbers of youths, such as pool halls, roller rinks, and other popular hang-outs. Juvenile specialists should be well trained and understand adolescent development and the psychosocial factors that may influence human behavior. Brandstatter and Brennan have identified six primary facets of police prevention work with youngsters:

1. Survey of prevention problems: determining the most common offenses, location, and physical characteristics of the delinquent enables juvenile workers to take preventive action at certain locales, orient themselves to crimes that are the most common and the groups of youngsters that are most likely to be offenders.
2. Prevention program authority: the legislative body, whether local, state, or federal, that has established and given authority to the juvenile crime prevention agency as a separate program within a department.
3. Determining a policy of prevention: specifically defining responsibilities of the juvenile specialist and stating priorities of the program that can be accomplished through management by objectives.
4. Police prevention as related to projects of other community agencies: consideration of supplemental community-based programs and the cooperation of police with these programs in combining efforts to prevent crime without duplication of services.
5. Department structure and prevention: amount of specialization within a department; large departments, for example, will have contacts with youths limited to several designated persons who have special training and experience in this area, while small departments must rely on all personnel to work in all facets of police work.
6. Relations with the community: establishing and maintaining positive community relations with the police department. Methods to promote the police image, particularly with youth, should be a continuing interest for the juvenile specialist.[44]

[44]Brandstatter, A. T., and Brennan, J. M., "Prevention Through the Police," in W. E. Amos and C. T. Wellford, editors, *Delinquency Prevention: Theory and Practice.* Englewood Cliffs, N.J.: Prentice-Hall, Inc., 1967, pp. 200-204.

The role of the juvenile specialist in preventing crime is multifaceted. There must be clear lines of authority within each department concerning specific duties of the specialist, and he or she should be well trained and aware of which adolescent behaviors may potentiate crime. In addition, locations that may foster criminal activity must be identified and appropriate intervention taken while at the same time promoting a positive image of the police among juveniles.

**Police-clergy programs.** Utilizing the services of the clergy is a fairly new and different approach in the area of crime prevention but should prove to be of value, particularly in the area of community relations since members of the clergy are generally community-minded and have developed communication skills. After a police-clergy program is established, participating clergy members are teamed with patrol officers and accompany them on their rounds. Clergy should have emergency medical training so that they can be of assistance to their police partners during emergencies.

**Community service unit.** Some municipalities have established community services units in an attempt to reach out and help citizens who readily demonstrate antisocial behavior and also those who may be covertly in need of assistance. One such program was established in 1966 in the police department of Winston-Salem, North Carolina. This unit emphasized crime and delinquency prevention with particular attention to socially and economically deprived areas of the city.

**Liaison officers.** Liaison officers offer potentially great benefits to the community, its youth, and the police department by promoting police programs and activities. The liaison officer should be an experienced, high-ranking police officer, have good speaking abilities, and be able to positively influence his or her audience. The liaison officer should also take an active role in developing preventive activities for individual patrol officers as well as educating concerned citizens in crime prevention techniques at home or business.

**Crime prevention unit.** Every police department in the country, regardless of size, should have a crime prevention unit. At least one officer should be designated responsible for crime prevention functions. In small departments this officer may be in charge of crime prevention along with other duties of routine patrol and calls for service. While it is realized that this is not the ideal, practical budget limitations must also be kept in mind. Departments with fewer than fifteen members can usually not assign one specific person to a crime prevention unit, and the responsibility must be shared by all. In larger departments the need for specialization arises and one or more officers must be designated as crime prevention officers. Specialization is also necessary within the crime prevention unit of large departments; some officers will be designated to head crime prevention for juveniles, for example, while others may specialize in business security, residential security, or crime prevention for the elderly.

All crime prevention officers should be familiar with basic crime prevention measures and be able to implement programs for crime prevention and security awareness. These should include home security surveys, business security surveys, neighborhood watch programs, operation identification, citizens reporting projects, liaison projects, and techniques to improve personal security for the especially vulnerable. If budget and manpower appropriations permit, other programs described throughout this book should also be implemented.

Even the smallest police department can afford to have at least one officer assigned to the crime prevention functions.[45] The crime prevention officer should carry increased rank and salary. The job should be made a high-status position, which in turn will attract more highly qualified individuals, and boost the program's respect within the community. The crime prevention officer should be willing to accept the major responsibility for controlling crime within a particular area. In a large city, one officer may be responsible to certain neighborhoods and blocks while in less populated areas one officer may be responsible for the entire town. Officers should determine the time and place at which they will concentrate their efforts and also the most effective tactics that can be used against a particular crime problem. A variety of methods are used by crime prevention units to prevent crime. These include:

- □ Detailed security surveys.
- □ Preventive patrol on the streets during periods of high criminal activity, attempting to maximize the concept of omnipresence.
- □ Development of specialized prevention programs.
- □ Learning of potential problems through as much personal contact as possible with people met during patrols. The police can be informed of potential troublemakers and also can offer crime prevention advice.

In addition, specialized crime prevention officers need to be concerned with specific needs of the population they serve. Juvenile crime prevention officers, for example, should be concerned with the discovery of delinquents and conditions that promote delinquency, investigating delinquency cases, and protecting the welfare of children.

**Street crime units.** Street crime units generally concentrate on street crimes such as robbery, personal grand larceny, and assault. The New York

---

[45]Shelton, R. F., "Can a Small Department Afford a Crime Prevention Officer?" *The Police Chief,* March 1979, p. 16.

City Police Department has employed street crime units for several years. Officers disguised as potential crime victims are placed in areas where they are likely to be victimized. Plainclothes back-up officers wait nearby, ready to come to the decoy's assistance and make an arrest. The program has led to an overwhelming increase in the number of arrests for robbery and grand larceny and a parallel increase in convictions. Since cost of implementation is nominal, it promises to be a valuable tool in the fight against crime for not only New York but other police departments across the country as well.

**Hidden cameras project.** Seattle, Washington is one city that employs innovative hidden camera techniques to prevent crime. Primarily concentrating on the crime of robbery, the Seattle Police Department, in 1975, installed cameras in seventy-five commercial establishments identified as high-risk robbery locations. Hidden in stereo speaker boxes, the cameras are activated upon removal of a dollar "trip" bill from the cash drawer. As a result of this project, commercial robberies in Seattle significantly declined, and a significantly larger percentage of robbers at hidden camera sites were eventually identified, arrested, and convicted compared to robbers at other sites. The time span between arrest and conviction was also considerably shortened.

Programs such as this are apt to be well received by local merchants in any community; they also have the benefit of being relatively inexpensive to operate. The technical skills required to develop and print the film are usually readily available within the police department or can be learned fairly quickly. Therefore, this program could be easily implemented in both small and large communities.

**Other programs.** Other specialized police units include the following:

□ Alcoholism units that explain the relationship of alcoholism and crime.
□ Community affairs units that strive to improve overall police responsiveness to the community as well as ascertain how the community service officer can better serve the citizen.
□ Organized crime units that explain how organized crime affects the average citizen.
□ Special Investigation Units that are concerned with how the department investigates reports of corruption within the department and how citizens can report police corruption.
□ Senior citizens units that concentrate on crimes to which senior citizens are particularly vulnerable.

## Encouraging public participation

As mentioned at the beginning of this chapter, crime prevention cannot be left to the police department alone since the public's cooperation in prevention activities is not only desirable, but also imperative. Several policies and programs can encourage public participation, but first of all, a department must have good community relations and a positive image. To accomplish these things the public must have confidence that the police are working for them instead of against them. There must be channels of communication open, either through mass media or at public meetings, where representatives of the department can discuss their policies, actions, or inactions. A public relations department is essential for large-scale public participation in crime prevention activities. When a crime prevention program is established, most citizens, after seeing the potential benefits of *not* becoming a criminal or victim, should be particularly receptive. However, needs and desires of the community should always direct the establishment of such programs. Many different community resources (civic clubs, youth clubs, insurance companies, and parents' associations) are usually more than willing to volunteer their time and efforts to such projects. Programs in which public input has been included are more likely to be accepted by the general public than those entirely of police origin. Concerned citizens have been a virtually untapped resource that could have been used in the development of police programs for many years. Who is better able to recognize or understand what programs are needed in a particular area than concerned citizens residing in those areas? Fig. 14-3 illustrates an example of how a small sheriff's department encourages public participation through mailed invitations to citizens to assist in the formation of a county-wide crime prevention program.

Leonard states that, "Direct citizen action to support the police in the suppression and control of delinquency and crime has become an absolute necessity. In a number of instances, citizen crime commissions have provided forceful vehicles for proper and sustained citizen action."[46] Most police administrators are against a citizen crime commission scrutinizing their activities. Several legitimate objections can be raised. The first is that lay citizens are not cognizant of many police methods or procedures and may be overly critical. The second is that political hopefuls could use the commission for personal publicity. If a community decides to authorize a citizen crime commission, these factors must be taken into consideration.

There have been many police-community programs developed in the past decade that have had tremendous success in the area of crime prevention. Operation Identification, Neighborhood Watch programs, Senior Citizens Anti-Crime Network (SCAN), and "lock-it-and-pocket-the-key" campaigns are only a few examples. Since crime prevention is an increasingly important aspect of police functions, there promises to be further emphasis on developing new programs. A fairly recent idea for involving citizens in crime prevention, particularly youngsters at high risk for child molestations, was

---

[46]Leonard, op. cit., p. 150.

**WATAUGA COUNTY SHERIFF'S DEPARTMENT**
301 W. QUEEN STREET
BOONE, NORTH CAROLINA 28607

704-264-3761
704-264-6809

**WARD G. CARROLL, SHERIFF**

December 13, 1979

Dear Watauga Citizen,

    As a co-operative effort between local enforcement and the citizens of Watauga County, your name has been selected to serve on the newly organized Watauga County Crime Prevention Committee. This committee is being formed to study the factors which influence crime within our community, to discover ways to reduce crime in the county;attempt to measure the progress toward our goals; to suggest ways that citizens can help local law enforcement officers to discourage criminal activities within the area, and to study the community's response to victims of crime.

    You, as a member of the county wide Crime Prevention Committee will be fighting with us to prevent crime rather than reacting to crimes after they have been committed. All law enforcement officers can do a better job, and in a more professional manner when they have the support and assistance of the citizens of our communities.

    In the very near future a committee meeting will be held in the Watauga County Court House to listen to your thoughts and ideas on how to prevent crime that affects the citizens of Watauga County.

Yours in Crime Prevention

*Jerry W Vaughn*

Jerry W. Vaughn, Detective Captain

*Ward G. Carroll*

Ward G. Carroll, Sheriff of Watauga County

**Fig. 14-3.** Invitation to citizen participation in crime prevention.

devised by the Portland, Oregon Police Bureau's crime prevention unit. This highly successful program, known as the Blazer Crime Prevention Trading Card Program, provides youngsters with opportunities to collect free cards that feature pictures and autographs of Portland Trail Blazers basketball players on the front and a crime prevention message on the back. Thus the cards provide an important educational opportunity for children while helping to bridge the gap between youngsters and police. The messages printed on the back are based upon three themes: children as offenders, children as victims, and children as crime fighters.[47] The popularity of the cards is even greater than the Bureau anticipated.

The Greensboro, North Carolina Police Department developed a similar program in which one side of a bubble gum card portrays the shoulder patch of a North Carolina city police department, and on the reverse a crime prevention message is provided. Each city in the state of North Carolina is represented by these cards, and children are provided with opportunities to collect all cards free. Two examples of such cards are provided in Fig. 14-4.

**Decreasing citizen reporting time.** One of the most crucial factors found to be related to the clearance of crimes by arrest is the amount of time a victim or witness takes to report the crime after it has occurred. Many victims of rape, for example, will take a bath before calling the police. Although the former is a natural reaction, this not only destroys physical evidence but also significantly decreases the chances for police to apprehend the suspect before he leaves the crime scene. Also, many times a victim will call a relative, friend, or even an insurance company before calling the police. Therefore, the police need to actively encourage citizens to report crimes before contacting other sources of assistance.

**Decreasing police response time.** The amount of time it takes an officer to respond to a request for help needs close examination. The response time will be an important variable to the solution of crime but it is not as important as citizen reporting time. However, if the police are delayed in reaching the scene of a crime, important witnesses may have disappeared and physical evidence may be destroyed.

**Team policing.** Team policing programs are characterized by officers joining in a team effort to prevent and control crime. These officers promote police-community relations through regular meetings with residents and business owners to define area crime problems. Team policing units permanently or semipermanently stationed in one area can get to know the people of the area. Thus the people served by the teams are not just members of faceless crowds who perceive the police as unresponsive or perhaps fright-

---

[47]Chan-Martin, Waynette, "A Winning Combination." *The Police Chief*, March 1979, p. 30.

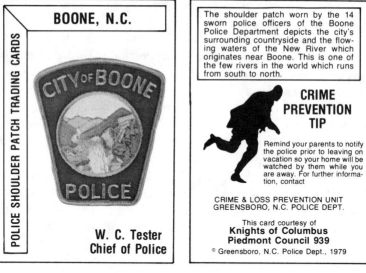

**Fig. 14-4.** Police shoulder patch trading cards.

ening. Problems within the area can be readily identified before they develop into potential crime-inducing or crisis situations. The officers assigned to a particular area should be responsible for control of crime within that area, while at the same time coordinating their efforts with other police personnel (such as plainclothes detectives) assigned to the same area.

Team policing has been implemented as a crime prevention measure in several cities. The fundamental concept pertains to the decentralization of police authority and responsibility. The team, consisting of patrol officers, detectives, support staff, and team supervisors, are responsible for practically all police services in their designated areas.

The purpose of team policing is to prevent crime and to secure a better image of the police through closer contact and association with the public. The general goals of team policing include: (1) an increased knowledge by the officer of the geographic, physical, social, and demographic composition of the area, (2) improved citizen understanding of the nature of police work, (3) citizen appreciation of the implications of an increased crime rate, (4) citizen recognition of proper crime reporting procedures and the operation of the criminal justice system, and (5) citizen comprehension of the overall personal and community benefits of police patrol. These goals, particularly that of getting to know the residents of an area, are furthered by foot patrol, bicycle patrol, horse patrol, and canine-accompanied patrol. This also shows that the key to developing a good relationship between the police and public does not always include extensive public relation campaigns or media advertising, but getting back to the friendly-cop-on-the-beat image that existed before the days of patrol cars. This does not mean that we should not use patrol cars, but rather we should maximize all advantages afforded by alternative patrols. The goal of prevention is also facilitated as team officers are motivated to prevent criminals from committing a crime in their assigned area.

The above objectives and priorities must be approved by the administration since it is the agency that is ultimately responsible for providing police services to a particular jurisdiction and not the team policing officers. Also, assigning the same officers to the same area for an extended period of time could open opportunities for corrupt practices by the officers; therefore, arrests, crime reports, and disposition reports of each area should be continually analyzed for inconsistencies that might indicate corruption.

**Special telephone line projects.** Another successful technique is the use of special telephone lines that allow citizens to report suspicious activity anonymously. The special telephone lines have a different number from the regular police emergency number, and these projects are usually publicized through billboards, newspapers, radio and television public service announcements, and by word of mouth through announcements made at crime prevention presentations at civic, service, or school group meetings. This type of project can be divided into two subtypes: (1) those that offer reward incentives, and (2) those that do not.

The special telephone line projects that offer rewards usually pay money for information leading to a conviction. The amount of the award is often decided upon by a committee of citizens. These reward projects are often operated by civilian agencies. A good example is WeTIP (We Turn in

Pushers) of Pomona, California, which is administered statewide by a non-profit private organization. The WeTIP project solicits narcotics information on an anonymous basis and informs the appropriate law enforcement agencies of tips received. Similar programs exist in most other cities with equal success. The WeTIP organization receives an average of 2300 tips per year. While many reward projects are directed only toward narcotics crimes, some solicit information on all types of crimes.

Special telephone line projects that do not offer rewards more often deal with information on all types of criminal activities. They are also more likely to be administered by law enforcement agencies than are reward projects. Some special telephone lines are manned by a twenty-four hour staff, while others are answered by recording devices that are checked frequently by agency personnel. The anonymous Crime Stop line of the San Antonio Police Department, for example, is operated by four civilians under the direction of a police lieutenant. An average of 28,000 calls per year is received by the Crime Stop telephone line. In Salinas, California, the police department has an automatic "tip line" that records anonymous nonemergency information about crime. This telephone recording device is monitored regularly by an officer from the Salinas Crime Suppression/Community Relations Unit, and information is channeled to the appropriate police division for investigation. A special telephone line that is answered by a recording device is well suited for nonemergency reports. In this respect citizens are taking the role of informants, particularly if a reward is offered.

A related service is the emergency police telephone number that has been implemented in many communities. The most common emergency number is 911, although some departments have designated other emergency numbers. By dialing the special emergency number, citizens can reach police, fire, or ambulance services in a matter of seconds. Emergency numbers should be advertised or otherwise promoted through postcards, telephone stickers, pamphlets, public meetings, newspapers, and other mass media sources. Citizens should be cautioned not to use this number to obtain information, to reach individuals, to complain about heat or electricity being turned off, and other nonemergency situations.

**Police Athletic Leagues (PALs).** There are over two hundred police athletic league programs currently in operation throughout the country. Two of their principal objectives are the prevention and reduction of juvenile delinquency and the promotion of better police-youth relationships in their communities.[48]

---

[48]Doeren, Stephen E., and O'Block, Robert L., "Crime Prevention: An Eclectic Approach," in *Introduction to Criminal Justice: Theory and Application*, Dae H. Chang, editor, Dubuque, Iowa: Kendall/Hunt Publishing Co., 1979, p. 319.

A fine example of a PAL program is the very successful Albuquerque, New Mexico Police Athletic League, which was organized in 1973. Today, the program employs five full-time police officers and utilizes the services of more than two hundred volunteers. Approximately six thousand youngsters in the greater Albuquerque area participate in over twenty-five annual police athletic activities. These activities include boxing, bicycling, wrestling, gymnastics, ballet classes, judo, karate, track and field, tennis, football, softball, chess, dog obedience training, photography, backpacking, camping, and motocross racing. The Albuquerque Police Athletic League is financially dependent upon community support in the form of contributions from citizens, businesses, and industries.

The underlying philosophy of PAL-oriented youth activities is to provide youngsters who have an overabundance of time and energy opportunities to participate in supervised sports activities instead of expending this energy in unsupervised and potentially delinquent activities. Close personal contacts with police officers during these activities is also thought to promote a positive police image with the youths and respect for the role the officer assumes in the exercise of authority. The program affords the officers the opportunity to relate to the youngsters as teachers, coaches, and friends, and to instill in the youngsters the principles of responsible and mature citizenship, goodwill, friendship, and sportsmanship.

Hopefully, by experiencing responsibility and success through sports and physical activity, the youths can begin to perceive themselves as responsible persons who are capable of achieving success through legitimate channels.

**Explorer Posts.** Many cities now have Explorer Post programs that give adolescents, usually between the ages of fourteen and nineteen, the opportunity to explore career opportunities through law enforcement activities. The New York Police Department's Law Enforcement Explorer Post program operates with participation of Boy Scouts of America and offers these youngsters many opportunities to become acquainted with realistic conditions and future potentials in business, industry, and the professions. Participants often are used by departments and civic groups to perform nondangerous functions. Many departments train Scouts in investigative techniques and other law enforcement duties as well as teaching them how to conduct a search for a lost child. A similar program has also been instituted for girls in many departments.

**Junior Deputies.** Junior Deputy Sheriff's Leagues are sponsored and promoted by the National Sheriff's Association but local sheriff's agencies actually establish the program and enroll young boys and girls to become Junior Deputies. This program had its roots established in 1936 by W. P. O'Neil, the first president of the National Sheriff's Association. O'Neil became concerned about high accident rates involving children attending rural schools in his county. He utilized a number of school children as extra "eyes" for watching and reporting careless motorists. Today most states have established Junior Deputy Leagues.

**Officer Friendly.** The Officer Friendly program, which originated in Oakland, California, strives to reach school children on a community-wide basis. The police department and the public schools cooperate to try to develop positive images of the police officer by elementary school children, and to reinforce rules and regulations that serve to modify children's behavior as they interact in their environment.

**Informants.** Informants can be used to prevent crime by tipping the police of potential crimes before they happen. The informant is usually on the fringes of criminal activity and is therefore able to provide police with specific information about criminal activity. There are a number of reasons why a person would become an informant. Although some people may feel it is their patriotic duty, most persons who become informants do so because they need the money offered by police for their information, or, more commonly, want to have some outstanding criminal charge against them reduced or dropped.

**Rewards.** Rewards are most often given by civic or private organizations, such as the WeTIP organization. However, in some cases, reward money is offered by police departments and state law enforcement agencies for information leading to the arrest and conviction of suspects of certain crimes. In this regard, a reward is different from money given to informants, since the reward is publicized and all citizens are encouraged to come forward if they have information of potential usefulness; informant money is usually kept confidential. Reward money can be donated by a private citizen or organization to be administered by the police department, or some departments set up special funds earmarked as reward money.

**Security inspections.** Several cities have made security inspections a routine part of their crime prevention programs while others may perform this service only upon request. All departments have the ability to perform this service, which would help to prevent both initial crimes and recurring crimes. However, to be effective, crime prevention officers must insist that their recommendations be implemented. Benefits of security inspections may go beyond the obvious potential of reducing vulnerabilities to crime. For example, lower insurance premiums may be given to persons who comply with suggested security improvements.

**Crime resistance.** Crime resistance is defined as an attitude on the part of citizens that manifests itself when citizens take measures to avoid becoming victims of crime and when they join with those in law enforcement in reacting to criminal activity when it occurs. Crime resistance does not involve any suggestion of ill-considered physical resistance to threats of force or violence, nor is it an invitation to vigilante groups to operate outside the law. It means resistance to the idea that everyone must live in isolation and shrink from contact with others.

The goal of crime resistance is similar to crime prevention—both seek to reduce crime. Crime resistance was a major project of Clarence Kelly, former director of the Federal Bureau of Investigation. Since his retirement, however, the movement has declined considerably, although any local office of the FBI can supply additional information concerning their crime resistance programs.

### Prevention training

It can almost be said that a person in criminal justice cannot receive too much training. Because of large sums of federal money made available to officers through the Law Enforcement Education Program, we now have the best educated police officers ever. It is not uncommon to find officers with bachelor's degrees, some with master's degrees, and a few with law or doctorate degrees.

Crime prevention as a subject should be incorporated into the curriculum of every police academy. Ideally, a minimum of forty hours of training should be spent on the subject. While this may seem to some like a lot of time, we should put it into perspective. Most states require less than 400 hours of training for a person to become certified as a police officer, but require 1500 hours of training for a beauty operator. Could it be that beauty is more important than the enforcement of laws and the prevention of crime?

It is no longer a debatable question as to whether or not specialized skills and knowledge are needed in the area of crime prevention. In addition to utilizing existing knowledge about prevention in developing expertise, research directed toward what is still not known about crime and delinquency could expedite further development of expertise both in the causes and prevention of crimes. Prevention courses should be mandatory for graduation from police academies as well as college or university criminal justice programs. This will help to assure that officers have received at least a minimum amount of training in this area, which should also reduce the possibility of producing pseudo experts who have not had proper training.

### FEDERAL AGENCY INVOLVEMENT

Getting crime prevention efforts underway has not been easy. Writing in the *Congressional Record*, Senator Birch Bayh detailed the history of the Juvenile Justice and Delinquency Prevention Act of 1974:

The passage of the 1974 act, which was opposed by the Nixon-Ford administrators of the LEAA, HEW, and OMB, was truly a turning point in Federal crime prevention policy. It was unmistakably clear that we had finally responded to the reality that juveniles commit more than half the serious crime.

Once law, the Ford administration, as if on cue from its predecessor, steadfastly opposed appropriations for the act and hampered the implementation of its provisions.

Despite continued stifled Ford administration opposition to this congressional crime prevention program, $25 million was obtained in the fiscal year 1975 supplemental. The act authorized $125 million for fiscal year 1976; the President requested zero funding; the Senate appropriated $75 million; and the Congress approved $40 million. In January, President Ford proposed to defer $15 million from fiscal year 1976 to fiscal year 1977 and requested a paltry $10 million of the $150 million authorized for fiscal year 1977, or a $30 million reduction from fiscal year 1976. On March 4, 1976, the House, on a voice vote, rejected the Ford deferral and the Congress provided $75 million for the new prevention program.[49]

The federal government, of course, plays a very dominant role in crime prevention activities. Through its various agencies it can provide both technical and financial assistance.

## Law Enforcement Assistance Administration (LEAA)

By far the federal agency that has spent the most time, effort, and money on crime prevention was the LEAA. The Office of Community Anti-Crime Programs of the LEAA was created by the Crime Control Act of 1976 to assist community organizations, neighborhood groups, and individual citizens become actively involved in activities designed to prevent crime, reduce the fear of crime, and improve the administration of justice.

The Office of Community Anti-Crime Programs also provided grants, fiscal and personnel management, community organization techniques, crime prevention methods, and coordinated program activities with local government agencies. Several of the programs presented in earlier chapters (see Chapter 13, for example) had been actively promoted by the LEAA.

The Federal Bureau of Investigation is involved to a lesser extent in crime prevention, as exemplified by its crime resistance program discussed earlier in this chapter.

## ROLE OF COURTS IN CRIME PREVENTION

Social mores or customs have traditionally exerted a strong but positive influence upon the behavior of members of a society, and because a majority of individuals behaved in compliance with these customs, there was little need for official state or national laws. Members who breached compliance

---

[49]Bayh, Hon. Birch, *The Congressional Record.* Vol. 123, No. 47, March 17, 1977, S4239.

generally were ousted or received other negative social sanctions of sufficient seriousness to make it clear that such actions were not to be tolerated within the social unit. However, a gradual relaxation of these mores or a decline in their effectiveness, possibly because these values are not shared equally by members within a large society, has resulted in increased deviant behavior within the society as a whole, and thus the need for increased state and national laws. Therefore, enforcement has been gradually delegated to the criminal justice system. As Manning states, "Social control was isomorphic with one's obligation to family, clan, and age group, and the political system of the tribe. In a modern, differentiated society, a minimal number of values and norms are shared. And because the fundamental, taken-for-granted consensus on what is proper and respectable has been blurred or shattered, or, indeed never existed, criminal law becomes a basis of social control."[50]

Social control on the state and national levels has not proved to be as effective in preventing crime as were the strict mores and customs of small subunits of a society. Therefore, we must strive through the courts to return social control to the community, the family, and the individual. This does not mean that we should cancel all of our laws. Responsibility for control in a large society can never be totally turned over to its members, since many members of a society simply would not comply with customs unofficially imposed by other members. But the courts can begin to put more responsibility upon individuals and families for their behavior than is presently expected of them. This can be accomplished by such court actions as insisting upon restitution and compensation of victims of crimes by offenders. If the offender refuses to provide compensation or community service, jail sentences should be imposed as a final resort.

Unfortunately, the courts in general have been slow to respond to the need of displacement of social control and have continued to function much as they did hundreds of years ago. Although there are a few innovations in court adjudication (which will be discussed), court inefficiencies have been long recognized by many, including those persons closest to the courts. The famous attorney Clarence Darrow pointed out the lack of progress of lawyers and courts in treating offenders when he stated:

> If doctors and scientists had been no wiser than lawyers, judges, legislatures and the public, the world would still be punishing imbeciles, the insane, the inferior and the sick; and treating human ailments with incantations, witchcraft, force and magic. We should still be driving devils out of the sick and into the swine.[51]

---

[50]Manning, Peter K., "The Policeman as Hero," in *The Crime-Control Establishment*, Isadore Silver, editor. Englewood Cliffs, N.J.: Prentice-Hall, Inc., 1974, p. 101.

[51]Darrow, Clarence, *Crime: Its Cause and Treatment*. Reprinted by Patterson Smith, Inc., Montclair, N.J., 1972, p. 276.

## Problems within the court systems

Although the problem is not as extreme as that depicted by Darrow several decades ago, the courts are still faced with many problems and exhibit many inadequacies in treating or handling arrested individuals. According to the Chamber of Commerce of the United States, "The Criminal Court is beset with organizational fragmentation and rigidity, managerial and administrative anachronisms, and undertrained and poorly supported personnel who are frequently of less than mediocre caliber."[52] Perhaps the key word in this statement is *rigidity*, still reflecting the notion that the courts have not made necessary changes in order to improve their functioning. This rigidity, however, goes beyond the capacities of the court and affects the functioning of police and correctional systems as well.

The type and length of sentences given are directly related to the influence of the correctional system, and prolonging and delaying of court cases directly affects the efforts of police. Countless persons awaiting trial are given varying lengths of time back in the community while free on bail. Unfortunately, the longer this time period, the greater the likelihood that these individuals will commit additional crimes or "disappear," forfeiting the bail money. In addition, numerous delays also increase chances that small but significant details of the crime will be forgotten by witnesses and police, which also increases the chances of acquittal. It has been said that the most effective punishment is swift punishment, so that a criminal's life is drastically and rapidly altered within a period of days rather than gradually changed over months or years. Perhaps if individuals knew that as soon as a crime was committed the offender would be immediately punished, some crimes would be prevented. This does not mean that we should do away with due process or that one is guilty until proved innocent, but it does mean that court efficiency must be increased—by increasing court budgets and manpower, utilizing available manpower more efficiently, expediting jury selection, using better management procedures, and/or limiting the length and number of delays by requiring all pretrial motions to be set at once. Many of the problems plaguing courts today are not caused solely by a shortage of judges; inefficient management, archaic methods, and lack of adequately trained supporting personnel are also factors. According to the Chamber of Commerce of the United States, "Though, many judges, prosecutors, defense attorneys, and other lower court officials are as capable as their counterparts in felony courts, the descriptions generally applicable to lower court personnel are 'least capable,' 'most inexperienced,' 'lowest paid,' 'unprepared,' and 'poorly qualified'."[53]

---

[52]*Marshaling Citizen Power Against Crime.* Washington, D.C.: Chamber of Commerce of the United States of America, 1970, p. 38.
[53]Ibid, p. 42.

Low operating budgets also plague the courts, including the federal courts. As was noted by Chief Justice Warren E. Burger several years ago, "A single C-5A military plane cost $200 million, whereas the budget for the entire federal judiciary was $128 million."[54]

Inefficient court management is also a major problem with most courts. Managing the courts, a full-time job in itself, is often left up to the judges, who are already overburdened with court cases. In addition, judges often do not have management or administrative experience. Even if they were proficient in managing, there are too many administrative responsibilities for them to handle in addition to their primary responsibility of adjudication. Efficient managing of courts must include consideration of many factors, such as developing budgets, training supporting courtroom personnel, appropriating space and manpower in the most efficient way possible, record-keeping, supervising maintenance of facilities, public relations with community, police, corrections, and legislature, supervising collection of fines, scheduling cases, and observing job performance of courtroom personnel.

Courts that are poorly managed are likely to be characterized by numerous problems, including inadequate coverage by judges, inadequate staggering of personnel vacations, no procedures for replacing ill judges or assisting those with abnormally heavy caseloads, incomplete records, uncollected delinquent fines, inefficient use of courtroom space, inefficient scheduling and monitoring of cases, lack of procedures to assure that all parties involved in a trial will be present, and an inordinate number of continuances granted for frivolous reasons. To counteract these problems is the newly developing field of court administration. Active courts are in dire need of such professional services; judges could be relieved of many management functions, and efficiency of the courts would become the rule rather than the exception.

Another problem that indirectly impedes the prevention of crime is inappropriate sentencing and unequal sentencing for offenses of relatively similar seriousness. Judges should strive to see that the punishment fits the crime, but all too frequently this is not the case, especially in lower courts. Too often repeat offenders are given short sentences for armed robbery, for example, while a first offender may be given a sentence of several years for a relatively minor offense. Disparities in sentencing create further problems for police and correctional facilities since dangerous criminals are released upon society prematurely, and many defense attorneys delay trials until they can be heard with the more lenient judges presiding. Mere slaps on the wrist for serious offenses, as frequently occurs with white collar crimes (particularly when corporate management personnel are involved), presents a serious in-

---

[54]Ibid, p. 40.

justice to society by the very institutions that are entrusted with the responsibility of administering justice. It seriously undermines the deterrence factor of punishment and reduces the deterrence of police apprehension. In addition, correctional facilities that must house offenders given overly harsh punishments must often deal with persons who are hostile and rebellious toward treatment and rehabilitation, particularly when the offenders believe they are the victims of a judge's prejudices. This type of experience only serves to further predispose one to criminal activity as a result of unfairness of the judicial system itself.

Balanced sentences should reflect the seriousness of the crime, the need for rehabilitation by the defendant, and the need to protect the public. Consideration of all of these factors can come only if judges who impose the sentences carefully review and study pretrial motions, hearings, and trial records, including testimony by both defense and prosecution. In addition, the use of plea bargaining must be given careful consideration. The Supreme Court specifically approves of plea bargaining as essential to the administration of justice. However, abuses of plea bargaining or indiscriminate use increases recidivism.

Awareness of the inequities and mismanagement within our court systems led the President's Commission on Law Enforcement and the Administration of Justice to conclude several years ago that, "No program of crime prevention will be effective without a massive overhaul of the lower criminal courts."[55] As mentioned previously, there have been a number of innovative—and usually successful—programs that have attempted to improve the efficiency and fairness of court functions. Such programs are discussed below in greater detail.

### Programs to improve the courts

**Victim-witness assistance bureaus.** A number of district attorney's offices have established victim-witness assistance bureaus. These programs have proved very successful and popular. The basic idea behind the program is to aid both victims of crime and witnesses through the criminal justice processes that take place following a crime. These bureaus provide such individuals with counseling, transportation to the trials if needed, and information concerning their role in the trial. Individuals are told when and where to appear, the name of the prosecutor handling the case, and a phone number to call for updated information. This program also assists the victim or witness in being excused from work to appear in court. This is particularly important since a

---

[55]*Task Force Report: The Courts.* Washington, D.C.: President's Commission on Law Enforcement and the Administration of Justice, U.S. Government Printing Office, 1967, p. 178.

large number of criminal cases filed are dismissed because of lack of victim-witness cooperation. Judges cannot sentence criminals to jail without solid evidence of guilt.

This most successful program can aid in the conviction of offenders and should be incorporated into every district attorney's office. Many times the task of persuading reluctant witnesses to participate in trial proceedings could not be accomplished without such bureaus.

**Volunteers in court settings.** There may presently be well over 100,000 volunteers in service to over 1000 courts. Many of these volunteers are involved in probation work, but there is a wide variety of other opportunities for volunteer work within the court systems. These include the following jobs:[56]

- Advisory council member
- Arts and crafts teacher
- Home skills teacher
- Recreation leader
- Coordinator or administrator of programs
- Employment counselor
- Foster parent (group or individual)
- Group guidance counselor
- Information officer
- Miscellaneous court support services worker
- Neighborhood worker
- Office worker (clerical, secretarial, etc.)
- Volunteer for one-to-one assignment to probationers
- Professional skills volunteer
- Public relations worker
- Community education counselor
- Recordkeeping volunteer
- Religious guidance counselor
- Tutor, educational aide

It was found in at least one court that probationers who receive volunteer services are less hostile and demonstrate drastically lower recidivism rates than probationers who do not receive such services.[57]

**Court watching.** Court watching programs are still relatively new efforts aimed at improving court functioning. The first of such programs was developed in St. Louis through the efforts of the Women's Crusade Against Crime. Generally where court watchers are needed and utilized most is in the lower, overcrowded municipal and trial courts that handle cases related to traffic and small claims, simple assaults, and offenses involving drunkenness, as well as

[56]"A Call For Citizen Action: Crime Prevention and the Citizen." National Advisory Commission on Criminal Justice Standards and Goals, 1974, p. 9.
[57]Ibid.

more serious crimes. The cases heard in these lower courts do not attract much public attention, and therefore there has not been much monitoring of these courts. On the other hand, high courts, which handle more cases of public interest or cases that affect large numbers of people, have been closely watched for years by local bar associations and state legislative committees.

Presently, thousands of citizens are involved in court watching and serve to (1) monitor and evaluate the courtroom and its facilities, and the behavior of judges, lawyers, and prosecutors; (2) monitor and evaluate support facilities and services, such as juvenile treatment homes and parole officers; and (3) note the reason for delays and continuances, presence of bail bond solicitors, and consistency of sentencing for comparison purposes. In addition, court watchers typically attempt to determine the following information:

- Are courtroom personnel polite to witnesses and jurors?
- Are juries representative of the community?
- Are the lawyers for both sides prepared?
- Does court start on time?
- Are there unnecessary delays?
- Can the proceedings be heard throughout the courtroom?
- How many cases are continued and why?
- How long is the period between the date the crime was committed and the arraignment and trial?
- Is the sentence appropriate to the crime?

Court watchers have made slow but nevertheless significant and important changes within the court system. In many cases, they have improved courtroom facilities, established information centers outside courtrooms to assist victims, witnesses, and offenders in finding the proper courtroom, and ensured against arbitrary action by judges, overly harsh practices by prosecutors, or corrupt practices in general within the court.

**Citizen dispute settlement programs.** A new and informal approach to the resolution of minor disputes was initiated in Columbus, Ohio in 1971. This program, known as the Night Prosecutor Program, provides an out-of-court method of resolving neighborhood and family disputes through mediation and counseling. The objective is to arrive at a lasting solution to an interpersonal problem rather than a judgment of right and wrong. This program, which also handles bad check cases, relieves prosecutors, judges, police, and courtroom staff of the workload of minor cases.

Appropriate cases to be handled through this program are referred by the local prosecutor's office for a hearing within one week of the filing of the complaint. Law students trained as mediators meet with the disputants during convenient evening and weekend hours to help them solve their problems without going through formal court procedures.

The basic concept of the Columbus program has been duplicated in other areas, some of which are experimenting with the use of professional people or trained lay citizens as mediators. These programs show much success in reducing the number of minor court cases, and at approximately one-fifth the cost of a court trial.

**Innovative sentences.** Many judges are experimenting with the use of nontraditional sentences. For example, one individual was given a ticket for running a stop sign but claimed that the sign was so dirty that it could not be read. The judge sentenced the individual to go to that same stop sign every day for one week and clean it. Another innovation involving sentencing is direct restitution of victims by offenders. This practice is new but one that holds much promise. Instead of a jail sentence or a fine paid to the court, where no one benefits, the offender is ordered to repay the victim either in terms of money or by working for the victim. In cases where a jail sentence is absolutely necessary, offenders can be sentenced to jail from 6:00 PM to 7:00 AM, and allowed to go to work during the day. This way the offenders do not lose their jobs (assuming they have one), and there is still money coming in to support their families. When an offender is sentenced to jail full-time, his or her dependents usually must go on welfare. In this situation, it is a three party loss. First, the victim will not be compensated; second, the government (taxpayers) must pay for the offender's incarceration; and third, the state (taxpayers) is charged with an additional expense of paying welfare to dependents. Since there is a 75% recidivism rate for individuals discharged from prison, the chances of a fourth party losing—another victim—are high.

Another type of alternative sentencing for minor offenses is the use of weekend jail terms, usually given to first offenders who have a job and family. This type of sentence will give offenders a taste of jail without completely predisposing them to the many more damaging and "criminal-influencing" experiences of being in prison on a full-time basis.

**Career Criminals Program.** The Law Enforcement Assistance Administration launched a major effort at prosecuting repeat offenders, known as the Career Criminals Program. Through LEAA, money and extra attorneys were added to the district attorney's office to develop strong cases against career criminals. Further, when a bail hearing was held, the prosecution made it a point to be present and to demand that a high bail be set. The prosecutor also tried to ensure that the case was brought quickly to trial. Computer technology, known as PROMIS (Prosecutor's Management Information System) has also been used to assist prosecutors in handling career criminals. The system enables prosecutors to call for a criminal's arrest and conviction record. Also, PROMIS will list all other pending cases against the defendant and will show whether the offender is on parole or in violation of bail. The

PROMIS technique can also rate a criminal according to how dangerous he or she is.

For many years the criminal justice system, and perhaps the general public as well, has been at least unofficially aware that recidivists are large contributors to the amount of crime being experienced. The media in particular have helped to heighten this awareness and today, perhaps more than ever, police and government officials feel pressure from the public to do something about repeat offenders. Basically, it is difficult for the public, who do not understand the criminal justice system and problems of the courts, to see how an individual can be charged repeatedly with a number of offenses and still be free, as is so often the case. During the 1970s there was much emphasis on programs to combat criminal careers, and this emphasis should continue since there is a clearly defined target to which limited prosecutorial resources need to be directed. This emphasis should bring higher conviction rates with fewer pleas to reduce charges and fewer dismissals. In addition, longer sentences can be expected to be imposed since the repeat offender has shown over and over again that he or she cannot be trusted in society and must receive maximum penalties. However, this shift in prosecutorial emphasis may result in a greater number of first time offenders receiving lesser sentences through plea bargaining, or there may be more delays in prosecuting first offenders, which could ultimately increase the number of acquittals for these individuals. However, if estimates concerning the impact of the habitual criminal upon the total amount of crime are correct, increased prosecution of these individuals on a nationwide basis should result in an overall reduction of crime. As stated by Wilson, "Most serious crime is committed by repeaters. What we do with first offenders is probably far less important than what we do with habitual offenders."[58]

**Major Violator Unit.** A project funded by the Law Enforcement Assistance Administration's National Career Criminal Program, the Major Violator Unit (MVU), was established in 1975 in San Diego County, under the sponsorship of the district attorney's office. The MVU considers its top priority to be the reduction of robbery and employs a variety of techniques to enhance the probability of successful prosecution. These include:

- Using vertical prosecution, in which a single prosecutor handles a case through all its stages
- Reducing staff case loads to enable prosecutors to pay greater attention to each case
- Reducing the use of plea bargaining
- Recommending severe sentences for convicted defendants
- Employing highly experienced prosecutors

---

[58]Wilson, James Q., *Thinking About Crime*. New York: Basic Books, Inc., 1975.

The typical offender prosecuted through the major violator unit is a young white or black male with several prior arrests and about two convictions; he is single or divorced, on probation or parole, unemployed, and was armed with a firearm during the robbery. The program has resulted in a greater percentage of defendants being convicted without a reduction of the charge against them, a greater percentage of defendants being sentenced to state prisons, and defendants receiving an average sentence of 8.8 years compared to a previous average of 4.3 years for career criminals.

**Economic Crime Unit.** In an attempt to upgrade the investigation and prosecution of white collar crime and consumer fraud, the Connecticut chief state's attorney's office established a statewide program, the Economic Crime Unit (ECU), aimed at pinpointing and combating such crimes. The ECU operates in conjunction with an economic crime council, comprised of representatives of every regulatory, enforcement, and prosecutorial agency in the state. This comprehensive offensive against the white collar criminal means the ECU can gather evidence and present cases that might otherwise have been unprosecutable. The unit also provides ongoing statewide programs designed to teach police officials and line officers the applicable statutes for prosecution and how to identify various fraud schemes. Also deterring white collar crime in Connecticut is a public awareness campaign that includes wide dissemination of consumer alert bulletins, publication of a citizens' handbook on economic crime, and direct liaison with classified advertising departments of all major newspapers to discourage publication of false advertising.

Economic crimes and consumer frauds are also special targets of the Fraud Divisions of the King County (Seattle) prosecutor's office and the San Diego County district attorney's office. King County focuses on major economic crimes involving economic losses of millions, and the San Diego Fraud Division, armed with a large staff, deals with all citizen complaints concerning fraud. A large number of these complaints are settled outside the courts or through small claims courts. Both divisions show an impressive record of prosecutorial success.

**One day/one trial jury system.** A promising alternative to lengthy jury terms has been adopted by the Wayne County, Michigan courts. As the name implies, jurors are eligible for service for only one day. If they are chosen, they serve for the duration of the trial. If they are not selected, they have fulfilled their obligation for the year. This system increases by seven times the number of citizens contacted for jury duty, makes better use of their time, and saves money for the courts.

Computers maintain a current list of all registered voters for easy access when jury pools are drawn. All prospective jurors are prequalified through a personal history questionnaire. New jurors are acquainted every morning with the legal process and their role as jurors through the use of a short slide program. This system utilizes jurors more efficiently in that more people are sharing the responsibility of jury duty, and less of the juror's time is wasted while waiting to be impaneled on a jury.

**Community Arbitration Project.** A Community Arbitration Project (CAP) was initiated in Anne Arundel County, Maryland, in 1975 as an alternative to the overburdened juvenile intake office. The project was designed to alleviate the burden on the juvenile court while still impressing on the young offender the consequences of his or her behavior. Prior to its establishment, a child accused of a first or second offense typically waited four to six weeks before official action was taken on the case. By that time, it was difficult for the court to reinforce the concept that youths must accept responsibility for their own actions, and as the cases proceeded, offenders' parents and the victim became less and less involved. Many cases received only cursory attention, or were sent for formal adjudication.

Under the CAP, juveniles accused of misdemeanors are issued a citation that records the offense and schedules a hearing to arbitrate the case seven days later. The offender's parents and the victim receive copies of the citation and are asked to appear at the hearing. The hearing is informal but is held in a courtroom setting to impress upon the child the importance and seriousness of the procedure. An attorney with experience in juvenile cases serves as the arbitrator. He hears the complaint and reviews the police report. If the youth admits committing the offense and consents to arbitration, the arbitrator makes an informal adjustment, sentencing the child to a prescribed number of hours of community work and/or restitution, counseling, or an educational program. The case is left open, to be closed within ninety days upon a positive report from the child's field supervisor. If the offense is serious, if the youth denies committing the offense, or if the parents so request, the case may be forwarded to the state's attorney for formal adjudication.

## Juvenile court

Juvenile court, established over seventy-five years ago, had as its goal to individualize treatment and social services for children coming under the court's jurisdiction rather than primarily administering punishment. However, through the years, this goal has not been entirely successful. Juvenile courts sometimes create or magnify the problems they were intended to solve. Individualized treatment and service have become the exception rather than the rule.

Since about one-half of all crime is committed by youth, the juvenile court is going to have to be the focus of much change or alternative services.

Former Senator Birch Bayh cited inadequacies in the present juvenile justice system when he stated:

> ... the system of juvenile justice which we have devised to meet this problem has not only failed, but has in many instances succeeded only in making first offenders into hardened criminals. Recidivism among youthful offenders under twenty is the highest among all age groups and has been estimated, in testimony before our subcommittee, at between seventy-five and eighty-five percent.[59]

Some juvenile courts have responded to the need of developing better methods of handling cases. For example, teenage juries are now used experimentally in Clovis, New Mexico, and Deerfield, Michigan, and thus far have resulted in dramatic reductions of the incidence of juvenile crime. Perhaps this is a strong enough form of peer pressure to influence the young offenders to behave in socially approved ways. Teenage juries decide the sentence, usually in the form of probation or a number of hours that must be committed toward community service by the offender.

Another unusual method of sentencing juveniles recently involved the handling of two truancy cases by a juvenile judge in a small North Carolina town. Two male juveniles, ages sixteen and seventeen, were given a choice by the judge of whether they would like two-week sentences in a group home or whether they would prefer a harsh spanking to be administered by the boys' parents or guardian. Both boys chose the physical punishment over detention and one of the boy's grandmother promptly got up and used a belt to carry out the sentence in front of the court. After twenty-five lashings, the judge stated the punishment had been fulfilled. The other boy was to receive his punishment at home by his parents. This particular judge clearly reinstated social control to the family, and the negative social sanction (the whipping) given in front of the courtroom is not likely to be forgotten by these youngsters for some time. Only more research and time will tell if such techniques are helpful in long-term efforts to prevent crime.

Juvenile courts, despite their good intentions, have come under increasing attack in that the process of going through juvenile court in any fashion only serves to reinforce the child's image of himself as delinquent. Lemert notes, "There are many examples of how the stigma resulting from a delinquency record can produce multiplied handicaps: increased police surveillance, neighborhood isolation, lowered receptivity and tolerance by school officials, and rejection by prospective employers."[60] In addition, it has been

---

[59]Bayh, op. cit., S4236.

[60]Lemert, Edwin M., "The Juvenile Court—Quest and Realities." *Task Force Report: Juvenile Delinquency and Youth Crime.* Washington, D.C.: President's Commission on Law Enforcement and Administration of Justice, U.S. Government Printing Office.

said that experiences with the juvenile court system only increase one's chances of subsequent arrests.

In 1967, youth service bureaus were established across the nation in both large cities and rural areas in an attempt to provide an alternative to the juvenile justice system. The goals of such bureaus, as suggested by the President's Commission on Law Enforcement and Administration of Justice, were

JUST ISN'T WORTH IT

**TO CATCH A JUVENILE THIEF . . .**

By Tom Tiede

---

ROCKVILLE, Md. (NEA)—What follows is a personal story. I wish I could say it is also unique, but there is nothing extraordinary about crime in America. Neither is there anything novel about victim distress, police paralysis, judicial ineptitude and the triumph of malefaction over propriety.

It began for me a year ago. I had been away on a news assignment and when I returned to my home in the Washington suburbs I found it had been broken into and robbed. Thugs had entered through a window on the first floor; they apparently stayed about 30 minutes and took $2,000 in property.

Their loot was a curiously mixed lot. They took a valuable antique clock, and some cash, but they passed up gold and jewelry to fill their pockets with an assortment of trinkets. This indicated they were not professional thieves, and the suspicion from the first day was that they were juveniles.

The suspicion was based on statistics as well as evidence. Half of all serious crimes in the nation are now committed by people under the age of 18. The FBI reports that four of 10 thefts are occasioned by children; the figure for burglaries is almost 60 percent.

But age apart, the young crooks are no easier to nab. Police who investigated the crime in my home frankly admitted the chances of an arrest were not good. On the average, arrests are made in less than 20 percent of all juvenile crimes, which means about eight in 10 young felons operate with impunity.

In my case the police did have strong suspicions. And they also had a palmprint that had been deposited in my home by one of the burglars. But they were forbidden by law from pursuing the leads by questioning suspects; police may not question juveniles—and rightly so—on suspicion alone.

Therefore, I was forced to use other measures to get to the thieves. I posted a $200 reward in my neighborhood. Shortly thereafter a lad contacted me for collection. He was a decided rogue himself, a chronic delinquent, and, in effect, he turned in a colleague for a handful of silver.

I was of course delighted. So was the law. Police matched the palmprint with the suspect and a boy of 17 was booked. In time it was learned that the boy was part of a ring; police said he and his companions were probably responsible for at least 12 home burglaries in my neighborhood.

---

Reprinted with permission of the Newspaper Enterprise Association from the *Morning Sun,* to provide and coordinate programs for young people. A few years later these goals were expanded to include: providing alternatives for juveniles to the justice system, providing services to youth, coordinating both individual cases and programs for youth, modifying systems of services for juveniles, and fostering the development of individual responsibility and involving youngsters in decision-making. Presently, youth service bureaus do not seem to be

---

The boy did not go straight to jail, however. Although he confessed to four robberies, he could not be held without a court order, and he was released to await a juvenile hearing. While waiting he reportedly got a steady job; ironically, the rumor was that it was in a burglar alarm company.

The hearings were held six months later. From a victim's point of view they were far from satisfactory. There were numerous delays, for one thing. And too, neither court officers nor state attorneys bothered much with the victims; the latter were left to fend for themselves in the confusion.

But, dutifully, four victims arrived for each hearing, which is more than can be said for the prosecuting attorneys. For reasons never explained, there was a different prosecutor for each hearing. And, quite unfortunately, the second one did not know what the first one had done, etc.

Defense, however, was not so careless. The thief's lawyer brought a parade of witnesses to the stand to testify as to the boy's character. That seemed amusing, since the boy had pleaded guilty, but, then again, defense explained that his client never really meant to rob all the houses.

The character testimonials moved Judge Roslynn Bell. She declined to sentence the burglar. However, she did indicate that he should make some kind of restitution. That naturally delayed matters further, because defense believed it was grossly unfair.

In the end defense triumphed completely. The boy went scot-free. Two of the victims became so disgusted they dropped out of the proceedings. The thief was ordered to pay restitution to one victim, which he has not, and he was told to write letters of apology to the others, which he did not.

So much for justice, then. No one wanted the boy's blood, certainly, but neither was it felt he should escape penalty in total. I believe he should have worked off his debt behind a lawn mower in the community. As it is, the only lesson he learned was that thieves should wear gloves when they work.

But that's not the end of the story. The other day, exactly 12 months from the date of the burglary, my home was broken into and robbed again. Same way. Same hour. Only this year there was no palmprint. I'm not sure I'll try to catch the thief this time; my experience is it's not worth it.

---

Pittsburg, Kansas, July 19, 1979.

the most favorable delinquency prevention effort, since such programs number only about 150 throughout the country and federal monies for support of these bureaus is severely limited.

## ROLE OF CORRECTIONS IN CRIME PREVENTION

Some would contend that describing the nation's correctional system as ineffective is more than a generous assessment. It is no secret that frequently the correctional system does more harm than good. No doubt the serious student of criminal justice and even laymen are aware of the countless inmates whose criminal tendencies have only been perpetuated by the correctional system, not inhibited. Prisons often do not rehabilitate or change inmates for the better, but instead may release hardened, frustrated, and alienated persons back into society. Unable to cope, perhaps even more so than before sentencing, such individuals quickly return to their former patterns of deviance. The role of the courts in determining an equitable sentence and the necessity, amount, and type of rehabilitation has a direct influence on the effectiveness of corrections. The courts must begin to differentiate those offenders who can best be served by social agencies and those who must be institutionalized. Persons who really do not belong in jail would no longer be shuffled in and out of correctional facilities, since they would be referred rather than sentenced to a jail term. This would eliminate more contact with criminal influences and at the same time give the person a real chance of solving his or her problem. Of course, this is only possible for offenders who do not pose a direct threat and not those who have committed serious crimes against society for which the public demands institutionalization. However, since this is not being done with even moderate frequency, it must be concluded that our correctional facilities do not correct.

This conclusion is hardly a new evaluation of the effectiveness of correctional facilities. In 1913, Mosby wrote:

> The penitentiary is an anachronism. It does not belong to modern civilization. It belongs to the day of the Bastile. It has destroyed more men than it has ever made, and wrecked more lives than it has ever saved. A few have been reformed in spite of it; none because of it."[61]

In 1920 O'Hare wrote:

> Pioneer work must be done in the investigation of the life histories of individual inmates of penal institutions in order to determine, if possible, the forces that foster the inception and development of criminalistic careers. No progress can be made in reducing the appalling social waste due to crime until it is accurately determined to what extent crime is an individual reaction, separate and apart from social causes, and to what extent there are causes external to the

---

[61] Mosby, Thomas S., *Causes and Cures of Crime*. St. Louis: The C. V. Mosby Co., 1913, p. 335.

individual as sure to produce crime and criminals, as unsanitary conditions are sure to produce physical disease. . . .[62]

. . . I recognize the fact that crime and prison systems have their causes deeply laid in the economic conditions of modern society and that prisons are merely the cesspools of our mal-adjusted social system. I believe that crime will not be considerably lessened until the economic struggle for existence is mitigated and the living conditions of the masses cease to breed human abnormalities. I believe that the ultimate goal must be, not the reformation of prisons, but the reconstruction of our whole system of dealing with unfit members of society; I realize that the prison as we know it today must go with all of its stupidities, crudities and cruelties, and that the reformative institutions of the future must be hospitals where trained physicians and psychologists, sympathetic and kindly nurses, cultured and understanding teachers shall deal with subnormals, not as criminals to be punished, but as unfortunate children upon whose helpless heads have fallen the "sins of the fathers." I understand quite well that "prison reform" is but a palliative, a sort of narcotic to ease the pain of unbearable social ills, but I also understand that there are conditions under which palliatives and narcotics must be made use of until time and progress have had an opportunity to work a cure.[63]

O'Hare was not only outspoken, but also willing to suffer for what she believed was right. Like many persons ahead of their time, she did have to suffer the consequences of rocking the status quo. On July 17, 1917, she made a speech in Bowman, North Dakota, the same speech she had given over 140 times. She talked about the inequities of women in society. She was accused of saying in her speech that "the women of the United States were nothing more nor less than brood sows, to raise children to get into the army and be made into fertilizer."[64] Some of the citizens of Bowman were less than gracious about her speech. They charged her with violating the wartime espionage act, and she was sentenced to five years imprisonment. She served her prison sentence and her experiences inspired her to write about the state of the prison system.*

---

[62]O'Hare, Kate Richards, *In Prison*. St. Louis: Frank P. O'Hare, 1920, p. 48.

[63]Ibid, p. 62.

[64]*Notable American Women, 1607-1950*, Vol. 1. Cambridge, Mass.: The Bellknap Press of Harvard University Press, 1971, pp. 417-420.

*Note: Kate Richards O'Hare Cunningham's story does not end there. After her release from prison she became very active in the Progressive Political Party, worked in Upton Sinclair's gubernatorial campaign, and in 1939 was appointed assistant director of the California Department of Penology. She introduced and implemented many reforms of the state's prison system. Incompetent officials were removed and prison administrative positions were placed under civil service. She eliminated the system under which juveniles were placed together with hardened criminals, established a new minimum security prison farm for young first offenders, and introduced a plan that made it possible for different types of offenders to be sent to different facilities. Kate Richards O'Hare Cunningham thus helped to change California's backward correctional system into one of the most progressive in the country. She died just nine years later at the age of seventy.

In addition to Kate O'Hare, there have been many other early advocates of prison reform. In 1929 Harry Elmer Barnes wrote:

> The possibility of maintaining one's self through lawful modes of activity should be assured by the teaching of a trade or profession to those not already thus equipped. After such a scheme of treatment the individual convict would then be in a position to be subjected to experimental release. There should be as thorough after-care for the discharged criminal as now accompanies the release of the inmate of a psychopathic hospital. Every effort should be made to secure employment for the discharged convict and to bring about adequate readjustment to normal social existence. In the case of a relapse, as demonstrated by the repetition of criminal conduct, the individual should be taken back for further treatment. If repeated experiments in this respect prove unsuccessful, then the individual should be permanently segregated.[65]

In 1931, Shaw stated, "Imprisonment as it exists today is a worse crime than any of those committed by its victims; for no single criminal can be as powerful for evil, or as unrestrained in its exercise, as an organized nation."[66]

Abrahamsen, thirty years later, likened the state of the art of treating prisoners to using kerosene lamps and the horse and buggy instead of electric lights and cars.[67] Through the years prison reform has occurred only after repeated exposure of the conditions of prison systems and their ineffectiveness by prison reform advocates, sometimes at great sacrifice.

Today there still exists much room for further changes in many areas, as several factors contribute to the problem of ineffective prisons. For example, there presently exists a lack of properly trained, high-caliber individuals who staff our correctional facilities, and many facilities still used to house prisoners were built at the turn of the century. There still exists a dire need for research, upgraded skills of persons working with prisoners, and a better understanding of the many complex problems that contribute to crime. Many career criminals, for example, apparently do not dread imprisonment, since in some cases it serves as a type of refuge. According to Mandelbaum, "prison is a place where some persons spend a majority of their adult lives, where their friends, if any, live, and a place where they can retreat again and again to obtain food, shelter, and clothing in addition to a well-ordered and restricted existence which they understand thoroughly."[68] The role of the correctional system as a refuge for career criminals certainly deserves further exploration,

---

[65]Barnes, Harry Elmer, *How to Deal with Crime*. Girard, Kan.: Haldeman-Julius Publications, 1929, p. 27. Little Blue Book No. 1468.

[66]Shaw, Bernard, *Doctors Delusions, Crude Criminology, and Sham Education*. London: Constable & Co., 1931 (reprinted in 1950), p. 171.

[67]Abrahamsen, David, *Who Are the Guilty: A Study of Education and Crime*. New York: Rinehart & Co., 1952, p. 306.

[68]Mandelbaum, Albert J., *Fundamentals of Protective Systems*. Springfield, Ill.: Charles C Thomas, Publisher, 1973, p. 30.

as obviously this is not its intended purpose. Another area that must be researched further is the adaptation process that (hopefully) occurs when ex-offenders return to the community. "The outside world can be variously indifferent, contemptuous, tough, even cruel, to the probationer, parolee, or ex-convict. If no one picks up the slack between the two worlds, we can expect these people to become still further alienated from society, and the lines on crime graphs will continue to rise."[69]

In addition to these age-old problems, there are many things that can and are being done to improve the operations of correctional facilities, so that perhaps they can actually correct without merely confining. Several programs dealing with education and job training, convicts helping convicts, and the concept of community-based corrections promise new hope for the actual correction of convicts, thereby reducing crime by reducing recidivism. Several of these programs are discussed in the following pages.

**Educational programs**

The more enlightened prisons around the country have set up educational programs aimed at providing basic literacy for inmates. A large number of those persons convicted and sent to prison cannot read or write beyond the fifth grade level. With the body of an adult, and the skills of a child, it is no wonder these persons get into legal difficulty. However, illiteracy does not explain all crime, especially white collar crimes such as embezzlement. But it is comparable with Cloward and Ohlin's theory of differential opportunity. The hope is that by making more legitimate channels open so that the offender can satisfactorily survive within the community through his or her own legitimate resources, the tendency to choose the illegitimate path of existence will be decreased.

Educational programs in prisons have not always been well supported by the general public or even by early "fathers" of criminology. For example, Cesare Lombroso, the nineteenth century medical doctor who gave us the concept of "born criminals," regarded education as positively harmful for the ordinary criminals, since supposedly it would serve only as an additional weapon in carrying out their crimes, thereby making recidivists out of them. He further maintained that if education were extended to inmates, it ought to be for the purpose of correcting passions and instincts rather than developing the intellect.[70] Although this attitude is almost a century old, many persons still hold such beliefs.

---

[69]Scheuer, James H., *To Walk the Streets Safely*. Garden City, N.Y.: Doubleday & Co., 1969, p. 177.

[70]Lombroso, Cesare, *Crime, Its Causes and Remedies*. Montclair, N.J.: Patterson Smith, Inc., reprinted 1968, p. 114.

## Job training programs

The notion of finding employment for prisoners is not new. In the Gaol Act of 1823, justices of any prison were authorized to forward prisoners to places where they could find employment.[71] It is recognized today that preparing prisoners to take a job during their sentence, and assisting them in this respect upon release, is one of the most important aspects of the adaptation process. This must be successfully accomplished if the ex-prisoner is to be permanently grafted within the community. Prostitutes, for example, who are released from prison with no money, no job, and no shelter very often are quickly—and not surprisingly—rearrested for that same crime. Finding employment for ex-prisoners takes much effort, time, and money. Prisoners who are released without prior arrangements for employment will need money for (1) food and shelter while looking for employment, (2) transportation, (3) decent clothing, (4) joining a union (which is often a necessity), and (5) perhaps buying supplies or tools. There must be some kind of assistance or program to meet these needs; otherwise the ex-prisoners may be forced to resort to crime again in order to provide themselves with these most basic necessities. Job training is also important. It teaches prisoners the routine of getting ready and going to their assignment every day. For some this is a major task to learn. Job assistance for the inmate must go beyond monetary assistance and the actual training since neither will do any good if there are no employment opportunities for ex-convicts.

Although employers cannot legally discriminate against applicants on the basis of arrest records in hiring, the Manpower Administration found that in the New York City area 75% of employment agencies ask applicants about arrest records and, as a regular procedure, do not refer any applicants with a record, regardless of whether or not the arrest was followed by a conviction.[72] If such is the case throughout the country, the odds for finding a job are definitely against an individual who has been arrested or convicted, even though he or she may have since been rehabilitated and has appropriate qualifications for the job sought. In all fairness to ex-convict applicants, employers should give consideration to their job qualifications, age at the time of the offense, present possibilities of risk in relation to the job in mind, and their overall characteristics.

The number of employers who will consider ex-prisoners is obviously limited and a large number of these consider ex-convicts for menial jobs in places such as car washes, restaurants, and similar businesses in which the

[71] Ducane, Sir Edmund F., *The Punishment and Prevention of Crime.* London: Macmillan & Co., 1885, p. 196.
[72] *Employment of the Ex-Offender.* Washington, D.C.: Manpower Administration, United States Department of Labor, RSVP Kit #5227-0 (mimeograph), p. 1.

employee is not likely to stay. However, a few corporations and companies have made special attempts in job placement for persons with troubled histories. The Teamsters Transportation Opportunity Program in Los Angeles estimates that the vast majority of its trainees have arrest records, and corporations such as Lockheed Aircraft Corporation administer special programs for the hard-core unemployed in which a large percentage of the enrollees have criminal records.[73] These businesses realize that ex-convicts who have served their sentences are deserving of a chance; also, many crimes committed by ex-convicts were the result of early deviant behaviors, which may have long since been abandoned by the individual in favor of socially approved behaviors.

A measure taken by the federal government to encourage hiring is the Federal Bonding Program, which provides bonding coverage to persons who cannot obtain suitable employment because they have police, credit, or other records that prevent their being covered by the usual commercial bonds. This program is made available by the Manpower Administration of the Department of Labor but is administered through local offices of state employment agencies. Persons eligible for this assistance must be qualified for the job and unable to obtain bonding under ordinary circumstances. In addition, many civic organizations such as the Jaycees have contributed many volunteer services to readjustment efforts and hiring of ex-convicts.

### Corrections-oriented programs

There are various programs, mostly volunteer, now in existence that attempt to help juvenile and adult correctional institutions prepare offenders for useful and successful lives in society. Many of these are concerned with job training and placement of ex-offenders, such as the Man-to-Man and Woman-to-Woman programs of Seattle, Washington. Others attempt to increase the offender's sense of self-worth and contact with the outside world. Examples include the Partners Program of Denver, Project Self Respect of Memphis, the Prison Pen Pal program headquartered in Cincinnati, and the Friends Outside program of Los Angeles. Osborne Association, Inc., a national nonprofit organization based in New York, is involved in guiding reforms and reorganization of state prisons and also in counseling and helping released offenders find jobs.

Another approach involves convicts acting as counselors to discourage criminal behavior. Such is the main tactic of the Scared Straight program of Rahway State Prison, New Jersey, where "lifers" use rather convincing methods to show young delinquents what prison life is really like. Some

---

[73]Ibid, p. 3.

researchers believe that rewarding juveniles, many of whom have serious behavior problems themselves, to assist younger juveniles with such things as schoolwork results in improved attitude and behavior of both the helper and the helped. Cressey believes that the best way to rehabilitate Offender A is to have him try to rehabilitate Offender B.[74]

## Conjugal visits

The question of providing conjugal visits is presently highly controversial. For the most part the general public is apathetic about conjugal visits, but there are a few who advocate maintaining a tough attitude and punishing prisoners in whatever way possible. Others, including personnel and researchers concerned with correctional policies and the inmates themselves, feel that conjugal visits should not be denied as a form of punishment for several reasons.[75] First, by denying conjugal visits the correctional system is helping to promote and encourage homosexuality, rape, unnatural acts, and violence in the prison. The prisoner exposed to such violence becomes more hostile, more aggressive, and more willing to retaliate against anyone who crosses him. Secondly, if conjugal visitations are denied as a deterrent to wrongdoing, then these rights should also be denied to civil law breakers as well. Third, denial of conjugal visits has been claimed to be cruel and unjust punishment to those awaiting trial, still presumed to be innocent of wrongdoing. It has also been claimed by some inmates to be a violation of the constitutional right to religious freedom.

Despite the arguments in favor of conjugal visitation rights, reform in this area of corrections is not expected to come immediately, and probably will come only as a result of much research indicating that these visits contribute to a reduction of prison violence and a lowering of the number of attempted escapes.

## Improving services at local jails

Local jails and correctional facilities have been called "storage bins for humans,"[76] "human warehouses,"[77] and the "most glaring inadequate institution on the American correctional scene."[78] Despite these shortcomings, the jail is the oldest of all correctional institutions and is still the most crucial

---

[74]Scheuer, op. cit., p. 174.
[75]Ibid, p. 175.
[76]Rottman, D. B., and Kimberly, J. R., "The Social Context of Jails." *Sociology and Social Research*, 1975, pp. 344-361.
[77]Glaser, D., "Some Notes on Urban Jails," in *Crime in the City*, D. Glaser, editor. New York: Harper & Row, Inc., 1970, p. 242.
[78]McGee, R. A., "Our Sick Jails." *Federal Probation Quarterly*, Vol. 35, March 1971, p. 3.

of all correctional facilities. It is here that the individual receives his or her first experience of involuntary confinement whether it be pretrial detention or serving a sentence. It is the most common type of residential facility, tending to have the smallest capacity, and is administered by local or county officials rather than by the state or federal government. The jail serves the dual role of detaining both persons awaiting trial and those convicted serving sentences.

The training of jail administrative and custodial personnel is a major and immediate thrust for improving this criminal justice subsystem. Law enforcement personnel have had much more opportunity and have been required to obtain much more training and education than have correctional personnel. This is unfortunate since the jail is the first exposure the arrested offender has with the correctional system, and this experience in jail may be extremely influential in molding future attitudes toward law enforcement, correctional rehabilitation, and the community in general.

As attention toward improved jail facilities increases and as treatment programs for offenders become more sophisticated, the need for trained correctional officers will become even more urgent. This need can be satisfied by developing programs that focus on educating jail security personnel, improving the conditions of jails through physical and architectural innovations, and by participating in the many programs that assist inmates in readjusting to society.

### Community-based corrections

Community-based corrections is an aspect of the correctional field that is likely to receive much more attention in the future as a preferable alternative to jails. Those on probation or parole or in halfway houses make up a significant number of the correctional population, and their presence in the community rather than in jail is likely to increase in years to come. The shift from the traditional penal institution toward community-based corrections is occurring for a variety of reasons. First of all, any restriction of freedom, such as that applied to individuals on probation and parole, is a form of punishment. In many cases, this type of punishment is sufficient without resorting to the physical confinements of jails and prisons. This in turn prevents contact with prison inmate subcultures, which have only proved to expedite the development of criminal or antisocial behavior among its members. Aggressive inmates, even in the best supervised correctional facilities, generally manage to impose their attitudes (usually negative ones) upon the others, and thus an informal prison code develops among the inmates, which is followed by most of them until they are released. This type of experience would tend to have extremely adverse effects upon the first offender and certainly undermines respect for authority and the effectiveness of rehabilitative programs among all offenders.

In addition, individuals who are not institutionalized face fewer problems with the readjustment process than do offenders who have had even minimal contact with the outside world. Those undergoing community-based correction generally are employed and do not feel as strongly alienated from society in general as do institutionalized offenders. One can maintain contact with family, relatives, church, and various other social organizations, which can all play supportive roles throughout a probationary or parole period.

Another positive result of community-based corrections is that it is much less expensive to operate than a large institution, thus saving tax money or making possible the rechanneling of funds into other needed areas of criminal justice. The parolee or probationer can most likely continue working, which should help to prevent a sense of failure and boost self-esteem and self-worth. Providing that case workers are not overworked, the community-based correctional population should also receive more contact and helpful supervision than the institutionalized correctional population who are often handled indiscriminately without much contact with correctional personnel. Thus, there is more guidance at less cost, in addition to many psychologic benefits afforded the individual being supervised.

However, despite its many advantages, community-based corrections is not the total answer since, obviously, many criminals pose grave threats to society if not institutionalized. Therefore, perhaps the solution lies in balancing the two alternatives and making more correct decisions in the courtroom as to which persons should be sentenced to penal institutions and which should be in community-based programs.

## CONCLUSION

Law enforcement, courts, and corrections cannot totally be separated when discussing crime prevention efforts. Although these agencies all have distinct roles in crime prevention, the actions and policies of each indirectly affect the success or failure of the others in efforts to prevent crime.

The development of crime prevention programs has perhaps been dominated by police agencies, influenced by leaders such as the Fieldings and Sir Robert Peel. Today in every police department across the country there exists some effort to prevent crime. Even the small departments whose main police function is motor patrol are making passive efforts to prevent crime. However, crime prevention must go far beyond this, and most departments, particularly large ones, have established multifaceted and highly successful campaigns to prevent crime.

The role of the court in crime prevention has been somewhat obscured since the importance of such measures as sentencing, granting delays, and the use of plea bargaining—not to mention the mismanagement of courtroom facilities and personnel—are not readily recognized as factors with potential to cause crime. However, as we have attempted to point out, courts play a very vital role in crime prevention.

Correctional facilities also play a vital role in crime prevention. Actual correcting of prisoners must take place if recidivism is to be prevented. There are many factors involved in the rehabilitation of prisoners, and there are still many gaps in our knowledge concerning the correct methods of rehabilitation. This must be researched if we are to maximize the potential of correctional efforts. Overall, we must particularly encourage needed changes in court and correctional policies, since traditionally, these two areas have been the slowest to respond to needed reforms.

Chapter 15

# New directions in crime prevention

The previous chapters have provided a look at a number of different crime prevention strategies. None of these topics is stagnant; each provides much fertile ground for further exploration and research. There are still other approaches and prospects on the horizon that may prove successful in limiting certain types of crime. However, it should be remembered that any large-scale crime prevention effort will not be without critics.[1]

## GRASS ROOTS CRIME PREVENTION

A comprehensive crime prevention program based in Washington, D.C. will never work. The only effective approach will be at the grass roots level. The federal government is starting to move in the direction of block grants on the state level and to provide consultation on which programs are effective and which are not. In addition, evaluation and methodologic assistance, as well as direct financial assistance to researchers developing and testing experimental crime prevention programs, is provided. Kentucky established a successful statewide crime prevention program and enhanced the grass roots approach by:

1. Establishing a statewide advisory committee on crime prevention
2. Establishing regional advisory committees on crime prevention
3. Developing a statewide association of crime prevention officers
4. Developing a media master plan for crime prevention
5. Developing police officer training programs in crime prevention
6. Developing a model security code for presentation to the state legislature.[2]

---

[1]Silver, Isidore, editor, *The Crime-Control Establishment*. Englewood Cliffs, N.J.: Prentice-Hall, Inc., 1974.

[2]Curtis, W. B., and Curtin, M. E., *Kentucky Statewide Crime Prevention Program*. Washington, D.C.: National Criminal Justice Reference Service, LEAA, U.S. Department of Justice, Aug. 4, 1976.

### Efforts of minority groups in
### crime prevention

Since members of minority groups occupy an unequal share of the lower socioeconomic category, they are more frequently victims of street crimes. For this reason, blacks and other minorities in many areas of the country have begun their own self-help programs, including Crime Stoppers, Afro-American Group Attack Team, RAP (Regional Addiction Prevention), and others. Parker and Brownfeld outline many successful strategies that blacks can utilize in crime prevention.[3] This is in line with the grass roots approach since statistics clearly indicate that, year after year, victims are usually members of the same ethnic or racial group as the offenders. Therefore, blacks, hispanics, and other groups will need to identify their particular problems or vulnerabilities to crime and develop and participate in specially designed crime prevention campaigns based on these particular problems and needs. The goal of such specialized programs should be a reduction of victimization rates for these groups.

## EXPANDING ROLE OF PRIVATE SECURITY

The field of private security has been growing at approximately 10% a year, and its continued growth seems inevitable. Private security has always had as its goal the prevention of crime, whereas the general goal of police departments in the past has been the enforcement of the law and the apprehension of criminals. Over the last ten years this industry has been largely responsible for most of the technical innovations in the field of crime prevention with the development of various electronic and mechanical devices. Private security has also been in the forefront of alerting businesses to the various preventive techniques that are available. Over the coming decade private security will play an even greater role in the protection of residences, businesses, and individuals.

## RURAL CRIME PREVENTION

Crime has been increasing in rural areas at a faster rate than in any other segment of society.[4] This has been taking place for a variety of reasons. Some scholars argue that it is a result of displacement, while others maintain that it is an indication of perceived opportunity. Still others believe that the rise in

---

[3]Parker, J. A., and Brownfeld, Allan C., *What the Negro Can Do About Crime.* New Rochelle: Arlington House, Inc., 1974.

[4]Phillips, G. Howard, "Rural Crimes and Rural Offenders." *Ohio State University Bulletin*, Ohio Cooperative Extension Service, June 1976.

rural crime only reflects better crime reporting and record-keeping techniques. Regardless of the reasons, preventive measures must be developed to deal with rural crime. The leader in this area has been the National Rural Crime Prevention Center, located at Ohio State University. The center has conducted several scientific studies in the area of rural crime prevention.[5,6] Much more research of this type needs to be conducted.

## REEVALUATION OF CRIMINAL STATUTES

Since crime is what we define it to be, we need to take a thorough look at our definitions of criminal behavior to see if they are adequate to the present needs of society. As advances in our knowledge of the causes of crime take place this knowledge must in turn be reflected in the laws governing criminal behavior and correction. Barnes, in 1929, stated:

> If the ignorance of the public and the bigotry, intolerance and stupidity of lawyers and judges so obstructs the progress of intelligence and science in the field of the repression of crime that the increase of crime comes to be markedly greater than the advance of science in this field, we may well expect the ultimate extinction of the social order and the gradual disappearance of human society. Hence, the worst enemies of society would appear to be the modern criminologist to be, not so much the degraded felon, as the conventional jurist and lawyer who consciously or unconsciously is doing his level best, through defending archaic methods, to increase the number and permanence of the delinquent class in contemporary society.[7]

Crime must be looked at in structural terms. In our definitions of crime (the legal codes) we determine what is and what is not a crime. Many argue that certain behaviors should not be defined as criminal acts. Indeed many types of relatively minor offenses that are handled through the criminal court system are responsible for clogging the courts and taking away time for more serious matters. Drunkenness, which in most locales is now considered a medical problem instead of a criminal offense and is treated as such, is one example of a change in the definition of criminal behavior. Perhaps chronic gambling and drug dependence should also be considered as medical or psychologic problems rather than as criminal acts, although decriminalization is not the solution to the underlying problem.

---

[5]Phillips, G. Howard, *Crime in Rural Ohio* (final report), Columbus: Ohio State University, Department of Agriculture Economics and Rural Sociology, March 1975.
[6]Phillips, G. Howard, and Bartlett, Kaye F., *Vandals and Vandalism in Rural Ohio*. Wooster: Ohio Agricultural Research and Development Center, Research Circular 222, Oct. 1976.
[7]Barnes, Harry Elmer, *How to Deal with Crime*. Girard, Kan.: Haldeman-Julius Publications, 1929, p. 32. Little Blue Book No. 1468.

## GUN CONTROL

Most Americans would favor legislation to keep firearms out of the hands of the violent and the criminal while allowing the law-abiding public to exercise its constitutional right to "keep and bear arms." However, gun control as such is simply impossible. Even if strict gun control legislation were passed in which citizens could no longer bear arms, there are at least 100 million hand guns, rifles, and shotguns presently in the possession of private citizens of the United States. There is no way the public would turn in their guns nor would it be possible to search every house and building and confiscate them. Further, most gun control advocates forget how relatively simple it is to make a fairly accurate gun. Many persons already do this as a hobby and any semiskilled machinist has the necessary tools in his shop to construct an accurate firearm. The control of the manufacture of firearms is not feasible in a democratic society.

The evidence is conclusive, however, that firearms play an important role in serious crime.[8] Therefore, there is a definite dilemma: impossible to confiscate or control, yet firearms present the greatest threat in the commission of a crime. The establishment of a reasonable waiting period and a thorough background check for criminal behavior or violent activity, which some cities have as ordinances, should not offend anyone's constitutional rights. In addition, some states, such as North Carolina, have passed laws that require mandatory seven-year prison sentences for persons convicted of committing a robbery with a gun.

Research regarding such practices needs to be conducted and expanded to determine if such sentences result in significantly fewer crimes involving firearms. This type of law will probably have no effect on family dispute situations in which one family member shoots another during an argument. Perhaps a law stating that guns kept at home must be unloaded and locked up would help prevent some of these occurrences; however, it would be impossible to enforce. Presently, background checks for criminal behavior coupled with across-the-board mandatory prison sentences for gun-related crimes appear to be the best alternatives to the control of firearms.

In the future, with the increased development of technology, the advent of nonlethal weapons will be upon us. When nonlethal weapons, such as Star Trek's "phaser," actually exist and become available to the public, there will be no need for anyone to possess deadly firearms for self-protection. It appears to be a matter of time and technology. The federal government should substantially increase its research into nonlethal weapons.

---

[8]Newton, George D., and Zimring, Franklin E., editors, *Firearms and Violence in American Life, A Staff Report.* Washington, D.C.: U.S. National Commission on the Causes and Precaution of Violence, U.S. Government Printing Office, 1969.

## RESEARCH
### Criminal behavior

The idea that at least some forms of criminal behavior can be caused by physiologic conditions has yet to be disproved. In fact, this area offers great challenges for future researchers. Some researchers have recently speculated that diets with predominately large amounts of sugar are a leading cause of crime. Therefore, changes in diet should reduce criminal activity. The theory postulates that sugar and other similar substances are the major cause of hyperactivity and that hyperactivity, especially in delinquents, is the chief reason children get into trouble. Others say that bad nutrition and bad behavior are closely linked.

Dr. Linus Pauling, the only man to ever win two Nobel prizes in different fields, originated the term "orthomolecular psychiatry" to describe the effects of the body's physical condition on behavior. Many orthomolecular psychiatrists believe that low blood sugar, deficiencies in vitamins $B_6$ and $B_{12}$, caffeine dependency, and alcoholism can all cause criminal behavior.[9] A lawyer and a psychologist recently founded an organization that is advancing forensic habilitation. This organization seeks to help young delinquents change their lives for the better through improvement in nutrition. This organization believes that hypoglycemia is a leading cause of antisocial behavior.[10]

The reader should note that both deficiencies and overabundances of certain chemicals have been offered as possible causes of criminal behavior. For example, both low and high blood sugar are considered as possible contributors to criminal activity by different researchers, and it could well be that both factors will be found to contribute to criminal activity but perhaps in different ways.

The old adage "you are what you eat" appears to be true.[11] This area opens a whole new dimension to crime prevention and should be carefully and systematically researched before conclusions are drawn and recommendations proposed.

### Criminal justice

It almost goes without saying that the level and quality of criminal justice research are getting better but there is room for improvement. As early as 1928 Benjamin Glassberg wrote, "Instead of analyzing the situation to find out whether in truth there is a crime wave, whether crime is on the increase,

---

[9]Yates, John, "Diet Goes on Trial." *Prevention Magazine*, Dec. 1979, p. 97.
[10]Ibid, p. 98.
[11]Gottlieb, Bill, "The Way They Ate Was a Crime." *Prevention Magazine*, May 1979, p. 64.

glib generalizations are hastily embraced and then hawked throughout the country."[12]

The established physical sciences have developed fairly universal procedures concerning methods of inquiry. The behavioral sciences, still in their infancy, have not yet evolved enough to develop research methodologies comparable to those used by the physical sciences. In most criminal justice degree programs only one survey course of research methods is required, and there are still some programs that do not require any course on research methods. This is quite puzzling since all persons engaged in criminal justice are involved in research, either as users or conductors of research. At the minimum, all students enrolled in a bachelor's degree program in criminal justice should be required to take one course in statistics and one in research methods. These future criminal justice practitioners need to be familiar with the following research techniques: survey, field observation, questionnaire, interview, laboratory observation, simulation, psychophysiologic testing, records, self-report, published sources, nonprobability sampling, probability sampling, census tract, bivariate test, multivariate test, and hypothesis testing among others.

The importance of research in crime prevention or any other field cannot be overemphasized. Real research in the area of crime prevention is almost nonexistent and when the government does let go of a few dollars, most funding is for applied rather than basic research.

A report from the President's Crime Commission states, "There is probably no subject of comparable concern to which a nation is devoting so many resources and so much effort with so little understanding of what it is doing." Indeed, it boggles the mind to think of the massive sums of money being spent on crime control. Just the salaries of the 500,000 or so police officers are staggering, let alone all the equipment and support services at the city, county, state, and federal levels. We seem to forget that we are paying the bills for this with our taxes while innovative research projects are sometimes scoffed at. Clearly, more emphasis is needed in the field of research.

Crime prevention theories with practical hypotheses need to be developed and tested in a rigorous and scientific manner, so that there can be straightforward answers as to which practices work and which do not. This research should be written up following proper scientific methodology but the conclusion section needs to be devoid of jargon, so that practitioners in the field can have immediate benefit of the results of the research. A national

---

[12]Glassberg, Benjamin, et al., *Prisons or Crime Prevention?* Girard, Kan.: Haldeman-Julius Publications, 1928, p. 1. Little Blue Book No. 1271.

journal devoted to crime prevention research is not presently in existence but perhaps the establishment of such a journal, federally funded, would serve as the best vehicle to disseminate research data across the country.

Presently, more funds need to be appropriated to research projects. According to a Presidential Commission, "A small fraction of one percent of the criminal justice system's total budget is spent on research. This figure could be multiplied many times without approaching the three percent industry spends on research, much less the fifteen percent the defense department spends; the Commission believes it should be multiplied many times."[13]

In addition to severe limitations on funding, there are also many methodologic problems that exist in research dealing with crime prevention. For example, the secrecy of the participants, the confidentiality of the materials collected by law enforcement and investigative agencies, and the various filters or screens on the perceptive apparatus of both informants and investigators pose serious methodologic problems for the social scientist who would change the state of knowledge about organized crime.[14]

Ultimately in dealing with such complex problems as crime and deviant behavior, research efforts comparable to those of the National Cancer Institute and the American Cancer Society will need to be developed in the area of criminal justice. In this way, behavioral scientists and scholars with various backgrounds and expertise can come together in an unpressured environment to engage in pure and applied research, oriented toward discovering new approaches and evaluating the effectiveness of present crime prevention activities. While a number of universities have attempted to formulate an institute of some kind for the study of crime, most are plagued with funding problems as well as the fact that researchers' time and efforts are diverted toward heavy teaching assignments and the sundry other academic pressures that take time and energy away from research efforts. Only when a final commitment and a unified effort are made with better communications and sharing of data can meaningful progress through research be made.

## COMPUTERIZATION

The computer will play an ever greater role in crime prevention during the coming decade. Second generation alarm systems will increasingly use microchips and computer technology. The identification of career criminals through computer files is being approached on several fronts, among them the

---

[13]*The Challenge of Crime in a Free Society*. Washington, D.C.: U.S. Government Printing Office, 1967.

[14]Cressey, Donald R., "Methodological Problems in the Study of Organized Crime as a Social Problem." *Annals of the American Academy of Political and Social Sciences*, Vol. 374, Nov. 1967, p. 101.

computerization of criminal history information. While at the outset this sounds like a good idea, there are many legal and ethical questions concerning violation of privacy acts. Through such vehicles as Project Search and the National Crime Information Center, experimental use has been made of computerized criminal history information.

Computers can aid in other aspects of crime prevention including manpower planning, patrol assistance, synthesis of intelligence information, and basic research into the causes of criminal behavior. The fundamental problem with the use of the computer is incomplete or inaccurate records. Careful controls must be established to ensure that valid information is put in the computer so that reliable data can be obtained.

## PREDICTION

Over the last fifty years there have been many unrelated individual attempts to develop a scientific procedure to predict criminality. As Kerlinger states, "A theoretical explanation implies prediction. And we come back to the idea that theory is the ultimate aim of science. All else flows from theory. This is perhaps what is meant by the expression 'There is nothing more practical than a good theory.'"[15] As explained by Zwanenburg, "One of the basic ideas is the logical equivalence of explanation and prediction: if one is able to explain why or through which circumstances an empirical phenomenon had to occur, it means that, given those circumstances, this particular phenomenon was to be expected and thus predictable."[16]

Efforts to predict crime have ranged from some early primitive attempts to very complex statistical techniques requiring the use of highly detailed computer programs. Prediction has most often emphasized identifying those persons likely to have a criminal career, and pinpointing the location, date, and time of a criminal occurrence. Victimologists also use prediction in attempts to determine which individuals will become the victim of a criminal attack.

The earliest and longest continuous scientific research in the field of crime prediction was undertaken by Eleanor and Sheldon Glueck of Harvard University. Through their book, *Unraveling Juvenile Delinquency*, they spurred world-wide interest in the subject. By taking an eclectic approach the Gluecks developed their "social prediction table," which is still one of the most accurate instruments to date, although certain administration problems

---

[15]Kerlinger, Fred N., *Foundations of Behavioral Research*. New York: Holt, Rinehart, & Winston, 1973, p. 10.

[16]Zwanenburg, M. A., *Prediction in Criminology*. Nijmegen: Dekker & Van de Vegt, 1977, p. 53.

exist. Other approaches have been undertaken that are purely psychologic or purely statistical.

Predicting the success of probation and parole should be regarded as an aid to judges, correctional officers, and society. If there did exist an accurate method of determining who would not repeat a crime, then the recidivism rate could be cut to zero. According to the Federal Bureau of Investigation's *Uniform Crime Reports,* approximately 75% of all felonies are committed by persons who have previously committed a felony. Therefore, a quite obvious benefit from probation and parole prediction is apparent.

The prediction of crime and criminality should also be differentiated. Prediction of crime involves more of a demographic approach and tends to be less specific than prediction of criminality. Research in the prediction of crime usually involves the use of computers. By feeding in the report of the crimes that have already occurred, crime analysts try to determine patterns of crime and to extrapolate from these data where the next incidence of crime will occur. They then use this information to determine how many officers will be assigned to each shift and to what beats. More officers will be assigned to vicinities of the highest level of expected crime. This method enables the most efficient employment of manpower, and the response time for officers to arrive at the scene of a crime is reduced.

The prediction of criminality differs in approach in that it is much more specific. Prediction of criminality involves trying to determine what specific individuals have a greater tendency to become criminals. Scientists in this field are developing instruments that, if perfected, would tell us which specific individuals will have "problems" with the criminal justice system. This research is being carried out with the hope that once a person (usually a juvenile) prone toward criminality becomes known, then preventive help can be provided, much in the same way that a person who is prone to heart disease is provided with preventive medical treatment. The "criminality-prone" could be provided with counselors, special teachers, psychologists, and social workers, with the aim of preventing criminal behavior. Research in the prediction of criminality could then eventually lead to a significant increase in the prevention of crime.

It should be apparent that the relatively unknown area of crime prediction holds almost unimaginable benefits to society, as well as possible dangers. The results of a prediction instrument could be misused in the case of those individuals who showed an extremely high tendency to lead criminal careers. Would these individuals be jailed for life before they even committed an offense because some instrument or panel of professionals indicated they would eventually rob banks? Would they be forced to live in a residential-type treatment facility, or forever be chaperoned by a probation officer? As reflected by these questions, there will always be many problems with criminality even if it is predicted.

Questions as to the constitutionality of such predictive instruments could be raised. For example, are these instruments an invasion of one's privacy? Would they interfere with one's right to pursue happiness? As the validity and use of the instruments progress, these are questions that must be dealt with and answered. It is up to scholars, practitioners, and the public to critically scrutinize the work in this area to make sure that it is used properly.

## PERMANENT CRIME PREVENTION ORGANIZATIONS

The crime prevention movement is starting to establish itself through a number of organizations that have set up permanent offices. Examples include the United Nations Office of Crime Prevention, the Justice Department's Office of Community Anti-Crime Programs, the National Council of Crime and Delinquency Office of Crime Prevention, the Minnesota Crime Prevention Center at Minneapolis, the University of Louisville National Institute of Crime Prevention, the Ohio State University's National Rural Crime Prevention Center, and the National Center for Community Crime Prevention at Southwest Texas State University. Many other national, union, trade, and professional associations are actively involved in the crime prevention movement. Most states have now set up statewide offices of crime prevention. The movement of crime prevention will expand tremendously over the next decade since the establishment of permanent offices to promote crime prevention services has become a part of the criminal justice system.

## INTERNATIONAL CRIME PREVENTION

Crime is an international problem and therefore the battle is being waged in many countries. The first real crime prevention efforts have roots that can be traced back to England. The British Home Office continues to be one of the world leaders in crime prevention. The United Nations Office of Crime Prevention also actively seeks international cooperation in efforts to prevent crime.[17] In addition, the International Police Organization (Interpol), while primarily an information-gathering and disseminating agency, is concerned with the problems of crime prevention. The Secretary-General of Interpol has its headquarters in St. Cloud near Paris. It implements the decisions of the General Assembly and the Executive Committee and is a major influence in the fight against international crimes. It maintains files, cards index systems, and collections of fingerprints and photographs, and sends out

---

[17] Schaffer, Richard B., "Crime Prevention and Criminal Justice: Is There An International Dimension." LAE *Journal of the American Criminal Justice Association*, Vol. 41, No. 2, Summer 1978, p. 7.

information on criminals wanted for extradition as well as information about crime prevention.[18]

Other countries are also taking various crime prevention approaches. The Japanese police spend time and resources in activities to provide assistance and services to the public.[19] They also maintain telephone consultation services to give advice and assistance to callers regarding their concerns and problems. Japan is also the best example of a very decentralized police force. Even with a very large, high-density population, Japan manages to keep a much lower crime rate than the United States. Although this probably has roots in part in the cultural prohibition against dishonoring one's family or oneself, the use of the police box is also largely responsible.[20] The police box basically is a small station where one or several officers spend their shift. Such boxes are placed every few blocks and citizens can go to the local police box and conduct any business that could be transacted at the larger headquarters located downtown. This puts the local officers in touch with the neighbors and they can take immediate action to handle complaints.

The world approach to crime prevention will be limited by several factors. Constraints such as language barriers, communications, internal and external conflict of nations, and different morals, customs, and mores leading to different definitions of crime may all contribute to a lack of progress regarding the international scope of crime prevention.

### Technology transfer

The idea of technology transfer to lesser developed nations has been around for a number of years, usually practiced in the area of agriculture and industrialization. The concept of technology transfer is now coming into play in crime prevention. The exchange of information across cultures is beneficial to all nations involved. With the practice of technology transfer, existing programs in America or England, for example, can be shared with lesser developed countries; technological information can also be exchanged between developed or industrialized nations. Crime prevention programs found to be successful in one country might also be effective in a different country. Therefore, knowledge of this nature should be exchanged among nations to benefit all mankind.

### PLANNING

The purpose of planning is to determine the best possible use of resources for the accomplishment of predetermined goals. Before actual plan-

---

[18] Agarwal, R. S., *Prevention of Crime*. New Delhi: Radiant Publishers, 1977, p. 68.
[19] Ibid, p. 68.
[20] Clifford, William, *Crime Control in Japan*. Lexington, Mass.: Lexington Books, 1978, p. 78.

ning can commence, there must exist a clear understanding of the problems and goals to be achieved. The usual approach is to break down a given problem into subproblems or subgoals. Clifford notes that the deficiencies in planning for future crime prevention control have resulted from a lack of crime prevention knowledge and a lack of technical information necessary for crime prevention planning. Being aware of crime trends has not always been the same as knowing what to do about them.[21] The planner will have to look at a number of variables besides rates of crimes reported to the police. The planner must also examine the amount of unreported crime, the public's attitude toward crime, the perceived level of security, and the social and economic benefits, as well as manpower, budgets, resources, and capability.

## EVALUATION

Closely related to planning is the process of evaluation. Evaluation is of utmost importance to crime prevention because it is through evaluation that we determine which approaches and programs work.

Evaluation has been defined as:

> . . . a systematic procedure which attempts to appraise and measure the actual inputs, processes, outcomes, and operational settings of one or more on-going programs or policies in order to compare these findings with those which were anticipated or assumed. It then seeks to explain the discovered differences and to suggest alternatives for improvements.[22]

In general, there are two major reasons why evaluation is critical:
1. To increase the efficiency and performance of the criminal justice system
2. To identify those programs and strategies that are effective in the control, reduction, and prevention of crime and delinquency

Between 1968 and 1980, the Law Enforcement Assistance Administration (LEAA) awarded about $6 billion to state and local governments to prevent and reduce crime and delinquency. However, what impact have these funds had on crime and the performance of the criminal justice system? Which specific strategies and programs have been effective in reducing, controlling, and preventing crime and delinquency? The answers to these questions remain unknown. Evaluation in crime prevention as well as in criminal justice in general is about on the same level as crime prevention theory—a very sad state of affairs. A special report to Congress by the Comptroller General concluded that the government's evaluation activities and information were not meeting planning, decision-making, and policy-making needs of users at dif-

---

[21]Clifford, William, *Planning Crime Prevention*. Lexington, Mass.: Lexington Books, 1976, p. 2.
[22]"Evaluation and Analysis To Support Decisionmaking." Washington, D.C.: U.S. Government Printing Office, GPO Report PAD-76-9, Sept. 1, 1976.

ferent levels of the intergovernmental block grant Crime Control Act Program:

- ☐ The amount and types of evaluation work had not been adequate.
- ☐ The quality of evaluation activities and products was questionable.
- ☐ The needs of those using the evaluation information were not being met.
- ☐ The allocation and management of evaluation resources need improvement.
- ☐ Better coordination of evaluation program efforts was needed.[23]

The report also concluded that outcome evaluation is particularly necessary to decision-makers, planners, and those responsible for formulating and/or changing criminal justice program policies and establishing priorities for funding consideration. Outcome evaluation is designed to determine objectively a program's progress toward an overall goal, for example, reduction of new offenses through successful criminal rehabilitation.

Some of the major problems with evaluations that have been conducted regarding a particular crime prevention program include inaccurate evaluation findings, with conclusions and recommendations that have had little usefulness for planning, decision-making, or policy-making. There has also been an inability to interpret the meaning of evaluation results and to draw valid conclusions. This in turn restricts the formulation of appropriate recommendations for the implementation of crime and delinquency programs, and sometimes the result is more expense by local and state governments to conduct another feasibility study. Some of these evaluation inadequacies may result from a lack of standards and procedures for reporting evaluation results or for determining the validity and reliability of evaluation findings.

The LEAA had been encouraging evaluation actively.[24-27] It will take the federal government's leadership and funding at the national level to further

---

[23]"Evaluation Needs of Crime Control Planners, Decisionmakers, and Policymakers are not Being Met." Washington, D.C.: U.S. Government Printing Office, GAO Report GGD-77-72A, Summary, July 14, 1978, p. 3.

[24]*Evaluation in Criminal Justice Programs: Guidelines and Examples.* Washington, D.C.: Law Enforcement Assistance Administration, National Institute of Law Enforcement and Criminal Justice, U.S. Government Printing Office, Stock No. 2700-00210, 1973.

[25]Albright, Ellen, *Evaluator's Manual for Anti-Crime Impact Projects—National Impact Program Evaluation.* Washington, D.C.: Law Enforcement Assistance Administration, National Institute of Law Enforcement and Criminal Justice, U.S. Government Printing Office, Microfiche (NCJ 34430), 1973.

[26]*Intensive Evaluation for Criminal Justice Planning Agencies.* Washington, D.C.: Urban Institute, Law Enforcement Assistance Administration, National Institute of Law Enforcement and Criminal Justice, U.S. Government Printing Office, 1975.

[27]Boston, Guy D., *Techniques for Project Evaluation—a Selected Bibliography.* Washington, D.C.: Law Enforcement Assistance Administration, National Institute of Law Enforcement and Criminal Justice, U.S. Government Printing Office, Aug. 1977.

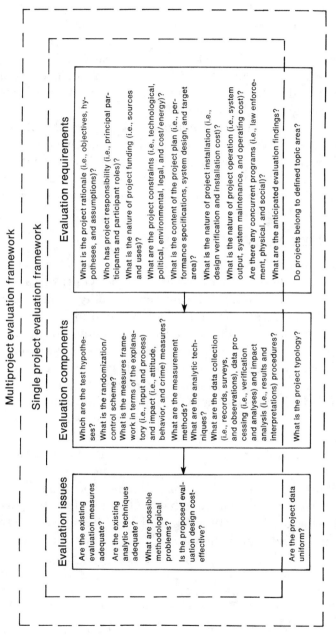

**Fig. 15-1.** Evaluation frameworks: a dynamic roll-back approach. (From *Street Lighting Projects*. Washington, D.C.: National Evaluation Program, Phase I Report, Series A, No. 21, National Institute of Law Enforcement and Criminal Justice, Law Enforcement Assistance Administration, U.S. Department of Justice, Jan. 1979, p. 39.)

promote the concept of evaluation. One of the principal objectives of evaluation efforts is to have performance information used at different governmental
levels and across criminal justice agencies, in policy formulation, planning,
decision-making, and related management functions, to achieve mandated
goals. Evaluation, therefore, is viewed also as a management tool and is required by federal guidelines.[28] Hackler has suggested five separate approaches to evaluation: (1) changes in official rates, (2) subjective opinion,
(3) changes as predicted by the theoretical framework, (4) a test of theoretical
ideas, and (5) the integrity of the program.[29]

   Glaser feels that criminal justice evaluation research would differentiate
offenses and offenders on the basis of causal theory and would interrelate
several levels of abstraction.[30] A number of different evaluation strategies are
being devised, as Fig. 15-1 indicates. However, standard methodologic procedures for evaluation must be uniformly adopted in order to correctly evaluate success of a particular project.

## INCREASING CITIZEN ACTIVITY

   With few exceptions, citizens, citizen committees, and other civic groups
have not made a bona fide effort to monitor the activities of various law
enforcement agencies. There is a certain amount of apathy characterizing the
average citizen, which tends to discourage involvement in law enforcement
activities. But it is this same apathy that encourages both corruption within
the police agencies and inability to progress with crime prevention efforts.
Once apathy has contaminated local governmental agencies, it can more easily infiltrate state and federal governmental agencies. Thus the average citizen plays a vital role in the prevention of many forms of corruption and also in
helping to preserve the idea that "the people are the police." If citizens do
not support or are apathetic about law enforcement activities, the police are
likely to be hampered in their crime prevention efforts both internally and
externally.

   In addition, both the police and victims of crime depend on the willingness of the average citizen to become involved, either to call for help, assist in
emergencies, or act as a witness. Being a good samaritan in such cases is a
volunteer effort, not mandatory, which is in sharp contrast to the days of the

---

[28]Ibid, p. 30.
[29]Hackler, James C., "Evaluation of Delinquency Prevention Programs," in *Prevention of Delinquency, Problems and Programs*, John R. Stratton and Robert M. Terry, editors. New York: The
Macmillan Co., 1968.
[30]Glaser, Daniel, "Remedies for the Key Deficiency in Criminal Justice Evaluation Research."
*Journal of Research in Crime and Delinquency*, Vol. 11, No. 2, July 1974, pp. 144-154.

Old West when citizens were deputized and compelled to become members of posses. Today citizens may refuse to aid police or may even obstruct the police in the carrying out of their duties. The solution to such apathy or hostility lies in positive police-public relations and an improved image of the police as well as good samaritan laws that protect citizens from possible legal actions as a result of their intervention. In addition, public education campaigns to instruct citizens on how to be good witnesses and how to give assistance in emergencies would be of benefit as would witness compensation programs and measures to protect the anonymity of some witnesses.

## Individual responsibility

In our discussion of crime prevention we cannot leave out the most important factor in the commission of crime—the criminal. Persons who commit crimes are some of the best rationalizers around. They can give a hundred reasons why they are not to blame for the commission of their offenses. The emphasis of crime prevention generally stresses the failure of the police or the mire of court procedures and the inability of corrections to correct. However, the area of individual responsibility, or accepting responsibility for one's own actions, is seldom mentioned. Dr. Karl Menninger and others have stressed the idea of being responsible for one's own actions. In his book, *Whatever Became of Sin?*, Menninger wrote, "The disappearance of the word 'sin' involves a shift in the allocation of responsibility for evil. Perhaps some people are convinced of the validity of the Skinnerian thesis, and no longer consider themselves or anyone else to be answerable for any evil—or any good."[31]

O. W. Wilson would have agreed with this view. While superintendent of police in Chicago, he said that one of the causes of the increasing crime rate was:

> . . . a breakdown in family control. We have an undisciplined society, and it's undisciplined because people seem more concerned with discovering some excuse for the behavior of an individual than anything else. Having discovered there is an explanation for his behavior, they use that as an excuse for the misbehavior. I don't think our forebears were ever concerned about *why* a person misbehaves. If he misbehaved, this called for a remedial action. *We are straying away from the principle of holding the individual responsible for his conduct, and are excusing his conduct in all too many cases—some very serious cases.*[32]

---

[31] Menninger, Karl, *Whatever Became of Sin?* New York: Hawthorn Books, 1973, p. 17.
[32] *U.S. News and World Report*, Vol. 61, Aug. 1, 1966.

Similarly, Reckless notes that supplementary to the evolution of a better role structure for youth is the need for young persons themselves to develop inner controls that are capable of steering them away from pitfalls.[33]

Noting the ineffectiveness of maintaining an attitude of rationalization, Shaw stated that the root of the evil lies in maintaining superficial virtues: "All communities must live finally by their ethical values; that is, by the genuine virtues. Living virtuously is an art that can be learnt only by living in full responsibility for our own actions."[34]

According to these views, rationalizations have played a dominant but ill-fitting role in the treatment of suspects and criminals. There will always be myriad conditions that promote criminal behavior, but most individuals know right from wrong and in the end are able to have the final say over their own behavior. Therefore, the concept of individual responsibility must not be camouflaged by excuses that tend to lessen the seriousness of the deviant behavior.

### Renewal of patriotism

For crime to be radically decreased it will also be necessary for a new sense of patriotism to sweep the country. Until government employees and citizens feel a sense of responsibility and gratitude to their country, certain types of crimes will persist, especially those relating to corruption and misfeasance of responsibility. The type of unity that existed during the American hostage situation in Iran in late 1979 and into 1981, which drew the people together for a common purpose, is an example of such patriotism. If this same type of unity could exist even briefly in the crime prevention movement, it could radically reduce crime.

### Renewal of religion

The subject of crime cannot be studied totally in a cold scientific manner. Principles of right and wrong and morality also come into play. In the simplest sense, if individuals would not break the Ten Commandments, we would not have crime.

The role of religion has been diminishing in recent years with respect to moral training. With our highly complex, mobile society, people find they do not have time for religion; it is interesting to note that at the same time the crime rate has been increasing. Although it is difficult if not impossible to

---

[33]Reckless, Walter C., and Dinitz, Simon, *The Prevention of Juvenile Delinquency, an Experiment.* Columbus: Ohio State University Press, 1972, p. 33.

[34]Shaw, Bernard, *Doctors Delusions, Crude Criminology, and Sham Education.* London: Constable & Co., 1931 (reprinted in 1950), p. 228.

draw direct causal relationships in the social sciences, this situation is one that bears further investigation.

The religious institutions can and should instill moral principles of conduct into individuals of all ages, including respect for others' property, the difference between right and wrong, and making amends when another is injured or wronged.

A spiritual reformation would bring about a whole new moral awakening. Strengthening of families, along with a decline in the rates of divorce, abuse of alcohol and drugs, gambling, and promiscuity would reflect a return to morality. Individuals would also have a greater sense of responsibility and self-control, thus strengthening the notion of accepting blame for one's actions. The church could also serve as a place for anticrime education where methods of coping with the complexities of modern day living could be explored, rather than trying to prevent crime through fear of punishment or actual punishment.

### Increasing the sanctity of life

We will always have crimes of violence as long as we have no respect for the sanctity of life. Our society and government continue to rationalize, legalize, and justify the taking of human life. Until we condemn the taking of life in all forms, from capital punishment to the killing of animals for sport, we will continue to have a massive amount of violence in the world.

## A SYSTEMS APPROACH

A systems approach will also be necessary if crime prevention is to make a significant impact. For example, many of the recommendations made in Chapter 5, Home Security, will have to be mandated in the form of building codes to be incorporated into all new construction. In addition, some of the methods of personal security need to be taught as early as elementary school. Cutting crime off at the roots will happen only when the majority of citizens take an enlightened approach to the causes of crime and delinquency. Children must be taught respect for others and their property; parents should have the opportunity to learn and develop effective parenting techniques.

## EMPLOYMENT OPPORTUNITIES IN SECURITY AND CRIME PREVENTION

The security industry has fluctuated and will continue to do so with changes in social behavior. Those in the security field are becoming increasingly aware of the impact of technologic development. Firms are turning to the use of closed-circuit televisions, UHF two-way communication, card-operated access control systems, microwave intruder sensors, plus a variety of fence, door, and window alarms. Future security managers and personnel, if not directly responsible for the implementation of such systems, will certainly benefit from being aware of the operational principles of their use.

Changes are also apparent within individual segments of the security industry. Presently, the private guard industry has grown to number more than one million security and crime prevention–related personnel. There is also an increasing demand by firms for contract security services rather than directly employing security officers. In some areas there are as many contract forces as in-house guards.

Career possibilities in the security field, like the industry itself, are on the upswing, both in numbers and stature. While the top positions have generally become more demanding in terms of intelligence, education, and experience, increases in industry size have multiplied the number of avenues to the executive positions.

The seven major industries generally in need of security services include: research and development, medical care, retail trade, government and military, transportation, security services contractors, and industrial. Security directors for major United States corporations generally hold the highest security position in terms of esteem, responsibility, and salary. The position directly under the corporate security director is generally the division-level security manager. There may also be positions for staff assistants to the top-level security directors and managers in medium-sized companies. Usually these individuals are specialists in one or more security skills. The security manager for the middle-sized firm typically must be a generalist, assuming complete responsibility for the firm's security within a local or regional area and managing a guard force. Often the support staff will be limited to clerical assistance in addition to the guard force.

Remaining positions in in-house security fields include jobs such as security manager for the larger retail merchandisers, hospitals, and the transportation industry. Retail is perhaps the fastest growing security market, but one that usually fills its higher security positions from within its own ranks. Hospital security administrators traditionally have been security managers for other types of industry. The transportation security field, generally considered to have originated with the advent of railroad police in the 1800s, is recognized as a forerunner in the security industry. Such events as airline skyjacking and bomb threats have imposed new federal regulations, thus adding to the increased need for security personnel.

Today more than ever, there is the need for contract guard services. Thousands of such companies are operating in the United States at the present time. Owning such a firm can be the most lucrative of security positions. Within the larger, more successful contract agencies there are a moderate number of salaried, middle management jobs of some promise and satisfaction. At the higher levels are the vice presidents of finance, operations, administration, personnel, and training, depending upon the structure and size of the company. Next are regional managers, covering several areas or even states, followed by area managers, who are usually responsible for the operation of a single office and are often responsible to a single, large client company. Between them and the posted security officers and patrolmen are several supervisors holding a variety of operational and clerical responsibilities.

All employers want to select the best qualified applicant for any position, and many firms are looking for persons with a non–law enforcement background because they want someone oriented toward prevention rather than enforcement. The indiscriminate hiring of retired law enforcement or military personnel to head a security unit can work both as an advantage and as a disadvantage. Many such officers already draw a good pension, and are going to just supplement it with a security position salary. In the long run, however, the smaller salaries paid to these retired persons may be false economy, since an employee who does not need a job may do a minimum of work because he has no need for advancement in salary or position. Also, former law enforcement officers often have had little or no experience in the security field and do not know how to develop a security program.

Salaries in security, particularly those of security guard personnel, have lagged far behind those of comparable vocations; therefore, the security industry at large has remained a second rather than first career choice for most individuals. Because of this the industry used to be most attractive to the person who had completed an earlier career in the military or one of the enforcement agencies and who was assured of at least moderate additional income such as a retirement pension. Salaries range from the minimum wage to $100,000 or more a year. However, there are only a few who draw an annual salary over $35,000 (and naturally they will also be in a better position to move up to the $100,000 range). The majority of security personnel make from $12,000 for a management trainee position to $25,000 for a director of security. This salary range includes investigators, polygraph examiners, interrogators, account executives, sales and marketing personnel, finance people, consultants, and assistant directors of security.

### Police department crime prevention units

Each year more and more police departments are recognizing the importance and benefits of a separate crime prevention unit. This will create more opportunities for employment in the crime prevention field. The crime prevention officer has the opportunity to make many positive contacts in the community with both residents and local business leaders. Within the next decade the majority of police departments will designate at least one member of the department as the crime prevention officer.

## Insurance industry

The insurance industry provides many positions for persons in the area of crime prevention. Among these are loss prevention consultants who conduct on-site security surveys, and insurance investigators, loss coordinators, and adjustors. The insurance industry has been quick to recognize the importance of loss prevention efforts.

## Other positions

There are a number of other positions open in the private security and crime prevention field, including engineering and designing of new products, especially in access control, and in selling of alarms and related products. It has been said that a salesman is never without a job. While some people have an inherent dislike of the word "sales," it can be a very prosperous occupation for an honest, energetic, and outgoing individual. Installation and service of security and crime prevention equipment will expand tremendously as the number of systems in use grows. The security and crime prevention field, given the numerous opportunities available, will be one of the best occupational fields a person can enter in the 1980s.

## CONCLUSION

It is not difficult to speculate about the future but it is difficult to accurately predict what will happen. Based on the intensive research that was conducted for this book, I believe that the future role of policing will change dramatically in the last part of this century and especially in the twenty-first century, less than twenty years away. There will still be a need for enforcement and investigators but the vast majority of emphasis by criminal justice will be on prevention.

We need a national commitment to crime prevention like our national effort in the space program to land a man on the moon. It is true that the LEAA has spent millions of dollars a year but we do not really have a national commitment. Many crime prevention programs or tactics are based on beliefs or ideologies rather than on substantiated data. We need more of a directed effort consisting of scientifically tested theories and alternate hypotheses. There is also a need for greater emphasis on methodology and evaluation. We must reject the archaic beliefs that society is too complex and that we will never be able to control crime. Indeed with that kind of negative attitude, we will not be able to control it. We must commit ourselves to basic research, to replication of that research, and then to dissemination of that information to legislators, scholars, criminal justice practitioners, teachers, and the public.

# Index

**B**

Background checks
  importance of in gun control, 421
  as preventive measure in employee theft,
    191-194
Backup power for alarms, 291-292
Bad checks, 169-171
Bait and switch, fraud involving, 131
Ball joint swindle, 132
Bank examiner confidence game, 129
Bankruptcy
  arson as means of avoiding, 177
  fraud involving, 174-175
Barriers
  environmental, 282
  perimeter, 282-285
  role of in environmental security, 308-314
Basement windows, vulnerability of to
    burglary, 100
Beat, analysis of, 378
Behavioral characteristics of abused child,
    73-74
Behavioral characteristics of child abuser, 74
Behavioral science research, 423
Bicycle patrol, use of by police in crime
    prevention, 369
Bicycle theft, 78
Big Brother/Big Sister programs, 10, 333-334
Billing, as health fraud practice, 151
Biology, as discipline of crime prevention,
    6-7
Blackmail, computer as vehicle for, 201
Blank check, fraud involving, 169-170
Blazer Crime Prevention Trading Card
    Program, 387
Block Mothers, 357
Block Parent Program, importance of in
    preventing crimes against children, 69
Block Watch, 341-349
Body alarm, as defense against robbery,
    76
"Boiler room," 241
Bonding, maternal, effect of on development
    of juvenile delinquency, 34
Bookmaking, gambling and, 181
Boxcar, theft of, 211
Boy Scouts of America, 334
Boys Clubs of America, 335
Break wire, use of in alarm sensors, 278-279
Bribery, 157, 220
Britain, crime prevention in, 367-368
British Home Office, 427
Broken beam detectors, use of in alarm
    sensors, 279
"Buddy Buzzer," 137
Budgets, influence of on efficiency of court
    system, 397
Building codes, importance of in
    environmental security, 322-323
Bureau of Child Welfare, importance of in
    prevention of child abuse, 74

Burglar
  behavior of, as factor in residential crime,
    89
  psychological profile of, 91
Burglary, 88-111, 157
  against elderly, 118-121
  business, 166-169
  mapping of by crime analysis, 378
  precautions against, 106-108
Business
  corruption in, 232-241
    oil industry, 233-236
    restraint of trade, 237-241
    techniques, 236-237
  crime prevention, 155-295
    corruption, 219-252
    security, 155-218
    security surveys, 253-269
    target hardening, 270-295
  fraud, 130-131
  influence of in preventing juvenile
    delinquency, 43
  security, 155-218, 261-266
  small, 156

**C**

Cable television security system, 277-278
Camera(s)
  automatic, as deterrent to business
    burglary, 168
  hidden, use of by police, 384
Camp-school programs, importance of in
    preventing juvenile delinquency, 49
Campaign expenditures, limiting, to prevent
    corruption, 227
Cancer drugs, fraud involving, 144
Canine patrol, use of by police in crime
    prevention, 370-373
CAP, 404
Capacitance detectors, 285
  use of in alarm sensors, 279
Capital punishment, deterrent effect of, 25,
    26
Card entry mechanical lock, 273-274
Career Criminals Program, 401-402
Cargo
  air, theft of, 210-211
  truck, theft of, 208-210
Carpetbagger era, 221
Casement windows, vulnerability of to
    burglary, 99
Causation, crime, theories of, 14
CB radios, use of in crime prevention,
    349-350
CCRP, 350-351
CCTV, use of as alarm system, 293-294
Central processing unit, computer crime
    involving, 202
Central station alarm systems, 277
Chain-referral scheme, 129-130
*Challenge of Crime in a Free Society*, 9